A *LEVEL*
ENGLISH

Rosemary Coxon
English Teacher and Head of Library
Myton School

EDUCATIONAL

Every effort has been made to trace copyright holders and to obtain their permission for the use of copyright material. The author and publishers will gladly receive information enabling them to rectify any reference or credit in subsequent editions.

First published 1983
Revised 1986, 1988, 1991, 1993, 1995
Reprinted 1992, 1993, 1994, 1996, 1997

Letts Educational
Aldine House
Aldine Place
London W12 8AW
0181 740 2266

Text © R Coxon 1993

Design and illustration © BPP (Letts Educational) Ltd

British Library Cataloguing in Publication Data
A CIP record for this book is available from the British Library.

ISBN 1 85758 337 X

Printed and bound in Great Britain by
WM Print Ltd, Frederick Street,
Walsall, West Midlands WS2 9NE

Letts Educational is the trading name of BPP (Letts Educational) Ltd

ACKNOWLEDGEMENTS

The author wishes to record her gratitude and thanks to Dr A Wheater, Mr BW Caws, Mr DF Mackenzie, Philip Robinson and Jacqueline Hughes-Williams for material help with the text of the book.

The author and publishers are grateful to the following for permission to quote copyright material (page numbers refer to this book unless stated):

AD Peters & Co Ltd (extract from *Brideshead Revisited* by Evelyn Waugh, reprinted by permission of AD Peters & Co Ltd, p. 132); Malcolm Bradbury and Martin Secker & Warburg Ltd (extracts from *The History Man* by Malcolm Bradbury, pp. 133 and 137–8); Penguin Books Ltd (extract from *Madame Bovary* by Flaubert, trans. Alan Russell, pp. 75–76 (Penguin ed.), Penguin Classics, 1950, Copyright © the Estate of Alan Russell, 1950, reprinted by permission of Penguin Books Ltd, p. 134); the Estate of the late Sonia Brownell Orwell and Martin Secker & Warburg Ltd (extract from *Animal Farm* by George Orwell, p. 135–6); Iris Murdoch and Chatto & Windus Ltd (extract from *The Sandcastle* by Iris Murdoch, p. 138); Weidenfeld & Nicolson Ltd (extract from *The Millstone* by Margaret Drabble, pp. 138–9); David Higham Associates Ltd (extract from *Billy Liar* by Keith Waterhouse, p. 141); Laurie Lee and The Hogarth Press Ltd (extract from *Cider with Rosie* by Laurie Lee, p. 143); Edward Arnold (extract from *A Passage to India* by EM Forster, p. 135); Elaine Greene Ltd (extract from *Death of a Salesman* published in Collected Plays by Arthur Miller, Secker & Warburg, *Death of a Salesman* Copyright © 1949 by Arthur Miller, pp. 92–3). Extract reprinted from "Yes, Do Have Those Bananas", by Jenny Bryan, June 26, 1992. Copyright 1992 by The Guardian. Reprinted with permission (p.186). "Turnip Heads" copyright Fleur Adcock 1991. Reprinted from *Time-Zones* by Fleur Adcock (1991) by permission of Oxford University Press (p.49). "Branch Line" copyright Anne Stevenson 1991. Reprinted from *The Other House* by Anne Stevenson (1990) by permission of Oxford University Press (pp.49–50). Extract reprinted from *Owners*, by Caryl Churchill, published by Methuen London. Reprinted by kind permission of Reed Consumer Books (pp.94–6). "Launderette" reprinted from *True Confessions*, by Liz Lochhead, published by Polygon. Reprinted with permission (pp.219–20). Extract from Chapter 5 of *Howards End* by E M Forster reprinted by kind permission of Kings College, Cambridge, and the Society of Authors as the literary representatives of the E M Forster estate (pp.216–7). Extract from *Uncertain Summer* copyright Betty Neels 1972. First published by Mills & Boon in 1972. Extract reproduced with the kind permission of Harlequin Books S.A. (pp.189–90). Extract reprinted from *Lipservice: The Story of Talk in Schools*, by Pat Jones, Open University Press, 1988. Reprinted with permission (pp.188–9). Photograph on p.116 by Angus McBean, reprinted by kind permission of the Raymond Mander & Joe Mitchenson Theatre Collection Ltd. All other photographs reprinted by kind permission of the National Portrait Gallery, London.

Thank you to the following Examination Boards for permission to reproduce their questions (NB any answers provided are the sole responsibility of the author and have not been provided by the Board in question):

Associated Examining Board
Northern Examinations and Assessment Board
University of London Examinations and Assessment Council
University of Cambridge Local Examinations Syndicate
Oxford Delegacy of Local Examinations
Welsh Joint Education Committee
Northern Ireland Council for the Curriculum Examinations and Assessment

Thank you also to my year 13 A-level students who allowed me to reproduce their essays: Andrew Greener, Radha Kumar, Claire Ashurst, Balwant Malhi and Rupinder Binning.

CONTENTS

SECTION 1: STARTING POINTS

SECTION 2: A-LEVEL ENGLISH

STARTING POINTS

HOW TO USE THIS BOOK

This book is not a text book, but has been written for English Literature and Language candidates at A- and AS-level and for the Scottish Higher Grade examinations. Our main objective has been to provide a book through which the student will gain skill and assurance in the techniques of A- and AS-level English and will be able to sit the examination with confidence. It is written by two practising teachers and examiners and has been compiled after carefully analysing the requirements of all the main A- and AS-level syllabuses. Our knowledge as examiners and our interpretation of Chief Examiners' Reports help us to provide you, the student, with the techniques and skills to make a success of your examination. You will find a summary of the syllabuses of the different boards in tabular form and the addresses of the main examination boards. This information may need checking from time to time as syllabuses change.

Although you will find reference to a wide variety of texts which appear on A-level syllabuses, this is **not** intended as a study aid to individual books or authors. It is a general guide to **transferable critical and study skills**. You should use the general advice given and **apply suggested methods of approach to your own set books**. You will find that we have used a wide range of approaches to different authors, genres and forms. You will get from this ideas on how to tackle your own study of individual texts. Close commentary, notes, the tracing of themes and diagrammatic aids are all represented.

THE STRUCTURE OF THIS BOOK

The key aim of this book is to guide you in the way you tackle A-level English. It should serve as a study guide, work book and revision aid throughout any A-level/AS-level English course, no matter what syllabus you are following. It is not intended to be a complete guide to the subject and should be used as a companion to your textbooks, which it is designed to complement rather than duplicate.

We have divided the book into three sections. **Section One, Starting Points**, contains study tips and syllabus information – all the material you need to get you started on your A-level study, together with advice on planning your revision and tips on how to tackle the exam itself.

Section Two, the main body of the text, contains the core of A-level English. It has been devised to make study as easy and enjoyable as possible, and has been divided into chapters which cover the themes you will encounter on your syllabus. The chapters are split into units, each covering a topic of study. A **list of objectives** at the beginning of each chapter directs you towards the key points of the chapter you are about to read. There are also **Question Banks**, with examples of different types of A-level exam questions for you to attempt.

In **Section Three, Test Run**, we turn our attention to the examination you will face at the end of your course. You should attempt the mock exam under timed conditions. This will give you invaluable examination practice and, together with the specimen answers specially provided by the author, will help you to judge how close you are to achieving your A-level pass.

USING YOUR SYLLABUS CHECKLIST

Whether you are using this book to work step-by-step through the syllabus or to structure your revision campaign, you will find it useful to keep a checklist of what you have covered – and how far you still have to go. Keep the checklist at hand when you are doing your revision, it will remind you of the chapters you have revised, and those still to be done.

The checklist for each examination – A, AS or Higher Grade – is in two parts. First there is a list of topics covered by this book which are part of the syllabus. When you have revised a topic make a note of the date in the column provided and, if there are questions elsewhere in the book, try to answer them.

The second part of the checklist gives you information about the examination, providing useful details about the time allocated for each written paper and the weighting of the questions on each paper. The different types of questions which may be set are explained under the heading The Examination.

COMMON CORE

ASSESSMENT OBJECTIVES

Literature

The examination will assess a candidate's ability to:

1. respond with understanding to texts of different types and periods;
2. understand the ways in which writers' choices of form, structure and language express meanings;
3. demonstrate knowledge of the contexts in which literary works are written and understood;
4. discuss their own and other readers' interpretations of texts;
5. produce informed, independent opinions and judgements;
6. communicate clearly the knowledge, understanding and insight appropriate to literary study.

Language

The examination will assess a candidate's ability to:

1. respond to, describe, explain and comment on examples of English from the present and the past;
2. know and use systematic frameworks for the study of language;
3. understand variations in the forms and meanings of language according to context;
4. understand concepts relating to language in use;
5. write for a variety of specific purposes and audiences;
6. communicate clearly the knowledge, understanding and insight appropriate to the study of language.

At AS and A level, all candidates must demonstrate study of at least one work of prose, one work of poetry and one work of drama and one play by Shakespeare, the first three of which should all have been written originally in English, include at least one written between 1370 and 1900, and be of sufficient substance and quality to merit serious consideration at A level.

SYLLABUS CHECKLISTS AND PAPER ANALYSIS

ASSOCIATED EXAMINING BOARD
A-level Syllabus 0623
ENGLISH LANGUAGE AND LITERATURE

Syllabus topic	Covered in Unit No	Completed on (date)	Questions attempted
Essay questions	All		
Poetry analysis	1.1		
Drama analysis	2.1		
Novel analysis	3.1		
Characters	1.1, 2.1, 3.1, 3.3		
Language	1.1, 2.1, 3.1, 3.3		
Themes	1.1, 2.1, 3.1, 3.3		
Shakespeare	2.5		
Settings	1.1, 2.1, 3.1, 3.3		
Language questions	4.4		
Essay	4.1		
Summary	4.2		
Comprehension	4.3		
Exam techniques	All		
Study skills	All		

Assessment Objectives

(i) In addition to the six core literature objectives this syllabus has four assessment objectives listed below:

7 make well-considered personal responses to prescribed texts;

8 understand the interplay between characters, plot and ideas in a text;

9 show how a writer involves different kinds of responses in readers or audiences;

10 discern and consider attitudes and values in texts.

(ii) Paper 1 tests core literature objectives 1–3; Paper 2 tests core literature objectives 3–6 and all objectives listed in note (i); Paper 3 tests core literature objectives 4–6 and all objectives listed in note (i).

Paper analysis

Paper 1   *2½ hours*   33⅓% of the marks
Section A
One essay on topics of general interest
Section B
A test of skills of summary writing

Paper 2   *3 hours*   33⅓% of the marks
Section A
Comprehension and analysis
Section B
Two essays, on set books – open book

Paper 3   *3 hours*   33⅓% of the marks
Set texts – two questions from Section 1
and two from Section 2 – open book.

ASSOCIATED EXAMINING BOARD
A-level Syllabus 0660C/0660W
ENGLISH LITERATURE

Syllabus topic	Covered in Unit No	Completed on (date)	Questions attempted
Essay questions	All		
Shakespeare	2.5		
Chaucer	1.7		
Poetry analysis	1.1		
Drama analysis	2.1		
Novel analysis	3.1		
Style & imagery	1.1, 2.1, 3.1, 3.3		
Comparison of two poems	1.1		
Themes	1.1, 2.1, 3.1, 3.3		
Settings	1.1, 2.1, 3.1, 3.3		
Literary criticism	1.1, 2.1, 3.1, 3.3		
Optional coursework	5.1		
Exam techniques	All		
Study skills	All		

Assessment objectives

(i) In addition to the six core literature objectives this syllabus has seven further assessment objectives. The candidate must demonstrate the ability to:

7️⃣ explore layers of meanings in text;

8️⃣ appreciate features of texts such as character, argument and imagery;

9️⃣ show how texts may excite emotions in readers or audiences;

🔟 make meaningful connections between texts;

⓫ explore works written for a different kind of society and in a different idiom from the candidate's own;

⓬ write effectively and appropriately in response to texts studied;

⓭ (optional coursework 0660) to show skill in presenting an oral response to a text.

(ii) Papers 1 and 2 tests core literature objectives 1–6 and objectives 7, 8, 9, 11 and 12 listed in note (i); Paper 3 tests all objectives except objective 13 listed in note (i); the coursework in syllabus 0660C tests all objectives.

Paper analysis

Syllabus 0660C

Paper 1   *3 hours*   40% of the marks
Section A
Unprepared poetry, one question from a choice of two
Section B
Unprepared prose, one question from a choice of two
Section C
Shakespeare, two questions on each of three Shakespeare plays, one question to be answered in total

Paper 2   *3 hours*   40% of the marks
                             Section A
                             Shakespeare, two questions on each of three
                             Shakespeare texts, one question to be answered
                             Section B
                             Drama, two questions on each of six drama texts,
                             one question to be answered
                             Section C
                             Poetry, two questions on each of six poetry texts,
                             one question to be answered
                             Section D
                             Prose, two questions on each of six prose texts,
                             one question to be answered

Paper 3   *Coursework*   20% of the marks
                             The whole folder should be between 2500 and 4000 words
                             For more detailed instructions send for a syllabus
                             from the Examining Board.

Syllabus 0660W
Paper 1 and Paper 2   Identical to Papers 1 and 2 in syllabus 0660C

Paper 3   *2¹/₂ hours*   20% of the marks
                             One question on each of two set texts,
                             one question on a free choice of text

ASSOCIATED EXAMINING BOARD
AS-level Syllabus 0986
ENGLISH LITERATURE

Syllabus topic	Covered in Unit No	Completed on (date)	Questions attempted
Essay questions	All		
Shakespeare	2.5		
Chaucer	1.7		
Poetry analysis	1.1		
Drama analysis	2.1		
Novel analysis	3.1		
Style & imagery	1.1, 2.1, 3.1, 3.3		
Comparison of two poems	1.1		
Themes	1.1, 2.1, 3.1, 3.3		
Settings	1.1, 2.1, 3.1, 3.3		
Literary criticism	1.1, 2.1, 3.1, 3.3		
Optional coursework	5.1		
Exam Techniques	All		
Study Skills	All		

Assessment objectives

(i) In addition to the six core literature objectives this syllabus has six further assessment objectives. The candidate must demonstrate the ability to:
  7 explore layers of meanings in text;
  8 appreciate features of texts such as character, argument and imagery;
  9 show how texts may excite emotions in readers or audiences;
  10 make meaningful connections between texts;
  11 explore works written for a different kind of society and in a different idiom from the candidate's own;
  12 write effectively and appropriately in response to texts studied.
(ii) Papers 1 tests core literature objectives 1–6 and objectives 7, 8, 9, 11 and 12; Paper 2 tests core literature objectives 2–6 and objectives 7, 8, 9, 10 and 12 listed in note (i).

Paper analysis

Paper 1   *3 hours*   80% of the marks
Section A
Shakespeare, two questions on each of three
Shakespeare texts, one question to be answered
Section B
Drama, two questions on each of six drama texts,
one question to be answered
Section C
Poetry, two questions on each of six poetry texts,
one question to be answered
Section D
Prose, two questions on each of six prose texts,
one question to be answered

Paper 2   *Coursework*   20% of the marks
The whole folder should be between 1500 and 2000 words
For more detailed instructions send for a syllabus
from the Examining Board.

ASSOCIATED EXAMINING BOARD
A-level Syllabus 0659
ENGLISH LANGUAGE

Syllabus topic	Covered in Unit No	Completed on (date)	Questions attempted
Essay questions	All		
Data response	4.3		
Phonology	4.5		
Spelling			
Lexis	4.6		
Semantics			
Grammar	4.6		
Discourse	4.1		
Language variations	4.4		
Language change	4.4		
Language development	4.4		
Language in society	4.4		
Language and social interaction	4.4		
Coursework	5.2		
Textual analysis	4.7		
Writing for audience	4.8		
Exam techniques	All		
Study skills	All		

Assessment objectives

(i) In addition to the six core language objectives this syllabus has four further assessment objectives. The candidate must demonstrate the ability to:

7 select information from a range of sources, interpret, adapt and re-present it for specific purposes and audiences;

8 understand and explain how meanings are conveyed through language choices at a variety of levels;

9 understand and act upon those social, personal and contextual factors which affect language use and its meaning;

10 evaluate the success of their own and others' language use.

(ii) Paper 1 tests core language objectives and all objectives listed in note (i); Paper 2 tests all core language objectives and objectives 7, 8, 9 and 10; Paper 3 tests all objectives.

Paper analysis

Paper 1   *3 hours*   40% of the marks
Two sections A and B, three questions to be answered, one from Section A, one from Section B and one from either Section A or B

Paper 2   *3 hours*   40% of the marks
Two sections A and B, two questions to be answered, one from each section

Paper 3   *Coursework*   20% of the marks
The whole folder should be between 2500 and 4000 words. For more detailed instructions send for a syllabus from the Examining Board

ASSOCIATED EXAMINING BOARD
AS-level Syllabus 0985
ENGLISH LANGUAGE

Syllabus topic	Covered in Unit No	Completed on (date)	Questions attempted
Essay questions	All		
Data response	4.3		
Phonology	4.5		
Spelling			
Lexis	4.6		
Semantics			
Grammar	4.6		
Discourse	4.1		
Language variations	4.4		
Language change	4.4		
Language development	4.4		
Language in society	4.4		
Language and social interaction	4.4		
Coursework	5.2		
Textual analysis	4.7		
Writing for audience	4.8		
Exam techniques	All		
Study skills	All		

Assessment objectives

(i) In addition to the six core language objectives this syllabus has five further assessment objectives. The candidate must demonstrate the ability to:

  7 select information from a range of sources, interpret, adapt and re-present it for specific purposes and audiences;

  8 understand and explain how meanings are conveyed through language choices at a variety of levels;

  9 understand and act upon those social, personal and contextual factors which affect language use and its meaning;

  10 evaluate the success of their own and others' language use;

  11 research and investigate independently and resourcefully.

(ii) Paper 1 tests core language objectives and all objectives listed in note (i); Paper 2 tests all objectives.

Paper analysis

Paper 1   *3 hours*   80% of the marks
Two sections A and B, three questions to be answered, one from Section A, one from Section B and one from either Section A or B

Paper 2   *Coursework*   20% of the marks
The whole folder should be between 1500 and 2000 words. For more detailed instructions send for a syllabus from the Examining Board

UNIVERSITY OF CAMBRIDGE LOCAL EXAMINATIONS SYNDICATE
A-level Syllabus 9004
ENGLISH

Syllabus topic	Covered in Unit No	Completed on (date)	Questions attempted
Essay questions	All		
Data response	4.3		
Phonology	4.5		
Spelling			
Lexis	4.6		
Semantics			
Grammar	4.6		
Discourse	4.1		
Language variations	4.4		
Language change	4.4		
Language development	4.4		
Language in society	4.4		
Language and social interaction	4.4		
Coursework	5.2		
Textual analysis	4.7		
Writing for audience	4.8		
Exam techniques	All		
Study skills	All		

Assessment objectives

(i) This syllabus has no additional objectives to the core language objectives.
(ii) Paper 1 tests core language objectives 1–6; Paper 2 tests core language objectives 1, 2, 4, 5 and 6; Paper 3 tests core language objectives 1, 2 and 5.

Paper analysis

Paper 1   *3 hours*   40% of the marks
Three questions from a choice of five.
All questions carry equal marks

Paper 2   *Coursework*   20% of the marks
A folder of written work of 3000–5000 words
and evidence of oral work

Paper 3   *3 hours*   40% of the marks
One question from three of the following areas:
(1) Language and persuasion
(2) Language and gender
(3) Language and identities
(4) Language at play

UNIVERSITY OF CAMBRIDGE LOCAL EXAMINATIONS SYNDICATE
AS-level Syllabus 8448
ENGLISH

Syllabus topic	Covered in Unit No	Completed on (date)	Questions attempted
Essay questions	All		
Data response	4.3		
Phonology	4.5		
Spelling			
Lexis	4.6		
Semantics			
Grammar	4.6		
Discourse	4.1		
Language variations	4.4		
Language change	4.4		
Language development	4.4		
Language in society	4.4		
Language and social interaction	4.4		
Coursework	5.2		
Textual analysis	4.7		
Writing for audience	4.8		
Exam techniques	All		
Study skills	All		

Assessment objectives

(i) This syllabus has no additional objectives to the core language objectives.

(ii) Paper 1 tests core language objectives 1–6; Paper 2 tests core language objectives 1, 2, 4, 5 and 6.

Paper analysis

Paper 1   *3 hours*   80% of the marks
Three questions from a choice of five

Paper 2   *Coursework*   20% of the marks
The whole folder should be between 3000–5000 words.
For more detailed instructions send for a syllabus
from the Examining Board

UNIVERSITY OF CAMBRIDGE LOCAL EXAMINATIONS SYNDICATE
A-level Syllabus 9000
ENGLISH LITERATURE

Syllabus topic	Covered in Unit No	Completed on (date)	Questions attempted
Essay questions	All		
Shakespeare	2.5		
Chaucer	1.7		
Poetry analysis	1.1		
Drama analysis	2.1		
Novel analysis	3.1		
Style & imagery	1.1, 2.1, 3.1, 3.3		
Comparison of two poems	1.1		
Themes	1.1, 2.1, 3.1, 3.3		
Settings	1.1, 2.1, 3.1, 3.3		
Literary criticism	1.1, 2.1, 3.1, 3.3		
Optional coursework	5.1		
Exam techniques	All		
Study skills	All		

Assessment objectives

(i) This syllabus has no additional objectives to the core literature objectives.
(ii) The seven papers test all core literature objectives.

Paper analysis

Paper 1   *3 hours*   33⅓% of the marks
Compulsory   Shakespeare and Other Authors
                        (pre-Twentieth Century) (books in)

Paper 2   *3 hours*   33⅓% of the marks
                        Eighteenth and Nineteenth Century Writing

Paper 3   *3 hours*   33⅓% of the marks
                        Twentieth Century Writing

Paper 4   *3 hours*   33⅓% of the marks
                        Topic Paper (books in)

Paper 5   *3 hours*   33⅓% of the marks
                        Open Texts (books in)

Paper 6   *1 hour*   20% plus Paper 7 13⅓%
                        Coursework plus Comment and Appreciation
                        (Set Text) (book in)

Rules of combination

Paper 1 plus any two of: 2, 3, 4, 5, 6+7
Number of Routeways – 10

1+2+3	1+2+5	1+3+4	1+3+6+7	1+4+6+7
1+2+4	1+2+6+7	1+3+5	1+4+5	1+5+6+7

No alternative routes of assessment are available. For more detailed instructions send for a syllabus from the Examining Board.

UNIVERSITY OF CAMBRIDGE LOCAL EXAMINATIONS SYNDICATE
A-level Syllabus 9505
AS-level Syllabus 8570
ENGLISH LITERATURE (MODULAR)

Syllabus topic	Covered in Unit No	Completed on (date)	Questions attempted
Essay questions	All		
Shakespeare	2.5		
Chaucer	1.7		
Poetry analysis	1.1		
Drama analysis	2.1		
Novel analysis	3.1		
Style & imagery	1.1, 2.1, 3.1, 3.3		
Comparison of two poems	1.1		
Themes	1.1, 2.1, 3.1, 3.3		
Settings	1.1, 2.1, 3.1, 3.3		
Literary criticism	1.1, 2.1, 3.1, 3.3		
Optional coursework	5.1		
Exam Techniques	All		
Study Skills	All		

Assessment objectives

(i) This syllabus has no additional objectives to the core literature objectives.

Paper analysis

The modular scheme consists of six modules for A-level (each carrying equal weighting) and three modules for AS (each carrying equal weighting).

Module 4481   *2 hours*   Shakespeare and Other Authors
                              (pre-Twentieth Century) (books in)

Module 4482   *2 hours*   Eighteenth- and Nineteenth-Century Writing

Module 4483   *2 hours*   Twentieth-Century Writing

Module 4484   *2 hours*   Topic Paper (books in)

Module 4485   *2 hours*   Open Texts (books in)

Module 4486*   Coursework (Literary Texts)
     OR
Module 4487*   Coursework (Creative Writing)

Module 4488†   *1¹⁄₂ hours*   Comment and Appreciation (Unseen)

Module 4489†   *1¹⁄₂ hours*   Imaginative Response

Note: All modules except 4486 and 4487 are assessed by end of module examination.

Module 4481 is compulsory for both A- and AS-level.

* available at A-level only.

† Candidates must take either module 4488 or module or module 4489 as a final synoptic module.

ENGLISH LANGUAGE
A-level Syllabus 9001

Paper analysis

Paper 1   *3 hours*   40% of the marks
                         Passages for comment and adaptation

Paper 2   *3 hours*   40% of the marks
                         Essays
Either
Paper 3   *2 hours*   20% of the marks
                         Special topic paper
Or
Paper 4   *Coursework*   20% of the marks
                         Option A: Creative and informative writing
                         (maximum 5,000 words)
          OR   Option B: Project (maximum 5,000 words)

AS-level Syllabus 8440

Paper analysis

Paper 1   *3 hours*   80% of the marks
                         Passages and essays

Paper 4   *Coursework*   20% of the marks
                         Option A: Creative and infromative writing
                         (maximum 3,000 words)
          OR   Option B: Project (maximum 3,000 words)

UNIVERSITY OF LONDON EXAMINATIONS AND ASSESSMENT COUNCIL
A-level Syllabus 9174
ENGLISH LANGUAGE

Syllabus topic	Covered in Unit No	Completed on (date)	Questions attempted
Essay questions	All		
Data response	4.3		
Phonology	4.5		
Spelling			
Lexis	4.6		
Semantics			
Grammar	4.6		
Discourse	4.1		
Language variations	4.4		
Language change	4.4		
Language development	4.4		
Language in society	4.4		
Language and social interaction	4.4		
Coursework	5.2		
Textual analysis	4.7		
Writing for audience	4.8		
Exam techniques	All		
Study Skills	All		

Assessment objectives

(i) This syllabus has no additional objectives to the core language objectives.

(ii) Papers 1, 2 and 3 test all objectives.

Paper analysis

Three papers to be attempted, Papers 1 and 2 compulsory; **either** Paper 3C **or** 3E to be answered.

Paper 1   *3 hours*   40% of the marks
                            One question from Section A and
                            two from Section B

Paper 2   *3 hours*   40% of the marks
                            Three questions, two to be answered

Either
Paper 3C   *Coursework*   20% of the marks
                            In the form of 2–3 mins of tape-recorded speech
                            and a project of 2000–3000 words
                            (see Examining Board syllabus for further guidance)
Or
Paper 3E   *1½ hours*   20% of the marks
                            Two questions, one to be answered

UNIVERSITY OF LONDON EXAMINATIONS AND ASSESSMENT COUNCIL
A-level Syllabus 9171 (modular or terminal examination)
ENGLISH LITERATURE

Syllabus topic	Covered in Unit No	Completed on (date)	Questions attempted
Essay questions	All		
Shakespeare	2.5		
Chaucer	1.7		
Poetry analysis	1.1		
Drama analysis	2.1		
Novel analysis	3.1		
Style & imagery	1.1, 2.1, 3.1, 3.3		
Comparison of two poems	1.1		
Themes	1.1, 2.1, 3.1, 3.3		
Settings	1.1, 2.1, 3.1, 3.3		
Literary criticism	1.1, 2.1, 3.1, 3.3		
Optional coursework	5.1		
Exam techniques	All		
Study skills	All		

Assessment objectives

(i) This syllabus has no additional objectives to the core literature objectives.

(ii) The syllabus is modular, each module tests all assessment objectives.

Paper analysis

Module 1   *2 hours*   20% of the marks
Two sections, one question to be answered from each section

Module 2   *3 hours*   30% of the marks
One question to be answered from compulsory section A,
one from section B and a third question from
either section B or section C

Module 3   3C *coursework*   3C 20% of the marks
OR   The whole folder should be between 3000–4000 words.
3E *2 hours*   For more detailed instructions send for a syllabus
from the Examining Board
3E 20% of the marks
Eight texts are normally set and candidates must
answer two questions

Module 4   *3 hours*   30% of the marks
One question from section A, two questions from section B

UNIVERSITY OF LONDON EXAMINATIONS AND ASSESSMENT COUNCIL
AS-level Syllabus 8171 (modular or terminal examination)
ENGLISH LITERATURE

Syllabus topic	Covered in Unit No	Completed on (date)	Questions attempted
Essay questions	All		
Shakespeare	2.5		
Chaucer	1.7		
Poetry analysis	1.1		
Drama analysis	2.1		
Novel analysis	3.1		
Style & imagery	1.1, 2.1, 3.1, 3.3		
Comparison of two poems	1.1		
Themes	1.1, 2.1, 3.1, 3.3		
Settings	1.1, 2.1, 3.1, 3.3		
Literary criticism	1.1, 2.1, 3.1, 3.3		
Optional coursework	5.1		
Exam techniques	All		
Study skills	All		

Assessment objectives

(i) This syllabus has no additional objectives to the core literature objectives.

(ii) The syllabus is modular, each module tests all assessment objectives.

Paper analysis

Module 1   *2 hours*   40% of the marks
One question to be answered from section A
and one from section B

Module 2   *1 hour*   20% of the marks
                           One question to be answered from section B

Module 4   *2 hours*   40% of the marks
                           One question to be answered from section A
                           and one from section B

UNIVERSITY OF LONDON EXAMINATIONS AND ASSESSMENT COUNCIL
AS-level Syllabus 8177 (modular or terminal examination)
ENGLISH

Syllabus topic	Covered in Unit No	Completed on (date)	Questions attempted
Essay questions	All		
Data response	4.3		
Phonology	4.5		
Spelling			
Lexis	4.6		
Semantics			
Grammar	4.6		
Discourse	4.1		
Language variations	4.4		
Language change	4.4		
Language development	4.4		
Language in society	4.4		
Language and social interaction	4.4		
Coursework	5.2		
Textual analysis	4.7		
Writing for audience	4.8		
Exam techniques	All		
Study skills	All		

Assessment objectives

(i)   This syllabus has no additional objectives to the core language objectives.
(ii) Papers 1, 2 and 3 test all objectives.

Paper analysis

Three papers to be attempted, Papers 1 and 2 compulsory; either Papers 3C or 3E to be answered.

Paper 1   *3 hours*   80% of the marks
                           For more detailed instructions send for a syllabus
                           from the Examining Board

Paper 2C   *Coursework*   20% of the marks
                           For more detailed instructions send for a syllabus
                           from the Examining Board

NORTHERN EXAMINATIONS AND ASSESSMENT BOARD
A and AS-level Syllabuses
ENGLISH LITERATURE

Syllabus topic	Covered in Unit No	Completed on (date)	Questions attempted
Essay questions	All		
Shakespeare	2.5		
Chaucer	1.7		
Poetry analysis	1.1		
Drama analysis	2.1		
Novel analysis	3.1		
Style & imagery	1.1, 2.1, 3.1, 3.3		
Comparison of two poems	1.1		
Themes	1.1, 2.1, 3.1, 3.3		
Settings	1.1, 2.1, 3.1, 3.3		
Literary criticism	1.1, 2.1, 3.1, 3.3		
Optional coursework	5.1		
Exam techniques	All		
Study skills	All		

Assessment objectives

(i) This syllabus has no additional objectives to the core literature objectives.
(ii) All papers test all objectives.

Paper analysis

Section A   60 marks

1 **Coursework Folder: Extended Literary Studies** comprising a study of at least three texts

OR 2 **Examination: Unseen Critical Appreciation** a choice of passages (poetry and prose) for critical appreciation.
NB this component may not be taken with Lit C4 (Critical Explorations).

Section B   each component 80 marks

Examination: Shakespeare requiring the study of two set plays. Either Traditional exam (2 questions), or Open book (2 questions).

Section C   each component 80 marks

1 **Examination: Selected Texts** requiring the study of two set texts. Either Traditional exam (2 questions), or Open book (2 questions).

2 **Examination: Selected Texts** requiring the study of two set texts. Either Traditional exam (2 questions), or Open book (2 questions).

3 **Examination: Linked Texts** requiring the study of two set texts. Either Traditional exam (2 questions), or Open book (2 questions).

4 **Examination: Critical Explorations** two questions on 'seen' passages from a choice of 'packages' covering a range of literary and critical forms.
NB this component may not be taken along with Lit A2 (Unseen critical appreciation).

Combinations

A-level   Lit A1 or Lit A2 + Lit B + 2 from Lit C.
NB Lit A2 may not be taken with Lit C4.
AS-level   Lit A1: reduced length + Lit B: 1 question (1 hour) + Lit C1 or Lit C2.

For more detailed instructions send for a syllabus from the Examining Board.

NORTHERN EXAMINATIONS AND ASSESSMENT BOARD
A and AS-level Syllabuses
ENGLISH LANGUAGE

Syllabus topic	Covered in Unit No	Completed on (date)	Questions attempted
Essay questions	All		
Data response	4.3		
Phonetics	4.5		
Grammar	4.6		
Language variations	4.4		
Language change	4.4		
Language development	4.4		
Language in society	4.4		
Language acquisition	4.4		
Case study	4.8		
Coursework	5.2		
Exam techniques	All		
Study skills	All		

Assessment objectives

(i) This syllabus has no additional objectives to the core language objectives.
(ii) All papers test all objectives.

Paper analysis

Components

Unless otherwise stated all components are of two hours' duration.

Language

Section A	60 marks	1 **Coursework Folder: Language and Its Uses** comprising either a language investigation or original writing (plus commentary)
Section B	each component 80 marks	**Examination: Language Issues and Stylistics** two questions to be answered on the theoretical knowledge and understanding essential to the study of English Language
Section C	each component 80 marks	1 **Examination: Language and Its Uses** requiring candidates to undertake *either* an investigation of linguistic data *or* original writing plus commentary *2 hrs 30 mins*
		2 **Examination: Case Study** requiring the candidate to create a new text by representing pre-released material *2 hrs 30 mins*

Combinations

A-level   Lang A1 + Lang B + Lang C1 + Lang C2
               NB Candidates may not offer the same alternatives in both
               Lang A1 and Lang C1

AS-level   Lang A1: reduced length (investigation alternative only available)
               Lang B: 1 question (1 hour), Lang C1 (original writing) or Lang C2

For more detailed instructions send for a syllabus from the Examining Board.

NORTHERN EXAMINATIONS AND ASSESSMENT BOARD
A-level Syllabus
ENGLISH LANGUAGE AND LITERATURE

Syllabus topic	Covered in Unit No	Completed on (date)	Questions attempted
Essay questions	All		
Poetry analysis	1.1		
Drama analysis	2.1		
Characters	1.1, 2.1, 3.1, 3.3		
Language	1.1, 2.1, 3.1, 3.3		
Shakespeare settings	2.5		
Language questions	1.1, 2.1, 3.1, 3.3		
Essay	4.1		
Language change	4.4		
Language in society	4.4		
Language variations	4.4		
Language acquisition	4.4		
Grammar	4.6		
Phonetics	4.5		
Case study	4.8		
Coursework	5.2		
Exam technique	All		
Study skills	All		

Assessment objectives

(i) This syllabus has no additional objectives to the core literature and language objectives.
(ii) All papers test all objectives.

Paper analysis

Components

Unless otherwise stated all components are of two hours' duration.

Literature

Section A	60 marks	1	**Coursework Folder: Extended Literary Studies** comprising a study of at least three texts
		OR 2	**Examination: Unseen Critical Appreciation** a choice of passages (poetry and prose) for critical appreciation. NB: this component may not be taken with Lit C4 (Critical Explorations)
Section B	each component 80 marks		**Examination: Shakespeare** requiring the study of two set plays. Either Traditional exam (2 questions), or Open book (2 questions)
Section C	each component 80 marks	1	**Examination: Selected Texts** requiring the study of two set texts. Either Traditional exam (2 questions), or Open book (2 questions)
		2	**Examination: Selected Texts** requiring the study of two set texts. Either Traditional exam (2 questions), or Open book (2 questions)

3 **Examination: Linked texts**
requiring the study of two set texts.
Either Traditional exam (2 questions), or
Open book (2 questions)

4 **Examination: Critical Explorations**
two questions on 'seen' passages from a choice
of 'packages' covering a range of literary and
critical forms. NB. This component may not be
taken along with Lit A2 (Unseen critical
appreciation)

Language

Section A	60 marks	1	**Coursework Folder: Language and Its Uses** comprising *either* a language investigation *or* original writing (plus commentary)
Section B	each component 80 marks		**Examination: Language Issues and Stylistics** two questions to be answered on the theoretical knowledge and understanding essential to the study of English Language
Section C	each component 80 marks	1	**Examination: Language and Its Uses** requiring candidates to undertake *either* an investigation of linguistic data *or* original writing plus commentary *2 hours 30 mins*
		2	**Examination: Case study** requiring the candidate to create a new text by representing pre-released material *2 hours 30 minutes*

Combinations

Either   Lang A1 or Lit A2 + Lang B + one Lit component + 1 Lang component
(Excluding Lang A1 and C1 investigation option)
NB Lit A2 may not be taken with Lit C4

Or   Lang A1 + Lang B + two Lit components (excluding Lit A1 and Lit A2)

For more detailed instructions send for a syllabus from the Examining Board.

NORTHERN IRELAND COUNCIL FOR THE CURRICULUM EXAMINATIONS AND ASSESSMENT
A-level Syllabus
ENGLISH LITERATURE

Syllabus topic	Covered in Unit No	Completed on (date)	Questions attempted
Essay questions	All		
Shakespeare	2.5		
Chaucer	1.7		
Poetry analysis	1.1		
Drama analysis	2.1		
Novel analysis	3.1		
Style & imagery	1.1, 2.1, 3.1, 3.3		
Comparison of two poems	1.1		
Themes	1.1, 2.1, 3.1, 3.3		
Settings	1.1, 2.1, 3.1, 3.3		
Literary criticism	1.1, 2.1, 3.1, 3.3		
Exam techniques	All		
Study skills	All		

Assessment objectives

(i) This syllabus has no additional objectives to the core literature objectives.

(ii) All papers test all objectives.

Paper analysis

Paper 1   *2½ hours*   30% of the marks
Section A
A compulsory practical criticism question on unseen poetry
Section B
Two essay questions on prescribed texts

Paper 2   *2½ hours*   30% of the marks
Candidates will answer three questions
Section A
A compulsory practical criticism question on unseen prose
Section B
Two essay questions on prescribed texts

Paper 3   *3 hours*   40% of the marks
Candidates will answer four questions
Section A
Candidates must answer one question on each of the two prescribed Shakespeare texts. There will be a choice of gobbet-style questions on one text and essay-type questions on the second. Either text may be examined in either question format
Section B
Two essay questions on prescribed texts

UNIVERSITY OF OXFORD DELEGACY OF LOCAL EXAMINATIONS
A and AS-level Syllabuses 9903
ENGLISH LITERATURE (modular or terminal examination)

Syllabus topic	Covered in Unit No	Completed on (date)	Questions attempted
Essay questions	All		
Shakespeare	2.5		
Chaucer	1.7		
Poetry analysis	1.1		
Drama analysis	2.1		
Novel analysis	3.1		
Style & imagery	1.1, 2.1, 3.1, 3.3		
Comparison of two poems	1.1		
Themes	1.1, 2.1, 3.1, 3.3		
Settings	1.1, 2.1, 3.1, 3.3		
Literary criticism	1.1, 2.1, 3.1, 3.3		
Exam techniques	All		
Study skills	All		

Assessment objectives

(i) These syllabuses have no additional objectives to the core literature objectives.

(ii) These syllabuses are modular and follow teaching units, each unit tests all assessment objectives.

Paper analysis – A-level teaching units

The A-level English Literature syllabus consists of eight Units. For an A-level Certificate candidates must do Units 1, 3, 5 and **three** other Units. **No** candidate may do **both** Unit 7(a) **and** Unit 8(a).

AREA 1 Close Readings	AREA 2 Wider Writings	AREA 3 Texts and Interpretations	AREA 4 Coursework
Unit 1 Shakespeare and The Drama	Unit 3 Poetry and Prose	Unit 5 Complementary Studies	Unit 7(a) Literature Coursework
Unit 2 Critical Appraisal	Unit 4 Writers of the Later Twentieth Century	Unit 6 Further Reading	Unit 8(a) Experiments in Writing Coursework

Assessment components

Teaching Units 1 to 6 are assessed by written question papers 9903/1 to 6 respectively and each paper is 1½ hours duration. Unit 7(a) and Unit 8(a) each comprise study leading to coursework which is assessed by the teacher and moderated by Oxford. All assessment components have 16.67% weighting.

During the examination the pairs of question papers for the same Area of study will be timetabled consecutively in three 3 hour sessions.

• Candidates working both papers may take a rest break of no more than 10 minutes between papers.

• Candidates working one paper of the pair must be in the examination room only for the appropriate 1½ hour period.

Paper analysis – AS-level teaching units

The AS-level English Literature syllabus consists of Units 1 to 4 and Unit 6 of the A-level English Literature syllabus.

For an AS-level certificate candidates **must** do Unit 1 and Unit 3 and **one** other Unit which must **not** be Unit 5 **nor** either of the coursework Units 7(a) and 8(a).

Assessment components

Teaching Units 1 to 4 and Unit 6 are assessed by written question papers 9903/1 to 4 and 9903/6 respectively, and each paper is 1½ hours duration. All question papers have equal weighting.

During the examination the pairs of question papers for the same Area of study will be timetabled consecutively in three 3 hour sessions.

- Candidates working both papers may take a rest break of **no more** than 10 minutes between papers.
- Candidates working one paper of the pair must be in the examination room **only** for the appropriate 1½ hour period.

UNIVERSITY OF OXFORD DELEGACY OF LOCAL EXAMINATIONS
A and AS-level Syllabuses 9905 (modular or terminal examination)
ENGLISH LANGUAGE AND LITERATURE

Syllabus topic	Covered in Unit No	Completed on (date)	Questions attempted
Essay questions	All		
Poetry analysis	1.1		
Novel analysis	3.1		
Characters	1.1, 2.1, 3.1, 3.3		
Language	1.1, 2.1, 3.1, 3.3		
Themes	1.1, 2.1, 3.1, 3.3		
Shakespeare settings	2.5		
Language questions	4.4		
Essay	4.1		
Summary	4.2		
Comprehension	4.3		
Coursework	5.2		
Exam techniques	All		
Study skills	All		

Assessment objectives

(i) In addition to the core literature and language objectives these syllabuses have eight further objectives. The candidate must demonstrate the following:

⑦ an ability to respond with understanding to a variety of texts including both literary and non-literary material;

⑧ an understanding of the ways in which writers' choices of form, structure, style and vocabulary may express meanings;

⑨ an ability to discern and consider attitudes and values in texts;

⑩ an ability to produce informed, independent opinions and judgements;

⑪ knowledge of, and the ability to use, systematic frameworks for the study of language;

⑫ an understanding of variations in the forms and meanings of language according to context;

⑬ an ability to express themselves clearly and effectively for a variety of audiences and purposes;

⑭ an ability to communicate the knowledge, understanding and insight appropriate to literary study and the study of language.

(ii) The syllabuses are modular, called teaching units, each unit tests all assessment objectives.

Paper analysis – A-level teaching units

The A-level English Language and Literature syllabus consists of ten Units. For an A-level Certificate candidates **must** do Unit 9 **and** Unit 10 together with **either** Unit 1 **or** Unit 3 and **either** Unit 7(b) **or** Unit 8(b) and **two** other Units.

AREA 1 Close Readings	AREA 2 Wider Writings	AREA 3 Texts and Interpretations	AREA 4 Coursework	AREA 5 Language
Unit 1 Shakespeare and The Drama	Unit 3 Poetry and Prose	Unit 5 Complementary Studies	Unit 7(b) Language and Literature Coursework	Unit 9 Approaches to English Language
Unit 2 Critical Appraisal	Unit 4 Writers of the Later Twentieth Century	Unit 6 Further Reading	Unit 8(a) Experiments in Writing Coursework	Unit 10 Language and Presentation

Assessment Components

Teaching Units 1–6 and Unit 9 and Unit 10 are assessed by written question papers 9905/1–6 and 9905/9 and 9905/10 respectively. Each paper is 1½ hours duration. Unit 7(b) and Unit 8(b) each comprise study leading to coursework which is assessed by the teacher and moderated by Oxford. All assessment components have 16.67% weighting.

During the examination three pairs of papers for the same Area of study will be timetabled consecutively in three 3 hour sessions.

• Candidates working both papers may take a rest break of no more than 10 minutes between papers.
• Candidates working one paper of the pair must be in the examination room only for the appropriate 1½ hour period.

AS-level teaching units

The AS-level English Language and Literature syllabus consists of Units 1 to 4, Unit 6, Unit 9 and Unit 10 of the Advanced English Language and Literature syllabus.

For an AS-level certificate candidates **must** do Unit 9 **or** Unit 10 with **either** Unit 1 **or** Unit 3 together with **one** other Unit which may **not** be Unit 5 **nor** either of the coursework Units 7(b) and 8(b).

SCOTTISH EXAMINATIONS BOARD
Higher Grade Syllabus
ENGLISH LANGUAGE AND LITERATURE

Syllabus topics	Covered in Unit No	Completed on (date)	Questions attempted
Essay question	All		
Discussion of quotation	1.1, 2.1, 3.1, 3.3		
Main characters	1.1, 2.1, 3.1, 3.3		
Minor characters	3.3		
Style and imagery	1.1, 2.1, 3.1, 3.3		
Comparison of two poets	1.1		
Treatment of themes	1.1, 2.1, 3.1, 3.3		
Settings	1.1, 2.1, 3.1, 3.3		
Autobiographical and narrative detail	1.1, 2.1, 3.1, 3.3		
General historical/literary essays on a period			
Literary criticism	1.1, 2.1, 3.1, 3.3		
Poetry	1.1–1.8		
Prose	3.1–3.3		
Drama	2.1–2.5		
Language questions	4.4		
Essay	4.1		
Summary	4.2		
Comprehension	4.3		
Personal studies folio	5.1, 5.2		
Creative work			
Unprescribed writing task			

Paper analysis

Personal studies folio	Candidates will submit two pieces of writing: i) a review of personal reading ii) either a piece of imaginative writing or a piece of discursive writing

Paper 1   *2 hours 5 min*   33% of the marks
Section A
Unseen prose
Section B
Candidates will be required to study several
related tasks and produce a report

Paper 2   *1 hours 35 min*   33% of the marks
Part 1
Either Section A
Practical criticism, one question to be answered
Or Section B
Answers on a key passage in prose or drama
taken from set texts
Part 2
Section C
Critical essay – a substantial piece of continuous prose on 1 of
a range of literary and media topics

NB There are also certificates of the sixth-year studies. The requirements of these must be
applied for from the board.

OXFORD AND CAMBRIDGE SCHOOLS EXAMINATION BOARD
A and AS-level Syllabuses 9620/8395 (modular or terminal examination)
ENGLISH LITERATURE

Syllabus topic	Covered in Unit No	Completed on (date)	Questions attempted
Essay questions	All		
Shakespeare	2.5		
Chaucer	1.7		
Poetry analysis	1.1		
Drama analysis	2.1		
Novel analysis	3.1		
Style & imagery	1.1, 2.1, 3.1, 3.3		
Comparison of two poems	1.1		
Themes	1.1, 2.1, 3.1, 3.3		
Settings	1.1, 2.1, 3.1, 3.3		
Literary criticism	1.1, 2.1, 3.1, 3.3		
Optional coursework	5.1		
Exam techniques	All		
Study skills	All		

Paper analysis

A-level English Literature 9620

Unit 1	*2½ hours*		30% of the marks
			1 Shakespeare and the Drama
Unit 2	*2½ hours*		30% of the marks
			2 Texts for close reading and critical analysis
Unit 3	*2 hours*		20% of the marks
		either	4 General literature
	Coursework	or	5 Literature in translation
		or	6 Coursework (texts), 3000–5000 words

Candidates offering Coursework may write either on Component 4 texts or on Component 5 texts or on a self chosen book list approved by the Board provided that the core requirements are thereby satisfied

Unit 4	*2½ hours*		20% of the marks
		either	8 Comment and Appreciation
		or	9 A-level Coursework (Project)
	Coursework		Option 1: 3 pieces of Creative Critical Writing
			Option 2: A Long Essay (3000 words)
			Option 3: A Theatre Project (3000 words)
Unit 0	*3 hours*		100% marks
			Special Paper

Units 1 to 4 are compulsory.

Coursework may be offered in either Unit 3 or Unit 4 but not in both.

Coursework is only available to candidates entered through a centre whose scheme has been approved by the Board.

Choices of texts within units are subject to core reading requirements (see syllabus for details).

The Special Paper (Unit 0) is available only to candidates entered for the Advanced level.

AS-level English Literature 8395

Unit 1
		60% of the marks
	2¹/₂ hours	either 1 Shakespeare and the Drama
	2¹/₂ hours	or 2 Texts for Close Reading and Critical Analysis

Unit 2
		40% of the marks
	2 hours	either 4 General Literature
	1 hour + coursework	or 7 AS General Literature with Coursework (Texts)

Candidates must take both units.

The coursework option (Component 7) is available only to candidates entered through a centre whose scheme has been approved by the Board.

Choices of texts within units are subject to core reading requirements (see syllabus for details). Centres should take particular care that AS courses cover these requirements. If, for example, Component 1 is not taken, Shakespeare must be studied for another component.

UNIVERSITY OF OXFORD DELEGACY OF LOCAL EXAMINATIONS
A and AS-level Syllabuses 9621/8396 (modular or terminal examination)
ENGLISH LITERATURE AND LANGUAGE

Syllabus topic	Covered in Unit No	Completed on (date)	Questions attempted
Essay questions	All		
Poetry analysis	1.1		
Novel analysis	3.1		
Characters	1.1, 2.1, 3.1, 3.3		
Language	1.1, 2.1, 3.1, 3.3		
Themes	1.1, 2.1, 3.1, 3.3		
Shakespeare settings	2.5		
Language questions	4.4		
Essay	4.1		
Summary	4.2		
Comprehension	4.3		
Coursework	5.2		
Exam techniques	All		
Study skills	All		

Paper analysis

A-level English Language and Literature 9621

Unit 1	*3 hours*	30% of the marks English Language
Unit 2	*2¹/₂ hours*	30% of the marks either Shakespeare and the Drama or Texts for Close Reading and Critical Analysis
Unit 3	*2 hours*	20% of the marks General literature
Unit 4	*Coursework*	Language – up to 3,000 words
Unit 0	*3 hours*	100% of the marks Special Paper

29

AS-level English Language and Literature 8396

Unit 1	*3 hours*	60% of the marks English Language
Unit 2	*2 hours*	40% of the marks General Literature
	OR	
	1 hour + coursework	20% + 20% of the marks AS General Literature with Coursework

WELSH JOINT EDUCATION COMMITTEE
A and AS-level Syllabuses
ENGLISH LITERATURE

Syllabus topic	Covered in Unit No	Completed on (date)	Questions attempted
Essay questions	All		
Shakespeare	2.5		
Chaucer	1.7		
Poetry analysis	1.1		
Drama analysis	2.1		
Novel analysis	3.1		
Style & imagery	1.1, 2.1, 3.1, 3.3		
Comparison of two poems	1.1		
Themes	1.1, 2.1, 3.1, 3.3		
Settings	1.1, 2.1, 3.1, 3.3		
Literary criticism	1.1, 2.1, 3.1, 3.3		
Exam techniques	All		
Study skills	All		

Assessment objectives

(i) In addition to the six core literature objectives this syllabus has two further assessment objectives. Depending on options chosen, candidates may be required to demonstrate:
   1 a spontaneous engagement with, and interpretation of literary texts based on a wider reading;
   2 an understanding of the writing process through an ability to produce their own texts.

Paper analysis

A-level

Paper 1	*3 hours*	40% of the marks Candidates must answer four questions, one from each of the following sections: Section A: Shakespeare play Section B: Poetry Section C: Prose Section D: Drama (open book)
Paper 2	*3 hours*	40% of the marks Four questions on at least four texts chosen from a reading list of fifteen (open book)

Either Paper 3		20% of the marks
	2¹/₂ hours	Three questions on unseen passages from a range of historical periods, two questions to be answered
OR	*Coursework*	The whole folder should be between 3000–4000 words. For more detailed instructions send for a syllabus from the Examining Board

AS-level

Paper 1	*3 hours*	80% of the marks
		Candidates must answer four questions, one from each of the following sections:
		Section A: Shakespeare
		Section B: Poetry
		Section C: Prose
		Section D: Drama
Either Paper 2		20% of the marks
	1¹/₄ hours	Three questions on unseen passages, one question to be answered
OR	*Coursework*	20% of the marks
		The whole folder should be between 1500–2000 words, comprised of either 1 long piece or 2 short pieces.
		The pieces may reflect textual study and/or personal writing.

31

EXAMINATION BOARDS AND ADDRESSES

AEB   The Associated Examining Board
                              Stag Hill House, Guildford, Surrey GU2 5XJ

                              01483 506506

Cambridge   University of Cambridge Local Examinations Syndicate
                              Syndicate Buildings, 1 Hills Road, Cambridge CB1 2EU

                              01223 553311

NEAB   Northern Examinations and Assessment Board
                              Devas Street, Manchester M15 6EX

                              0161 953 1180

NICCEA   Northern Ireland Council for the Curriculum Examinations
                              and Assessment
                              Beechill House, 42 Beechill Road, Belfast BT8 4RS

                              01232 704666

Oxford   University of Oxford Delegacy of Local Examinations
                              Ewert House, Ewert Place, Summertown, Oxford OX2 7BZ

                              01865 54291

Oxford and Cambridge   Oxford and Cambridge Schools Examination Board
                              (a) Purbeck House, Purbeck Road, Cambridge CB2 1PU
                              (b) Elsfield Way, Oxford OX2 2BZ

                              01865 54421

SEB   Scottish Examinations Board
                              Ironmills Road, Dalkeith, Midlothian EH22 1LE

                              0131 663 6601

ULEAC   University of London Examination and Assessment Council
                              Stewart House, 32 Russell Square, London WC1 5DN

                              0171 331 4000

WJEC   Welsh Joint Education Committee
                              245 Western Avenue, Cardiff CF5 2YX

                              01222 265000

STUDYING AND REVISING ENGLISH

THE DIFFERENCE BETWEEN GCSE AND A/AS-LEVEL STUDY

1 There is a great deal more freedom attached to A-level work and students who embark upon A-level direct from GCSE will find it bewildering that they have the responsibility to discipline themselves. Much reading, research and note-taking has to be done in the candidate's own time and many of the least successful A-level candidates have failed to organise their time properly and thus have not prepared themselves adequately for the examination.

2 The A-level examiner will expect more of you in terms of breadth and depth of knowledge as you are only studying three, or at the most four, A-level subjects instead of up to ten or eleven GCSEs. Also, because of your increased maturity and your obvious desire to pursue this subject in depth, the A-level examiner will expect you to apply this knowledge to specific questions which will not be as straightforward as GCSE questions. There is more about this under Point 3.

3 The different approach to A-level questions is apparent in the vocabulary used in the questions. At GCSE the most common directions are 'describe', 'give an account of', 'account for'. At A-level these words can recur, but they are more often replaced by **'assess'**, **'discuss'**, **'compare'**, **'contrast'**, **'comment on'**, **'critically examine'** and **'to what extent would you agree with'**. It is a good idea to underline these key words which tell you *how* to answer the question and to ask yourself whether you are being relevant to these key words all the way through your answer. Always bear in mind that A-level demands an increased sophistication in the way you answer the question.

4 Another major difference between GCSE and A-level study is the difficulty of the set texts. Although GCSE literature is by no means 'easy reading', the language of the novels is usually fairly straightforward, and the Shakespeare and poetry should present little difficulty to the average student if they are thoroughly taught and the student conscientiously prepares him- or herself for the examination.

A-level texts usually offer more scope for appreciation and thought along the lines of themes, imagery, moral or political ideas, symbolism and other such more intellectual considerations. Understanding of a more complex field of interrelationships of character, ideas or language is required. Collections of poems by a single poet, often of a more demanding degree of difficulty, are set, rather than selections from groups of different poets, with a more superficial reference to their subject matter, which is sometimes classified in the anthology rather loosely.

The immediate practical result of all this for the student is that he or she has to consider the texts, looking more closely for such things and considering them more deeply; he/she may have to find advanced books of criticism or biography on the set author. The former are unfortunately often harder to grasp than the author's work itself; the student will need guidance and help in this. Intense and appreciative reading by a student comparatively widely read already, especially in the works of the set author or his period, is in the end the best preparation. Ability to write on the question well is then rather a matter of an ability to form connections, select relevant material and discuss intelligently the prescribed topic, as well as of mere memory.

The following thoughts will be a useful guide to any student embarking upon an A-level English course after having prepared him- or herself for a GCSE examination. In general, GCSE tests competence in the appreciation and knowledge of three sections (i) Shakespeare, and sometimes other drama; (ii) prose works, usually novels and (iii) poetry. Emphasis is placed on a sensitive and informed response to the text. The standard derives from a requirement that candidates should have sound understanding of the text and thorough knowledge of individual details such as character portraits and features of the language. Where references to other matters are made or unusual words used, candidates are expected to be able to explain them.

When a context passage is introduced, the questions concern what light the passage throws on the character, what it reveals about the character's feelings, what the candidate finds worthy of note in the situation, characters or speech of the passage. Relevance is required and vigilance to select all the evidence present.

This type of question is unlikely at A level. The philosophy behind A-level questions on set passages is, 'you have been trained to write about passages like these; you have had experience in appreciation; now do it'. There is little further guidance except in A-level language comprehension papers (see p. 170). All the writing is left to the candidate who must therefore be well practised in analysing unseen or seen passages. Useful advice on this can be found in the chapters on practical criticism. A study of these chapters should give the candidate certain ideas of technique and terminology which have to be acquired.

GCSE asks for evidence of knowledge of incidents and facts concerning the story, characters and language of the printed passage or whole text. A level tests the ability to organise and select from one's knowledge. What you must not do is reproduce it uncritically or in narrative sequence. An A-level candidate must try to adjust his or her thinking to the actual requirements of a question that turns on ideas and implications deriving from the book.

Although GCSE candidates are required to think as well as remember, they are usually only asked to apply directly and immediately to their knowledge as a source for the relevant material, not to use it for evaluations or discussions of any controversial or debatable nature. For A-level work a higher degree of appreciation, critical awareness and subtlety in marshalling the points of discussion is expected.

At GCSE the books or authors chosen need only be sufficiently known and understood on a basic level, not necessarily commented upon or appreciated in any depth. A level will presume a knowledge of good criticism, whether written for sixth formers or more advanced students; biographical background which throws light on the work and literary history, all of which can be valuable in an A-level essay. Also at A level there is room for intelligent comparison or contrast with other works not specifically prescribed for study, by the same or related authors. What is not prescribed at A level can often be enlisted to support essays on what is. One need only have knowledge of the texts alone at GCSE. Revision aids for the texts are helpful, but often summarise or give simplified synopses of the texts or paraphrases of poems and are too simplistic for much use at A level.

Modular courses

Some examining boards now offer modular courses as a flexible scheme which allows you to follow a variety of different routes in order to achieve an AS or A level. The syllabus is divided into small units (modules), each of which is examined by an end-of-module test. These tests may be taken at appropriate times throughout the course or, if preferred, at the end of the course. The advantages of taking the tests throughout the course are that there is regular feedback on how well you are doing and there is the possibility of retaking modules in order to improve your grade. Furthermore, the results of modular tests may be 'banked', and then 'cashed-in' at some time within four years to obtain an AS or A level. This allows for a break in a course of study without loss of the credit already obtained. Some modules are compulsory, others may be selected from a list of optional ones. At the end of a modular course there may be a synoptic assessment. This is a test made up of questions which are taken from across the compulsory modules.

STUDY STRATEGIES AND TECHNIQUES

Far from being an easy option, A-level English is a difficult subject. It will test intellectual ability and maturity. Maturity of judgement and maturity of emotion are called for. Literature must not just be **read**, it must be **studied**. This means that you must consider not only **what** the writer has achieved, but **how** he or she has achieved it. You must try to **understand** the author's intentions and to respond intellectually and imaginatively to the written word.

Knowledge of what happens in the text and a few thoughts on the characters is not enough. You must also have a close, first-hand knowledge of your texts – second-hand knowledge, i.e. critics and 'crib' notes – can be useful to support first-hand knowledge, but is no substitute for it. Critics are helpful, provided that you understand what they are saying. Half-understanding leads to gibberish in the examination. Have your own thoughts and your own opinions, but make certain they are based on close study and careful thought.

A space of your own

You must find a place where you can work quietly, without distraction. One of these places should be at home, and another at school. Don't make the place too relaxing – it must be shut off from social life and social noises, e.g. television and chatter. You need the minimum of a desk, a chair, good lighting, shelves for books, files (with dividers) for notes and pens and paper.

Once you have your place for study, organise your time. Don't just drift through the school day, the evening and weekends, without a clear work plan. If you have a part-time job, make sure it doesn't affect your studies. The little amount you gain at the local supermarket is 'peanuts' compared with what you can gain from good A-level results. If you do have a part-time job, you should think seriously of giving it up in the second year of study.

Promise yourself time off at the end of a period of study. Make sure that your notes are up to date, legible and well set out and your texts are well annotated.

Remember A levels are two-year courses; you will not do well if you only work hard at the end of them. Like a marathon runner, you have to learn to pace yourself and bring out the final burst of energy to break the tape at the end.

A last thought – use your library! Remember public libraries usually open late at least two or three evenings a week. Your school library should also be a quiet place to work and you should always be able to find reference books and dictionaries to hand.

Note taking

Annotate your set books freely and conscientiously. Look up any difficult words in a glossary or in the notes at the back of the book. This particularly applies to books where the language is difficult, like Shakespeare, Chaucer and Milton. Make brief notes of what your teacher says in lesson or lecture time and read them through in your own time, making sure that you fully understand them.

If you make notes from any other source, i.e. a novel by the same author or a critical work on a set book, make sure that you record the author and title. Sometimes the page number is also useful for future reference. Do not lose yourself in detail. Keep the main issues and the important questions clear. This is particularly important in the study of Chaucer and Shakespeare, where the language is often a barrier to understanding

Making the best of your set texts

You will find that your A-level teachers will usually decide which editions of the set texts they wish to use for A-level study. These should be clearly printed, with useful introductions and a clear glossary or explanatory notes on the foot of each page, by the side of the text or at the back of the text.

The books which form the basis of your study of A-level English set texts should never be 'clean' copies by the end of your course. In every lesson you should have a pencil handy to annotate it thoroughly, either by underlining words, phrases or sentences and/or making notes by the side of the text.

All A/AS level reading is an ACTIVE process. You are not just reading for pleasure as you might do on holiday or on a journey. You must always read with a questioning mind and a pencil in your hand. As well as your text, always have a sheet of file paper handy on which to make notes to amplify what you have been reading.

Use the glossary and a dictionary to look up any difficult words or allusions to mythology, the Bible and so on. Don't be lazy over this. Come to your lessons prepared to offer explanations of anything obscure in the text.

When you have read the whole text, make further notes under separate headings of character, narrative, themes, style, setting. Re-read the text several times; the last time being before your final examination. In this way, you will be able to read critically with both accuracy and speed.

Use your teacher and fellow students to help you study

Each week you will probably spend 3–4 hours in class for each of your A-level subjects. Taken over a two-year course, this represents a considerable amount of time for you to use or misuse. To make optimum use of this class time, follow the guidelines below.

❶ Never be tempted to skip lessons. Your teacher can cover more ground in an expert and informed way than you can yourself, and you may miss vital tests, essays, discussions and hand-outs.

❷ Always bring your set text and a plentiful supply of pens, pencils and file paper to each lesson, plus a dictionary and any critical works you have been reading. BE PREPARED.

❸ CONTRIBUTE IN CLASS. Be prepared to offer ideas for discussion. Don't sit there like a soggy sponge, soaking in your teacher's ideas and those of your more vociferous fellow students without being prepared to give anything of yourself. Your ideas are just as valid as anyone else's – so have a go!

If you have prepared yourself as you have been advised in previous paragraphs, you will do yourself credit.

❹ Make thorough notes in the text and on file paper. BE ACTIVE in writing down everything necessary for future recall.

❺ After the lesson, re-read all your notes. Make sure they are legible, well ordered and full enough to prove useful for revision. If you are unhappy with your lesson notes take action to remedy the situation NOW – never leave it until another day – a procrastinating student never achieves his potential.

❻ Talk to your fellow students about your work and bounce ideas off each other. This will give you fresh insight into your texts and make your study more enjoyable – don't work in isolation.

❼ Make use of your teacher – listen and question if you do not understand. Ask for help, advice on further reading, or extra work if you feel you need it.

Study aids

These come in many forms and can also be called 'crib notes'. Some students find these an invaluable prop or crutch, but they can never be a substitute for the text itself. Many contain pre-digested theories about characters, themes, plot, etc. which the weaker student may try to pass off as his or her own, but the examiner is skilled in detecting such plagiarism.

The A-level examiner is looking for original response and personal ideas, so don't resort to crib notes as a substitute for the text. The text itself is the bed-rock of your A-level work and you should never forget this.

Works of criticism

These are more commendable to read than crib notes, containing useful theories about your set texts by academics whose comments hold credibility amongst teachers and examiners alike. Often quotations from such works are used as a basis for A-level questions.

However, the same warnings apply. Don't accept them blindly. Your ideas and opinions are what is being sought. Never copy them slavishly. Never assume they are a substitute for the text. Your ability to name-drop and quote from critics is far less important than your knowledge of the text.

Essay-writing skills

Learn to construct an **argument**. A-level questions will not ask you 'what happened'. They will ask you to 'discuss' an issue or give your opinion. Underline the key words in the question and make sure you do 'discuss' or 'compare' or 'contrast' all the way through.

Be **relevant**. Learn to use the text to support your argument; give it some thought before you start and then keep it clear and concise. English examiners are very used to dealing with waffle and object to answers which are ill-prepared and irrelevant.

Never try to bend a question to suit the answer you wish to write. However brilliant an essay you may have written for your teacher during the year, you must answer the question asked, otherwise the examiner's red pen will be drawn through your brilliantly written but irrelevant essay.

During an A-level course, take some pride in your own writing. Try to develop an appropriate style which is neither too pompous nor too colloquial. If you have something to say, say it as neatly and effectively as possible. If you have nothing to say, then do not write anything until you have.

Long, memorised chunks of quotations are neither necessary nor helpful. This advice applies to exams of traditional character, but obviously more will be expected of you if you are allowed to take books into the exam. Your aim should be to know the works you are studying so well that you can refer to any section to support the points you are making. Close reference is usually enough – no one expects you to memorise a novel! Complete accuracy in direct quotation is, of course, necessary if you are using the quotation as a detailed illustration of style.

Learn to write to a particular length. An A-level paper of three hours with four questions gives you about 40 minutes per question, allowing for reading and planning. This is about 500 words. Learn to say what you have to say within specified limits. This will help to stop the woolly, wandering approach that examiners so often meet. Finally, take pleasure in the subject. It is a privilege to be given time to explore the great writers. Read around your texts, on such themes as biography and social history, but always come back to the texts as the centre of your study. Increasing familiarity will bring increased understanding, and increased understanding greater confidence. This will be reflected in the examination. In this way you will have the double reward of pleasure and success.

Critical terminology

A-level students are often uncertain how to make the best use of critical books written on their prescribed texts or authors. The use of critical terminology can be another stumbling block for the student.

Technical critical terms are like a workman's tools, in that if handled well they carry out a task expertly and swiftly, but if mishandled, or especially if the wrong tools are chosen, the results are disastrous. It is not enough that terms should be learnt; they should also be seen working in good critical language, and used in one's own criticism until by experience their use is exact and appropriate. It is best not to use a word from the bank of critical terminology unless its use is natural and well tested.

Some terms have special and obvious applications, such as the names of various verse forms and metres. Others have a wider application outside the world of literary criticism and you must be careful to use properly words such as 'satire' and 'didactic' when applying them within a critical literary context.

On p. 235 of this book there is a Glossary. You should use this to discover the meaning of terms new to you and to check that you understand fully the meaning of terms with which you are already familiar. Words emboldened in the text are explained in the Glossary.

Open Book Techniques

A great many Examination Boards now include the option of taking your set texts into the examination room with you. This provides the candidate with more preparation time, since less emphasis is placed on memorising the set texts. However, a more genuine exploration of text and appreciation of literature is required, along with evidence of relevant wider reading.

Points to remember in open book examinations:
- Find out from your teacher or exam syllabus what you are and are not allowed to do in annotating the text.
- Be clear in your annotation. Use highlighter pens (if the book belongs to you!).
- Know your way round the book, so you don't waste valuable time as you must be able to find what you want straight away.
- You need to be selective in the material you use and quote in your essay – there is no point in copying great chunks, either of text or introduction.

Above all – ask for advice from your teacher, and GUARD YOUR TEXT WITH YOUR LIFE!

REVISION TECHNIQUES

You really need to start thinking about revision in the Easter holidays before your examinations. You will already have had an examination in Year 12 and a mock in Year 13. Your notes and text books should be fully organised and annotated.

Before you start your revision, make yourself absolutely familiar with the syllabus. Check which of your texts are on which papers and see where the choices lie. Also, see what sort of questions are set on each text – and whether there are any short-answer or context questions.

Do not decide to 'drop' or abandon one of your set texts. You may not like any of the questions on your favourite text and love the questions on the text you have not studied. Make sure you know how many questions you have to answer and the amount of time to be spent on each of them.

Do not try to 'spot' or predict questions as there is little chance that you will guess correctly.It is an excellent idea to ask your teacher if you can look at the examiners' reports of the last two years, as these give useful advice on how to achieve good grades. The value of trial essays should be mentioned here. These could be in the form of skeleton outlines of responses to important topics. In a sense, whether they 'come up' or not is unimportant – it's the practice you get in adapting your knowledge to the demands of the particular question that's important.

Planning your revision

Find out when your exams are and make a revision timetable – this should show when you intend to revise each text and should cover the period between Easter and the exams in June. Don't set yourself unrealistic aspirations and don't be disappointed if you miss the odd revision session.

Just like dieting, one episode of back-sliding doesn't mean you have failed altogether. Give yourself treats at the end of each session and talk to your parents, friends and teachers about your work and progress.

A piece of good advice – revise your least favourite and least remembered texts first. You will then feel a sense of achievement right at the beginning of your revision. Try to watch a film or video of your text or see the play. This will be an enjoyable and useful way of reinforcing your revision.

Remember to practise timed essays under strict exam conditions, with or without your text, according to the rubric of the examination. Try to get a teacher to mark it for you or, if that is difficult, give it to a classmate to read. Re-read all your texts and list quotes which you know you will be able to learn. Know the key passages and episodes of the text very well.

THE EXAMINATION

Accuracy and language skills

However well you may have prepared for the examination, your efforts could be frustrated by illegible writing or faulty spelling.

All English A- and AS-1evel exams, whether they be in language or literature, highlight the importance of good language skills. The key word is 'communication'.

If your handwriting, spelling or style impedes communication, your mark will be lowered. Never misspell names of characters; aim for short, clear sentences; pay attention to poor phrasing; quote briefly and accurately and make sure your writing can be read quickly. An examiner with 200 to 300 scripts will easily be annoyed with illegible scrawl to mark!

Lastly –
• Keep calm
• Sleep and eat well
• Talk out your problems with someone
• Avoid stressful personal relationships
• Refuse time-consuming part-time jobs
• Take exercise
• Treat yourself

And remember – it's only an exam, **not** the end of the world!

A-LEVEL ENGLISH

Each chapter features:

- *Units in this chapter:* a list of the main topic heads to follow.

- *Chapter objectives:* an introduction to the topics covered in the units.

- *The main text:* this is divided into numbered topic units for ease of reference.

- *Question bank:* a selection of actual examination questions, to help you appreciate the kinds of approach examiners require.

POETRY

Units in this chapter

Chapter objectives

School students see plays and read novels, but, like many of their parents and teachers, never read poetry in their free time. Further, they do not hear it read today, except with varying success at school. It inevitably becomes more neglected even in the last outposts of our former literary culture, possibly still taken seriously only because A-level English syllabuses devote about a third of their attention to it.

With the invasion and flood of other, more immediately satisfying art forms, much prejudice and many erroneous ideas about poetry have grown up. There is no indication that poetry can be appreciated with any less ease than the novel or drama and no examining board seems inclined to be influenced by its relative unpopularity. Discovering poetry can be one of the great pleasures of A-level English.

Many would claim that the peculiar pleasure of poetry does not derive primarily from its thought. Nevertheless, a grasp of the ideas of a poem may simplify the reader's appreciation and clear the way to enjoying other more important qualities. In trying to disentangle the 'thought' or 'idea' of a poem we may be in danger of knocking to pieces those elements which are arranged in a pleasing way for their sound, colour and rhythm.

A good poem does not depend for its worth on originality of ideas; it often prefers its ideas to be already well understood by the audience, in order the better to embody them in the most excellent language, that synthesis or pattern of words called a poem. We may feel, understandably, that it is necessary to clarify whatever thought a poem contains, as one of the simplest ways of approaching it. However, it is important not to fall into the trap of neglecting style and language but to work towards a full response to the poem, noting meaning and form.

Some poems can be left to speak for themselves. For example, Burns's *O my luve's like a red, red rose* would need little or no analysis of its meaning as it conveys an immediately communicated experience. In contrast, Yeats's *A Nativity*, a shorter poem, cannot be appreciated fully without a knowledge of other poetry and prose by Yeats. It is the business of the A-level student to work towards a 'full response' to a poem, whether it be lyric or epic. In the section on approaches to poetry at the beginning of this chapter, you will find basic guidelines suggested to help you approach each new poem you encounter.

1.1 APPROACHES TO POETRY

Practical criticism is a method of revealing to the student-critic the significance of the structure of words which make up a poem. Everyone reacts to reading a poem in different ways but even the right reactions or feelings may be too simple and not further our understanding of the poem a great deal. In order to know how to go further, the student needs to know how to tackle the skills of practical criticism. A simple reaction to a poem: 'I like it', or 'It doesn't do anything for me', is too simple a form of criticism. Through practical criticism you can refine and deepen your appreciation of the poet's skills.

When reading a poem, the first thing you should try to do is grasp the meaning and mood the poet is creating. Repeated readings will improve your first impressions. Gradually, ideas that seemed obscure will become clear. The relevance of particular words or images will manifest themselves. You should have a knowledge of the technical skills of manipulating rhythm and language and, through this knowledge, a deeper understanding of the poem will be achieved.

The 'meaning' of a poem is conveyed by the arrangement of chosen words on paper and the kind of arrangement or pattern the poet has given them. How a poet like Keats, Siegfried Sassoon, Ted Hughes or TS Eliot writes is his own distinctive trademark. A poem is a personal communication with words chosen to suit a variety of purposes and the words so chosen have to be comprehended if we are to get from the poem as much meaning as the poet intended. Each poet agonises over the correct choice of words and nothing happens by accident. Therefore the student must treat the poem as a deliberate artistic creation with intent behind it, and not a random happening.

Each reader brings to the poem his or her own store of knowledge, his or her own preferences, perceptiveness and degree of response to words. A poem is like a looking glass where everyone sees his or her own reflection. We probably respond best to poems written in our own time which contain words whose meanings we are familiar with. For your criticism to be worthwhile you should be familiar with the cultural background of the poem. There is no substitute for wide reading among the best authors as a way to acquire sensitivity. The section which follows this general introduction will help with these skills.

One of the aspects of poetry we are seeking to understand is meaning. We cannot find the total meaning without getting inside the head of the poet. The tone of the words and choice of words help to convey the poet's meaning. We must also look at the sounds of the words and the effect they have on us. A third source of consideration is the grammatical arrangement of words into a meaningful pattern. If your judgements are to arouse the approval of your teacher and the person who marks your examination paper you must learn to look carefully and methodically at what poets do.

METHOD OF TACKLING A POEM

1. **Understanding** At the first reading, concentrate on understanding the poem. Try to establish the theme of the poem: the kind of experience the poet is dealing with, and the sequence of thoughts or images which are being communicated to you. You may find, when you read the poem again, that you discover more meaning than you had done originally, and this may cause you to alter your ideas of the content and meaning of the poem. However, candidates can get very hung up on the problem of meaning, of needing to get it absolutely clear throughout the poem. In modern poetry, this is simply impossible. They need to be prepared to live with the likelihood that not every detail will be understood, that some parts of the poem may communicate without clear meaning, that some details will inevitably remain obscure. There's a danger that they will come to see the poems as puzzles that have to be solved and become despondent when the whole solution seems elusive. They need to be prepared to risk tentative suggestions and partial understanding, to offer alternative readings – to take chances in fact.

2. **Voice** Asking questions about voice can be very helpful when tackling a poem. Who is speaking here? The poet? Someone else? If the latter, then who and in what circumstances? What kind of a poem are we dealing with here? Reflective, argumentative, lyrical, persuasive, dramatic?

Note – the question of meaning and voice are dealt within the two students' answers on the Sylvia Plath poems which follow this section.

3 **Rhythm and metre**   Read the poem out loud to yourself with the kinds of emphasis and pauses intended by the poet. Through this, you are likely to become aware of some of the uses of sound and grammatical structures utilised in the poem's construction. Use the parts of this book on rhythm and metre which will help you. There is no point in identifying rhythm, metre or rhyme for its own sake. They are all used to add something to a poem – mood, an atmosphere, a purpose. Examples of useful comments on rhyme, rhythm, metre and structure will be included in the students' answers which follow and explanations of words in bold will be found in the glossary.

4 **Use of literary devices**   Literary devices are used deliberately and contribute to the total significance of the poem. Decide and comment on those you find distinctive and consider why the poet uses the literary devices he or she has chosen. Use the parts of this book on literary devices which will help you.

5 **Themes or experiences communicated**   Discuss whether the poem makes any comment on the poet's attitudes and give your opinion on the value of the poem's themes.

6 **Structure**   How does the poem divide up? Not just in terms of stanzas and verses, but in terms of progression of its ideas. How does the poet signal these changes and boundaries through pointers in the use of words such as but, now, yet?

All these points lead to the importance of overview, a sense of the poem's wholeness. Of course, detail is important, but an overview can help to put troublesome individual pieces, however obscure or elusive, into some coherent shape or pattern.

COMMENTARIES

An example of 'making sense' of a difficult poem follows – Andrew Marvell's *The Definition of Love* and a detailed commentary on rhythm, rhyme, structure and technical imagery in *The Darkling Thrush* by Thomas Hardy. Read these carefully. Any technical vocabulary is highlighted in bold and found in the glossary.

The Definition of Love

My Love is of a birth as rare
As 'tis for object strange and high:
It was begotten by despair
Upon Impossibility.

5   Magnanimous Despair alone
Could show me so divine a thing,
Where feeble hope could ne'r have flown
But vainly flapt its Tinsel Wing.

And yet I quickly might arrive
10   Where my extended Soul is fixt,
But Fate does iron wedges drive,
And alwaies crouds it self betwixt.

For Fate with jealous Eye does see
Two perfect Loves; nor lets them close:
15   Their union would her ruine be,
And her Tyrannick pow'r, depose.

And therefore her Decrees of Steel
Us as the distant poles have plac'd,
(Though loves whole World on us doth wheel)
20   Not by themselves to be embrac'd.

Unless the giddy heaven fall,
And Earth some new Convulsion tear;
And, us to joyn, the World should all
Be cramp'd into a *Planisphere*. ¹

25   As Lines so Loves *oblique* may well
Themselves in every Angle greet:
But ours so truly Paralel,
Though infinite can never meet.

Therefore the Love which us doth bind,

30   But Fate so enviously debarrs,

Is the Conjunction of the Mind,

And Opposition of the Stars.

Andrew Marvell

(Text from Helen Gardner's *Metaphysical Poets*, Penguin)

[1] flat two-dimensional projection of the two hemispheres to show appearance of heavens

Commentary on *The Definition of Love*

Marvell's poem is consecrated to human love, a subject which ranks equal with religion as a subject for **metaphysical** poetry.

Its theme of hopeless, star-crossed love is familiar and easily recognised, and its argument not difficult to follow in outline. The poet claims a special distinction or pre-eminence for his love precisely because it is, and must for ever be ungratified. In lines 9–10 there is a hint that the lady, if she were free to do so, would requite his passion, but Fate intervenes and forbids what would be a perfect union – why or how, we are never told. Only if the world were turned upside down in some cataclysm could the lovers ever be united. They are destined, therefore, to remain united in mind but eternally separated in body by a greater power than they can contradict.

The verse form of the poem, too, requires no elaborate commentary. It is in simple **quatrains** of alternately rhyming lines of equal length, the individual lines having four **iambic feet** – a verse form familiar in English poetry.

The distinctive feature of the poem, of course, is its accumulation of ingenious and elaborate **imagery**. It opens with a cluster of **personified** abstractions: his love has two unusual and distinguished parents, Despair and Impossibility, as is only fit, considering the 'strange and high' quality of its object. (Is this a conventional compliment to the lady, or a more specific, if veiled allusion to her superior rank?) Only Despair, described as 'magnanimous', i.e. generous, could have directed his affections to 'so divine a thing' – could have made him love a goddess. Hope could never have flown so high on its 'Tinsel Wing': we perhaps picture Hope as a glittering but feeble insect. In effect, in lines 1–8, Marvell formulates a paradox: Despair inspires him to higher ambitions than Hope could ever do.

Nevertheless, he continues, he could quickly gain possession of the person of the lady to whom his soul, having gone forth out of his body, is already 'fixt', i.e. attached (note the delicate circumlocution of the language here), did not Fate, like an officious or bullying meddler, 'croud', i.e. thrust itself between, to separate them. Alternatively, Fate is thought of as parting them by driving 'iron wedges' between them, of the kind quarrymen and stonemasons use to split rock: the image suggests both the solidity of the bond and the force employed to break it. Similarly, a little later, the strength of Fate is conveyed in 'her Decrees of Steel' (line 17). The fanciful, as opposed to the practical reason for Fate's hostility is given in lines 13–16: she rules the world as a tyrant, and the union of two lovers she has forbidden to marry would overthrow her despotic power. (The political image must have come naturally to Marvell, who lived through the period of the Civil War and held a public appointment under Cromwell.)

In lines 17–24 the poet develops an elaborate image based on geography and astronomy – a true '**conceit**', as this kind of unexpected, ingenious and detailed comparison is usually called. The lovers have been placed by Fate at the opposite poles of the world of love – poles apart, in fact; and just as the North and South Poles of the world's axis can never meet, no more can they, though the whole world of love revolves around them – unless, indeed, there were to be a universal collapse into chaos in which the spinning ('giddy') heaven should fall and the earth be torn apart by some new convulsion. (There was a good deal of speculation in the seventeenth century about the possible floods, eruptions, and the like which Earth might have suffered in its earlier history.)

In short, (lines 23–24) the lovers could only be joined if the whole round world, here completely conflated with the world of love, were to be 'cramp'd into a *Planisphere*', i.e. reduced to a flat two-dimensional projection of the two hemispheres, so arranged that the two poles are brought together. (Do not be alarmed by this complex and highly technical image. Where such an **allusion** appears in an appreciation paper, the examiners would feel bound to give an explanatory note. If you were being examined on a prescribed poem, of course, you would be expected to know what was meant.)

Having thus, with typical **metaphysical** panache, elevated his frustrated love to the cosmic scale, Marvell descends, in lines 25–29, to the merely geometrical. As two straight lines which are oblique to each other converge to form an angle, so may those lovers converge who are naturally drawn together and encounter no opposition; but he and his lady are like parallel lines which, though produced to infinity, never meet. The very long-windedness of this explanation reveals the compression of Marvell's style.

Finally, in lines 29–32, the poet introduces the language of astrology. The lovers are joined in soul like planets in 'Conjunction', i.e. in the same sign of the zodiac, but their stars are in 'Opposition'.

Looking back, we can now see that there is more depth of meaning in the title than at first appears. Marvell is not just 'defining' love in the modern sense of the word; the love the poem deals with is, in any case, untypical, as he is at pains to point out. 'Definition' seems to be used rather with the meaning of 'fixing boundaries'. Perhaps the title might be best rendered in modern English as 'The Limitation of Love'; for the lovers, Fate has 'set a bourn how far to be belov'd.'

The poem we have considered may be seen as essentially a literary exercise, taking up the well-worn theme of unrequited or hopeless love and tricking it out with the kind of decoration the taste of the day approved. It may be a conscious imitation of Donne's earlier and more celebrated poem, *A Valediction: forbidding mourning*, which is also about lovers parted (at least for a time), employs the same verse-form, and is equally profuse in learned, 'scientific' **images**. Certainly, to some readers, it may seem to have more of art than of nature. For all that, it is possible that it has some relationship to such known facts in Marvell's life as that he lived through the Civil War, when many family and personal links were broken up by political discord (Milton's first marriage is a case in point), was for a time tutor to Lord Fairfax's daughter, and seems never to have married. If he was disappointed in love, he might well, as a clever young man, have found relief in composing a highly wrought and sophisticated poem in which he positively glories in the hopelessness of his aspirations.

Speculation and reference to biographical background, though often tempting, must be kept under control. You may allow yourself a little, but your first and main concern must always be with the text, and with what may fairly be deduced from it.

The Darkling Thrush

I leant upon a coppice gate
When Frost was spectre-grey,
And Winter's dregs made desolate
The weakening eye of day.
5   The tangled bine-stems scored the sky
Like strings of broken lyres,
And all mankind that haunted nigh
Had sought their household fires.

The land's sharp features seemed to be
10   The Century's corpse outleant,
His crypt the cloudy canopy,
The wind his death-lament
The ancient pulse of germ and birth
Was shrunken hard and dry,
15   And every spirit upon earth
Seemed fervourless as I.

At once a voice arose among
The bleak twigs overhead
In a full-hearted evensong
20   Of joy illimited;
An aged thrush, frail, gaunt and small,
In blast-beruffled plume,
Had chosen thus to fling his soul
Upon the growing gloom

25   So little cause for carolings
Of such ecstatic sound

> Was written on terrestrial things
> Afar or nigh around,
> That I could think there trembled through
> 30   His happy good–night air
> Some blessed Hope, whereof he knew
> And I was unaware.

Thomas Hardy

Commentary on *The Darkling Thrush*

This poem expresses the desolation of a late afternoon in mid-winter, with whose grim aspect the poet's own mood is in complete harmony. The first verse describes the isolation of the writer, who is portrayed as a solitary human being, chilled and dreary like the winter and the frost.

In the second verse, the grim reality of the poem is reinforced by the widening of the scene. Hardy compares the whole landscape with the dead body of the century, bare with the sharpness of death. The earth lies under the cloudy skies and the wind is in mourning for the passing of the century. The vitality of life seems numbed and the deadness of the world is matched by the apathetic and uncommunicative state of the poet's mind.

The third stanza introduces a new element, for the song of the thrush bursts into the gloom of the evening: his joy contrasts sadly with the barren scene. However, the poet feels that the scene is so desolate that the thrush's outburst is from an inspiration known only to him and hidden from the pessimistic poet.

The poet brings a universal significance to the song of the thrush in the winter time. The end of the year makes most men feel pessimistic. The poet wonders whether the creator of the universe has any interest in the life of any human being, and it is typical of Hardy's philosophy that he feels the weather is a cruelly ironical background against which man plays his part.

The pattern of the **metre** is flexible; although the rhyme scheme is rigid, thus underlining the firmness of purpose in the passage, there is considerable use of run-on lines, especially in verses three and four, where feelings run more freely.

The use of **figures of speech**: 'spectre-grey', 'the weakening eye of day', 'like strings of broken lyres' intensifies the gloomy scene of the first stanza. In the second stanza, the **similes** and **metaphors** indicate that the poet feels sepulchral like the landscape. Note also the **alliterative** use of 'dregs made desolate', 'Century's corpse', 'crypt the cloudy canopy'. The corpse of the old dead century seems to be leaning uneasily outwards, a ghastly reminder of the passage of time and the inevitability of death.

The final impression of the poem is sombre. If readers have some knowledge of the novels of Thomas Hardy, such as *Tess of the D'Urbervilles*, they will realise that a pessimistic attitude to life is common in his work. However, it is reasonable to conclude that the poet recognises the thrush has an intuitive sense of joy and 'blessed Hope' which he himself lacks, but which *may* be immanent in the universe.

Finally, practise what you have read in writing a commentary on *Torrey Canyon*.

The poem below is by Jack Clemo, who was born in 1916 in Cornwall, where he has spent nearly all his life. The title of the poem refers to an oil tanker, the *Torrey Canyon*, which caused the worst oil spillage ever in the English Channel when it sank in 1967.

Read the poem carefully, and then write a critical commentary of it, paying particular attention to **theme**, **imagery**, use of language, mood and **tone**, but also mentioning anything else you find particularly interesting. How far do you think the poet is successful?

Torrey Canyon

> One thick black patch, then another,
> Pushing coastward greedily
> In crude menace that leaks from a gored tanker;
> Night's raping crust on the noon sea,
> 5   The prance and song of spring waves
> Stilled by the belch and stench of that spreading mouth.
> Fish die where the poison reaches
> Under the floating mounds of oil that soil
> Soon the crunched tongues of shingle.

10   Yet men have said, through bleared piety,
            That the wreck of our fuel-laden dreams
            Cleanses the soul's tides and beaches...
    Oh bright gulls smeared, sinking with grease-deadened screams,
            Unwinged in the crash-bred slough!
15   Fuel-film rotting the seaweed, the smothered cockle;
        Rocks daubed, mere slime-heaps, though the rollers' sport
        Rinsed them while the tanker ploughed towards port.

Jack Clemo

COMPARING POEMS

Often in poetry papers, two or three poems with similar themes are chosen for the candidate to compare and contrast. This type of answer involves careful planning as you have to cross-reference between one poem and another. However, you can still treat each poem under the headings given in 'Method of tackling a poem', but remember not to write your commentary under headings. It is perfectly permissible to say which poem you prefer, as long as you support your opinion with detailed reference to and quotation from the poem.

We have given you three famous poems on autumn to consider. Choose two of the three and try to compare and contrast them as though you had been asked to do this in an examination. You could look back on the commentary on *The Darkling Thrush* to see how Hardy deals with the seasonal description in the poem. This may help you to discuss these three poets' treatment of autumn weather. No other guidance should be necessary at this stage, but ask yourself all the time whether you are comparing the two poems and not just writing separate commentaries on each one.

To Autumn

            Season of mists and mellow fruitfulness!
            Close bosom-friend of the maturing sun;
            Conspiring with him how to load and bless
        With fruit the vines that round the thatch-eaves run;
5   To bend with apples the mossed cottage-trees,
            And fill all fruit with ripeness to the core;
            To swell the gourd, and plump the hazel shells
            With a sweet kernel; to set budding more,
            And still more, later flowers for the bees,
10   Until they think warm days will never cease,
        For Summer has o'er-brimm'd their clammy cells.

            Who hath not seen thee oft amid thy store!
            Sometimes whoever seeks abroad may find
            Thee sitting careless on a granary floor,
15   Thy hair soft-lifted by the winnowing wind;
            Or on a half-reaped furrow sound asleep,
        Drowsed with the fume of poppies, while thy hook
        Spares the next swath and all its twined flowers;
            And sometime like a gleaner thou dost keep
20   Steady thy laden head across a brook;
            Or by a cider-press, with patient look,
        Thou watchest the last oozings, hours by hours.

            Where are the songs of Spring? Ay, where are they?
            Think not of them, thou hast thy music too,
25   While barred clouds bloom the soft-dying day,
            And touch the stubble-plains with rosy hue;
            Then in a wailful choir, the small gnats mourn
            Among the river sallows, borne aloft
            Or sinking as the light wind lives or dies;
30   And full-grown lambs loud bleat from hilly bourn;
            Hedge-crickets sing; and now with treble soft
            The redbreast whistles from a garden-croft,
            And gathering swallows twitter in the skies.

John Keats (1795–1821)

November

The shepherds almost wonder where they dwell.
And the old dog for his right journey stares;
The path leads somewhere, but they cannot tell.
And neighbour meets with neighbour unawares.
5   The maiden passes close beside her cow,
And wanders on, and thinks her far away;
The ploughman goes unseen behind his plough
And seems to lose his horses half the day.
The lazy mist creeps on in journey slow;
10   The maidens shout and wonder where they go;
So dull and dark are the November days.
The lazy mist high up the evening curled.
And now the morn quite hides in smoke and haze;
The place we occupy seems all the world.

John Clare (1793–1864)

No!

No sun – no moon!
No morn – no noon –
No dawn – no dusk – no proper time of day –
No sky – no earthly view –
5   No distance looking blue –
No road – no street – no 't' other side the way' –
No end to any Row –
No indications where the Crescents go –
No top to any steeple –
10   No recognitions of familiar people –
No courtesies for showing 'em –
No knowing 'em –
No travelling at all – no locomotion,
No inkling of the way – no notion –
15   'No go' – by land or ocean –
No mail – no post –
No news from any foreign coast –
No Park – no Ring – no afternoon gentility –
No company – no nobility –
20   No warmth, no cheerfulness, no healthful ease.
No comfortable feel in any member –
No shade, no shine, no butterflies, no bees,
No fruit, no flowers, no leaves, no birds –
November!

Thomas Hood (1799–1845)

Specimen commentary

There follows an A-level student's attempt to discuss ideas of power and freedom from four of Sylvia Plath's poems. These poems are to be found in her anthology, *Ariel*, often set for A-level examinations and chosen for coursework. In this essay, the mock grade and teacher's comments follow the essay.

The Bee Meeting, The Arrival of the Bee Box, Stings, and *Wintering* are said to be the exploration of the meaning of power and freedom. By detailed reference to the poems give your reactions to this statement.

In the four poems, Sylvia Plath links power and freedom with almost every aspect of her life, in order to explore their meanings. One of the first topics she touches is the idea of protection. In her 'sleeveless summery dress' she has no protection. This takes away her power, because without protection, she could not deal with the bees and so she has no power over them. It is noticeable that she feels 'freer', without the heavier garments holding her down, yet she has no real power.

Further down, we find love linked with protection. In the same line, Plath links her feelings of vulnerability with the feeling of not being loved. 'I am nude as chicken neck, does nobody love me?' With the backing of the love of her fellow villagers, she has the power to live with confidence. However, they are also able to take her power away by not loving her. Because there are more of them than her, they form the majority, and so have the power to accept or reject her. She is literally at their mercy. They can make her life easy or unbearable.

Knowledge is also a form of power, according to Plath. Because the villagers know more than the 'I' person, she must submit to their power and trust them to look after her. Again she is at their mercy. Knowledge also brings freedom. If she knew how to look after bees, she would be able to do it herself and would not have to rely upon others to help her. She is constantly saying 'they are making me one of them', 'they are leading me', 'I cannot run', and it is quite clear that in relying on them she is submitting to their power and therefore losing her freedom.

In *The Arrival of the Bee Box*, we see a slightly different view of power and freedom. To begin with, we see the power of tradition. To break free from tradition means that you must expect the scorn of 'these women who only scurry!' These women are afraid to break out themselves. Sylvia, or the 'I' person, wants to be daring, to lead a special life, to break free from normality and to assert her own power and femininity. Yet at the same time she wants to lead a traditional life, to get along with other women and to bring up a loving family. She admits in the first line that 'I ordered this, this clean white box'. Yet she feels it stifles her and her sexuality. She describes herself as 'milkweed silk'. Here we see the power of conflicting desires working in a person. She no longer truly knows what she wants. No wonder she looks on herself as a box, 'dark with the swarmy feeling of African hands … black on black, angrily clambering'. These conflicting desires have the power to cause mayhem within her and therefore take away yet more of her freedom. She cries in desperation, 'how can I get them out?' How can she answer such a question? She cannot.

The poem also highlights Plath's, or of course the 'I' person's, curiosity and the power even this has over her. She wants to leave the bees yet 'I wonder how hungry they are. I wonder if they would forget me…' Even though she wants to be free of it, her curiosity has power over her, therefore taking away her freedom.

Plath also explores the difference between real power and superficial power. She says 'They can be sent back. They can die, I need feed them nothing, I am the owner'. Yet it is quite obvious that in reality it is the other way around. They have the power to turn on her, to fill her with curiosity and to create mayhem. They really have power over her.

Towards the end of the poem *Stings*, Plath begins to explore the power and freedom of women over men. Speaking as a woman she says 'I have a self to recover'. She has to break out of what a male orientated society has made her and become her own identity. 'Is she dead, is she sleeping?' Next comes a real display of power. 'Now she is flying, more terrible than she ever was … over the engine that filled her, over the powers that held her captive.' At the beginning of *Stings* we see this power. She spends her time 'enamelling' the house with excessive love.

She works her life away for the house and then 'the man' comes and collects the result, the sweet 'combs' from her. Yet she has broken free from such powers and now has power over them.

In *Wintering* we see a woman who has left these ties that held her back along with her husband. Now she is alone, surviving the winter. She also speaks of bees being the women who have done the same as her. 'They have got rid of men.' Now they are sitting, simply surviving. Towards the end, she asks 'will the hive survive?' But 'The bees are flying. They taste the spring.' They see the easier times ahead and are determined to survive. Here we see one other source of power – determination. Because of their determination the women are able to have the power to survive on their own and so it also gives them freedom.

Sylvia Plath has opened many discussions and explorations into power and freedom. The importance of determination, protection, knowledge, collectiveness, tradition, curiosity, the difference between real and superficial power, the link between power and freedom, the power of men, desires and the power of women.

Yet the most important question, which comes in *The Bee Meeting*, is 'What have they accomplished?' Where has the power of men got them? Yet the same question can also be asked at the end of the four poems. Where has the power of women got them? True, they are free, yet they have no love with anyone but themselves and have simply entered a life of suffering. Sure, they have got rid of men, but what have they achieved? Perhaps happier days of spring will come for the women, a time where they can live in happy dominance. But they did not come for Sylvia Plath.

Teacher's comments

17/20 (A/B) Still more close references needed, but good detail and some valid individual perceptions.

Practice exercise

Here is a comparison of two 'unseen' poems for you to try yourself. Compare the following two poems, paying particular attention to such features as content, imagery, form and style. Feel free to express and explain a preference for one or other poem if you so wish.

Turnip-Heads

Here are the ploughed fields of Middle England;
and here are the scarecrows, flapping polythene arms
over what still, for the moment, looks like England:
bare trees, earth-colours, even a hedge or two.

5   The scarecrows' coats are fertilizer bags;
their heads (it's hard to see from the swift windows
of the Intercity) are probably 5-litre
containers for some chemical or other.

And what are the scarecrows guarding? Fields of rape?
10   Plenty of that in Middle England; also
pillage, and certain other medieval
institutions – some things haven't changed,

now that the men of straw are men of plastic.
They wave their rags in fitful semaphore,
15   in the March wind; our train blurs past them.
Whatever their message was, we seem to have missed it.

Fleur Adcock *Time-Zones* (Oxford)

Branch Line

The train is two cars linking
Lincoln and Market Rasen.

Late May. Proof everywhere from
smudged sunny windows
5   that the Economic Community
is paying the farmers for rape.

How unembarrassed they are,
wanton patches the colour of heat
dropped like cheap tropical skirts
10   on the proper wolds.

The trees have almost completely
put on their clothes.
They sway in green crinolines,
new cool generous Eves.

15   White hawthorns, too,
do predictable cold unclenchings.

As the train parts green field from gold
a spray of peewits fans up in a bow wave.

            Is that a factory out there
20   where the sea might be?
        A lighthouse? A tall methane candle,
            lethal if it were to go out?

        The train slowly judders and halts
            for no visible reason.

25   Rooks squabble in a maple.
    A blackbird ferries an enormous worm to a nest.
    Staring cows bend again to their munching.

    Meaningless life, I'm reading in the TLS,[1]
        a nexus of competing purposes ...

30   God is impossible.

            Life is impossible.

            But here it is.

Anne Stevenson The Other House (Oxford)

[1] TLS: Times Literary Supplement.

AEB 1994

POETRY CRITICISM BIBLIOGRAPHY

Bowra, C M	*The Romantic Imagination*
	From Virgil to Milton
Bradbrook, M C	*Andrew Marvell*
	British Poetry since 1970
Bronowski, J	*The Poet's Defence*
Day Lewis, C	*The Poetic Image*
Dronke, Peter	*The Medieval Lyric*
Durrell, Lawrence	*Key to Modern Poetry*
Dyson, A E	*Poetry Criticism and Practice*
Giddings, Robert	*The War Poets*
Graves, Robert	*The Crowning Privilege*
Heaney, Seamus	*The Government of the Tongue*
Longley, Edna	*Poetry in the Wars*
Melchiori, Barbara	*Browning's Poetry*
Partridge, A C	*The Language of Renaissance Poetry*
Press, John	*Poets of World War I*
Reeves, James	*The Critical Sense*
Riding, Laura	*A Survey of Modernist Poetry*
Sisson, C H	*English Poetry, 1900–1950*
Spearing, A C	*Criticism and Medieval Poetry*
Spender, Stephen	*Poetry since 1939*
Sullivan, Sheila	*Critics on T S Eliot*
Tillyard, E M W	*Poetry and its Background*
Williams, John	*Twentieth-Century British Poetry*
Wood, Jeffrey	*Cambridge Poetry Workshop*
Young, Andrew	*The Poet and the Landscape*

1.2 THE METAPHYSICAL POETS

THE METAPHYSICAL POETS OF THE SEVENTEENTH CENTURY

In poetry selections set at A level, as few as two and as many as seven of the Metaphysicals may be represented. Donne is often set alone, and single selections from Herbert or Marvell are also sometimes set. In any case the student can generally expect Donne, Herbert, Vaughan and Marvell to be favoured in any choice from the Metaphysical poets.

Definitions

Definitions of **Metaphysical** poetry or other significant material in the introductions to anthologies or single poet selections are always worth reading with a view to preparing material for your answers. Examination questions often rely upon the ideas put forward in such introductions, and you can use them as critical clues and leads. For example, you could consider the following definition, thinking of illustrations from the poems you are studying: 'The essence of a Metaphysical poem is a vivid imagining of a moment of experience or of a situation out of which the need to argue, or persuade or define, arises.'

If questions on the style or language are set, they are likely to hinge on that aspect which gives this type of poetry its title – Metaphysical. You should understand this term thoroughly, know the characteristics of the Metaphysical **conceit** and have plenty of examples ready. The term 'Metaphysical' was established in this connection by Dr Johnson. He was referring to Donne's habit of drawing images from all the sources of knowledge: scientific, theological and philosophical. Dr Johnson disapproved of the school, referring to the poets' 'heterogeneous' images 'violently yoked together' (*Lives of the Poets* 1779–81). You should ask yourself whether the **imagery** in the poems you are studying is, in your opinion, unjustifiably extreme, far-fetched or immoderate. You should prepare examples of types of imagery, showing how and where they are used in the poems.

A typical example of questions relating to the 'Metaphysical' label, what it means, and how far one or more of these poets conform to any definition, is:

From three poems in your selection, show how they represent the main characteristics of Metaphysical poetry.

Perhaps the question itself may select one or two of the characteristics, thus:

'Metaphysical poetry is concerned with the lack of coherence and certainty in this world.' Discuss.

Or:

'The Metaphysical poets set out to express and explore ideas and feelings about the complex and changing world in which they lived, and also about their own natures.' Of which poet do you think this is most true?

Themes

The variety of the work of different poets, and that of the work of a single poet, is commonly touched upon in A-level questions. For example:

'Poetry which has much variety must lack sincerity.' Discuss.

It would be the business of the essay to demonstrate, while showing a good understanding of the implication of the question, that 'sincerity' in Donne or Marvell, for example, need not be lacking though it is shown in poems which display a variety of forms, **themes**, and **tones**. Donne wholly changes from a man really interested in secular matters and earthly love, to one devoted to divine matters and love of God.

It is useful to prepare material on common themes in the work of the Metaphysical poets. A typical short list you might isolate, with illustrations, may include:

- Love
- Sin
- Grief
- Nature
- Hope

Love is especially important in Donne; nature in Vaughan (where it is used to express God), Marvell and Herrick (where the pastoral convention survives); and sin, hope and grief in Herbert where there is always a Christian context for them.

Sometimes special characteristics of the religious poems are asked for in A-level questions, e.g. their vividness, sincerity or the personal nature of most of them. If Donne's sonnet *Batter my heart, Three Person'd God* is studied in depth it will yield a good deal in answer to such generalised questions: its passionate tone and its appeal to God as though he were a great but familiar man. (Herbert also addresses God like a friend or a lover.) The close line of argument and bold but consistent imagery may be noted, and the firm, decisive final line. Last lines make an interesting study if compared with first lines, in poems by Donne and Herbert.

The theme of love in Donne

When studying Donne's commonly set *Songs and Sonnets* and *Elegies*, you should make a special analysis of every facet of their treatment of the beloved. There is a wide range of devices – arguments, celebrations, complaints, use of 'wit' (of which Donne is said to be 'the monarch'), despair, jokes and playfulness. Dryden said of Donne, 'He affects the metaphysics not only in his satires, but in his amorous verses, where nature only should reign, and perplexes the minds of the fair sex with nice speculations of philosophy.' (*Discourse of the Origin and Progress of Satire*, 1629)

The loved one seems at times merely to be the occasion for a string of extraordinary **conceits**; one poem (*The Indifferent*) begins jauntily:

> I can love both faire and browne

and so on, listing other types – so long as

> she be not true.

It proceeds with the idea that fidelity in love is a vice; and Venus, having heard that two or three lovers are daring to grow constant, goes off to let them know that,

> since you will be true
> You shall be true to them, who're false to you.

Fantastical and Wildean as this may appear, there is a serious point, passionately held even if disguised by Donne. The passion is expressed in the detail, the elaborations:

> Will it not serve your turn to do, as did your mothers?

The point is his favourite theme of 'no woman can be true', so brilliantly expressed in direct terms in *Song* (*Goe and catche a falling starre*).

Love's Growth as an example of Donne's general manner

Love's Growth

1	I SCARCE believe my love to be so pure
	As I had thought it was,
	Because it doth endure
	Vicissitude, and season, as the grass;
5	Methinks I lied all winter, when I swore,
	My love was infinite, if spring make it more.
	But if this medicine, love, which cures all sorrow
	With more, not only be no quintessence,
	But mixt of all stuffs, paining soul, or sense,
10	And of the Sun his working vigour borrow,
	Love's not so pure, and abstract, as they use
	To say, which have no Mistress but their Muse,
	But as all else, being elemented too,
	Love sometimes would contemplate, sometimes do.
15	And yet no greater, but more eminent,
	Love by the Spring is grown;
	As, in the firmament,
	Stars by the Sun are not enlarg'd, but shown.
	Gentle love deeds, as blossoms on a bough,

```
20        From love's awakened root do bud out now.
             If, as in water stirr'd more circles be
           Produc'd by one, love such additions take,
         Those like so many spheres, but one heaven make,
             For, they are all concentric unto thee;
25        And though each spring do add to love new heat,
              As princes do in times of action get
             New taxes, and remit them not in peace,
            No winter shall abate the spring's increase.
```

The poem *Love's Growth* offers the simple proposition that in spring love grows, a theme dear to the hearts of medieval people, although they would not have much appreciated Donne's handling of it. Donne begins by affecting surprise that what he thought was already infinitely great in winter, actually grows further in spring, like the grass – he must have 'lied' in winter! He continues almost as an aside, that since love is not therefore an ultimate substance incapable of change, but a mixture that is given energy by the sun, it is not such a pure abstraction as poets (whose only mistress is their Muse) like to suppose. Since love has material substance it will at times be passive and, at other times, active. Returning to the main subject, he reflects that love does not become any bigger, but becomes more evident, in the way that stars are revealed by the sun (the reflected light of the planets), not enlarged by it. Then (in a couplet, 19–20, like one from a Shakespeare song), he compares love's deeds to blossom in the spring, opening from the 'awakened root'. Love increases as rings in water do, when the water is 'stirr'd', making many 'spheres' but still one universe ('heaven'), all concentric to love itself. Donne concludes with an image not taken from nature: each spring causes an increase in love, just as princes raise new taxes in wartime. Princes do not cancel the source of expanded revenue when peace comes, and no winter reduces spring's growth.

The proposition is teased out in a mock-serious way, sustained by a series of images that surprise and yet compel acquiescence in their validity, indeed their choice is psychologically right, even if on the surface incongruous. It is like hearing a brilliantly persuasive lawyer prove a point with frequent recourse to **metaphor** and **simile**, with this difference: a real lawyer needs to establish a conclusion and so will not break up the direct flow of his argument till he has made his point; the poet has already won his point by declaring it; he now appears to argue it, but it is merely for the sake of a display of wit as he does so; this does not appear to hold up or break up the process of proving the point, because it is already accepted.

Further than this, the images are actually integral to the argument; the beginning or middle do not exist for the end, any part exists for any other. Thus in other poems the point, or series of points, may emerge as the poem proceeds, by way of the images; images and meaning become fused. As Donne writes in another context:

```
                    … Nor must wit
          Be colleague to religion, but be it.
```

Particular themes of Marvell

Marvell's verse shows many of the characteristics of Metaphysical poetry already discussed, particularly his use of **wit** and his choice of love as a theme for many of his poems. (On pp. 43–4 there is a critical commentary on one of his love poems.) There are two other areas which are particularly his: poetry in the **pastoral** tradition and political **satire**.

Marvell combines an instinctive liking for nature with the ready-made use of it as in pastoral poems like those of Spenser and Milton, which themselves owe much to Greek and Roman eclogues. Rustic figures in rural settings may be made the mouthpiece of satire or meditation or even wit in the Metaphysical manner. Like Donne, Milton, and to a lesser degree, Herbert (although the last named was connected to a great aristocratic family), Marvell was involved in public affairs. His poetry reflects this in satire which was formidable in its time, though less interesting now, and in formal set pieces in honour of Admiral Blake and Oliver Cromwell, and of Lord Fairfax, his patron, whose daughter he taught and whose great house and garden he describes. There is an interesting contrast, therefore, between the private, introspective musings and relationships, and the public, man-of-affairs aspects in Marvell's poetry.

1.3   AUGUSTAN POETRY

We have chosen to concentrate here on Pope rather than Dryden, as his poetry is more commonly set at A level.

For many, Pope (1688–1744) stands as the most perfect representative of the **Augustans** in poetry as does Congreve in drama and Swift in prose. His verse, almost entirely composed in **heroic couplets**, is the most finished and inspired of any **satire** using that medium. Poems most often prescribed at A level are: *The Rape of the Lock, Epistle to Dr Arbuthnot, Eloisa to Abelard*, the first *Epistle of Essay on Man*, the second, third and fourth of the *Moral Essays*, one of the books of *The Dunciad*. Although it is seldom actually set, it is also a good policy to read the *Essay on Criticism*. This will give a good idea of Pope's range, variety, and special strengths. He also produced a translation into couplets of the whole of Homer, but Pope as a translator has not yet featured in A-level syllabuses. It should be noted that *The Rape of the Lock*, our language's greatest example of **mock-heroic** satire, is the poem most commonly set.

Pope's background

Questions on how the Augustan age is reflected in Pope's poetry are common at A level and you should understand something of the time at which he was writing. As well as studying your set poems, you would benefit by looking at other work by him, such as *The Epistles*, springing directly from the social, artistic, intellectual and political life of the time. A useful background book for the period is Basil Willey's *Eighteenth Century Background*.

Pope's satire

A-level questions on Pope's satire usually concentrate on his targets and how he hits them, and in a similar vein questions such as: Is the satire too bitter, angry or personal? What is the mock heroic mode? Illustrate its nature, variety and range.

You should be able to give examples of the range of Pope's satire, including illustrations of the power and effectiveness of some of his character sketches such as 'Atticus and Sporus', or groups of people such as the Grub Street scribblers in *The Dunciad*, with examples of the grotesque, or humorous, methods of satirising them. There is venom and contempt in some of the lines against those whom Pope particularly disliked, and follies he was most scornful of, but in general it may be seen that, ferocious and cutting as the satire is, the targets are anonymous, generalised, or disguised (if often thinly: note the Atticus–Addison equivalent), and the purpose not animosity or vengeance, but the preservation of moral, aesthetic and social standards. Pope wrote that his satire was published 'in the cause of virtue, to mend people's morals'.

The variety of Pope's satire may be illustrated by his use of:
- humour
- serious moral indignation
- bitterness
- prejudice
- contempt
- bawdiness (*The Dunciad*)
- scorn
- personal animosity
- social criticism

You should find illustrations for each mode or for those you consider important in your set poems. For example, you may show Pope's bitterness against aspects of his society by quoting from *The Rape of the Lock:*

> The hungry Judges soon the Sentence sign,
> And Wretches hang that Jury men may dine.

Humour lies everywhere in Pope, and everyone must have his or her favourite illustration of it, whether subtle or crude:

> Or stain her honour, or her new Brocade,
> Forget her Prayers or miss a Masquerade.

(The Rape of the Lock)

The mock-heroic mode

The mock-heroic joke can be seen in Dryden's work and is developed effectively by Pope. Note Dryden's use of incongruity in this couplet from *Absolem and Achitophel*:

> The midwife laid her hand on his thick skull
> With this prophetic blessing: be thou dull

The mock-heroic mode is adopted to make a trivial subject seem grand and in this way to satirise it.

The Rape of the Lock is acknowledged as the greatest example of the mock-heroic epic, satirising triviality by treating it in the lofty style of the classical epic. The machinery of interfering gods and goddesses from classical epics are reduced to 'sylphs' and 'gnomes'. The main characteristics of the classical poem are parodied, from broad effects to the smallest details such as verbal mannerisms and formulae. The variety and foppery of men and women are shown and, more profoundly, love and honour (the grand themes of classical epic) are debased to flirtation and fatuity.

The non-satiric Pope

A-level questions often ask candidates to assess how far Pope was a satirist only. You need to be familiar with the non-satiric aspects of his work in order to consider this question. You may also be asked whether Pope has ability as a love poet, and the nature of serious moral purpose in his work. There may be an opportunity on your paper to refer to the earlier pastoral work of *Windsor Forest*, but there is much other material to illustrate his non-satiric side, for example, the literary criticism of *Essay on Criticism*, the philosophy of *Essay on Man* (although all the thought is second-hand, whether from Boileau or Horace or Lord Bolingbroke, Pope's restating of it is valid for discussion on the kinds of his poetry). There is also pure fun without special satiric intent, and, perhaps most important, the poems of compliment to men of whom he approved, such as Richard Boyle, Allen Bathurst or Noble the landscape gardener. A common question on *The Dunciad* and *The Epistle to Dr Arbuthnot* asks what permanent appeal (if any) the poems have now the issues and people written about are almost totally forgotten. You must be aware of what other qualities the poetry possesses, and whether sins and follies common to every age lurk behind Pope's satirical targets.

Pope's style

Some questions at A level relate to Pope's style, and particularly whether Pope was a man of genuine imaginative power, or merely of surface brilliance. This entails a full description and appreciation of Pope's style; his mastery of the heroic couplet and his range of language to suit various modes of writing. It also requires attention to the more creative aspects of Pope's writing: his ability to control the structure of *The Rape of the Lock* and *The Dunciad* and the deeper themes in these and other poems; the morality, as well as the satire of more superficial matters, and the originality and appositeness of the imagery. The felicitous balance of language with content in Pope is exemplified as well as expressed in the couplet:

> True wit is nature to advantage dress'd
> What oft was thought but ne'er so well expressed

If *The Essay on Criticism* is included in your prescribed poems, then there may be a question related to Pope's ability in criticism. It is mainly a matter of what the above couplet expresses: well-known critical theory very neatly rewritten for the delight as well as the instruction of the early eighteenth-century audience.

1.4   THE ROMANTIC SCHOOL

Background – what is Romanticism?

The usual limits for this period are from Blake (first poems 1783) to the first volume of Tennyson (1830).

It is notoriously difficult to set limits to the romantic spirit in art, literature, or even poetry. The Romantic poets are lumped together for convenience mainly because they lived at the same time, with not more than a generation between them; but also because they were able to benefit by a shift in attitude and literary technique which occurred at the close of the eighteenth century.

This new attitude is complex in origin and nature, but broadly speaking it coincided with a revolutionary fervour, with new value given to the ordinary people of the poorer class, and to dignity and freedom of the individual. There occurred also a revival of interest in **romance**, especially medieval romance, the supernatural, and the mystery of life.

Romantic sensations, such as the love of the mysterious, and yearning for the unknown or the strange, the regard for uncultivated nature, the emphasis on the individual and his liberty, and other similar characteristics of the romantic school, were all present earlier, in varying degrees and forms and in other arts. For example, James Thomson's *Winter* was composed in 1725 and Dyer's *Grongar Hill* published the following year. Three books of Young's *Night Thoughts* were brought out in 1742. Collins's *Odes* were published in 1746.

In music, Haydn's *Seasons* were suggested by Thomson's completed poem of the same name (published 1730) and many of Mozart's tunes and opera airs are equally 'romantic'.

Painters such as Rembrandt in the mid-seventeenth century, but especially Watteau, Fragonard, Chardin (whose landscapes anticipated the Impressionists a century later), together with that seventeenth-century pair, Claude and Poussin, all had an incalculable influence on the nature poetry of the eighteenth century. Keats's poetry especially owes much to visual art.

A sense of striving, quest and the urge to discover are strong in romantic writing; the ideal to be won was 'beauty', or the expression by the creative faculty, called 'imagination', of high forms of love (as in Shelley), and 'sublimity'. Such ambitious aims often fell short, turning into romantic self-regard, or **solipsism**. 'Imagination' tended to take too high a place in man's existence; the virtues of social life were underestimated, and romantic love exaggerated. Stories of sensational magic, or exotic scenes, weakened allegory or more purposeful narrative.

Crabbe

George Crabbe (1754–1832), three years older than Blake, is the oldest of the poets writing during this period. He chose to continue in the old **heroic couplet** metre, writing verse tales, and became an anachronism, out of the main tradition of the other great romantics. His poetry is still very interesting and occasionally set for A level. There are two good modern selections: those of John Lucas in the Longman English series, and of Geoffrey Newbold in the Macmillan English Classics series. The *Letters and Tales* reveal great powers of observation, both for scenery and psychology of character, with an unerring ability in narrative, an overriding intelligence and a sure sense of dramatic situations.

Blake

In the case of William Blake (1757–1827) the longing for an ideal world is transmuted into that for an innocent past or a glorious future. Blake differed from Wordsworth in that he thought that the human heart was innately evil: man must purge himself to become innocent. For Wordsworth, Nature was Man's *alma mater*: for Blake she was a whore. Both poets saw eighteenth-century England as oppressed by tyranny and loss of human dignity. Machinery and the factory were the symbols of this.

Blake is often represented in the syllabuses by his famous collection, *Songs of Innocence and Experience* (1789). These poems are designed as counterparts or contraries: each state (and 'innocence' thus implies also 'inexperience') comments critically upon the other; pairs of poems are matched, and even printed thus in some editions. Each state embodied in the pairs is a necessary condition of the soul, but inadequate alone. Blake's prophetic and mystic side later possessed his mind and work, but he remains the first to attack reason, advance the imagination, and emphasise the importance and purity of man's natural desires which become corrupted by the various oppressions of society. Similar attitudes were taken by Gray (*Ode on a Distant Prospect of Eton College*, 1742) and later on by Wordsworth in his *Ode: Intimations of Immortality*.

Blake's short lyrics contain visionary power and unusually penetrating psychological insight. His gift was for bringing an inventiveness of concepts to bear upon a prophetic purpose – prophetic in the manner of Isaiah, Ezekiel and the later Milton. Indeed, a knowledge of the Authorised Version of the Bible, and of Milton, is almost indispensable to an understanding of Blake. Indeed, Blake's prophetic poetry is a sustained and major effort to equal Milton and the Biblical prophets, rather than merely to follow their lead as his contemporaries were apt and content to do. Scientific historicity had no interest for Blake; on the contrary he actually held history to blame for most of the world's evils. The Bible for him was a great document of the imagination; its truth lay in its vision. It is not what the eye sees that is important, but what the inner eye perceives; hence his easy movement among symbols.

Blake abhorred the scientific and analytical world of the Royal Society. He considered that the Augustan poets were in league with it, and later poets of refined sensibility, such as Gray and Cowper, too weak to counteract it. He symbolised this repressive world as *The Accuser of Sin*, who persecuted the people of 'Albion'. The elaborate structures of Blake's symbolism and myth-making are hard to appreciate, which is why the earlier, lyrical poetry is more popular.

Blake's use of symbols When studying Blake's poetry, it is important to acquaint yourself with the main symbols he uses and apply the 'meanings' to the poems in which they occur. You may find it helpful to group symbols as in the examples given below. However, it is important to remember that every poem with its symbols stands alone and that the meaning of symbols may change from poem to poem. A general grouping can only give a rough guide.

- Innocence, ignorance or inexperience
  Represented by: children, flowers, birds, sheep, fields, dew, spring
- Parental, religious or political oppression
  Represented by: priests, forests, clouds, thunder, stone, iron, mills, mountains
- Joyful or over-possessive sex
  Represented by: roses, gold, moonlight, nets, arrows, branches
- Creative or heroic energy
  Represented by: tigers, lions, eagles, forges, swords, spears, chariots, sun, fire

Wordsworth

William Wordsworth (1770–1850), if not the greatest of the Romantics – a position challenged by Keats alone – produced the most considerable body of great poetry. In 1798 he announced to the world his revolutionary manifesto for a new kind of poetry – the Preface to the *Lyrical Ballads* by himself and Coleridge. This condemned to outer darkness all 'Arbitrary and capricious habits of expression in order to furnish food for fickle tastes and appetites'. Wordsworth's aim in his *Lyrical Ballads* was to take natural subjects from common life and to find a less obviously 'literary' medium for their expression. When studying Wordsworth it is useful to look at the Preface and pick out a few helpful quotations to illustrate Wordsworth's ideas. (You may not feel these are always put into practice in the poems.) Examination questions on Wordsworth sometimes quote the Preface, for example:

'A selection of language really used by men'. Is this what Wordsworth used?

As with most great writers, the parts of Wordsworth's best work fit into a coherent whole; he had something of major significance to communicate, and for thirty years until his powers flagged, he managed to say it in a great many different kinds of poem, in which he effected a fusion of moral feeling and a sense of the greatness and beauty of Nature, by establishing his conviction of the interaction of Nature and human nature.

The air of philosophy in Wordsworth's work led his admirer Coleridge to encourage him to write a philosophic poem, whose 'Prelude' was completed in twelve books, sufficient for such philosophy as Wordsworth had to express in the personal, autobiographical manner; but continued and completed in the nine books and nearly ten thousand lines of *The Excursion*. This poem is a discursive meditation on the same themes as *The Prelude* (not published till after Wordsworth's death), *Tintern Abbey* and the *Ode: Intimations of Immortality*.

Questions on Wordsworth at A level regularly turn on the morality or the aesthetic qualities of the poems, or the two combined. All his conclusions derive from observed life, especially his own, or that of his sister Dorothy. Philosophy and morality have to be tested against what has been perceived; consequently there is a strong autobiographical element in all his poetry. This is the 'egotistical' half of Keats's phrase describing Wordsworth's remarkably sustained and unified vision: the 'egotistical sublime'. The exploration of his vision of Nature would not have yielded anything of great value had it not been linked with 'human nature' as he observed this in himself and the characters and behaviour of simple working people, especially solitary ones. His **pantheism** is no more than his conviction that Nature in her sublime as well as her most lowly states (the violet, celandine, bunch of knot grass, meanest flower, daisy, etc.) radiates a power that meets and inter-operates with a corresponding spirit from the observing man: this power is given various names: 'soul', 'glory' or simply 'power'. *Tintern Abbey* shows this belief in its most intense and lyrical form. About the senses of eye and ear, he writes of:

> ...what they half create
> And what perceive

Both sides contribute equally to the glory; that which *Ode: Intimations of Immortality* while lamenting its loss, again affirms.

The 'inner' contribution is not simply a wise passiveness, but heightened awareness and response, the 'leap' of the heart at a rainbow. Most typically, he conveys the action of memory on scenes, the recreation of perception in the transfiguring heart or 'inward eye'. So we return to the poet's words in the Preface:

> the poet possesses an ability of conjuring up in himself passions, which are indeed far from being the same as those produced by real events, yet do more nearly resemble the passions produced by real events, than any thing which, from the motions of their own minds merely other men are accustomed to feel in themselves; whence ... he has acquired a greater readiness and power in expressing ... those thoughts, and feelings which ... arise in him *without immediate external excitement*. (Our italics.)

This helps to correct any tendency to suppose that Wordsworth's original stimuli (for 'passions', read 'sensations' and for 'events' read 'phenomena') produced unusual or idiosyncratic responses. All his actual experience was normal – we may all have access to his inner life, and may go away the richer for having shared his vision.

Coleridge

The more interesting period of Samuel Taylor Coleridge's life (1772–1834) was linked with Wordsworth and his sister Dorothy. The most fruitful time was that after their first meeting in Nether Stowey, north Somerset, where Coleridge was living. Wordsworth took a house nearby called Alfoxden, and the two poets began a series of conversations during their walks over beautiful Exmoor. The result was *Lyrical Ballads* (1798) containing, with a few other contributions by Coleridge, his remarkable *The Rime of the Ancient Mariner*.

Coleridge was a voluble and fascinating talker; he read very widely and took an interest in almost everything: theology, philosophy, criticism, political theory – all of which he later planned to work up into a major prose work (never completed). The main topics of his discussions with Wordsworth were, 'the power of exciting the sympathy of the reader by a faithful adherence to the truth of nature, and the power of giving the interest of novelty by the modifying colours of imagination'. Wordsworth's concern was for the 'things of every day', to which he was to add the 'charm of novelty' and to direct the mind to the 'loneliness and wonder of the world before us'. Coleridge was to turn his attention to supernatural events, yet so as to 'transfer from our inward nature a human interest and semblance of truth.'

Coleridge was not, like Wordsworth, primarily reflective or meditative. Coleridge was a myth-maker, expressing his ideas as symbols which exist as potent images independently of any of their likely 'meanings'. This was no doubt designed to bring such poems into congruity with Wordsworth's poems illustrating the truths of human nature.

Byron (1788–1824)

Shelley declared that Byron's *Don Juan* was the greatest poem of the age. Today Byron is reckoned to be an 'original' poet in some of his long poems (the last two cantos of *Childe Harold's Pilgrimage*, *Beppo*, *The Vision of Judgement* and *Don Juan* itself). Without doubt *Don Juan* is one of the best comic poems in English and examination questions often ask candidates to assess its comic power. Even TS Eliot, who wrote that if Byron had distilled his verse there would have been nothing left, admitted that *Don Juan* is an original poem. It is very readable for its **wit**, colloquial diction, skilful narration and expertly handled metrics. The poem has precision of statement and description, though no great penetration into human nature or motive. It expresses eloquently a sincere contempt for hypocrisy in the last cantos. The first stanzas of dedication to Robert Southey are 'one of the most exhilarating pieces of abuse in the language' (TS Eliot's words).

Byron was a great admirer of Pope, Scott and Rogers, some of whose virtues he himself displays:

> Then roll the brazen thunders of the door,
> Which opens to the thousand happy few
> An earthly paradise of Or Molu.

The colloquial and narrative technique was established in *Beppo* (1818):

> Now Laura, much recovered, or less loth
> To speak, cries 'Beppo! what's your pagan name?
> Bless me! your beard is of amazing growth!'

In this poem he also switched from the **Spenserian stanzas** of *Childe Harold* to the *ottava rima* metre whose potential for narrative he had discovered from Italian poetry. **Ottava rima** was better suited to his style and subject matter: the final couplet in particular was often used to give a special 'snap' to the humour or vigour of the stanza.

In *The Vision of Judgement*, written in 1822 during the time of composition of *Don Juan*, Byron perfected his satiric skill and power. He disliked and dispensed with systematic, structured plots:

> I take a vicious and unprincipled character, and lead him through the ranks of society whose high external accomplishments cover and cloak internal and secret vices, and I paint the natural effects of such characters.

Don Juan, although often referred to as an 'epic', is more akin to the **picaresque** novels of Sterne and Fielding, being a highly diverse, rambling but effective criticism of society.

The incidental comment of the author takes the prime place in the poem. The forceful, vivid nature of this comment, its satirical and shocking turns, looks back to the best of the eighteenth-century writing, and forward to Browning and Wilde. Much twentieth-century poetic and dramatic satire and wit also is owed to this tradition. Society is asked to reassess some of its perhaps too complacently held values. Byron had fallen out of favour with society himself, having contravened some of its cherished taboos; he wrote his best poetry while ostracised from it. This may have added the air of indignation and rebellious aggression to some of the satire, but he knew and preserved in all his mockery the difference between immorality, reprehensible behaviour and humbug. His influence, both as a writer and as a character, proved to be very great on the continent of Europe, and a revival of interest in this country with the evaporation of irrelevant controversy about Byron the man, has accompanied a more attentive reading of his later work.

Shelley

Some knowledge of Shelley's 'romantic' life is useful as a background to an understanding of his poetry. Percy Bysshe Shelley (1792–1822) was born into the minor gentry, educated at Eton where he felt very isolated, and at Oxford from where he was expelled for circulating a pamphlet, 'The Necessity of Atheism', to the Heads of the colleges. He eloped with Harriet Westbrook, but left her for Mary Godwin after entering the Godwin circle, with its intense revolutionary, anti-royalist opinions. The couple visited Byron in Switzerland, frequented Leigh Hunt's company at home, and revisited Byron in Venice. The rest of Shelley's life was spent in Italy, and most of his best work was done during this period. He was drowned while out at sea in a small boat, alone.

Shelley is famous for what has been called the pure lyric: a short poem celebrating nothing but the poet's own soul, with few or no attendant circumstances. He was very well-read, and at one time thought about taking up metaphysics and politics; failing to come to terms with society, however, he decided to write poetry as a full-time task, but his intellectual interests found their way into the poetry with a seriousness of purpose and even **didacticism** that may surprise those who think of him as merely a lyricist. He adopted Godwin's views, which were founded on **rationalist** principles and the importance of individual liberties, but more as a bulwark against his own chaotic imagination, and the philistinism he saw in the world.

The images in Shelley's lyric poetry are usually only loosely connected with one another, or with the theme: they seem to float free, yet they still manage to convey a coherent effect overall. The exact meaning of many images does not bear close analysis, nor should they receive it. They should be read in the spirit of the entire poem to which they contribute a part of the aura or atmosphere of the poem. In the same way, each stanza of *To a Skylark* bears little or no relation logically to those before and after, yet the poem as a whole has an undeniable effect, and a unity. A notorious image in *Ode to the West Wind*, severely censured by Leavis in *Revaluation*, refers to an approaching thundercloud thus:

> ...there are spread
> On the blue surface of thine aery surge,
> Like the bright hair uplifted from the head
>
> Of some fierce Maenad, even from the dim verge
> Of the horizon to the zenith's height,
> The locks of the approaching storm.

This strange simile is no more inappropriate or badly visualised than any other image in this great poem; it takes its place in the turbulent stream of emotionally grounded images in the stanza and the whole poem: colourful, energetic, and verbally 'right'.

When studying Shelley, it is useful to look at his essay *The Defence of Poetry*. Again, it provides a useful source of stimulating quotation for the examination boards. Shelley regards poetry as subordinate to 'moral or political science' (his early love); it has a mission and a responsibility to 'reform the world' by the power of imagination. Beauty is an absolute, to which all the arts aspire: the poet may come nearest – he may express truth in beauty's form, giving all uncorrupted people pleasure. Not only can poetry do this; it can even initiate law and lay the foundations of society: 'poets are the unacknowledged legislators of the world'. This ambitious idea lends at least part of the peculiar excitement of *Ode to the West Wind*.

Keats

Questions on Keats (1795–1821) at A level fall into three main categories: questions on the odes, questions on the unfinished epic *Hyperion* and questions asking for discussion of his narrative craft. Keats's letters, prescribed by some boards, are interesting and useful reading for any student studying the poems.

The odes In 1811 Wordsworth wrote a sonnet, remembered by Keats when the younger poet came to compose the *Ode on a Grecian Urn*, on a painting by his friend Sir George Beaumont. After describing:

> The Bark upon the grassy flood
> Forever anchored in her sheltering bay

the poem concludes:

> (thou) Here ... has given
> To one brief moment caught from fleeting time
> The appropriate calm of blest eternity.

The theme of transience and permanence which struck Keats in Wordsworth's poem, forms the leading theme in the Odes. This may be followed through in all except *Ode to Psyche*. The crowning ode, *To Autumn*, may be seen as a satisfying, albeit temporary, suspension in the continuing debate between the two states, in this case emblemised by the sequent seasons. A respite is achieved though even here the problem is not entirely solved:

> Where are the songs of Spring Ay, where are they?
> Think not of them...

In *Ode to a Nightingale* the permanent element is the bird's song, and the emphasis is on the beauty of this and its rural setting. The bird is subject to change but does not in the poem appear to be; it is unseen and identified with its eternal song. The real victims are men who:

> sit and hear each other groan

Sorrow and despair reign where neither love nor beauty nor joy can last. There are hints that the nightingale's song symbolises poetry itself, especially in the fourth stanza where there is an apparent reference to Edmund Spenser, once Keats's favourite poet.

In *Ode on a Grecian Urn* the dichotomy is seen as being between 'life' (which is transient) and Art (which is permanent). There is a 'teasing' illusion of life about the scene on the urn – but all its thronging, celebratory and amorous activities will never proceed to any conclusion. Permanence exacts its price; the moulded scene will outlast 'breathing passion', the 'high sorrowful' heart and (like the spectre-thin youth of *Ode to a Nightingale*) the fevers men die of. But it is cold and has an aesthetic message that is uncompromising and exclusive, as Keats later showed in *Ode on Melancholy* and *The Fall of Hyperion*, and even the 'Bright star...' sonnet. However, if the last two lines of *On a Grecian Urn* are taken as the urn's complete message to us, then the conclusion is coherent. Beauty is the whole story; permanence wins.

> "Beauty is truth, truth beauty," – that is all
> Ye know on earth, and all ye need to know.

So far we see that the two states are unreconciled and tragically separate. In *Ode to a Nightingale*, permanent song is clearly superior, and it is unqualifiedly sad for the vision to withdraw, as 'Forlorn', the word like a melancholy bell, indicates; in *Ode on a Grecian Urn* permanence is equivocal; art is long, but dead in itself, though beautiful. In the *Ode on Melancholy*, a synthesis is attempted and achieved; the thematic problem is solved by identifying the principle of beauty and therefore joy (even love) with transience itself. This ode, which significantly concludes the set, Keats's greatest achievement, expresses a vision of those beauties so characteristic of art, visions which are incapable of gaining their effect unless perceived as fleeting. Hence 'melancholy', after being associated with passing things: the morning rose, the rainbow in seaspray, an emotionally aroused lover, is then said to occupy the very throne in 'the temple of delight', and the rhetoric of the last stanza achieves authenticity not only by its own argument, but by the treatment of themes in the other odes.

Hyperion There are three dominant divinities in this unfinished epic: Saturn and Hyperion share equally the leading interest of Book I; Saturn controls the debate in Book II, but at the end attention is once more diverted to Hyperion who arrives to:

> oppose to each malignant hour
> Ethereal presence.

However, he proves to be ineffectual, only revealing the terrible scene more clearly to the fallen gods. When the poem opens, Saturn is revealed alone, dignified and majestic still in defeat; Thea comes to rouse him, reminding him of his past glory, but he is unheeding in his profound sleep, and Thea can only sigh and weep. When he awakes, he reveals his impotence, with 'palsied tongue' and 'aspen malady'. Surely some figure more powerful and active must be the hero of the epic? We are introduced to Hyperion himself – still, indeed, unfallen in his sun palace, but everything foreshadows disaster for him too:

> horrors, portion'd to a giant nerve
> Oft made Hyperion ache

The palace is full of frightful omens: his servants stand clustered in fearful groups expecting the worst. All this makes Hyperion apprehensive and angry, and he defies that infant thunderer, rebel Jove; challenging him to try and unseat him. However, his heroic defiance only makes the lurking Phantoms rise against him more chokingly; he runs to start the new day, but Fate is against him, and he can only stretch himself 'in radiance faint' in the sky. At this the father of the Titans, Coelus or Uranus, speaks to him, and the speech underlines the new situation, but advises him to oppose the rebellion while he is still able to 'move about, an evident God'.

From this, at the close of Book I, it may be inferred that Hyperion is to become the hero of the epic, opposing himself titanically against the already successful rebellion of Jupiter and the Olympians, rather as Satan did against God and His Creation in Milton's *Paradise Lost*.

The great debate in Book II, so clearly modelled on the similar Council in *Paradise Lost* Book II, is stimulated, begun and conducted by Saturn, hailed by Enceladus:

> Titans, behold your God!

Saturn can see no reason why they should be in their plight: nor, being there, why they should accept it and remain there. The speeches that follow are in response to Saturn's appeal for opinions on what they should now do. One of these speeches, that of Oceanus, predecessor of Neptune, tries to establish a truth they must all accept: that as they superseded Coelus and Gea, who themselves followed Chaos and Darkness, so there must follow a new set of gods, who will exceed them far in 'Beauty', and:

> 'tis the eternal law
> That first in beauty should be first in might.

This principle, fatal for Saturn, Hyperion and all the old crew, is then given sharper point by Clymene who in her speech mentions for the first time who must be considered to be the probable hero of the poem if it had been finished: Apollo, the God destined to take Hyperion's place. She demonstrates the law of greater beauty putting the lesser to flight, in her story of Apollo's music, sounding across the sea from Delos to where she was attempting to make melody from breathing into a seashell. Apollo's was the brilliant music of his lyre, invented by him – a discovery described in Book III. Apollo, and his name reiterated five times in three lines, is therefore well prepared for.

Enceladus, like the ignorant Moloch in *Paradise Lost*, advocates violent resistence in similarly thundering but mindless terms; he serves also to direct attention to Hyperion, but the still-active god shows rather the hopelessness of the situation.

In Book III, which breaks off after only 136 lines, the epic takes the new but anticipated turn. Apollo, described on his island of Delos prior to the time of his deification – the event which closes the poem – clearly assumes the leading role. He is at the centre of the epic's theme: that of the necessity of superiority in Beauty superseding the old, outworn and outclassed regime.

As Hyperion is seen to approach his fate, toppling into the same sad, sunken vale as Saturn, so Apollo is described as learning from Mnemosyne, ('Memory', the mother of the Muses), his imminent apotheosis as Hyperion's successor.

In the story of the poem, therefore, there may be three leading figures or 'heroes'; but in the dimension of the theme, there is one: Apollo.

Keats's narrative skill Keats, unlike his contemporary Shelley, loved poetry above any other reading, and his early delight in Spenser's *Faerie Queene*, the tales of Chaucer and the plays of Shakespeare, all made him naturally inclined to try his hand at writing long poems in which he might 'have a little region to wander in where they may pick and choose and in which the images are so numerous that many are forgotten and found new in a second reading: which may be food for a week's stroll in the summer.'

The earlier attempts are consequently rambling and plotless: *Sleep and Poetry* in the 1817 volume was followed by *Endymion* in 1818. Some sketch for a narrative thread was provided, but this is swamped by the discursive descriptions of the arbitrary scenes; 'As I proceeded my steps were all uncertain' the poet says about its composition, and this is the effect the narrative has on the reader. There is an interesting symbolic level, however, and this may be summarised as the pursuit of Beauty by the enamoured soul.

The poem which formed the transition to the maturity of *The Eve of St Agnes* is *Isabella*, which Keats, again his own best critic, later called 'weak-sided…with an amusing sober-sadness about it.' In it, however, Keats tackles new themes in a new way: human love, tension and enmity, grief. He chose, probably mistakenly, the Byronic *ottava rima* to be the metre, but lacked Byron's polished use of the final couplet for neat conclusions to the stanza. Published revisions demonstrate that he eliminated many of the vague phrases, imprecisions, sentimentalities and the like. Several remain, as well as the overall 'inexperience of life' and the incongruity of the gruesome story and the gentle, ornate descriptive style.

Lamia is a much finer poem: its couplets proceed more steadily and purposefully; the whole is less sentimental, indeed its theme includes the idea of the necessary, if cynical, rejection of sentimental self-delusion. There are some wonderful passages of rich but exact description, with a most economical use of words to evoke an atmosphere; for example, Lycius's entry into Corinth, and the description of Lamia's house, especially the banqueting hall.

The Eve of St Agnes reveals Keats's poetical and narrative powers to the full; the poem is as near perfect as such can be: the setting, moods and technique chime together in an unflawed whole.

1.5   THE VICTORIAN POETS

Tennyson and Browning are almost exactly contemporary and their lives squarely occupy the nineteenth century from the first decade to the last. Tennyson, Browning and Hopkins occupy the leading positions in examination syllabuses for Victorian poetry.

Tennyson (1809–92)

Questions on Tennyson at A level often reflect some still-persisting critical doubt about his greatness, suggesting sympathy but not enthusiasm. Here is a selection:

Consider the variety of Tennyson's subject matter and style.
Has Tennyson's emotion any intensity?
Consider the aspects of Tennyson's narrative skill.

It would be hard to assess the nature of Tennyson's claim to greatness in his poetry from such questions; nor are the editors of selections much more helpful in their introductions; the following questions all receive different answers:

Are Tennyson's moral concerns provincial or outdated, or are they still vital today?

Are his truths 'commonplace' (as Hopkins said), or 'profoundly simple' (Christopher Ricks)?

Is his famed facility in language, and smoothness of texture, merely skilled versification, or is it more?

Tennyson had a huge audience in his day, but his contemporary critics and writers were not so sure of him. The popular journals were wholly enthusiastic and reflected the taste of their readers; later, a reaction against him joined that against other Victorian idols. Very many of Tennyson's readers would have read his work aloud to each other, and this can be the best way to experience Tennyson's poetry, providing a clue to his once huge popularity. You may find it helpful to read aloud the poems you are studying. It is still not easy to know what to make of a poet who can as readily write:

> Sons be welded, each and all
> Into one Imperial whole,
> One with Britain, heart and soul!

> One life, one flag, one fleet, one Throne!
> Britons, hold your own!
> And, God guard all!

(did the Headmaster declare it in assembly, or the Colonel in the mess?); as, at an advanced age:

> Naay, but tha *mun* speak hout to the Baptises here i'the town,
> Fur moast on 'em talks agean tithe, an' I'd like tha to preach 'em down,
> Fur *they've* bin a-preachin'*mea* down, they heve, an I haates 'em now
> Fur they leaved their nasty sins i'my pond, an'it poison'd the cow.'

except to say that if one man wrote both, he was clearly a skilled writer who could and did turn his hand to almost any theme, and publish it. This artistic flexibility may obscure the fact that some things did move him more deeply. He was moved by death, for which he found it expedient in his poetry to provide some trappings of Christian doctrine: compare the second stanza with the first, for example, of *God and the Universe*. He was particularly affected by the death of a great friend, Arthur Hallam, in 1833. He was moved by the idea of a stoical advance into a dark and uncertain future. The music of his lines may suggest a process of escape. They sometimes seem to exist only to create an imaginative auditory effect, and not to respond at a deep and perhaps painful level to the subject of their composition.

When, with the most congenial subjects, Tennyson's polished and perfected technique joins with a strong, purposeful voice saying something that matters, even if, as Hopkins complained, nothing fresh or original is said, we have poetry of which it would be churlish to ask more. For example, for the humour of rustic dialogue, the poem from which the Lincolnshire dialect lines from *The Churchwarden and the Curate* above are taken do all that may be expected of such verse anecdotes. In a poem of the same late period, *Crossing the Bar*, we have: (at death may there be)...

> such a tide as moving seems asleep,
> Too full for sound and foam
> When that which drew from out the boundless deep
> Turns again home.

This is fine enough, although flawed for the modern sensibility by the Victorian nod to 'my Pilot' (i.e. Christ) who as in Victorian hymnals, following St Paul, may at last be seen 'face to face'. There is a more convincing note of genuine inner struggle in these quatrains:

> I falter where I firmly trod,
> And falling with my weight of cares
> Upon the great world's altar-stairs
> That slope thro' darkness up to God,
>
> I stretch lame hands of faith, and grope
> And gather dust and chaff, and call
> To what I feel is Lord of all,
> And faintly trust the larger hope.

Browning (1812–89)

With Robert Browning we meet quite different problems associated with the different quality and content of his poetry. In the first place, it should be stressed that Browning was not smug or complacently optimistic: the familiar lines:

> God's in his heaven –
> All's right with the world.

are like much else in this poet's work, another's words and sentiment; the song of an Italian girl, Pippa, as she passes by different men and women. She sings songs that affect their attitudes and opinions, thus innocently influencing them.

Browning is famous for his dramatic monologues which are collected in *Men and Women* (1855), and *Dramatis Personae* (1864), the two most commonly used works in prescriptions from Browning. His variety, fertility of imagination and robust energy are shown to the full in these 'personae' or masks of characters put on by Browning for the dramatic purpose of rendering the different characters immediate, life-like and convincing. This aspect is emphasised in many questions, often quoting one of the editors of editions of his verse:

'Browning could reveal in a flash the motives which make men and women behave as they do.' To what extent is this contention borne out in the selection?

The method of preparing for this type of question is to make a complete note on what the motives of all the characters are, by asking yourself the question, why do they speak and act as they do? Then pinpoint the lines and phrases which best communicate such motives.

Hopkins (1844–89)

Gerard Manley Hopkins is in many ways the most congenial poet to the modern sensibility. He is considered by many A-level candidates to be 'difficult', but he need not be so to those prepared to follow Hopkins's own advice and 'open' their ears.

Robert Bridges, Hopkins's friend, fellow poet and constant correspondent, preserved his poetry, as well as at times attempting to rewrite it into Victorian-style stanzas! He prepared the first edition of Hopkins's verse, published in 1918, 29 years after Hopkins's death. It was not until the second edition of 1930 that, with the 'moderns' then mostly published, the public could begin to recognise Hopkins's great and original talent.

Bridges wrote of his friend's verse:

> occasional affectations in metaphor ... perversion of human feeling ... efforts
> to force emotion into theological or sectarian channels ... the unpoetic line –
> His mystery must be instressed stressed –
> ... the exaggerated Marianism ... the naked encounter of sensualism and asceticism.

Bridges' phrase, 'the naked encounter of sensualism and asceticism' refers to *The Golden Echo*, a good test piece for an appreciation of Hopkins. The poem is counterpointed with its companion piece, *The Leaden Echo*.

All this from a *contemporary* poet indicates the reception Hopkins might have expected if he had been read earlier. It also helps to make clear how far the 'modernist' movement of the 'twenties brought about a revolution in the sophisticated audience's expectations.

Bridges in his preface goes on to refer to the 'oddity and obscurity' of Hopkins, of which the first 'provokes laughter' when he is 'always serious', while the second must prevent his being understood when he 'always has something to say'.

For modern readers used to the practice of Yeats, Eliot, Auden or Dylan Thomas, there is very little to hold them up when approaching Hopkins. If such handicaps still exist, it is best to approach the poet by way of some of the better apprentice-work poems, such as *Heaven Haven* or *The Habit of Perfection*; or good fragments such as *Moonless darkness stands between* or the more characteristic *The Woodlark*, and the remarkably interesting narrative style opening to *Epithalamium*, a very late poem scribbled in pencil on a University of Ireland candidates' examination paper in 1888. The poem was to have been an ode on his brother's marriage, but he only got as far as creating a set of emblems and images for the occasion, worked up into a kind of allegory.

A-level questions may well refer to Hopkins' great feeling for natural beauty, for his most observant eye, and fresh, sensuous response which is reminiscent of the best of Keats. Almost every poem illustrates these characteristics, often by way of brilliant images that by a flash of insight reveal and glorify the real scene and experience:

(on stars):	'Flake-doves sent forth at a farmyard scare!'
(on blossom):	'When drop-of-blood-and-foam dapple Bloom lights the orchard apple'
(on a clutch of eggs):	'Thrush's eggs look little low heavens'
(on the kestrel):	'Then off, off forth on swing As a skate's heel sweeps smooth on a bow-bend'
(on the sound of waves):	'the tide that ramps against the shore with a flood or a fall, low lull-off or all roar'

This last is a good example of Hopkins's management of exact words rather than images, to render an exact impression.

Hopkins's 'difficulties' are sometimes singled out for special treatment in essays. You should decide if you think these are due to 'mangling' of the English language (see Bridges's lack of sympathy), or whether his poetic techniques may be viewed as brilliant handling of the medium, combining choice of vocabulary, rhythm (special notes are needed on 'sprung' rhythm), metre and imagery, for fully justified effects.

A final word on Hopkins's religion which is ubiquitous in his poetry, and the mainspring of most of it. Hopkins's religious experience was without question genuine, sincere and turbulent. It is quite as evident as his delight in nature. One question on this is:

'We see more of the terror than of the beauty of religion in Hopkins's poetry.' Do you agree?

The reference to the 'terror' may lead the student to the theme and much of the language and imagery of *The Wreck of the Deutschland*; the nuns 'fought with God's cold', and in the introductory stanzas:

> Thou has bound bones and veins in me, fastened me flesh,
> And after it almost unmade, what with dread,
> Thy doing...

In *Carrion Comfort*, after a record of a terrible night of doubt,

> That night, that year
> of now done darkness I wretch lay wrestling with (my God!) my God.

To set against these, there is the more typical sense of God's praiseworthiness:

> Glory be to God for dappled things!

finishing 'Praise Him'; and:

> Christ plays in ten thousand places
> Lovely in limbs, and lovely in eyes not his...

1.6 TWENTIETH-CENTURY POETRY

The works most often set at A level from this century, judging by recent papers of all the Boards, are:

TS Eliot[1]	WB Yeats
Anthologies[2]	Poets of the First World War
Philip Larkin	Louis MacNeice
WH Auden	Ted Hughes
Dylan Thomas	Thomas Hardy
Robert Lowell	DH Lawrence
AE Housman	

[1]including two widely used selections – Faber's *Selected Poems* and *Four Quartets*
[2]especially George MacBeth's *Poetry 1900–65*, and since that edition, *Poetry 1900–75*

Other modern poets are introduced each year, recent examples being Seamus Heaney and Sylvia Plath. In the past there has been more Dylan Thomas, and Edwin Muir, Robert Graves and Thom Gunn have all been represented, and no doubt will be again. It is noteworthy that MacBeth has included Hardy in *Poetry 1900–75*, presumably because of his growing reputation as a very good poet of this century. American poets continue to creep into anthologies used in schools, and as single poet selections for examinations, though anthologies of American poets alone are not set and the policy is not consistent. The two leading poets of the century are American and Irish born, though they have joined the main tradition of European if not English poetry. Both Eliot and Yeats, however, retain many characteristics derived from their background.

Most of the poets listed above have produced prose of high quality in essays and criticism, and in some cases have also been great novelists (Hardy, Lawrence), or good ones (Larkin, Graves) or playwrights (Lawrence, Yeats, Eliot). It need not be emphasised that the prose or drama of prescribed poets is very valuable supportive reading and in some cases greatly enlightens one's understanding of the poetry (Hardy, Yeats, Lawrence, Eliot, Auden, Dylan Thomas, MacNeice's autobiography, Ted Hughes's stories and essays). Because of the high incidence of Yeats's and Eliot's appearance on the syllabuses, we will consider them separately below, but first we will refer briefly to two poets of the second rank, but still of sufficient merit and interest to warrant a prominent place in present and future A-level work – Auden (1907–1973), and Ted Hughes (1930–).

A note on Auden and Hughes

Any poem from, say, the last collection of each of these poets, if contrasted, will illustrate the difference between this pair. In *Archaeology* (Auden's *Thank you Fog*), one of his multitude of manners, he takes a topic and launches into a series of easy, seemingly casual comments, turning it over as if it were a subject for after-dinner conversation; but the three-line stanzas each contain a separate idea, like a string of matched beads, finishing with a sudden insight into the similarity yet dissimilarity between barbaric rites and Christ's crucifixion. Then in a coda, like an afterthought, casually added, he clinches the discourse on *Archaeology* with a moral proposition that is not only worthy of thought but offers a key to the previous, apparently inconsequential string of variations. Such is the geniality of tone, it is difficult to notice that Auden has used ten coined parts of speech – mainly new verbs from adjectives or nouns; two coined phrases and one word (unless 'stumper' is a slang word like 'poser').

Auden continues the tradition of English poetry from Pope to Browning, with fresh access of tone from American poets such as Marianne Moore. Ted Hughes intensifies the sensuous apprehensions explored by Keats, Hopkins, and DH Lawrence to such a degree that it is difficult to conceive how this can be taken further; a poem on catching fish in the style of *Earth Numb* (*Moortown*) could not be improved upon. In place of Auden's urbanity, and deceptive simplicity:

> Poets have learned us their myths
> But just how did They take them?

We have this of Ted Hughes:

> As the eyes of incredulity
> Fix their death-exposure of the celandine and the cloud,

to end the poem with the landing of the fish.

Set in their contexts, the first quotation excites the assent of the reader, with gratitude for the friendly, good-humoured tone, the graceful wit; the second excites at a more mysterious level – the sources of the emotions. As in all the best **romantic** poetry, nothing can be specifically isolated or defined concerning the response to the poems of Wodwo, Crow or Moortown, but it is as valuable as that of one's intelligence. Indeed it is a kind of intelligence of the emotions, when these are ordered and evoked in good poetry of this type. It is a mere falsification to label as 'horror' the emotion aroused by:

> The spider clamps the bluefly – whose death panic
> Becomes sudden soulful absorption

> (Lumb's songs in the Epilogue to *Gaudete*)

And the emotion evoked in:

> He saw the stars, fuming away into the black,
> mushrooms of the nothing forest, clouding their spores, the virus of God–

A single line from *Crow Alights* is similarly transformed, though the next line states Crow's own reaction:

> And he shivered with the horror of Creation

We may shiver, but more from the imaginative power of verbal creation.

Yeats (1865–1939)

If Hopkins was received by the modern age as a long-lost father, WB Yeats and TS Eliot may be regarded as the founding fathers of twentieth-century literature and modern poetry.

No poet's output has been so complex, yet so deliberately unified as that of WB Yeats, whose whole life's work in poetry, prose and drama has together expressed that life from youth to old age, and made of it a unity. He has stated that a writer should 'hammer his thought into

unity'; he himself set out with remarkable dedication to apply this principle to himself. Thus to read any one, even a major example of his poems, is not such an enriching experience as to read the same poem in the light of all the rest, a piece of a coherent whole much greater than the sum of the parts taken separately. Many of the shorter pieces indeed do not make much sense until read in this context.

To aid this process, Yeats developed a network of symbols, images and areas of reference that interact, and thereby gather power. Beneath all he writes lies the biography: his country and background, especially Galway; his friends and family; Irish mythology and literary or political heroes, and the development of a philosophical theory, which for Yeats, who said, 'I am a very religious man', took the place of orthodoxy.

Irish history and especially current Irish life are most important for Yeats, and not merely, as for Joyce, convenient material for more universal truth. At the same time, as for Joyce's Dublin, so for all the Irish matter in Yeats, readers may see that there are parallels between provincial affairs and personal passions, and those that concern everyone.

Themes There is a wide scope for choice of themes on Yeats, but some of the most obvious may be selected. For example, the thinking which was eventually 'codified' in the prose *A Vision* (1925), even if at first weird or nonsensical to the student, well repays investigation: a great many poems owe their imagery and even explanations to it. A good clear note should be prepared on the theory of millennial cycles and their association with 'Subjective' and 'Objective' eras, these also being linked to sun and moon symbolism. Also an elaborately worked out set of characteristics for the different stages of a millennium related to different types of person, is symbolised by the 28 phases of the moon. In the 'subjective'–'objective' contrast above there is implicated another major area of thought; that of the 'antinomies' or opposites, represented by an inner man and his 'antithetical' mask.

In particular, significant events in the crucial stages of the world's history should be noted, and the places associated with these events, which are of a strongly supernatural kind, as the idea of fate is apt to be, if taken seriously. James Joyce develops another cyclical view of man's progress through the world's history in his last novel, *Finnegans Wake*.

If this approach does not appeal to you, then a far different area may be profitably explored: that of Yeats's friendships. He has written a considerable number of great poems about different men and women whom he knew and loved: Maude Gonne, Major Robert Gregory (the poem in memory of whom contains stanzas recalling other earlier companions), Mabel Beardsley (the sister of the artist Aubrey Beardsley) who died courageously: 'When she meets our gaze her eyes are laughter lit'.

The poem to her, *Upon a Dying Lady*, should be read alongside two letters which contain enlightening comments: those to Lady Augusta Gregory of 8 January and 11 February 1913. Other poems to friends may be added to form a special study of this fruitful theme.

Other themes include: meditations on Eastern mysticism, and the Western philosophy opposed to it; life and art; gaiety in the teeth of tragedy both in art and life; myth and anthropology (as by Eliot, Graves and others, a rediscovery of this source of poetry was furthered by Yeats) – see, for example, *Leda and the Swan* in *The Tower* (1928), *Vacillation* in *The Winding Stair* (1933) and a host of others. Also, there are: magic and the occult, and Irish politics (e.g. *Easter 1916*).

Of course, examples of these and other themes are to be found in all combinations in the poetry and by no means separated into compartments; very often one theme serves to illustrate or expand others – they are all parts of Yeats's complex but unified world. Yeats's interest in magic is common to his people, he met it at the home of George Pollexfen, his maternal uncle in Sligo, whose servant, Mary Battle, possessed the power of 'second sight'. Her vision of horsemen with swords swinging, riding over the slopes of Ben Bulben, was remembered by the poet when he wrote his epitaph at the close of *Under Ben Bulben*. After some experiments with theosophy under Madam Blavatsky and Rosicrucianism, which resulted in some poems and images, Yeats's interest in spiritual second sight revived when, after his marriage, he found his wife exercised the power of automatic writing. Much more imagery flowed from this, from 1917 on, and the book, *A Vision*, was a result of it. This imagery, and much of the esoteric business, had already been seen in some of Yeats's poetry, e.g. *Ego Dominus Tuus* and the prose of *Per Amica Silentia Lunae*: there is no traumatic change between these ideas and the concerns of *The Second Coming* (1921), or *Byzantium* (1933). They are linked with Yeats's developing thought, which is merely given more images and symbols by Mrs Yeats, when the interest returns with great power in poems from his volume *A Full Moon in March* (1935), especially Ribh's 'holy book' in the twelve 'supernatural songs', really meditations on the nature of love and its relationship to sex. The 'gyres' or wheeling of time, return in the last, *Meru*, where man returns or is returned, at last, to 'The desolation of reality'.

From the 'system', the 'Great Year' or double millennia, linked with the 'Great Wheel', or phases of the moon, we may note in particular the revelations that begin and end such eras. Christ came at the close of a subjectively controlled period, and inaugurated its converse, 'fabulous darkness', and that which:

> Made all Platonic tolerance vain
> And vain the Doric discipline.

So in our present century, once more the gyres whirl to their close and renewal:

> Things fall apart; the centre cannot hold;
> Mere anarchy is loosed upon the world

and at the mid point, the time of Byzantium's zenith as a city, there is a state of perfect balance and supernatural revelation. Yeats wrote:

> Each age unwinds the threads another age had wound, and it amuses one to remember that before Phidias and his westward moving art, Persia fell, and that when full moon came round again, amid eastward-moving thought, and brought Byzantine glory, Rome fell; and that at the outset of our westward moving Renaissance Byzantium fell; all things dying each other's life, living each other's death

Some ideas in both *Byzantium* and the late poem *The Statues* will be illustrated by this, as well as *The Gyres*, and many lesser poems such as *Two Songs from a Play*.

By reference to theory from the 'system' of *A Vision*, interesting connections can be established between poems to their mutual advantage, and ours in their appreciation; for example, *Leda and the Swan*, on more available levels a vividly effective and dramatic sonnet, also announces the beginning of an era which closes with the birth of Christ; here *Two Songs from a Play* will lose much of its obscurity; the process reaches a further transition in *The Second Coming*.

Style Yeats's poetry has three clearly distinguishable styles, depending roughly on whether it is of his early, middle, or late writing periods. The first, sometimes called his 'Celtic Twilight' phase, may be illustrated by poetry and prose to about 1910, and the poems of *The Green Helmet*, and is characterised by dreaminess, vagueness and sensuality.

The middle period, regarded by many as his best, is represented by volumes from *Responsibilities* (1914), to *The Tower* (1928), which contains 20 poems, more than half of them great ones and most of those as well-known as anything Yeats wrote. The poems are mostly characterised by a new bitterness, but expressed in a vigorous, direct and eloquent style. In this period he developed the 'public' utterance so impressive in poems such as *In Memory of Major Robert Gregory* and *A Prayer for My Daughter*, as well as those of *The Tower*. Yeats owned the tower (in Galway) in which he wrote many of these poems, and noted:

> My poems attribute to it most of the meanings attributed in the past to the Tower – whether watch tower or pharos, and to its winding stair those attributed to gyre or whorl.

His next volume, *The Winding Stair* (1933), and the rest of his books in the 'thirties until his death, result from a huge burst of creative energy that led him into new paths. The public tone vanished, except in some deliberate revivals such as *The Circus Animals' Desertion* or *The Municipal Gallery Revisited*, and its place was taken by short lines, quatrains, haunting refrains, a new fervour and bluntness, and a final mystic wisdom.

Yeats's poems: a summary

1. Yeats's poems are usually clear and effective when read in the light of the rest of his work. His entire output constitutes a whole which strengthens and illuminates the separate pieces.

② The achievement of this unity is assisted by Yeats's use of a 'system' of symbols and of mythologies such as the Irish-Celtic and Greek.

③ Irish political and social history is also an important element, and a unifying influence in Yeats's work.

④ There is a need to be acquainted with Yeats's 'system' as, for example, set out in *A Vision*: the phases of the Moon, the mask and anti-mask, the cyclical 'gyres'; subjectivity and objectivity, and the application of all of them to world history and public and private people.

⑤ Yeats wrote for and about people he knew: their celebration by Yeats often assumes a symbolic character. Knowledge of such persons and the poems written in their honour is an important aspect of the study of Yeats. For example, Maude Gonne lies behind the heroine of *Cathleen ni Hoolihan*, as well as behind many other poems.

⑥ Other themes include life and death, art, magic and occultism, and the supernatural.

⑦ Magic and 'The System'. A thread of interest in magic runs through Yeats's life and work, developing from early fascination with Irish superstition to wider application of images used as symbols from his wife's automatic writing. The interest centres on the nature of the relationship between the living and the dead, or perhaps we should say 'the other world'.

⑧ It is important to note in particular the revelations that occur at the close and new beginning of the cycles of human history.

⑨ Yeats's work can be seen in three periods:

(a) the early period – 'Celtic Twilight' phase: poetry and prose to about 1910 and *The Green Helmet*;

(b) the middle period – characterised by bitterness and 'public' utterance: from *Responsibilities* (1914), to *The Tower* (1928);

(c) the late period – characterised by 'gaiety': from *The Winding Stair* (1933) to Yeats's death in 1939.

⑩ It is useful to read Yeats's essay *JM Synge and the Ireland of his Time* (1910). It shows again the unity of Yeats's thought.

TS Eliot (1888–1965)

This century's greatest poem of horror, despair and boredom, a terrifying vision of the paralysis and spiritual bankruptcy of modern life, is TS Eliot's *The Waste Land*. The immediate background to this poem is the postwar London of the early nineteen-twenties, when it was begun, but there are strong personal springs running into the poem's creation.

Prufrock had been dedicated to a poet, and friend of Eliot, who had been killed in 1915 in the Dardanelles; Mrs. Eliot was receiving treatment for nervous disorders that later resulted in her confinement to a mental hospital; Eliot himself was finding the necessity of working in a bank harder to bear, and there were even other anxieties, such as the effort to found a literary magazine, the death of his father, and the near-impossibility of travelling to see his mother in the USA. He was approaching a psychological collapse, and in such circumstances *The Waste Land* was conceived and begun, continued at Margate where Eliot was sent to rest, and completed at Lausanne by Lake Geneva – the 'waters of Leman' of Part III of the poem.

Personal and intellectual motives, therefore, combined to give the poem its sombre theme; Eliot assembled a large number of primary and secondary allusions to assist in expressing this, as well as forming part of the structure, and serving as thematic metaphors in very many of the lines; a small selection is explained in Eliot's own notes, most of which are helpful, but some of which are mild leg-pulls.

The most useful guide to this and the other poems in *Selected Poems* is BC Southam's *A Student's Guide*, if this is read with the poems open; help may also be obtained from George Williamson's *A Reader's Guide to TS Eliot*, which is a 'poem-by-poem' analysis; a general introduction to the poems from one or two of the 'profiles' particularly suitable for A-level students is advisable, such as Northrop Frye's in the Writers and Critics series, or TS Pearce's in *Literature in Perspective*.

Eliot had already made use of many allusions in most of the *Poems 1920* collection, but the technique is carried to an extreme in this poem, and not employed again except in a far more subdued and sparing way. The allusions in *The Waste Land*, although they are drawn from an amazing range of historical periods, foreign literatures and different cultures, are all carefully chosen for their power to illuminate the main themes of the poem from different angles, and to aid in the overall structure. The demonstration of erudition is not mere exhibitionism nor as random as it may seem. The diverse 'sources' have been thoroughly assimilated into the poem.

Questions sometimes ask for those passages that are most effective, in the candidate's opinion; or most lyrical, or most descriptive. Before choice is made of such passages the poem should be grasped as a whole, and all its parts seen as taking their fit places. The allusions, the imagery, and different spokesmen are all methods that Eliot uses to achieve his 'objective correlatives' as he called the process of finding a fit equivalent to his meanings and feelings. Typical questions you may come across are:

'Eliot's poetry attempts to find striking though indirect ways to express personal feeling in impersonal terms.' Discuss.

'These poems are a progress from despair to faith. Eliot looks only for the sordid and depressing.' Is this fair comment?

Other questions may more specifically refer to *The Love Song of J. Alfred Prufrock*, or *Portrait of a Lady*. For example:

'There is a coldness and shrinking from emotion, a fear of life in Eliot's poetry.' How far is this true?

Ideas and images from these poems, together with *Preludes* and *Rhapsody on a Windy Night*, will help you to answer such questions as this:

'There is a sense of either elusive beauty or menace in *Selected Poems*.' Do you find this so?

Questions which refer to the content of the poetry may also ask for Eliot's 'social comment', for which the choruses of *The Rock* and the answering Workmen are a good source. Another question might ask:

What distinguishes Eliot's early from his later poems?

This is asking about Eliot's changes of style as well as more obvious progress of his philosophy from doubt, disgust, realisation and resolution to faith and assurance.

Finally, there are the questions relating more specifically to style and language. Selective quotation with comment is always important here. It is interesting to note the number of lines in this poetry which are variants of the regular **iambic pentameter** and how the verse subtly echoes the metre that is well-established in the ear of the readers of Shakespeare, Chaucer and most English poetry. It is the poetic 'norm' for the verse.

In *Poems 1920* there is a change into tight quatrains similar to those used by seventeeth-century metaphysical poets. Their characteristics are incisive wit and economy of diction, with reliance on the exactitude of metre and rhyme.

The experiment in *The Waste Land* was to try to achieve the same unity and synthesis in a long poem, whose five parts are stuffed with broken 'fragments' from other literature, the knowledge of which is required as background for the reader. If it is known, haunting echoes and reinforcements of sensibility are achieved; if not, then only confusion. The experiment was not repeated by Eliot, nor by other poets in poems of equivalent status, with the exception of Ezra Pound in the *Cantos*.

TS Eliot: A Summary

❶ *The Waste Land*:
- The circumstances of its composition.
- The peculiar form and style of the poem.

❷ Eliot's allusiveness: its purpose and justification.

❸ The place of *The Waste Land* in Eliot's oeuvre: its thematic links with *Gerontion* and *Ash Wednesday*.

❹ Eliot's search for apt images to express his concerns: his use of 'voices', and notorious employment of sordid images and situations.

❺ Questions relating to the early poetry: the theme of evasion or moral failure or weakness; moral decay.

⑥ Eliot's social concerns: neglected churches and the state of the true 'church'; leaderless masses (*The Rock*).

⑦ Eliot's change of poetic method and style as these accompany the transitions into new themes: a steady progress from doubt and despair through conversion to serene faith and meditative Christian philosophy.

⑧ Eliot's style: free verse and the tight stanza.

⑨ The variety and degrees of Eliot's stylistic method, especially in *The Waste Land*. Recurrent images as 'motifs', e.g. that of the city.

⑩ Later abandoning of allusiveness: interrelation of imagery and motif increased in *The Hollow Men* and *Ash Wednesday*, culminating in the 'figure in the carpet' complexity of *Four Quartets* (for example, use of 'turn' motif in *Ash Wednesday*).

⑪ Eliot's concentration on the more unpleasant aspects of contemporary life in his references and imagery: its decrease after *The Waste Land* and the growth of Eliot's religious faith.

⑫ Eliot's serious purpose in his most allusive poems, e.g. *Burbank with a Baedecker*. This poem should be analysed closely in order to show the justification for the presence of the plethora of allusions.

1.7 CHAUCER

BIOGRAPHICAL BACKGROUND

Our literature begins with Chaucer, and it is a divine start. There are some fine things in late Middle English literature, notably *Sir Gawain and the Green Knight*, *Pearl*, Langland's *Piers the Ploughman* and a collection of fresh old **ballads** and **lyrics**, but they pale into insignificance beside the great work of Chaucer. His creative genius was seemingly boundless, his learning huge, especially where this country's literature so much needed it – in other European literatures, ancient and recent. The Classics, the great Italians of the emergent Renaissance, the French – he was acquainted in their own languages with them all and probably met several, such as Petrarch in Padua.

Chaucer thus rightly enjoys special status in all the boards' syllabuses, with Milton as a close second, outside Shakespeare. He is still read with the highest pleasure and appreciation, in spite of the slight difficulties of the dialect barrier. To be more precise, the dialect is the one he has handed down to us – the London and East Anglian – not even his own native Kentish – but the intervening six hundred years have removed or altered the meaning of many words, and slightly affected the grammar and syntax too. To counteract the sense of 'strangeness' many candidates feel when encountering Chaucer at A level, it is often helpful if they begin by making themselves familiar with his life.

Geoffrey Chaucer was born in or near 1343. He was a page in the household of Elizabeth, Countess of Ulster, wife of Duke Lionel, Edward III's third son. This was at Hatfield, in Yorkshire. John Chaucer, his father, was relatively wealthy, a vintner and collector of wool duties.

When Chaucer was about 15, he was in France as a squire, on a military operation in which he was taken prisoner. The king paid £16 towards his ransom. He held a number of positions at court and in the king's service, and travelled abroad on numerous diplomatic missions. French would have been the accepted language at court; the Queen, Philippa of Hainault, was a Frenchwoman. When 25 he accompanied John of Gaunt (the King's fourth son, and with the death of the Black Prince, probably the most powerful man after the King), on a raid in Picardy.

Then in 1372 Chaucer went on a more important and, for his vocation as a poet, very significant journey to Italy. The purpose of the visit was to negotiate with the Doge of Genoa a port of entry in England for Genoese merchants. He went to Florence on the King's business and probably other places – he is reported to have met Petrarch in Padua. Italian literature from then on took its place as a major influence on Chaucer's developing art: the whole of *Troilus and Criseyde* and several of *The Canterbury Tales* have their origins in Boccaccio's work, whom he might also have visited.

After this, Chaucer moved from Westminster to the City, where he became Controller of Customs of wool, skins and hides in the Port of London. His connection with John of Gaunt's household was particularly strong, as his wife's sister became the Duke's third wife, in 1396. Chaucer had probably known John of Gaunt since boyhood, from the time of his service at Hatfield. They were more or less the same age. John of Gaunt's first wife, Blanche, had died in 1368, and Chaucer wrote his first major poem, *The Boke of the Duchesse*, in her honour, shortly afterwards. As John was extremely attached to Blanche, the poem was clearly designed to please him.

In 1382 he was made Controller of the Petty Customs on wines and other goods, and in 1385 on wool; he was made a JP and member of Parliament as a Knight of the Shire of Kent. From 1374 he lived in a house over Aldgate, in the east wall of the City. There he read and wrote, after his day's work at the wool wharf near the Tower.

In 1386 he lost his job due to a change of favour under the new young King Richard II, John of Gaunt's nephew. John of Gaunt was out of the country and new men were in favour, opposed to the king's powerful uncle. Then Chaucer's wife died, and the poet began to devote himself and the rest of his life to organising and completing *The Canterbury Tales*. In 1389 Richard II decided to favour the poet, making him Clerk of the King's Works; responsible, that is, for the building and repair of all the King's properties (the Tower of London, Westminster Palace and eight royal manors). He performed this duty for two years, and then received the sinecure of a forestry officer for Petherton in Somerset. He was over 50, and virtually in retirement. The last year of his life was spent in a new house close to Westminster Abbey, where he died on 25 October 1400, and was buried in Poet's Corner.

THE CANTERBURY TALES

Apart from *The Canterbury Tales* only *Troilus and Criseyde* is set at A level. This is because Chaucer's last work is his best, and there is plenty of superlative material to choose from. Space for more than a minor proportion of his work is limited, usually to one story and the *General Prologue* set as a choice, against other major authors, usually including Milton. Also, most of the best stories are of a convenient overall length, though at times they are cut. The *Knight's Tale* is one of the best, but is over two thousand lines long; the *Physician's*, *Prioress's* and *Manciple's Tales* are too short; the *Miller's*, *Reeve's* and *Summoner's* are sometimes neglected because of their scurrility.

The parts most often selected for study are: the *General Prologue*; the *Pardoner's Prologue* and *Tale*; the *Wife of Bath's Prologue* and *Tale*; the *Nun's Priest's Tale* (sometimes known as 'The Cock and the Fox'); and the *Franklin's Tale*. Those tales set less often are: the *Man of Law's Tale*; the *Clerk of Oxford's Tale* ('Patient Griselda'), and part of the *Knight's Tale*. Others are never set at all: the two prose tales (even though one excellent one is delivered by the author), the *Monk's*, *Cook's*, *Shipman's* and the rest.

The various boards differ in one method of approach: that of either setting merely essay questions, or a printed passage to turn into clear modern English, and perhaps an essay as well. Usually with Chaucer a fair breadth of choice is given, either to choose one of two passages, or to prepare for and so choose a different major author, not only in the sections containing the 'passage' type of question but in those with essay questions. Oxford is the most traditional in that it sets only three authors: Chaucer, Milton and one other, from which two must be chosen.

THE *GENERAL PROLOGUE*

The Canterbury Tales is not the first work to link a sequence of stories by bringing together a group of different characters as the tellers – Boccaccio's *Decameron* has the ladies of Florence exchanging a hundred stories to pass the time in a local villa while the Plague rages in the city below. Nor is Chaucer the first to introduce himself as a persona and participant in a dramatic poem: Dante does so in his *Divine Comedy*. Both these works were well known to Chaucer. *The Canterbury Tales*, however, is the first work in literature to give all the speakers a single purpose within a carefully organised diversity of occupation, character and dress:

> whiche they weren and of what degree
> And eek in what array that they were inne.

Organisation

The *General Prologue*, which presents the tellers of the tales, is carefully organised. In the introductory section, which ends at line 42, Chaucer concisely describes the setting. The time of the year, with its strong associations of rebirth and renewal, life and joy, is significant, for it is a time at which men and women stir themselves and, whoever they might be, whatever they might do, first turn to unite in a common enterprise of pilgrimage, to worship at a famous shrine. They gather in Southwark at the Tabard Inn, kept by a known Londoner, Harry Bailley; walk along a known path through North Kent to Canterbury, on a well-known annual pilgrimage, and on the road exchange stories according to a set of simple rules set by their host and judge, Bailley. All this is perfectly realistic, as are the characters themselves, and the experience of telling and hearing such stories, most of which were very well known either from other literature or the common stock of folk story. Chaucer's art appears in almost casual details such as calling March a month of 'drought' (only by classical literary convention considered to be such), or rhetorical devices such as referring to spring by zodiacal allusions ushered in with a classical Greek breeze. Then there are broader designs, such as the careful selection of people; representative types of laymen and clerics, good folk and bad, low born or gentlefolk. But the fellowship of all is established at the outset, and Chaucer's plan to make each pilgrim tell two stories on the way, and two more returning, is put into Bailley's proposal for the competition at the end of the Prologue. This would have made 116 tales from the 29 pilgrims (assuming that there is only one Nun's priest and not three). In fact we get only 20 completed and two uncompleted stories, as well as two, the Monk's and Chaucer's own, which the host cuts short. There obviously was also to have been a link between each, provided by conversation between the host and the pilgrims, or between themselves, but several of these links are missing and the order of the whole is therefore in doubt.

Nearly half the number of lines of description are given to religious figures: Friar, Parson, Pardoner, Summoner, Monk, Prioress and Clerk. All the characters display good and bad traits. The order in which they are described repays consideration. For example, the Miller, Manciple, Reeve, Summoner and Pardoner are all rogues in various respects, but the Manciple is a cunning operator in contrast to the more extroverted ruffians he is placed between. Similarly, of the first three related types, the Knight rightly takes first place. Then the Prioress should preceed the Monk, who in turn takes precedence over the Friar. The professional men are separated from from more workaday types by the five Gildmen. The last two, the Summoner and Pardoner, are a pair of unholy friends; the Pardoner's tale, because of its position at the end (his tale is also the last one, as indeed, the Knight's is the first), is rendered more memorable.

Although all the characters are realistically presented to the reader, and the details of their descriptions confer a vivid life on each, even though some are quite short, these types are not commonplace people: each one is exaggerated in some way – in fact, in as literary a creation as any in Shakespeare or Dickens. The Knight is worthy and honourable; the Squire a young, brightly singing lover, the Prioress a fastidious aristocrat, and so on. Characteristic traits, such as the Pardoner's hypocrisy, are strongly highlighted. The evidence of characters in their various fields is often asked for in A-level questions. There are also various details which reveal the characters as living people, for example the Friar's 'wanton' (affected) lisping, the Miller's big nostrils, and the Wife of Bath's scarlet stockings and partial deafness. The *General Prologue* is wonderful in itself, but even more impressive as an integral part of the tales which follow: there are very interesting relationships between the characters as sketched in the Prologue, and their subsequent tales.

Note on satire

The expert economy of Chaucer's satirical hints in many of his short descriptions of the pilgrims in the *General Prologue* is to be noted in any study of his text. Chaucer likes to use humorous or sly innuendo; at times the reader is left to make his own deductions about character from styles of dress, equipment, horses or even facial appearance. The description of the Prioress is a masterpiece in this way, but we will illustrate it by four lines on the Man of Law:

> So greet a purchasour was nowher noon,
> Al was fee symple to him in effect,
> ...Nowher so bisy a man as he ther nas
> And yet he semed bisier than he was.

The first line hints, under the guise of praise, that the sergeant, using his wealth, snapped up property; the second suggests that he perhaps fraudulently converted partly bought interests into outright possession, probably to anticipate legal moves to deprive him of it; the fourth line suggests that he put on an act to impress his clients.

COMMON QUESTIONS ON *THE CANTERBURY TALES*

The following areas of Chaucer's art are commonly touched upon in A-level questions:
1. narrative skills
2. scene painting and character sketching ability
3. creation of dramatic interest
4. realism in dialogue
5. maintenance of plot interest

For example, on the *Wife of Bath's Tale* there are often questions on the status of The Prologue to her tale: whether it is a tale in its own right, or theoretically linked to the tale that follows; whether the Wife expresses her feminism in both, and how; the role of the 'sermon' embedded in the conclusion; the humour and fairytale element; the marriage debate advanced by probing the question of who should hold 'maistrie' or sovereignty. (The Middle Ages, following St Paul, assumed this should be the husband; we today accept equality of partnership; Chaucer was thinking it through – see also the *Franklin's* and *Clerk's* tales.)

Questions on other tales follow these general lines. Some single out the use of irony in Chaucer's writing. It is usually linked with humour and innuendo. Because of this, it is sometimes considered to be 'gentle' irony, but this is a misnomer for its understated, modest subtlety. Chaucer always had high regard for the intelligence of his audience: he seldom laboured his points except for the purpose of character representation.

HINTS ON TRANSLATION

When 'translating' Chaucer, the first thing is to establish the most exact modern equivalents to the very different words, and then suitable modern phrases for the outdated expressions that still bear some recognisable meaning. In the example below, 'lye' illustrates the first, 'up peril of my lyf' the second. The first operation depends on careful preparation of the text with the glossary and notes, the second more on a weighing of what is being expressed, and rendering the meaning rather than the words. Glossaries are not much help, only other prose translations may supply deficiences here. It is not advisable, though, to try to learn other translations wholesale, the way students sometimes will with a Latin text.

In writing the final modern version, care should be taken *not* to translate line-by-line if meanings continue on subsequent lines. The right method is to translate by unit of meaning, whether this ends with a full stop, semi-colon or dash; *not* normally a comma, even at the line-end. Sentences should be grammatical and well-constructed; slang should be avoided. Any taint of archaism or false romanticism should be avoided, such as poetic inversions of word order.

Here is a short extract from a recent paper to demonstrate some of this; it should also serve to remind you that Chaucer is essentially an English, not a foreign poet. Nor is he so remote in the past that he cannot speak to us in living language and with fresh thought. Reading his verse aloud often resolves specious difficulties. Try 'translating' the following passage yourself, before looking at the version below.

> Taak fyr, and ber it in the derkeste hous
> Betwix this and the mount of Kaukasous,
> And lat men shette the dores and go thenne;
> Yet wole the fyr as faire lye and brenne
> As twenty thousand men myghte it beholde:
> His office natureel ay wol it holde,
> Up peril of my lyf, til that it dye.

> Take some fire, carry it into the darkest house between here and the Caucasus, and then shut the door and leave; the fire will still blaze and burn as well as if twenty thousand men could see it; I may dare swear that its very nature is always to do what it must, until it dies.

It is fair to expect A-level students to show their competence to modernise Chaucer. Perhaps the exercise offends those who dislike interfering with poetry, weakening it to no good purpose, but if this objection were pushed too far, Neville Coghill's monumental translation into couplets (published by Penguin) might be called a travesty. The justifiable hope is that after the exercise one may read Chaucer in the original with the same delight and ease experienced in reading Spenser.

We would advise a student to try learning a good passage of between 35 and 40 lines by heart, and reciting them aloud. Apparent obscurities fall into natural, satisfying music. For example, two fine openings are suitable: the first 18 lines of the *General Prologue*, and the first 25 lines of the *Wife of Bath's Tale*.

It is not necessary to try to fill up every line into a decasyllabic count. Although Chaucer, influenced by French poetry, might have been aiming for metrical 'correctness', we are not now so obsessed with this; many modern poems are deliberately unpolished for greater strength and rhythmic interest. It is still possible that Chaucer did the same service for his music. The flexible and varying narrative and tones of different speaking characters in the tales are more aptly conveyed by light-stress variations. Thus:

Citees, Burghes, Castels, hye toures

is ancephalous and possibly robbed of the fifth foot's light stress; it might practically be read as:

Cities, boroughs, castles, high towers

which the modern ear might prefer to some expletive syllable as in 'lofty towers'. Should the editor (or printer of the examination paper) print the 'e' of 'hye' as a dotted 'e', it is thought in that case to be sounded lightly, and render the line metrically 'regular'. It is true that French poetry prefers to retain sounded final 'e's' for this reason, and Chaucer may be extending this practice to English.

The essay questions deal with such matters as the content of the tale, including its elements of suspense, surprise, climax, revelation, complication, character interactions, passages of argument, preaching, philosophising, rhetorical amplifications such as sententiae (moral generalisations) and exempla (illustrations by reference to related incidents), digressions and the relevance of all these to the theme.

1.8 MILTON

TYPES OF QUESTION SET

When passages of Milton, usually from 25 to 30 lines, are printed on the paper, the procedure for questions on them varies. The WJEC asks for specific questions under the passage to be answered: candidates are asked to explain phrases and groups of lines, or imagery and allusions; the context may be asked for, and deductions drawn from the passage. The SEB prints the passage together with others from Shakespeare and Chaucer, asking for only one to be considered in terms set for them all – 'Write critical comment; explain anything not readily understood today; give the significance of the passage in its relationship to the whole work.' The choice is wide and a virtually free hand is given to the candidate. NICCEA sets questions on 16 set texts, including one on Milton, asking for comment on four of them.

The Oxford Board gives a smaller choice – either Chaucer or Milton or a major novel, and where the choice is two of the three, the questions on Milton are more precise, e.g.

Explain or give the meaning of the italicised words and phrases; say what you find most noteworthy in its style and thought. (The context is not required.)

Three phrases are printed in italics; twelve marks are awarded overall (about one-ninth of the marks available for this paper.)

AEB stipulates that Milton may be chosen *instead* of Shakespeare: the choice is two books from six authors who include Shakespeare and Milton. Oxford and Cambridge Board sets a compulsory Chaucer passage with questions beneath, an essay on the same text, and then a choice of one from three passages, including one from Milton, and later a similar choice from essays on the three texts from which the passages were chosen. In this case, the Milton texts chosen included *Lycidas* and *Comus*, or *Samson Agonistes*. Questions are set beneath the passages from Milton, asking for specific issues to be explained and for discussion of the context, or other detailed matters.

From this it may be observed that on the whole Milton has held his place in papers which deal with authors of special importance: these always include Chaucer and Shakespeare plus one or two others – a great novel or a poet, for example, a Dickens or a Hardy novel, or poems of Keats or TS Eliot.

Whether the passages are from books of *Paradise Lost*, or from the greater of the earlier poems, the questions expect a close knowledge of the text, an ability to explain allusions and obscurities of diction, and a general appreciation of the content. The Oxford Board also asks for the style to be discussed.

BIOGRAPHICAL NOTE

John Milton was born in 1608 in London, and educated at St Paul's School and Christ's College, Cambridge, after which he spent six further years educating himself along carefully planned lines. During this period he wrote *Comus* (1634) and *Lycidas* (1637). He then spent a year and a half in Italy. He embarked on a decade of political pamphleteering, supporting the Puritan faction against the bishops, and defending the execution of Charles I (1649), in *Defence of the English People*, on behalf of Oliver Cromwell, in 1651. The next year he went blind.

Upon the Restoration of the monarchy in the person of Charles II (1660), Milton was imprisoned in the Tower for several weeks. He now devoted himself to the composition of the epic which has secured his immortality, *Paradise Lost*, published in 1667. Four years later *Paradise Regained* followed, and *Samson Agonistes*, his only play, based on Greek classical models, was also published, but it may have been written much earlier. In 1674 he died at his home in Chalfont St Giles.

PARADISE LOST

The books most regularly set at A level are 1 and 2, 4, and 9 and 10. It is ideal, though not essential at A level to read through all the other books, perhaps in the summer vacation, to place the set book in its proper context. No balanced view of this extraordinarily well-constructed epic can be gained by reading only one book, or that and a prose summary of the others. The poem's structure, like that of its models (the *Iliad* and the *Aeneid*), gives it a well-proportioned shape that can only be appreciated by reading the whole for oneself. Homer and Virgil have always suffered from piecemeal study: the obstacle of the language even necessitated losing the sense of the single book's structure and form. Although Milton's language is very Latinate, it still may be read easily enough. We suggest that when reading the non-prescribed books as background, you should suspend reference to critical apparatus and explanations, as much of the poem's shape is the result of the continuous flow of thought and sound.

Useful background reading

Among the best introductory criticism of *Paradise Lost* is Addison's set of *Spectator* essays on the poem for new readers. It is recommendatory criticism at its best; the quotations he selects are all worth memorising for use in examination questions. It is simple, direct appreciation which was given at a time when the reputation of the poem was at its height.

In this century, an equally inspiring and more penetrating critical introduction to the poem was provided by CS Lewis's *Preface to Paradise Lost*, written at a time when it needed defence against powerful critical attack.

Among the critical editions provided for schools and colleges, the oldest still in regular use is EMW Tillyard's editions of Books 1, 2, 9 and 10 (1960). Tillyard is the author of standard criticism published before the war. The introduction to these texts is clear, useful and simple; the notes quite adequate for the student's ordinary purposes.

Two later editions are more detailed and elaborate, designed more for A-level and university students. The Macmillan edition of the whole poem began publication in 1970, each book annotated and introduced by a different scholar. A biographical outline is followed by an introduction that is sufficiently thorough; the text has notes printed on the facing page, in line with the latest practice for Shakespeare texts. These are full and detailed when appropriate. Appendices contain further useful notes, sources (e.g. the first three chapters of Genesis are given) and a reading list which is the only one in any of these three editions of any practical use.

The last, most recent edition is JB Broadbent's (author of *Some Graver Subject*, 1960), *Cambridge Milton for Schools and Colleges*. This series has a separately published Introduction to the whole poem, and has been brought out as one volume per pair of books, six in all. The most notable features of this series are its originality of approach, the detailed analyses of the texts, and its combination of vigour and good scholarship. In the Notes, almost complete ignorance in the reader is assumed. In the intriguing Appendices, themes such as 'Light', 'God', 'Free Will and Predestination', 'The Son and Redemption' and so on are discussed, and there is wide reference to other literature which is related in theme or ideas.

Common themes in examination questions on *Paradise Lost*

Questions on Milton usually include the following themes:

1. the ways in which the book set may be part of an epic – the nature of a classical epic and how *Paradise Lost* conforms to it; what the epic form contributes to the set book;
2. who is the hero – surely not Satan? How is Satan made to have heroic stature? This is applicable especially to Books 1 and 2, but to achieve a sense of proportion it is necessary to read the rest;
3. Milton's sources for his allusions and how he makes use of them;
4. what is the nature of Milton's sublimity, and what does this term mean (often used to describe *Paradise Lost*);
5. what ideas and desires are expressed and how powerfully, by Satan and his friends in Hell; what they really suffer – physical, mental or spiritual torment; how they manage to convey the impression of being newly fallen angels; how the confrontation between Satan, and Sin and Death proceeds;
6. what qualities Milton's verse has; the range of description and imagery, and the appropriateness of these to the book's theme – these last subjects particularly require quotations.

Questions that apply to Book 4 include:

Discuss Milton's power to make us believe in Paradise.

How is Satan presented to the reader?

How are ideal nature and ideal humanity linked?

How are Adam and Eve presented to us?

For this see, for instance, the lines beginning:

> Two of far nobler shape erect and tall,
> Godlike erect with native honour clad
> In naked majesty seemed lords of all…

For Books 9 and 10, consider the following themes:

1. How well does Milton unfold the tragic themes of these books? How well does he evoke the bliss of Eden?
2. How far is Satan degraded by his obsession?
3. What is Satan's role in Book 9? Can he be the total embodiment of evil now? (Note here the contrast to Satan's heroic stance in Books 1 and 2; after the courageous and amazing voyage past the Gates of Hell, through Chaos to the Universe, we arrive at the story of the Fall, via the narration of his earlier rebellion and battle against God.)
4. What imagination is present in the scenes of Hell? (This applies to the language used as well as the scenes.)
5. In what ways does Milton please our senses and minds by this poetry?
6. How does Milton reconcile his theological interest in the Fall with the demands of dramatic narrative?
7. How far is the Fall the result of 'Man's First Disobedience', and how far due to other sin?

MINOR POEMS

Occasionally, instead of books chosen from *Paradise Lost*, texts are set from Milton's earlier or later work. The earlier is best represented by *Comus*, and *Lycidas*, the elegy written for a Cambridge friend, Edward King, drowned in 1637.

Comus

Comus, A Mask presented at Ludlow Castle, specially written for performance by the children of the Earl of Bridgwater, the new Lord President of Wales, is more literary than earlier masques by, for example, Ben Jonson. The latter were essentially spectacles, with elaborate machinery (designed by Inigo Jones), dance, costume and music. Milton's masque contained some of these elements, especially the music written by one of his favourite composers, Henry Lawes, but it went further in its craftsmanlike text and its fine poetry. It is a dramatic poem. In it, the theme of chastity is debated. The moral is that virtue and temperance triumph. As in *Lycidas*, Christian tones and ideas develop from classical elements, which dominated earlier masques.

Lycidas

Lycidas is written in a carefully constructed mode of **pastoral** convention, the **elegaic** tone being generalised rather than attached to a personal grief and loss. The real themes are other than specific lament – Milton was anxious to write a significant and recognisably great poem. The scenes expand beyond those of one individual dying in the Irish Sea, into wider realms of time and space.

One last observation is that the poem contains a basic uncertainty of philosophy. This springs from Milton's adoption of, on the one hand, pastoral procedures, the classical machinery of Phoebus, Jove, the inexorability of Fate and the mystery of death. On the other hand, and progressively gathering strength in the poem, is the assumed truth of God's dispensation, and Christ's salvation, where Lycidas is without doubt saved (he was Christian in his own person of Edward King), and in heaven. There would be no need for mourning in the pastoral mode, with its doubts and despondency, if these assurances were established at the beginning. Milton's classical learning and interests were in this instance rather at odds with his Christian faith.

Question bank

CHAUCER: *The Franklin's Tale*

1 **Either**, (a) Is it a relevant criticism of *The Franklin's Tale* to say that it is 'sexist'? Base your answer firmly on the text.

   Or, (b) Look at the passage from line 785 ('Thus pleyned Dorigen a day or tweye') to line 826 ('And whan that ye han herd the tale, demeth'). How sympathetic to his characters is Chaucer's portrayal of their relationship here?
   Note: Line numbers may vary slightly depending upon the edition being used.

ULEAC 1994

CHAUCER: *The Wife of Bath's Prologue and Tale*

2 **Either**, (a) Re-read the last 37 lines of *The Wife of Bath's Tale* (from 'This knight aviseth him...' to the end) before answering the following question:
   Using these lines as your starting point, consider the proposition that no clear moral emerges from *The Wife of Bath's Prologue and Tale*.

Or, (b) There is general agreement that the Wife of Bath is a woman of great spirit. How does Chaucer create this impression of her in the Prologue and Tale?

Oxford 1994

MILTON: *Paradise Lost, Books I and II*

3 Either, (a) Many readers see Satan as an heroic figure in *Paradise Lost, Books I and II*. Do you?

Or, (b) There are four speakers in the Infernal Debate. Look closely at Mammon's speech: Book II, lines 229–283. ('Either to disenthrone the king of heav'n'...'All thoughts of war: ye have what I advise.') Summarise the reasoning here and comment on the speech's persuasiveness.

ULEAC 1994

4 Either, (a) By a close comparison of Satan's first speech in Book I (lines 84–124: 'If thou beest he, ... the Tyranny of Heaven') with his last speech in Book II (817–844: 'Dear Daughter ... all things shall be your prey') consider whether or not our understanding of Satan changes in the course of these two books.

Or, (b) Having considered writing *Paradise Lost* in dramatic form, Milton finally decided to write it as an epic. Using your knowledge of Books I and II, discuss the wisdom of his decision.

Oxford 1994

ANDREW MARVELL: **Selected Poems of Andrew Marvell** (ed. B Hutchings)

5 Either, (a) How far does Marvell's poetry suggest to you that he believes conflict to be inevitable in life?

Or, (b) 'Marvell's poetry displays both moral seriousness and adventurous wit.' Discuss and illustrate this statement.

AEB 1994

ALEXANDER POPE: **Selected Poems of Alexander Pope** (ed. J Heath-Stubbs)

6 Either (a) 'The proper study of Mankind is Man,' wrote Pope. Examine the applications of this principle in your text.

Or, (b) 'Pope's fiercest criticisms are kept in check by his good humour.' Do you agree?

AEB 1994

WORDSWORTH AND COLERIDGE: **Lyrical Ballads** (ed. W Owen)

7 Either, (a) According to Wordsworth, 'Poetry is the spontaneous overflow of powerful feelings.' How well do you think 'Lyrical Ballads' illustrates this definition? Refer to at least three poems in your answer.

Or, (b) Wordsworth proposed in 'Lyrical Ballads' 'to imitate, and, as far as possible, to adopt the very language of men ...' How successful has he been?

AEB 1994

KEATS: **Selected Poems and Letters** (ed. Gittings, Heinemann)

8 Either, (a) Robert Gittings, in the Introduction to this selection, states that Keats's 'real qualities' are 'strong thought, direct apprehension of beauty and vivid concrete imagery'. Choose one of these three qualities and discuss it in relation to Keats's poetry. You should illustrate your answer by reference to at least three poems.

Or, (b) Consider the nature of Keats's achievement in *Lamia* (pages 130–151 of the Heinemann edition).

ULEAC 1994

Scars Upon My Heart (ed. Reilly, Virago)

9 Either, (a) Jon Silkin, writing of First World War poetry, has said: 'The danger with compassion is that it can tend to self-indulgence'. How far do you think that this danger has been avoided in 'Scars Upon My Heart'?

Or, (b) Compare the work of Vera Brittain with any other writer in this anthology.

ULEAC 1994

CHARLES CAUSLEY: Secret Destinations

10 Either, (a) Causley's earliest poems arose from wartime experience in the Royal Navy. Do the poems in 'Secret Destinations' convey to you the flavour of writings directly inspired by stressful events?

Or, (b) Causley praises St Anthony. 'Who asked for, and received, nothing.' Does 'Secret Destinations' suggest a similar attitude in its author?

AEB 1994

TED HUGHES: Selected Poems 1957–1981

11 Either, (a) 'Only birth matters.'
To what extent might these words serve as a motto for Hughes's poetry?

Or, (b) '...they fit themselves to what has happened.'
Examine the ways in which Hughes explores ideas of adapting to experience.

AEB 1994

HEANEY: New Selected Poems (Faber)

12 Either, (a) Heaney has defined poetry as being 'a point of entry into the buried life of the feelings'. Do his own poems support this description?

Or, (b) Look at *Personal Helicon* and *North* (in 'Selected Poems 1965–75' on pages 27 and 105; in 'New Selected Poems 1966–87' on pages 9 and 56). How have content, form and language changed in the years that divide these two poems?

ULEAC 1994

DOUGLAS DUNN: Selected Poems 1964–1983

13 Either, (a) Do you agree that the best work in 'Selected Poems' is that which is least self-centred?

Or, (b) 'Truth is known only to its victims.'
Where in Dunn's poetry have you found truth associated with suffering?

AEB 1994

DRAMA

Units in this chapter

2.1   *Approaches to drama*
2.2   *Elizabethan and Jacobean drama*
2.3   *The comedy of manners*
2.4   *The modern period*
2.5   *Shakespeare*

Chapter objectives

This chapter gives a brief survey of the main areas of drama set at A level. It will help you to place your own set plays in context. It is always useful to 'read round' a set play, either by looking at other plays by the same author or at others of the same period. The A-level examination boards concentrate on three periods of drama: Elizabethan and Jacobean; the 'comedy of manners' (Restoration theatre) and the modern period. The first and third are the richest fields. The second is almost entirely absorbed by Congreve's *The Way of the World* and Wycherley's *Country Wife*. Very often, also, those later eighteenth-century revivals of the comic spirit of the seventeenth century, Sheridan's *The School for Scandal* (1777) and Goldsmith's *She Stoops to Conquer* (1773) appear on the syllabuses.

Non-Shakespearian drama is usually prescribed for general literature papers, where candidates are not necessarily expected to show quite the same intimate knowledge of texts as that required on the Shakespeare papers. This does **not** mean that superficial knowledge is sufficient.

- The text should be studied with care, making full use of notes and editorial material in annotated editions.
- You should form some picture of the state of the theatre at that time, what was being written for it, and how the prescribed work fits into the general picture.
- Try to fix the outline of the plot firmly in your mind, preferably by making your *own* summary.
- Note the main features of characters, and how they are revealed in speech and action.
- Look out for the ways in which atmosphere is created and themes developed.
- Try to see a production of any play you are studying, otherwise try to listen to a recording.

Your preparation should equip you to answer general questions and also passage-based critical appreciation questions in which both close analysis of an extract and ability to relate it to the rest of the play will be required.

2.1 APPROACHES TO DRAMA

INTRODUCTION

In drama, writers have only the actual words spoken by their characters through which to tell their story and make their effects. Of course, when the play is seen on the stage, it receives a great deal of help from the skill of the actors, the interpretation of the producer and the lighting, set, costumes and music.

In practical criticism of drama, you are faced with the words alone. The basis for whatever you say in your analysis of the passage must come from the text.

In any passage of drama, the dramatist tries to include the following:

1. General atmosphere of the scene, e.g. the three witches on the heath at the beginning of *Macbeth*.
2. Indications of actions, past, present and future.
3. Indications of character by what the characters say themselves, what is said about them and their actions.
4. Indications of the moral attitude of the dramatist through the speeches and actions of the characters and the implied beliefs of the dramatist him- or herself. Most writers – and this applies to dramatists as well as to novelists – are not just telling stories or creating characters; they are also indicating attitudes to life which they feel are right and which they want us to share.

It is very difficult, if not impossible, to comment on a passage from a play in isolation from the rest of the work. Where the passage to be discussed is from a play prescribed for an examination, no difficulty should be experienced by a candidate who has prepared it thoroughly. Passages of drama are not often set 'unseen' in Appreciation papers; where they are, examiners will supply the appropriate background information. In presenting the passages in this book, some account of the plays from which they are taken is given. In the detailed comments, incidental reference to events elsewhere in the play should suggest how this could be done most effectively in an examination answer. We hope that the passages are sufficiently interesting in themselves to inspire you to go on and read the complete plays. Your background knowledge will benefit from this, even if none of them is in your examination syllabus.

In the following passages from well-known plays, which have frequently been set for A level, an A-level examiner has given a commentary for each passage, bringing out the main areas a candidate should examine when preparing an A-level answer. They are *not* 'model answers'. As in most exercises on practical criticism, *practice* is the key word. Too often candidates feel they will achieve a good grade by natural flair and ability without any previous experience of writing commentaries in examination conditions. Try to read the passage aloud to yourself as though you are acting it. It will help to supply the right dramatic intonations. Check up on your ideas of what the playwright is trying to do and make your own notes with the text to help you.

Passages in chronological order with commentaries
Christopher Marlowe   *Edward II*
Ben Jonson   *Volpone*
William Congreve   *The Way of the World*
Arthur Miller   *The Death of a Salesman*

ELIZABETHAN AND JACOBEAN

Violent death on stage was an obligatory feature of the Elizabethan or Jacobean tragedy. We give here a death-scene from a play often prescribed for A level: Marlowe's *Edward II*.

Note We will sometimes refer to aspects of the play outside the passage quoted. If you have prepared a play for A level, you ought to be able to do this, and will probably be expected to do so.

Edward II by Christopher Marlowe

(**Synopsis of previous events** Edward, unable to control his turbulent barons, humiliated by his defeat at Bannockburn, and accused of taking advice only from his homosexual lovers, has been imprisoned in Berkeley Castle by the ambitious Mortimer and the Queen, now Mortimer's mistress. Attempts to bring about his death by subjecting him to humiliating maltreatment – shaving off his beard with ditch-water, keeping him in the castle sewers – having failed, Mortimer has engaged an assassin, Lightborn, to murder him. Matrevis and Gurney are two gentlemen acting as the King's keepers. Just before this passage, Lightborn has hypocritically pretended to pity him.)

King Edward Weep'st thou already? list a while to me,
   And then thy heart, were it as Gurney's is,
   Or as Matrevis', hewn from the Caucasus,
   Yet will it melt ere I have done my tale.
   This dungeon where they keep me is the sink
   Wherein the filth of all the castle falls.

Lightborn O villains!

King Edward And there, in mire and puddle, have I stood
   This ten days's pace; and, lest that I should sleep,
   One plays continually upon a drum;
   They give me bread and water, being a king;
   So that, for want of sleep and sustenance,
   My mind's distemper'd, and my body's numb'd,
   And whether I have limbs or no I know not.
   O, would my blood dropp'd out from every vein,
   As doth this water from my tatter'd robes!
   Tell Isabel the queen, I look'd not thus,
   When for her sake I ran at tilt in France,
   And there unhors'd the Duke of Cleremont.

Lightborn O, speak no more, my lord! this breaks my heart.
   Lie on this bed, and rest yourself a while.

King Edward These looks of thine can harbour naught but death;
   I see my tragedy written in thy brows.
   Yet stay a while; forbear thy bloody hand,
   And let me see the stroke before it comes,
   That even then when I shall lose my life,
   My mind may be more steadfast on my God.

Lightborn What means your highness to mistrust me thus?

King Edward What mean'st thou to dissemble with me thus?

Lightborn These hands were never stain'd with innocent blood,
   Nor shall they now be tainted with a king's.

King Edward Forgive my thought for having such a thought.
   One jewel have I left; receive thou this: [*Giving jewel*]
   Still fear I, and I know not what's the cause.
   But every joint shakes as I give it thee.
   O, if thou harbour'st murder in thy heart,
   Let this gift change thy mind, and save thy soul!
   Know that I am a king: O, at that name
   I feel a hell of grief! where is my crown?
   Gone, gone! and do I [still] remain alive?

Lightborn You're overwatch'd, my lord: lie down and rest.

King Edward But that grief keeps me waking, I should sleep;
   For not these ten days have these eye-lids clos'd.
   Now, as I speak, they fall; and yet with fear
   Open again. O, wherefore sitt'st thou here?

Lightborn If you mistrust me, I'll be gone, my lord.

King Edward No, no; for, if thou mean'st to murder me,
   Thou wilt return again; and therefore stay. [*Sleeps*]

Lightborn He sleeps.

King Edward [*waking*] O, let me not die yet! O, stay a while!

Lightborn How now, my lord!

King Edward Something still buzzeth in mine ears,
   And tells me, if I sleep, I never wake:
   This fear is that which makes me tremble thus;
   And therefore tell me, wherefore art thou come?

Lightborn To rid thee of life. – Matrevis, come!

Enter MATREVIS *and* GURNEY.

King Edward I am too weak and feeble to resist.
    Assist me, sweet God, and receive my soul!
Lightborn Run for the table.
King Edward O, spare me, or despatch me in a trice!
[*Matrevis brings in a table. King Edward is murdered
    by holding him down on the bed with the table, and
    stamping on it*]
Lightborn So, lay the table down, and stamp on it,
    But not too hard, lest that you bruise his body.
Matrevis I fear me that this cry will raise the town.
    And therefore let us take horse and away.

Lightborn Tell me, sirs, was it not bravely done?

Gurney Excellent well: take this for thy reward.
[*Stabs Lightborn, who dies*]
    Come, let us cast the body in the moat,
    And bear the king's to Mortimer our lord:
    Away!

[*Exeunt with the bodies*]

Marlowe could count on two built-in advantages in choosing the reign of Edward II for his subject. Firstly, the 'fall of princes' was universally recognised as the great tragic theme, its awesomeness increased by the reverence for kings carefully inculcated in the subjects of our Tudor monarchs; secondly, Edward II was, like Shakespeare's Richard II, well known as one of the most unhappy of English kings, and the story of his troubled life and miserable end was a familar one.

It is easy to see how these advantages are exploited in the passage. Edward is made to dwell with much feeling on the contrast between his present wretchedness and the days when he cut a brave figure in the lists ('ran at tilt in France'). A more extreme change of fortune would be hard to imagine. Natural **pathos** is introduced by his implied hope that the Queen's heart may be softened towards him if she is reminded of other times. He laments the loss of his crown as if it were not just his most treasured personal possession, but rather the very principle of his life.

The human aspect of Edward's sufferings is, of course, greatly heightened by his fear that he will be murdered in his sleep, his wish to meet his end awake, so that his thoughts may be consciously directed towards God (a matter of importance in a religious age), and his parting with his last remaining jewel in the faint hope of bribing Lightborn, whose intentions he divines all too clearly, to spare him. Lightborn's own behaviour may not be altogether as easy to explain as at first appears. Certainly his professed sympathy and assurances that he means Edward no harm can be interpreted adequately enough as sadistic trifling with his victim for his own amusement and, as such, is dramatically effective in prolonging the tension of the episode and intensifying the atmosphere of cold horror that envelops it. His assertion that his hands 'were never stain'd with innocent blood' fits well with this view of his motives, as an example of devilish equivocation; as we have been told a little earlier, he specialises in murder by subtle means, not by crude blood-letting. Indeed, one reason for his wishing to lull Edward to sleep before he sets to work on him is, presumably, to avoid a struggle, with consequent marks of violence on the body. But are there perhaps other, almost instinctive reasons? If he kills Edward awake and calling on God, the murder becomes doubly heinous; there is the old belief that the image of the murderer is imprinted on his victim's open eyes; and finally, after all, Edward had been an anointed king, and to look such a person in the eyes and kill him was a fearful deed – one that Macbeth shrinks from. We can be pretty sure that thoughts of this nature were in the minds of Marlowe's audience as they watched the representation of the killing of a king with fascinated horror.

In any case, to treat a monarch disrespectfully on the stage (unless he were one of the officially labelled bad kings like Richard III) was a somewhat ticklish business, as Shakespeare's company found when the authority required the deposition of Richard II to be cut out of the printed version of the play, and there were limits to what could decently be shown on the stage. Marlowe has skirted round the peculiarly revolting way in which the chroniclers report that Edward was killed, though he drops hints that would have been readily taken in his day. Earlier, Lightborn has boasted to Mortimer that he knows 'a braver way' to kill a man, one that he intends to keep to himself as a professional secret, and has ordered Matrevis and Gurney to heat a spit red-hot. We are not shown it in use, but it is hard to imagine how Edward, in the process of being smothered, could emit the awful shriek which traditionally awoke the whole sleeping countryside, and to which Matrevis refers in

> I fear me that this cry will raise the town.

Background knowledge will help us to appreciate more fully the impact of this episode on Marlowe's contemporaries, but its dramatic power can still be felt by audiences today. The increase of tension and the drawing out of Edward's agony during his conversation with Lightborn has already been mentioned; the end, when it actually comes, is appalling in its sudden violence, following the dreadful words, 'To rid thee of thy life'. Note here the **irony**, whether conscious or otherwise: life has indeed become a burden to Edward, of which he has wished to be rid

> O, would my blood dropp'd out from every vein

though not by such means, and therefore, in a certain sense, Lightborn is doing him a service. The immediate killing of Lightborn in his turn, when he is expecting congratulation, does not indeed come as a complete surprise to the spectator, because we already know that this was part of Mortimer's plan; still, it remains a dramatically effective, if perhaps rather obviously contrived **peripeteia** (i.e. sudden change of fortune), and satisfies the moral sense by visiting immediate retribution on the murderer, even if at the hands of his accomplices.

No comment on the passage would be complete without reference to the language and versification. Despite the command shown elsewhere in Marlowe's work of high-flown **imagery** and exuberant **diction**, the style here, despite the emotionally charged content, is restrained, almost austere. Certainly this is not 'tragical rant'. There is hardly an **image** from beginning to end. Further, and most notably, the strict **iambic** measure is rigorously observed throughout, with a high proportion of **end-stopped** lines. Even in death, Edward keeps regular **metre**

> O, spare me, or despatch me in a trice!

– one almost feels that he might have added 'And in one line of five iambic feet'. The effect is very unlike natural speech, and indeed **naturalism** was not Marlowe's objective. Instead he depicts the atrocious action in language and verse which give it a kind of formal dignity; to adapt Hamlet's words about the kind of acting he approves, in the very torrent, tempest and whirlwind of passion, it begets a temperance.

Volpone (1605) by Ben Jonson

In *Volpone* there is not a great range of **humours** (see Glossary), as nearly all the personages are dominated by greed in a variety of forms. The scene is Venice, and they bear the Italian names of birds and beasts: Volpone (the Fox, celebrated for his cunning), Mosca (the Fly), Voltore (the Vulture), Corbaccio (the Crow), Corvino (the Raven) – all the last four having in common a propensity to feed on carrion. In the play, Volpone is a wealthy nobleman in the prime of life, with a highly developed appetite for sensual pleasure, but above all else a worshipper of gold, to which he prays as to a god every morning. Assisted by his parasite or hanger-on, Mosca, he pretends to be at death's door in order to attract a crew of legacy-hunters, each of whom believes that he is to be Volpone's sole heir.

In the following passage Corvino, a merchant, has just entered with rich gifts for Volpone, who lies motionless in bed, his face plastered with ointments, while Mosca plays the intermediary.

> *Corvino* Say,
> > I have a diamond for him, too.
> *Mosca* Best shew it, sir;
> > Put it into his hand; 'tis only there
> > He apprehends: he has his feeling, yet.
> > See how he grasps it!
> *Corvino* 'Las, good gentleman!
> > How pitiful the sight is!
> *Mosca* Tut! forget, sir.
> > The weeping of an heir should still be laughter
> > Under a visor.
> *Corvino* O, my dear Mosca! [*They embrace.*] Does he not perceive
> > us?
> *Mosca* No more than a blind harper. He knows no man,
> > No face of friend, nor name of any servant,

Who 'twas that fed him last, or gave him drink:
Not those he hath begotten, or brought up,
Can he remember.

Corvino Has he children?

Mosca Bastards,
Some dozen, or more, that he begot on beggars,
Gypsies, and Jews, and black-moors, when he was drunk.
Knew you not that, sir? 'tis the common fable.
The dwarf, the fool, the eunuch, are all his;
He's the true father of his family,
In all, save me: – but he has given them nothing.

Corvino That's well, that's well!
Art sure he does not hear us?

Mosca Sure sir! why, look you, credit your own sense.

[*Shouts in Volpone's ear.*]

The pox approach, and add to your diseases,
If it would send you hence the sooner, sir,
For your incontinence, it hath deserv'd it
Thoroughly, and thoroughly, and the plague to boot!
You may come near, sir. – Would you would once close
Those filthy eyes of yours, that flow with slime,
Like two frog-pits; and those same hanging cheeks,
Cover'd with hide instead of skin – Nay, help, sir –
That look like frozen dish-clouts set on end!

Corvino [*aloud.*] Or like an old smoked wall, on which the rain
Ran down in streaks!

Mosca Excellent, sir! speak out:
You may be louder yet; a culverin
Discharged in his ear would hardly bore it.

Corvino His nose is like a common sewer, still running.

Mosca 'Tis good! And what his mouth?

Corvino A very draught.

Mosca O, stop it up –

Corvino By no means.

Mosca 'Pray you, let me:
Faith I could stifle him rarely with a pillow,
As well as any woman that should keep him.

Corvino Do as you will; but I'll begone.

Mosca Be so:
It is your presence makes him last so long.

Corvino I pray you, use no violence.

Mosca No, sir! why?
Why should you be thus scrupulous, pray you, sir?

Corvino Nay, at your discretion.

Mosca Well, good sir, begone.

Corvino I will not trouble him now, to take my pearl.

Mosca Puh! nor your diamond. What a needless care
Is this afflicts you? Is not all here yours?
Am not I here, whom you have made your creature?
That owe my being to you?

Corvino Grateful Mosca!
Thou art my friend, my fellow, my companion,
My partner, and shalt share in all my fortunes.

Mosca Excepting one.

Corvino What's that?

Mosca Your gallant wife, sir, – [*Exit Corvino*]
Now is he gone: we had no other means
To shoot him hence, thus this.

Volpone My divine Mosca!
Thou hast to-day outgone thyself. [*Knocking within.*] – Who's there?
I will be troubled with no more. Prepare
Me music, dances, banquets, all delights;

> The Turk is not more sensual in his pleasures,
> Than will Volpone. [*Exit Mosca*] let me see; a pearl!
> A diamond! plate! chequines! Good morning's purchase.
> Why, this is better than rob churches, yet;
> Or fat, by eating, once a month, a man –

The most immediately striking aspect of this scene is the skill and malicious glee with which Mosca manipulates the dupe, Corvino. First, he assures him that he is to be the sole heir, and that they can speak and act with perfect freedom since Volpone sees nothing and knows nobody – not even 'those he hath begotten'. This seemingly artless mention of possible rivals for the inheritance alarms Corvino, as it is intended to do ('Has he children?'), but he is reassured by 'he has given them nothing.' The sneering references to Volpone's supposed offspring ('The dwarf, the fool, the eunuch' are members of a private circus of 'freaks' kept by Volpone for his entertainment) serve to confirm that the supposedly dying man is deaf as well as blind, which Mosca proceeds to demonstrate by bawling foul abuse into his ear, inciting Corvino to join in. He follows this up with the suggestion that he could very easily give Volpone the last little push to launch him into Eternity, and that, in the circumstances, Corvino being so close to realising his hopes, it is not worth troubling to prise the jewels out of Volpone's tenacious grasp. The precious pair then exchange vows of eternal gratitude, which Mosca cuts short by bringing in an allusion to Corvino's 'gallant (i.e. handsome and high-spirited) wife'. This sends the jealous husband packing.

Corvino, naturally, has the passive part of this conversation, but his thoroughly unpleasant character is strongly brought out. He is at first hypocritically conventional:

> 'Las, good gentleman!
> How pitiful the sight is!

but shows himself indecently ready to drop the pretence when convinced that Volpone cannot hear him; the meanness of his nature is thus demonstrated. He objects, for form's sake, to Mosca's suggestion of a little timely homicide ('By no means'), then immediately makes it plain that he has no real scruples, provided the deed is done discreetly, and not in his presence. His jealousy of his wife, played on at the end, introduces a new element in the plot, which is to assume major importance later.

The dramatic impact of the passage is undeniable. Note, first, that the whole comedy is enacted for the enjoyment of Volpone, and that we inevitably associate ourselves with him, however much we may dislike him, seeing it through his eyes, watching Corvino reveal his true self, and hugely relishing the way in which he is being gulled. After his departure, when Volpone throws off the disguise of sickness and exultantly devotes the rest of the day to pleasures more exquisite than those of the Grand Turk (i.e. the Sultan of Turkey), the atmosphere is swiftly and powerfully transformed. It is hard not to admire someone who is so uninhibited in his triumph over crawling baseness and his enjoyment of the accrued profits. The scene demonstrates rather strikingly at the end that we do not always have to find a character attractive in order to feel a degree of sympathy with him.

Apart from the major ironies, there are other subtler details which add depth and texture to the effect of the episode. Does it not seem, for example, that Mosca's reviling of Volpone goes rather beyond what the situation requires, and breathes a real hatred? Does Mosca in fact loathe his patron and the part he is obliged to play? Certainly he attempts to perpetrate an enormous double-cross at the end of the play. The allusion to Volpone's grasp of whatever is put into his hand ironically points to a real feature of his character, as well as to a kind of assumed 'rigor mortis'. Other seemingly incidental references suggest a background of a corrupt society in which cheating, and graver crimes, are commonplace. If Volpone (who can see perfectly well) can perceive 'no more than a blind harper', then it seems to follow that blind harpers, and similar itinerant musicians, were no more blind than Volpone really is. When Mosca says that he could stifle him

> with a pillow
> As well as any woman that should keep him

the casual tone of the comparison implies that it was quite usual for nurses to get rid of their patients this way.

I have referred to *Volpone* as a **comedy**, but – as the extract makes plain – it is a very black kind of comedy. All the main characters are morally vile (though there is a kind of depraved splendour about Volpone himself), and all, in the end, are exposed and sentenced by judges as corrupt as themselves to punishments which have little of the **comic** about them

– whipping and the galleys, imprisonment in chains, disbarring and banishment, confinement to a monastery, and the pillory.

The play is unlike Jonson's other major comedies in two ways. Firstly, it takes place, not in contemporary London, but in Venice. Why Jonson should have chosen this exotic location is not altogether clear. Venice certainly meant much to the English writers of his day – Shakespeare among them. To Jonson, the great merchant city may well have seemed to **symbolise** wealth, luxury, and depravity of morals, and by giving his work a foreign setting he may have intended to emphasise the international, indeed the universal nature of the human vices he **satirises**.

Secondly, *Volpone*, unlike the others again, is almost entirely composed in **blank verse**. It must be allowed that, in this passage, there is great energy and inventiveness in the language, especially in that of Mosca's longest speech. Whether it is the language of poetry may be disputed by those who think that poetry must be 'beautiful'. (Elsewhere in the play the style attains an undeniable splendour.) What must be allowed is Jonson's skill in the writing of lively dialogue in verse. The short exchanges between Mosca and Corvino look like prose, but a more careful examination shows that in fact they form perfect **pentameters**:

> Tis good! And what his mouth?/ A very draught.
> O, stop it up –/ By no means./ Pray you, let me.

(the unstressed extra syllable at the end of the second line being always permissible in dramatic blank verse). To combine such strict observance of **metre** with such racy freedom of speech may not be the most that poetry is capable of, but it is certainly craftsmanship of a very high order.

RESTORATION COMEDY

Restoration comedy may seem something of a misnomer for a play belonging to the first years of the eighteenth century, long after 'Good King Charles's golden days'. Nevertheless, the kind of comedy written during the fifty years or so after the restoration of the monarchy in 1660, though it certainly developed, did not change fundamentally during that period. For a full account of the new theatre which emerged in the 1660s you must consult a history of English drama.

The Way of the World (1700) by William Congreve

By common consent the finest example of its kind, this play has a very involved **plot**. There are many characters, and they are all engaged in elaborate schemes involving a great deal of doublecrossing – such, as Congreve suggests by the title, is 'the way of the world'. At the centre of the action is Mirabell's plan to marry the far-from-unwilling Millament despite the hostility of her aunt and guardian, Lady Wishfort, without whose consent Millament loses her fortune. In the passage that follows, Mirabell proposes, and is accepted – on certain conditions.

> *Millament* Ah! I'll never marry, unless I am first made sure of my will and
>   pleasure.
> *Mirabell* Would you have 'em both before marriage? Or will you be contented
>   with the first now, and stay for the other 'till after grace?
> *Millament* Ah, don't be impertinent – My dear liberty, shall I leave thee? My
>   faithful solitude, my darling contemplation, must I bid you then adieu?
>   Ay-h, adieu – my morning thoughts, agreeable wakings, indolent slumbers,
>   all ye *douceurs*, ye *someils du matin*, adieu – I can't do't, 'tis more than
>   impossible – Positively, Mirabell, I'll lye abed in a morning as long as I
>   please.
> *Mirabell* Then I'll get up in a morning as early as I please.
> *Millament* Ah! Idle creature, get up when you will – And d'ye hear, I won't
>   be called names after I'm married; positively I won't be called names.
> *Mirabell* Names!
> *Millament* Ay, as wife, spouse, my dear, joy, jewel, love, sweetheart, and the
>   rest of that nauseous cant, in which men and their wives are so fulsomly
>   familiar – I shall never bear that – Good Mirabell, don't let us be familiar
>   or fond, nor kiss before folks, like my Lady Fadler and Sir Francis: nor to
>   go Hide Park together the first Sunday in a new chariot, to provoke eyes
>   and whispers; and then never be seen there together again; as if we were

> proud of one another the first week, and ashamed of one another ever
> after. Let us never visit together, nor go to a play together, but let us be
> very strange and well bred: let us be as strange as if we had been married
> a great while; and as well bred as if we were not married at all.
>
> *Mirabell* Have you any more conditions to offer? Hitherto your demands are
> pretty reasonable.
>
> *Millament* Trifles, – as liberty to pay and receive visits to and from whom I
> please; to write and receive letters, without interrogatories or wry faces on
> your part; to wear what I please; and chuse conversation with regard only
> to my own taste; to have no obligation upon me to converse with wits that
> I don't like, because they are your acquaintance; or to be intimate with
> fools because they may be your relations. Come to dinner when I please,
> dine in my dressing-room when I'm out of humour, without giving a
> reason. To have my closet inviolate; to be sole empress of my tea-table,
> which you must never presume to approach without first asking leave. And
> lastly, wherever I am, you shall always knock at the door before you come
> in. These articles subscribed, if I continue to endure you a little longer, I
> may by degrees dwindle into a wife.
>
> *Mirabell* Your bill of fare is something advanced in this latter account. Well,
> have I liberty to offer conditions – that when you are dwindled into a wife,
> I may not be beyond measure enlarged into a husband?
>
> *Millament* You have free leave, propose your utmost, speak and spare not.
>
> *Mirabell* I thank you. *Imprimis* then, I covenant that your acquaintance be
> general; that you admit no sworn confident or intimate of your own sex…
> *Item*, when you shall be breeding –
>
> *Millament* Ah! name it not.
>
> *Mirabell* Which may be presumed, with a blessing on our endeavours –
>
> *Millament* Odious endeavours!
>
> *Mirabell* I denounce against all strait lacing, squeezing for a shape, 'till you
> mould my boy's head like a sugar-loaf; and instead of a man-child, make
> me father to a crooked-billet.

Here we can enjoy a lively example of that 'duel of the sexes' which is, and always has been, one of the mainstays of comedy (cf. Beatrice and Benedick in Shakespeare's *Much Ado About Nothing*). The duellists are well-matched: Mirabell, ('the admirable') and Millament ('she who has a thousand lovers'). Millament is presented as full of caprice and affectation, exceedingly self-centred, and determined to be as different as possible from conventional people. We see her first delighting in her indolent mornings abed – not forgetting to smatter a little fashionable French – and pretending that, if she is expected to give them up, that would be an insuperable objection to marriage

> I can't do't, 'tis more than impossible

though immediately afterwards she implies her consent with

> Positively, Mirabell, I'll lye abed in a morning as long as I please.

She expresses a comprehensive contempt for homely endearments ('that nauseous cant'), her list of 'trifles', taken as a whole, adds up to a declaration of domestic independence, and her reaction to the prospect of child-bearing, generally taken to be the whole point of marriage, is comically squeamish. Her professed ideal of the married state is given in

> Let us be as strange [i.e. distant] as if we had been married a great while; and as well bred as if we were not married at all

an ideal which, translated into practice, is summed up by

> Wherever I am, you should always knock at the door before you come in.

Mirabell, being an accomplished gentleman, takes all these airs and graces with imperturbable good humour, though he goes on to make a string of stipulations on his side, too long to be quoted here. Notice how the humour of the situation is enhanced by the legalistic turns of phrase – 'these articles subscribed', *'imprimis' 'item'*. From this point of view, the episode **parodies** the drawing up of a contract between two prospective business partners.

We may not share Mirabell's attitudes and conventions; but we find Millament enormously appealing. Why is this? It is not just because a beautiful young woman is traditionally allowed to be whimsical and capricious. The real reason is surely that, as so often in great comedy, there is seriousness – perhaps, indeed, **pathos** – underlying the **wit** and the high spirits. We reflect that Millament's freedom to tease and play hard to get depends entirely on youth, beauty, and her single state. The first two are proverbially transient, while the independence she enjoys and prizes while single was, in fact, incompatible in her day with marriage. However politely a wife might be treated, her property (apart from what might be reserved for her in the marriage settlement) became her husband's, and her personal freedom was restricted in many ways which were sanctioned both by law and custom. Congreve, we may be pretty certain, was perfectly aware of the reality underlying the parade of courtship and fine manners. He makes fun of Millament, true, but in a wholly unmalicious way. Despite the easy assumptions made today about the male-dominated society of other times, it is fair to say that his view of women – or, at least, of women in Millament's situation – is basically sympathetic.

As in so many Restoration comedies, we are here given some rather **satirical** glimpses of the social life of London and the current practices of the 'beau monde': driving round Hyde Park in one's 'chariot' to see and be seen, paying formal calls on acquaintances, going to the play, taking tea with much ceremony, and submitting to ferocious tight-lacing even during pregnancy.

When we compare the prose style of *The Way of the World* with that of the comedies of some sixty years earlier, we realise that a great watershed has been passed, and that what we have here, for all its elegance and its outmoded expressions, is essentially modern English. The sentence structure is neat and compact. The language combines colloquial ease with carefully studied effects, e.g. the **paradox** and **antithesis** in the sentence already quoted ('Let us be as strange…') or the delicate hesitations and qualifications of

> These articles subscribed, / *if* I continue to endure you a little longer, / I *may* / by degrees / *dwindle* into a wife. (Our italics)

Enough has been said to show why Millament should see marriage as a 'dwindling', a diminution. Note also how these two examples of Congreve's fine sense of style serve to bring important speeches to a decisive conclusion.

THE MODERN PERIOD

Death of a Salesman (1949) by Arthur Miller

Apart from a few exceptions like TS Eliot's *Murder in the Cathedral* and *The Cocktail Party*, poetic drama – if by that we mean plays written in verse – has failed to establish itself in the twentieth-century theatre. The medium of drama remains overwhelmingly prose. Nevertheless, there are many works by contemporary dramatists which are essentially poetic in their appeal to feeling and imagination and in their use of language, even when it is, in general, what Wordsworth called, in another connection, 'the language of conversation in the middle and lower classes of society'.

Among plays falling into this category are those of Arthur Miller, which, despite their distinctively American qualities, have quickly become recognised as modern 'classics' in the theatre of the English-speaking world.

Death of a Salesman presents the last days in the life of a 63-year-old commercial traveller, Willy Loman. Willy has 'worked' New England for 34 years as the representative of the New York firm of Wagner's. At one time he was – or so he says – so successful that the firm's founder, 'old man Wagner', virtually promised him a partnership. Now he is old and exhausted. His whole life has been founded on self-deception and illusion, and the pursuit of worthless and unrealisable aims. Moreover, his relationship with his two sons, still known by their family nicknames as Biff and Happy, for whom he also cherished high hopes, has gone sour – especially with Biff, the elder.

The play is a notable example of imaginative stagecraft. As the author himself has explained, it began from the presumption that the distinction we make between our past and our present is unreal: everything in our lives exists simultaneously in our minds. Indeed, Miller's first tentative name for the play was *The Inside of His Head*, and he pictured a set in the form of 'an enormous face the height of the **proscenium** arch which would appear and then open up, and we would see the inside of a man's head'. This was subsequently modified to a kind of vertical section through Willy's house in Brooklyn, overshadowed by a suggestion of more recently built apartment blocks, and with a front-stage acting area on which is performed everything that happens outside the house. Just as the location of events is supposed to alter as the play requires, without change of scene, so events from Willy's past and, in at least one case, events that never happened, fuse with the action in the present, showing how past and present coexist in Willy's mind.

A significant figure always in Willy's thoughts, particularly when he is most depressed, is his much older brother, Ben, who has recently died in Africa – where, we are told, he made a great fortune. Apparently he once visited Willy in Brooklyn on his way to complete a big deal in Alaska and – so Willy has convinced himself – offered him a job in that distant land of opportunity. Willy earnestly believes that Ben had the secret of success, and regularly wonders what it was, but Ben never gives him any real advice. All he will do is to pronounce a kind of magic formula:

> When I was seventeen I walked into the jungle, and when I was twenty-one I walked out. And by God I was rich.

Just before the extract which follows, Willy has gone to his firm's head office to ask if, in view of his long service, he can be taken off the road and given a permanent job in New York. Young Howard Wagner, who now runs the business, is much more interested in his latest gadget, a tape-recorder, than in Willy's problems. As Willy tries to press his point, Howard makes it increasingly clear that it is time for Willy to go for good. In the end, Willy is reduced to pleading to be allowed to make the trip to Boston he had hoped to avoid originally.

Willy [*grasping Howard's arm*] Howard, you've got to let me go to Boston!

Howard [*hard, keeping himself under control*] I've got a line of people to see this morning. Sit down, take five minutes, and pull yourself together, and then go home, will ya? I need the office, Willy. [*He starts to go, turns, remembering the recorder, starts to push off the table holding the recorder.*] Oh, yeah. Whenever you can this week, stop by and drop off the samples. You'll feel better, Willy, and then come back and we'll talk. Pull yourself together, kid, there's people outside.

Howard exits, pushing the table off left. Willy stares into space, exhausted. Now the music is heard – Ben's music – first distantly, then closer, closer. As Willy speaks, Ben enters from the right. He carries valise and umbrella.

Willy Oh, Ben, how did you do it? What is the answer? Did you wind up the Alaska deal already?

Ben Doesn't take much time if you know what you're doing. Just a short business trip. Boarding ship in an hour. Wanted to say good-by.

Willy Ben, I've got to talk to you.

Ben [*glancing at his watch*] Haven't the time, William.

Willy [*crossing the apron to Ben*] Ben, nothing's working out. I don't know what to do.

Ben Now, look here, William. I've bought timberland in Alaska and I need a man to look after things for me.

Willy God, timberland! Me and my boys in those grand outdoors!

Ben You've a new continent at your doorstep, William. Get out of these cities, they're full of talk and time payments and courts of law. Screw on your fists and you can fight for a fortune up there.

Willy Yes, yes! Linda, Linda!

Linda enters as of old, with the wash.

Linda Oh, you're back?

Ben I haven't much time.

Willy No, wait! Linda, he's got a proposition for me in Alaska.

Linda But you've got – [*To Ben*] He's got a beautiful job here.

Willy But in Alaska, kid, I could –

Linda You're doing well enough, Willy!

Ben [*to Linda*] Enough for what, my dear?

Linda [*frightened of Ben and angry at him*] Don't say those things to him! Enough to be happy right here, right now. [*To Willy, while Ben laughs*] Why must everybody conquer the world? You're well liked, and the boys love you, and someday – [*to Ben*] why, old man Wagner told him just the other day that if he keeps it up he'll be a member of the firm, didn't he, Willy?

Willy Sure, sure. I am building something with this firm, Ben, and if a man is building something he must be on the right track, mustn't he?

Ben What are you building? Lay your hand on it. Where is it?

Willy [*hesitantly*] That's true, Linda, there's nothing.

Linda Why? [*To Ben*] There's a man eighty-four years old –

Willy That's right, Ben, that's right. When I look at that man I say, what is there to worry about?

Ben Bah!

Willy It's true, Ben. All he has to do is go into any city, pick up the phone, and he's making his living and you know why?

Ben [*picking up his valise*] I've got to go.

Willy [*holding Ben back*] Look at this boy!

Biff, in his high school sweater, enters carrying suitcase. Happy carries Biff's shoulder guards, gold helmet, and football pants.

Willy Without a penny to his name, three great universities are begging for him, and from there the sky's the limit, because it's not what you do, Ben. It's who you know and the smile on your face! It's contacts, Ben, contacts! The whole wealth of Alaska passes over the lunch table at the Commodore Hotel, and that's the wonder, the wonder of this country, that a man can end with diamonds here on the basis of being liked! [*He turns to Biff*] And that's why when you get out on that field today it's important. Because thousands of people will be rooting for you and loving you. [*To Ben, who has again begun to leave*] And Ben! when he walks into a business office his name will sound out like a bell and all the doors will open to him! I've seen it, Ben, I've seen it a thousand times! You can't feel it with your hand like timber, but it's there!

Ben Good-by, William.

Willy Ben, am I right? Don't you think I'm right? I value your advice.

Ben There's a new continent at your doorstep, William. You could walk out rich. Rich!

[*He is gone*]

Willy We'll do it here, Ben! You hear me? We're gonna do it here!

Let us first consider the fluid treatment of time and place, and the significance of the stage properties and sound effects. The tape-recorder on its trolley locates the action in Howard's office. After he has wheeled it off, though Willy does not physically move, the scene changes to the Loman house in Brooklyn, and the time is now that of Ben's visit long ago. Ben's entrance is heralded by a musical theme (as in a Wagner opera, he has his *leitmotiv*); his case and umbrella indicate that he is just passing through, travelling from one end of the world to the other on his mysterious but profitable business. Ben can never stay long. When Linda, Willy's wife, enters 'as of old', i.e. as in former days, she is, of course, younger in appearance and carries a basket full of washing, symbolising her devotion to her household tasks. Finally, Biff appears as he was in his High School days, attended by his admiring and envious younger brother carrying his football kit – for there is to be an important game this afternoon, and Willy has already decided that Biff will be the hero of the match.

Notice next how the attitudes of the characters are conveyed. Howard is both embarrassed and irritated by Willy's desperate appeal to be allowed to go to Boston. As people in his position often do, he tries to put an end to the interview by claiming that he is a busy man. He appears to be worried about Willy – 'Pull yourself together, kid' – and hints that he *may* be able to do something for him when he feels better – 'Come back and we'll talk' – but we know that his real object is to get rid of Willy with as little fuss as possible. 'Stop by and drop off the samples' makes it very clear, despite the show of concern, that Willy is really being sacked.

In the conversation with Ben, who is throughout fidgeting to be off, Willy's inconsistency and his ability to swing round on a completely different tack are sharply revealed. At one moment 'nothing's working out' and he hears the call of the wide open spaces – 'God, timberland! Me and my boys in those grand outdoors!'; the next, he asserts that he is 'building something with this firm' and that he's 'gonna do it here'. All his aspirations are romantic dreams. The business success he yearns for is as far beyond his grasp as the new life on the Last Frontier. Ben jolts him by asking what solid achievement he can point to, but Linda – who at this stage is wholly converted to Willy's view of life – comes to his aid. She reminds him of a veteran salesman (his name is Dave Singleman) who can still make an easy living because of his contacts and popularity, which in turn prompts Willy to a rhetorical outburst celebrating 'the wonder of this country' where deals involving as much wealth as can be found in the whole of Alaska are settled over lunch in a New York hotel.

Running through most of the episode is the spurious claim that everything can be acheived if you are 'well liked'. Linda, no doubt echoing what she has so often heard from Willy himself, reminds him that he is well liked; evidently Dave Singleman at 84 is well liked; 'a man can end with diamonds here on the basis of being well liked' – he doesn't have to go to Africa, like Ben, to find them. (It is almost predictable, after all this, that not one of Willy's business acquaintances will turn up at his funeral.) Most of all it is important that Biff, Willy's golden boy – as he is, literally, in one way, his football helmet being lacquered gold – should be well liked. The game of football, as Willy sees it, is not just an important sporting event: it marks the beginning for Biff of a spectacularly successful career in which all doors will fly open before the popular young sportsman with the big smile and the wide circle of useful friends. Already, boasts the proud father, 'three great universities' are competing for the privilege of admitting Biff as a student. It is, of course, only natural that Willy's ambitions for Biff should lead him to preach the false gospel of success incessantly, and that a relationship, in which success is so important, will be greatly strained when success is not in fact achieved.

The conversation is carried on for the most part, in the everyday speech of contemporary New Yorkers. There are moments when it achieves great **pathos** by its simplicity:

> Oh, Ben, how did you do it? What is the answer? ... Ben, nothing's working out. I don't know what to do.

At other times, however, when Willy is carried away by his triumphal visions, his language is inspired rather as Volpone's is by the contemplation of his gold –

> And Ben! when he walks into a business office his name will sound out like a bell and all the doors will open to him!

One almost expects him to add that all the trumpets will sound for him on the other side – of the President's teak portals.

Miller has denied that the play is either an indictment of American capitalism or an analysis of family relationships gone wrong, though any reader or spectator is bound to feel that these are elements in it. His explanation of what he intended it to be about is a good deal more complex than the play itself. It is perhaps sensible to see it as primarily an attempt – a very powerful and moving one – to demonstrate what goes on in the mind of a man defeated by life and betrayed by the fantasies and illusions which have become necessary to him. Such people are to be found by the tens of thousands in all societies. Miller seems to think that Willy gains a kind of victory at the end by suicide, and that, while he is not a tragic figure in the **Aristotelian** sense, i.e. one who, before his downfall, is 'highly renowned and prosperous', he has the kind of tragic stature which our civilisation allows. However that may be, we can agree, in the 'century of the common man', that he is something of an Everyman figure ('Loman'–'Low man'?), and the play a modern **morality play**.

CRITICISM PRACTICE ON AN EXTRACT OF UNSEEN DRAMA

Marion, married to Clegg, a butcher, has purchased a house where a couple, Alec and Lisa, rent a flat and live with their sons and Alec's mother. Worsely visits the flat to persuade them to move out. Marion knew Alec previously...

Write an appreciation of the following extract paying particular attention to the ways in which the playwright creates atmosphere and character.

> Room, ALEC is on the bed and his MUM is in the armchair asleep. From time to time she slips down and has to be propped up. MARION is standing, eating a banana taken from a bowl on the table. She gives him an orange, which he takes but doesn't eat.
>
> *Marion* I'm always hungry. But thin. I don't put on. Nothing to show for it. Moving about
> 5   all the time is what does it. I eat in bed. I work at the table and sleep at my desk.
>   Burning it up.
> *Alec* Help yourself.
> *Marion* I do. Is something wrong with your legs?
> *Alec* No.
> 10 *Marion* Or your head?
> *Alec* No.
> *Marion* Why don't you get up?
> *Alec* If you like.
>   (He gets up.)

15 *Marion* Alec you know it's me that's bought the house.

Alec Lisa told me.

Marion Worsely acts for me.

Alec She said.

Marion I want vacant possession of my house.

20 *Alec* I gather.

Marion Lisa suggested I came and talked to you. I can offer alternative accommodation. I wouldn't have come otherwise.

Alec No.

Marion I would have come anyway.

25 *Alec* Yes.

Marion I knew you were here when I bought the house. That was why. Also the property itself. Desirable investment. How could I have bought it without knowing unless I'd forgotten the address and I couldn't do that. I've a great memory for details. All sorts of little details.

30 *Alec* Marion, what do you want?

Marion I'll give you a thousand pounds to go away.

Alec I don't want a thousand pounds.

Marion What do you want?

Alec Nothing at all. I try to want things for Lisa. For the boys. For mum even though
35   she's past wanting anything she can have. I don't know what I could lose that would make any difference to me.

Marion Lisa?

Alec No.

Marion You don't love her.

40 *Alec* I didn't say that.

Marion If you love someone you want to keep them. I want to. So not Lisa. Your mum? Lisa says you won't part with her. You won't let her go to hospital. Do you cling to your mum?

Alec She'll die soon.

45 *Marion* Are you sorry?

Alec Everyone dies. Unless they were never born.

Marion Are you glad then?

Alec No.

Marion Have you got no feelings at all?

50 *Alec* Not of indignation.

Marion But you wouldn't want to lose your children.

Alec No.

Marion There then.

Alec But children do die sometimes. It could happen. Why not to mine as much as
55   someone else's?

Marion But if it did happen to yours, that should be a horror for you. We're not talking about other people.

Alec I could probably bear it.

Marion I'll give you a thousand pounds for Lisa. For your mum. For the boys. Whatever
60   you like to think it's for. And find you somewhere to live. This flat is ridiculous.

Alec You seem to want this house very much.

Marion What I want is you to wake up. We were going to better ourselves. What did we go to evening classes for? We both felt we'd missed something. You were never sure what subject was the answer. Everything seemed to lead to something else you
65   wanted to get hold of. There were books in the bed. You couldn't let a single fact go.

Alec Learning things wasn't any use.

Marion If you wanted it to be some use you should have concentrated on one thing and got a qualification. I got on in the end in my own way. I always said I wasn't the butcher's wife. You could have done something even greater.

70 *Alec* But why should I?

Marion You've no stamina. [*Pause.*] I've got a garden flat you could have.

Alec Basement.

Marion Basement flat.

Alec Do you want us to go really?

75 *Marion* Two thousand pounds to get out of my house.

Alec Why do you think I want two thousand pounds?

Marion You should want it. For Lisa's sake. For your sons. What are you up to, Alec? Of

course it wasn't in your interest to go for two hundred or five hundred or whatever
little sum it was. Even a thousand doesn't touch the profit I'll make. I respect you

80   for hanging on. But two thousand? Two five.

Mum   Edie, Edie.

Alec   Hello there.

Marion   Are you Edie?

Alec   She likes someone to answer.

85   [*He goes over to MUM and props her up.*]

Marion   My God, I hope I don't live as long.

Alec   She's not in pain.

Marion   Marvellous.

Alec   It's a great deal.

90   *Marion*   But she doesn't know what's going on. Does she remember her own life? Does she
even know who she is? I'd kill myself if I felt my mind beginning to drop away like
that. Suppose I said, Alec, Alec, and someone else said Hello there. And I didn't
know it wasn't you. Because it would be you I called for even if I was eighty.

Alec   I've always thought of that as over. In fact I never think of it at all.

95   *Marion* My face will go like hers one day. I keep what I can. I don't want to die.

Alec   It was all here before you were born and you don't resent that.

Marion   But once you have things you don't want to give them up. It's quite different.

Alec   No, it's just the same.

Caryl Churchill
WJEC 1994

DRAMA CRITICISM BIBLIOGRAPHY

Benson, Eugene	*H M Synge*
Berlin, Normand	*Eugene O'Neill*
Bevis, Richard W	*English Drama: Restoration*
Billington, Michael	*Alan Ayckbourn*
Bordman, Gerald	*The American Theatre*
Bowers, Fredson	*Elizabethan Revenge Tragedy*
Bradbrook, M C	*Themes and Conventions of Elizabethan Drama*
Carson, Neil	*Arthur Miller*
Cunningham, John E	*Elizabethan and Early Stuarts*
Dean, Leonard	*Four Tudor Comedies*
	Elizabethan – Jacobean Drama
Dukore, Bernard F	*Harold Pinter*
Etherton, Michael	*Contemporary Irish Dramatists*
Ganz, Arthur	*George Bernard Shaw*
Glanakaris, C J	*Peter Shaffer*
Gray, Frances	*John Arden*
Leeming, Glenda	*Poetic Drama*
Lyons, Charles R	*Samuel Beckett*
McLuskie, Kathleen	*Renaissance Dramatists*
Mehl, Dieter	*The Elizabethan Dumb Show*
Miles, Rosalind	*Ben Jonson: His Life and Works*
	Restoration and 18th-Century Drama
Partridge, A C	*The Language of Renaissance*
Rossiter, A P	*English Drama from Early Times*
Rowse, A L	*Discoveries and Reviews*
Simpson, Percy	*Studies in Elizabethan Drama*
Thomas, David	*Henrik Ibsen*
Whitaker, Thomas R	*Tom Stoppard*
Worley, Demetrice	*African–American Literature*
Worth, Katharine	*Oscar Wilde*
Ure, Peter	*Elizabethan and Jacobean Drama*

2.2 ELIZABETHAN AND JACOBEAN DRAMA

BACKGROUND

In 1576 the first public theatre, called the Theatre, was built near the site of Liverpool Street Station and opened by James Burbage, its principal actor. This theatre achieved immediate popularity, and many more were constructed, including the Curtain, the Fortune, the Swan and the most famous of all, the Globe Theatre, built on the South Bank of the Thames near the site of the National Theatre today.

The theatres of Shakespeare's day were divided into private and public theatres. The private theatres were built indoors, usually in large houses and palaces. They were lit by artificial light and the audience sat on benches. The price of seats ranged from 6d to 2/6.

The public theatres were built with roofs that were open to the sky. The performances were always held in the daylight, usually in an afternoon. The seats were far from luxurious and the 'groundlings' sat on stools near the stage. These seats cost 1d.

Elizabeth I died in 1603 and James I's accession accompanied the great dramatic phase of the Jacobean drama. This included not only the greatest plays of Shakespeare and Jonson, but also the tragedies of Tourneur (*The Revenger's Tragedy*, 1607, *The Atheist's Tragedy*, 1608); Webster (*The Duchess of Malfi*, 1614, *The White Devil*, 1620); Beaumont and Fletcher (*The Maid's Tragedy*, 1601); Middleton (*The Changeling*, 1622); and the comedies of Dekker (*The Shoemaker's Holiday*, 1599); Beaumont and Fletcher (*The Knight of the Burning Pestle*, 1613), Massinger (*A New Way to Pay Old Debts*, 1625) and Ford (*Tis Pity She's a Whore*, 1627). It is important to get a feeling for the passion and the **realism** in the staging of drama of this period. You should make full use of the notes and introduction in individual editions of your set play and consult general background books.

CHRISTOPHER MARLOWE (1564–93)

Of the pre-Shakespearian plays, the most often set are Marlowe's *The Tragical History of Doctor Faustus*, *The Jew of Malta*, and *Edward II*.

Dr Faustus (written 1589, printed 1604)

Dr Faustus was a dominating character whose aspirations the author shared imaginatively, giving them a compelling power. The favourite Renaissance figure of the 'overreacher' (whose emblem was Icarus), is set in a play which owes much else to medieval morality drama. Marlowe follows in outline the English translation (from the German) of *The History of the Damnable Life and Death of Dr Faustus*, developed from the medieval legend of a man who sold his soul to the Devil. However, Marlowe's conception of Faustus is of a character far more complex than the legendary magician.

The hero's monopoly of the play's action, and the great struggle that goes on in him between good and evil, are to be specially noted. Typically for the earlier plays, the supporting characters are given little depth or life of their own. (Compare this with Shakespeare's treatment of his minor characters such as Kent in *King Lear*.) This is often highlighted in examination questions, such as:

'Dr Faustus dominates the action: there is no other developed character in the play.' Do you agree?

The Jew of Malta (c. 1590)

With *The Jew of Malta*, in the Senecan tradition of the revenge tragedy, Marlowe takes another step in the right direction of presenting none but immoral characters. Barabas is quite blatantly a bad man – but equalled in villainy by everyone else in the play. The central character, like earlier heroes, is distinct, functional, but lacking in all warm humanity and subtlety.

The role of humour in the play is a common topic for examination questions, for example:

'Primarily comic entertainment'. Is this an adequate description of *The Jew of Malta*?

You may not feel that the play is in any way comic. You should work out your views on this and note the reactions to the horrors of the play's characters within it. Barabas' servant Ithamore, for example, takes delight in his master's deviousness (Act III):

> *Itha* Why, was there ever seen such villany,
> So neatly plotted, and so well perform'd?
> Both held in hand, and flat both beguil'd

TS Eliot referred to the humour in the play as 'farce' and it is useful to read his opinion in his essay on Marlowe.

Edward II (c. 1591–2)

Edward II draws on a period of history that fascinated Elizabethan audiences: the Plantagenet wars, internal and external, leading to the Tudor accession. It is useful to acquaint yourself with the historical facts and compare them with Marlowe's version. Typically, Marlowe concentrates on his central character, the King, and shows how his ruin springs from his weaknesses.

Note that the striking heroic stanzas and tirades, even the lyricism, of earlier plays have largely disappeared from this stark play.

WEBSTER AND JACOBEAN TRAGEDY

Of the Jacobean tragedies, the two most frequently set at A level are those of Webster (c. 1580–1634). These may represent the gloomy, menacing tragedy of the Jacobean period. The horrors and claustrophobic atmosphere derive partly from the late Roman tragedian Seneca, partly from the changing mood of the audience and King James's love of magic and mystery, partly from the character of the authors. They had observed how much of a success Kyd's melodramatic *The Spanish Tragedy* had been two decades earlier, and how well this vein had been exploited by Shakespeare himself. As taste began to deteriorate and Shakespeare fell silent (*The Tempest* was produced in 1612, a year after *The White Devil*), so Tourneur, Webster and Massinger took over the stage until the Puritans closed it for twenty years.

Sometimes, in critical discussions of Jacobean tragedy, the impression is given that by the end of Elizabeth I's reign audiences had already supped so full of horrors that playwrights felt compelled to go on piling up the atrocities to make any impression at all on blunted sensibilities. This is not altogether true. Considered merely as anthologies of horror, there is not much to choose between *The Duchess of Malfi* and early plays like Kyd's *Spanish Tragedy* or Shakespeare's *Titus Andronicus*. What is different about Jacobean tragedies is not so much any increase in the number, or the essential bloodiness of the murders and maimings, but rather their more refined and ingenious nature, a greater psychological depth, and perhaps above all the more varied and expressive language employed.

The White Devil (1612)

Character *The White Devil* describes the central and all-pervading character, Vittoria Corombona. Questions set on the play at A level often concentrate on her. You should explore in detail her relations with the other characters, especially with her lover Brachiano and her brother Marcello. Marcello's character should also be studied carefully. Like Marlowe's megalomaniacs, Vittoria Corombona will perpetrate any crime to serve her ambitions.

Construction Editors have commented on how the scenes seem to blaze out of a dark background, so that the impression is not of a whole, but of a series of lurid, imaginatively realised episodes. Two scenes you may find rewarding to examine in particular detail are the trial scene (Act I, Sc. 2) for its revelations of character and the changing directions of the action, and the final scene (Act V, Sc. 6). Here you should assess the effectiveness of the ending and note a common element in Jacobean tragedy – courage in the face of death.

Themes *The White Devil* falls into the genre of revenge tragedy (cf. *The Spanish Tragedy* by Kyd and *Hamlet* by Shakespeare). You can trace in it the themes of justice and revenge. You should note also the modifications of ideas on right and wrong throughout the play and the theme of the corruption of the Court life.

BEN JONSON (?1573-1637)

The name of Ben Jonson is always associated with the **comedy of humours**, in which comic effects are achieved by bringing together a collection of eccentric characters, each dominated by a 'humour', i.e. a ruling passion. For Jonson's own definition of 'humour' you should consult the famous lines in the prologue to his play *Every Man Out of His Humour*:

Some one peculiar quality
Doth so possess a man, that it doth draw
All his affects, his spirits, and his powers,
In their confluctions, all to run one way.

Jonson was by no means the only dramatist of his age to exploit 'humour' on the stage, though he erected it into a theory of comedy. Shakespeare too had his 'humorous' characters; indeed, Hamlet implies that they were among the stock-in-trade of the drama: 'the humorous man shall end his part in peace' (*Hamlet*, Act II, Sc. 2). Note that the 'humorous man' was not a humorist in the popular modern sense; he aroused amusement by his oddity, but did not set out to be amusing.

The unities Jonson was a learned (although largely self-educated) man. He knew more of the ancient Greek and Roman literature than any other dramatist of his time. It is useful to note Jonson's adherence to the **classical unities** (see Glossary) of time, place and action – a discipline within which he worked skilfully in his comedies but which did not help him achieve tension in his one tragedy *Sejanus*.

The Alchemist and *Bartholomew Fair*

Jonson is above all a satirist of the morals and follies of his times. He called comedy 'A thing pleasant and ridiculous and accommodated to the correction of manners.' This is essentially how his comedy should be seen. Despite the large number of topicalities and ephemeral weaknesses that he satirised, there is plenty of recognisable satirical humour. Surly in *The Alchemist* says:

Must needs I cheat myself
With that same foolish vice of honesty?

Surly should be central to a study of *The Alchemist*. The rest of the characters are a nest of villains whose brilliant exposure by Jonson was said to have helped clear the streets of London of quacks and imposters. Lovewit, the master tricked by his roguish servants, does not seem much better than they. His attitude is conveyed in the line:

I love a teeming wit as I love nourishment.

Typical questions you might encounter are:

What effects does Jonson achieve in *The Alchemist* by setting his comedy in contemporary London?

Examine the part of Surly in *The Alchemist*, and say how you think Jonson's portrayal fits in with his dramatic purposes.

Bartholomew Fair may be less carefully constructed, but it is full of the keenest, most biting **satire** of which Jonson is capable, full of vigorous invective and City life in all its colourful diversity; the characters have amazing individuality: the Puritan, Zeal-of-the-land Busy; Ursula, the Pig Woman; Justice Overdo; Tom Quarlous and the rest, Littlewit and all, a fine Rabelaisian rout. Here is the comedy of social realism as well as the satire of manners.

Note Jonson's use of names to convey the disposition of humour of his comic characters – Zeal-of-the-land Busy, the puritan in *Bartholomew Fair*, is an extreme and colourful example. The same device is used in many of Charles Dickens's novels. Like Dickens, Jonson shows great **realism** in his portrayal of urban life, despite his use of caricature. In *Volpone* the characters generally take their cue from their suggestive names.

2.3 THE COMEDY OF MANNERS

Restoration drama or, as it is often called, comedy of manners, lasted the fifty years from 1660 to 1710, that is for four reigns in our history. (Charles II, 1660–85; James II, 1685–88; William III, 1688–1702 and Mary II, 1688–94; Anne 1702–14.) Its leading exponents were Etherege, Dryden, Wycherley, Congreve, Vanbrugh and Farquhar. Although the drama did not change or develop as markedly as the Elizabethan and Jacobean over a similar period of time, it did run into a general change of public taste by Queen Anne's time – a taste that was adequately guided and expressed by Sir Joseph Addison, whose essays in *The Spectator* began to appear in 1711.

Although Restoration comedy was a new phenomenon, it had certain links with the 'citizen' drama of Jonson, his use of names to indicate humours, or character traits, above the satirical drive. The style of the plays, however, was nearer to that of the comedy of Beaumont and Fletcher, where we also find some of the characteristics of the later drama, such as the 'gallant' – a lover more interested in conquests than marriage (e.g. Mirabel in Fletcher's *The Wild Goose Chase*). Shirley (1596–1666) also wrote plays in the 1630s in which couples similar to those in the 'comedy of manners' are to be found.

With the encouragement of the court newly returned from Paris, and an awareness of the comedies of Molière as they began to appear from 1662, the style of drama as critics now distinguish it began to take shape. The drama concerned itself exclusively with Londoners of the aristocratic class, or played off against country oafs. Ordinary citizens, when they appear, are often made to appear foolish, or even cuckolded. The gallants, rakes and idle rich are reluctant to marry but are liable to be 'caught' in the end (in which case one assumes they may settle down to a virtuous life). Wives are dissatisfied with husbands, and the dialogue often consists of witty exchanges like verbal fencing matches.

In theory, some of the writers of these comedies, such as Dryden, claimed that it was part of their satirical interest to hold up the rakes and libertines to criticism if not ridicule, but in practice such characters often stole the show and were clearly amusing if not admirable in their behaviour. The later dramatists, Wycherley and Farquhar, tried rather more than Etherege and Congreve to expose bad behaviour, in keeping with changing opinions. Victorian moral qualms put Restoration comedy right out of court, and when it returned to the stage in this century the productions tended to emphasise the externals of the age, in order to try and distance its immorality. There was also an unjustifiable tendency to treat the characters as though they were heartless or mere mouthpieces for a stream of **wit**. Recently there has been a better understanding and presentation of the **realism** and living qualities of the characters. As Congreve himself wrote, in defence of Valentine (*Love for Love*):

> He was Prodigal and is shown in the first Act under hard circumstances, which are the effects of his Prodigality.... In short, the Character is a mix'd Character: his faults are fewer than his good qualities: and, as the World goes, he may pass well enough for the best character in a Comedy: where even the best must be shewn to have faults, that the best spectators may be warn'd not to think too well of themselves.

We summarise below some key points to remember about the drama of this period.

General features of the Restoration theatre

1. It was now an indoor theatre on the contemporary French model, set back behind a proscenium arch with a curtain. Scenery and artificial lighting were employed.
2. For the first time in England, actresses appeared on the public stage. This gave dramatists wider scope in the writing of women's parts, and no doubt permitted a greater and more persuasive seductiveness in their interpretation. Many of the female roles in Shakespeare's comedies must have been played (by male actors, of course) in a somewhat tomboyish fashion, e.g. Rosalind in *As You Like It*.
3. Even more than in Shakespeare's day, the players depended on Royal and Court patronage. Going to see plays was a fashionable diversion, much favoured by those members of the upper classes who wished to celebrate their liberation from Puritan rule and by an even larger number of middle-class people seeking to imitate their social superiors. The diarist and civil servant Samuel Pepys was a keen playgoer.

Particular features of Restoration comedies

1 The plays were almost wholly in prose. In the best of them, the dialogue is splendidly polished and witty.

2 Some traces of the old 'comedy of humours' survive in the treatment of the more eccentric characters, and in the bestowing of 'characteristic' names on all the people in a play, e.g. Waitwell, a serving man; Fainall, an unscrupulous schemer; Gibbet, a highwayman.

3 The typical scene of the action is London and the leading characters are 'persons of quality'. Country life is viewed with exaggerated horror as a desert of unmitigated, uncouth boredom. It should be added that the London merchant – the 'City Knight' – is also made a figure of fun, existing only to be robbed of his money and his wife.

4 The attitude of the upper-class characters – especially, but by no means exclusively, the men – to sex and marriage is cheerfully cynical. The man of fashion devotes his time and energy above all to the pursuit of women, and the women are very willing to be pursued, and frequently overtaken. At the same time they profess a hypocritical concern for keeping up appearances – 'honour' and 'reputation' are words forever in their mouths. Among the men, even a husband who positively loathes his wife is still expected to fly into a fury at the prospect of being made, or reputed, a cuckold. Wives, like pheasants, have to be preserved from poachers.

5 Almost of equal importance to the fine gentleman is the repair of his shaky financial position. Money, and the law in connection with inheritance, dowries, marriage settlements, estates in trust, and so forth, bulk large in almost every play. For the Mirabells and the Aimwells, supreme happiness comes in the form of marriage to a beautiful heiress.

WYCHERLEY – *THE COUNTRY WIFE* (1675)

Examining two recent and typical questions on Wycherley's *The Country Wife*, we can explore some of the moral and social assumptions of Restoration comedy, touched upon in point 4 above.

'Wycherley's alleged immorality, in particular his failure to expose Horner's deception, has offended many'. Discuss.

'The good characters in *The Country Wife* are dull and colourless; the bad are grotesque but vital'. Discuss.

In this play, Pinchwife marries an ignorant woman in order not to be deceived, having had experience of 'whores'. He is duly well deceived, but in view of his motive for marrying, and other characteristics he reveals, no one could be entirely sorry for him. Horner says to him:

> So then, you only marry'd to keep a Whore to yourself.

He goes on to give a lesson to Pinchwife in better motives for marriage. In the next scene Pinchwife is seen spying on his wife, and in several ways treats her badly in a jealous humour. We can only approve, therefore, of Margery's success in deceiving him.

Horner himself has little difficulty in overcoming the 'honour' (which soon is exposed as a myth) of the various women he seduces by pretending to be a eunuch. He is not really a man to be approved of or condemned by the audience, being more of a dramatic tool used by Wycherley to satirise the society women who are his victims. These are the hypocrites and are strongly condemned. Margery is an exception, but her unfaithfulness is understandable.

In a subplot, the fop Sparkish is the rival to Harcourt, a man of good sense and virtue, for the hand of Pinchwife's sister Alithea. Although the two good characters are not too convincing, they are present as gauges of the moral temperature and do not need to do more than fulfil that role while Wycherley concentrates on the one (Horner), who exposes immorality. Sparkish is similarly exposed as an over-credulous fool.

In view of these considerations, we need not be indignant that the morally reprehensible Horner remains unexposed and unpunished. Present moral sensibility in such matters has tended to draw nearer to that of Wycherley's audience, rather than that of the more 'straitlaced' Queen Anne period: it may be remembered that the Victorians could not accept any Restoration comedy, on largely moral grounds. Witty rakes were commonly forgiven moral weaknesses for the sake of their ability to make the contemporary audience – and us – laugh, and as we have pointed out, since Horner is more of a function of the satire than a rounded character, we may trust the playwright's handling of his fate.

The immorality, so-called, of the good wife Margery has been explained, and in general the adultery and flirtations between lovers and married people in Restoration comedy, though certainly the product of a comparatively licentious 'upper-class' outlook on life, may stand today within their humorous and satirical contexts as possibly mildly shocking, but not necessarily to be imitated, regarded as the norm, or to be admired by the ordinary man. The same kind of moral anarchy, absorbed by elements of satire and crazy humour, are to be observed today in present drama, the theatre of the absurd or black comedy. We do not now believe that ordinary people will leave the theatre bent on imitating such behaviour, or admiring it. The moral tone of Wycherley and certainly that of later dramatists such as Congreve is close enough to that of, say, Marlowe or Webster, when good is known to be good, and bad, bad. Formerly, critics were also demanding why Autolycus of *The Winter's Tale* by Shakespeare did not receive his well-merited prison sentence.

It is, however, true that characters serving as gauges for virtue, such as Harcourt and Alithea, tend to be overshadowed in vigour and interest by rascals such as Pinchwife or those that fall into (albeit enforced) error, such as his wife.

CONGREVE – *THE WAY OF THE WORLD* (1700)

Manly Wycherley, the most robust and biting of the Restoration dramatists, was far surpassed by Congreve in plot organisation and effectiveness of dialogue. Violence gives way to more subtle satire, and Etherege's admiration of profligacy, to a firmer standard of morality. Congreve's masterpiece is *The Way of the World*, though in his time *Love for Love* was more of a success.

Mirabell, the 'hero' of *The Way of the World*, is a hero with a difference: he is not a saint, because of his past affairs; he takes easily to intrigue, and clearly the loss of his loved one's fortune is important to him – his first concern is to recover it. Yet he has warmth, magnanimity and a fine recklessness in his courtship of Millamant. There is none of the old lust in their relationship: they desire to be justified and their playful intrigues are a form of self-protection. This attitude operates even against each other, as in the wonderful 'proviso' or 'bargain scene' in which each has to promise the other not to behave as man and wife once they are married, if they are to agree to marry. This is a fairly well-worn convention, but the manner in which Congreve handles it surpasses all other examples. The wit is of the older Comedy of Manners; the serious intention to marry looks forward to the comedy of sentiment (see overleaf).

The style of the play has great variety: it is particularly skilled in giving an individual voice to each character, completely suited to that character, and varying according to circumstances. Here is Lady Wishfort being coy and assuming arch airs with her supposed suitor Sir Rowland, actually Mirabell's servant Waitwell:

> You must not attribute my yielding to any sinister appetite, or Indigestion of Widowhood; Nor Impute my Complacency to any Lethargy of Continence – I Hope you do not think me prone to any iteration of Nuptials

where Malapropism is surpassed by such pretentiousness.

Compare this with the fishwife aspect of Lady Wishfort driving away her maid, Foible, on the discovery of her plot with Waitwell:

> Out of my house, out of my house, thou viper, thou serpent, that I have fostered! thou bosom traitress, that I raised from nothing! – begone, begone, begone, go go! – that I took from washing of old gauze and wearing of dead hair, with a bleak blue nose, over a chafing dish of starved embers, and dining behind a traverse rag in a shop no bigger than a bird-cage. – go, go, starve again, do, do!

Both these manners are in character and the persons of the play are brought to life by such expert mimicry of speech-tone.

In his dedication to the play, Congreve, after saying that it was not dramatically interesting to portray pure fools, since one can only pity them, goes on:

> This reflection moved me to design some characters, which should appear ridiculous not so much through a natural folly ... as through an affected wit which at the same time that it is affected, is also false.

This definition only perfectly fits Witwoud, whom, Congreve complains, the audience actually mistook to be genuinely witty. It is interesting here to note Pope's comment, 'Tell me if Congreve's fools be fools indeed.'

GOLDSMITH AND SHERIDAN

A more sober social morality silenced the genius of Congreve and his fellow dramatists. Perhaps as a reaction against Restoration comedy, sentiment became more admired than wit, and licentiousness and blasphemy in drama were condemned. There followed a period where the dramatic vogue was for the 'sentimental comedy'. 'Sentiment' at this time implied the solemn and rather pious communication of morality and correct emotion – temperance and wisdom rather than light-hearted gaiety.

The true brilliance of the 'comedy of manners' was revived with Goldsmith and Sheridan and A-level questions sometimes refer to the view that their plays were meant to be 'anti-sentimental'.

Goldsmith describes the sentimental comedy thus,

the virtues of private life are exhibited, rather than the vices exposed, and the distresses rather than the frailty of mankind.

There are residual elements of the sentimental comedy in his play *She Stoops to Conquer* (1773). This play looks back to Shakespeare's romantic comedy and the exercise of pure humour rather than wit.

In the Prologue to *The Rivals* (1775), Sheridan asks whether we should expect the spirit of comedy to preach. The reference to the genteel comedy of the time is obvious.

Look on her well – does she seem form'd to teach?
Should you expect to hear this lady preach?
Is grey experience suited to her youth?
Do solemn sentiments become that mouth?

Sheridan's plays are much closer to the 'comedy of manners' tradition than to the sentimental comedy. He exploited the popular taste of his day for spectacle. *The School for Scandal* (1777) has a succession of well-managed and often spectacular scenes such as the visually effective 'screen' scene which, from the usual reaction of the audience, might be called the 'scream' scene.

2.4 THE MODERN PERIOD

'I can hardly form an estimate of a play merely by reading it' Chekhov once wrote, and this is probably nowhere more true than in modern plays. Where we do not have to study to understand the language or the social milieu, there is every reason for seeing the play performed and judging its impact in performance.

GB SHAW (1856–1950)

It is paradoxical that, while from the beginning of the eighteenth to the end of the nineteenth century the theatre grew and prospered as popular entertainment, few of the multitude of plays written during this period have found a place in the first rank of English drama. Certainly, apart from the comedies of Sheridan, they are unlikely to figure in A-level syllabuses.

The appearance of George Bernard Shaw as a new dramatist in the 1890s may be considered – certainly was considered by Shaw himself! – to have saved the English theatre from becoming merely a trivial amusement. Certainly, he dominated the stage during the first 30 years of this century. Shaw's earliest plays reveal a concern with social issues which, although his touch became lighter, he never lost. Indeed, he ostentatiously enjoys parading his didactic intentions; but he persuaded theatregoers to absorb, and indeed relish, long discussions of, for example, the 'Irish Question' (in *John Bull's Other Island*, 1904) or medical ethics (in *The Doctor's Dilemma*, 1906) by being enormously entertaining. Strongly outlined characterisation, sometimes verging on caricature, highly absurd – not to say farcical –

situations, and a splendid fluency and wit distributed impartially among nearly all his characters, ensure that a Shaw play hardly ever fails to hold even a juvenile audience. Moreover, Shaw writes for the reader as well as the spectator; and while he is no poet, his prose has at times, especially in *Saint Joan* (1923), an eloquence that is undeniably poetic in style and feeling.

Several of Shaw's plays appear regularly on A-level syllabuses: *Man and Superman*, *Pygmalion*, *Arms and the Man* and *Saint Joan*. The last play appears very frequently and may be his masterpiece, as it combines an intensely serious theme with an adequate historical story for it, excellent dialogue and fine construction. Shaw did not usually trouble much about this last quality; he liked to work through his argument till he was satisfied it was fully aired, and then stop. Shaw himself considered *Back to Methuselah* to be his best play, but this is seldom performed, is very long, and probably appealed to Shaw because it expounds in eloquent terms his final 'gospel': his theory of 'creative evolution' and belief in the 'life force'.

Shaw's Prefaces The most obvious way for students to approach the ideas in Shaw's plays is via the Prefaces. They make absorbing reading and are indispensable for those interested in Shaw's ideas.

The Prefaces range far beyond the actual concerns of the plays and to that extent may not be considered directly relevant. However, it is useful to measure the speeches and scenes which crystalise the ideas in the plays, against the points made in the Prefaces. In the Preface to *Major Barbara*, for example, Shaw, having railed against the critics for 'their habit of treating Britain as an intellectual void', attempts to compensate for their 'ignorant credulity' by providing a critique of his own play!

> It is this credulity that drives me to help my critics out with *Major Barbara* by telling them what to say about it.

Saint Joan

Every dramatic quality is given masterly expression in *Saint Joan*. Above all it works on the stage. Historical settings for plays of ideas are not out of favour in this century, as other excellent examples fully prove (Bolt's *A Man for All Seasons*; Shaffer's *The Royal Hunt of the Sun*; Eliot's *Murder in the Cathedral* as well as plays by Anouilh and Brecht). As usual with plays historically founded, there is a need to note how far in *Saint Joan* Shaw deviates from and manipulates the actual events: some light can thus be thrown on his special purposes in the theme, and his craftsmanship as a playwright. First he had to select the salient episodes from the events of February 1429 to May 1431, and then write appropriate dialogue which also conveys the themes.

No one, not even an historian, can be absolutely sure what historical characters were like; only deductions which do not offend common sense or contradict the evidence may be made. Within his historical framework, Shaw introduces a tremendous variety of characters: English and French, laymen and clerics, the base and noble.

It is sometimes said that Shaw uses his characters merely as mouthpieces for his own ideas. However, *Saint Joan* is a truly dramatic play with characters who are far more than 'dummies' to convey messages. Shaw has a fine sense of dramatic situation and can create a gripping tension of argument in a scene consisting solely of dialogue. An example of this in *Saint Joan* is Act I Sc. 4 – a dialogue between the Earl of Warwick and Bishop Cauchon with occasional explosions by Stogumber.

Sometimes the validity of the Epilogue is questioned and we may ask whether it is fair in modern drama to expect the audience to accept a living, cheerful ghost, apparently merely for the purpose of rounding off the debate of ideas. But it forms a kind of palinode, like that when Chaucer's Troilus, when killed, returns to shed ironic light on the futility of his sufferings. The justifiable design of Shaw's Epilogue was to establish the permanence of Joan's work and her own immortality. In this way the tragedy is technically almost turned into a comedy: the tone and content of Joan's speeches are as they were: friendly, provincial, simple, full of sense, of a pure integrity, of penetrating vision, above all of irrepressible good humour. The characters each come before Joan and make their excuses, then leave. The ordinary soldier, who gave Joan the cross when she was being burnt at the stake, has the last word which touches on an important theme:

> What I say is, you have as good a right to your notions as they (i.e. the captains and bishops and lawyers) have to theirs, and perhaps better.

OSCAR WILDE (1854–1900)

With Wilde, wit, missing for more than a century, returned to the English theatre. In 1892, the same year Shaw's early failure *Widower's Houses* was seen in London, *Lady Windermere's Fan* was produced. That Wilde fully realised how dependent such plays as his are on the qualities of the actors, is revealed by the remark he made in a letter to a newspaper:

> The personality of the actor is often a source of danger in the perfect presentation of a work of art. It may distort. It may lead astray. It may be a discord in the tone or symphony. For anybody can act. Most people in England do nothing else. … The actor's aim is, or should be, to convert his own accidental personality into the real and essential personality of the character he is called upon to personate.

Whether given superlative actors or not, the thing that made an immediate impact on the audiences of the nineties, and is still fresh now, is the sparkle of the dialogue. Many lines by Wilde are still quoted:

> What is a cynic? A man who knows the price of everything and the value of nothing.

> In this world there are two tragedies. One is not getting what one wants, and the other is getting it.

What makes so many of Wilde's paradoxes arresting is that they are not idle contradictions, but can be justified. In the same way it is an error to suppose that this play and the next two, *A Woman of No Importance* (1893) and *The Importance of Being Earnest* (1895) are mere gossamers of shimmering language spun by lightweight characters. Wilde's characters may sound unserious, even fantastic, but they are founded on types as real as those of the comedy of manners and express points of view as worthy of attention. The sustained epigrams should not dazzle us into supposing there is nothing to think about: they would hardly be as effective as they are if they were empty of ideas. The above examples alone demonstrate this, and although Wilde's plots do not work out, as Shaw's are designed to do, a strongly reasoned thesis about the serious concerns of life, they are well enough constructed and true enough to themes of human relationships to be good comedies.

TS Eliot (1888–1965) – *Murder in the Cathedral*

In the 'thirties, after a largely ignored effort by WB Yeats to re-establish poetic drama, Eliot began to produce successful plays in the verse play genre. Two or three of these plays are now classics of the theatre, and *Murder in the Cathedral* is the most commonly set at A level.

Thomas à Becket is the play's hero, and his heroic status is unusual. Many tragic heroes' deaths are forms of martyrdom: Becket's actually is one, but his willing acceptance of, indeed triumph in his death makes one wonder if he attains tragic dimensions.

The Tempters The conflict that normally leads to a hero's death is provided in this play by the four 'tempters' whose rising scale of credibility and power dramatically provides the opportunities for Becket to question his course of action. This action is merely to allow himself to be killed – to allow himself to be made a martyr for the *right* reason, that is, for the good of the Church and the glory of God; not for victory in his quarrel with Henry II, nor for future personal glory.

The fact that Becket was once a very worldly and ambitious man, who owed his elevation entirely to Henry's earlier support, helps to create in Becket a more interesting character when the tempters arrive. Not one offers an entirely idle temptation, although the first is little more than a reminder of luxuries and enjoyment long since given up. The next tempter also derives his allure from the past, but with a more serious proposition: to resume power by restoring the damaged relations with the King. The third tempter offers Becket the opportunity of aligning himself with those powerful elements that oppose the King: the feudal nobility. However, this intriguing against the central power would entail, apart from its innate immorality, the destruction of the order that Becket believes should prevail in the state. The fourth tempter creates a dramatic surprise by turning out to be Becket himself, underlining the extremely intimate nature of this temptation. His offer is what Becket secretly dreams of: the glory of martyrdom. He knows that the form of death that threatens him will ensure his veneration in Canterbury through all future ages of Christendom. As with the third tempter, Becket is shown a vision of the future that attends upon his acceptance.

Even more subtle is the further promise of a certain glorious place in Heaven. There seems to be nothing wrong with this, except what Becket is able to perceive: the motive would be wrong, spiritual pride is masked by the temptation. By being willing to reject this apparently God-willed solution, Becket has it restored to him: the purification of the motive makes the attainment possible.

The Chorus Many questions on this play understandably select the Chorus for special attention. Eliot has had almost obtrusive recourse to the practice and theory of Greek classical tragedy; for example, the machinery of *The Family Reunion* and the preservation of unities in all his plays. The Chorus appears in *The Family Reunion* in the choric speaking by all the characters present except the hero (a trick which can be very effective dramatically). Eliot employs the device of a Chorus in a manner which exceeds its use in Greek tragedy, where it links episodes by commentary such as might be expected by an articulate spectator. Its reactions guide as well as inform the audience's reactions.

In *Murder in the Cathedral* Eliot makes the Chorus an emotional, excitable group of female citizens of Canterbury. As such they express far more than comment: they try to sway Becket's behaviour, they mourn his absence, they provide emotion for the brooding menace, and the actual horror. Eliot exercises all his great poetic gift on their lines. One feels Eliot was so thoroughly at home in the medium of choral verse, that rather than assume a subordinate position, they appear in a fully functional role with at least equal status to the dialogue. In Part I the Priests scold them for 'immodest babbling', and later Thomas, more compassionately, tells them to be at peace; but the most remarkable and dramatically effective intervention of the Chorus in the action is when they speak antiphonally, or perhaps operatically, as in a trio, with Priests and Tempters. This emotionally heightened passage follows directly on from more extended observations by the three groups, and is followed by a long choric chant expressing dark horror, and a final speech of clear, calm resolution by Becket, to close Part I.

The Chorus also demonstrates that Becket's martyrdom is already doing for the people what Becket has declared that it should: bringing them back to a recognition of God's ways. They virtually turn the play into a modern morality, as well as underline the 'poetic' side of the drama. They also 'fix' moments of the action in the development of the content and reference; for example to open Part II, they are ironically looking towards a happy spring after Becket's Christmas sermon: there are signs of hope and regeneration; then there are the three agonised sections while Becket is being murdered; finally a *Te Deum* is chanted by them to return the play to its spiritual plane and historical distancing, after the blunt, stylistically modernised prose of the knights.

PLAYS OF THE FIRST AND SECOND WORLD WARS

First World War literature still holds a firm position of popularity and perhaps for that reason the admittedly sometimes brilliant but by no means first-rate *Journey's End* by RC Sheriff survives on A-level syllabuses. For its dramatic interest, good construction and accurate 'period' dialogue, Willis Hall's *The Long and the Short and the Tall* makes a fitting companion to Sheriff's play. The earlier play is about the strains between officers in a trench before an attack by the enemy; the later (produced 1958) presents a group of NCOs and men in a hut in the Malayan jungle, at the time of the Japanese breakthrough of the Second World War.

BECKETT (1965-89)

While the examining boards concentrate on the plays of Shaw and Eliot's *Murder in the Cathedral*, there are a considerable number of other major dramatists whose plays appear on the syllabuses. Samuel Beckett, otherwise neglected by theatregoers and readers alike, has been represented by *Waiting for Godot*, *Endgame* and *Happy Days*, plays which also are French Theatre classics, translated by the author into English. *Krapp's Last Tape*, *All That Fall*, *Embers* and others deserve equal attention.

Beckett concentrates his art most single-mindedly on the mystery of existence, the impossibility of making any rational explanation of time, birth or death, the ineffable nature of such matters, in short the essential incommunicability of much of the would-be material of art. Beckett's characters, or 'surrogates' of one character, are especially obsessed by the point or the pointlessness of death, its curiously unreachable nature; and therefore the absurdity and ennui of life: this takes on the character of a quite meaningless 'wait' for the end. One of the several intense frustrations of both character and creator is the less-than-satisfactory nature of the medium, words: these tend to be regarded with contempt as outworn, secondhand or even false counters of so-called communication: music or perhaps silence may do better; form, design and arrangements of characters or props on the stage; movements and sound effects, all tend to displace words; when used, words are often employed as elements for verbal games or for resonances beyond denotative meaning. Sometimes, as in *Play* or *Not I*, the words dominate the play, but only as pathetic droning or manic re-enactments of futile pasts. Syntax and sentence structures may be shattered, as in the long speech by the otherwise dumb Lucky (*Waiting for Godot*), which contains some satire on the language of academics. This Beckett had earlier satirised in the 'committee' sequence in *Watt*. However, the real point of the satire is, as usual in Beckett, more to do with the inanity of academic endeavour, in common with any other human enterprise. For Beckett, man is trapped in an inescapable dilemma: only God can authenticate life and death, but God, if he exists, has clearly chosen to pretend that he does not, leaving Man stuck in time and space, sometimes trying to pass the time with all sorts of foolish evasions or delusions. Some critics try to read existentialism, or the 'absurd', or even surrealism, into Beckett's work, but he eludes such labels. In such a predicament, Man may either weep or laugh; *Waiting for Godot* is described as a 'tragicomedy', and the detail, and much of the dialogue, in Beckett's plays is comic in various modes; the world view is intensely tragic. It is a case of laughing at or in spite of unhappiness, which Arsene, as he was leaving Mr Knott's service in *Watt*, said was the purest sort of laugh.

PINTER

Harold Pinter learned a good deal from Beckett, especially in the musical handling of dialogue, humorous effects such as ironic use of slapstick, and the presentation of only one or two characters in an enigmatic situation. Beckett derived his slapstick humour from the early cinema comedians: Buster Keaton, Charlie Chaplin, Laurel and Hardy and the Marx Brothers, but he was the first to adapt it to high drama. Pinter demonstrates that he can write dialogue in the peculiarly lyrical manner of Beckett:

> *Stanley* How do I know if I know them until I know their names?
> *Meg* Well … he told me, I remember.
> *Stanley* Well?
>   [*She thinks.*]
> *Meg* Gold – something.
> *Stanley* Goldsomething?
> *Meg* Yes. Gold …
> *Stanley* Yes?
> *Meg* Goldberg.
> *Stanley* Goldberg?
> *Meg* That's right. That was one of them.
> [*Stanley sits at table.*]
>   Do you know them?

The Birthday Party, 1958

Apart from this brilliant play, and the classic *The Caretaker*, Pinter's *The Homecoming* is now an established choice with A-level boards. Under the deceptive surface of absurd or virtually absurd humour, there is in Pinter's plays an undercurrent of horror, violence, menace or tenseness in relationships to the point of destructive eruption. The incompatibility of the old tramp, Davies, and the sinister Mick, in *The Caretaker*, in which normal, recognisable rascality is set against a weird malevolence, provides both the humour and the tension of this play. Similar tensions and menace are present in most of the other plays, as when Meg announces to Stanley in *The Birthday Party* the arrival of the two men who have come for him, and he first indicates to her his mental imbalance by the way he bangs the drum she has given him for a birthday present. The tension mounts in *The Dumb Waiter* as the two criminals await their orders via the dumb waiter. The eruptions, whether verbal or a stage effect, are all the more shocking because half-expected.

BOLT AND SCHAFFER

Robert Bolt's *A Man For All Seasons* is well established as one of the best modern historical dramas. It concerns Sir Thomas More's resistance of King Henry VIII on the grounds of personal conscience, and his consequent death. Another is *The Royal Hunt of the Sun* by Peter Shaffer, an epic-type drama based on the events in Spain and the Inca Empire of Peru between 1529 and 1533, the hero, of course, being Francisco Pizarro. The action turns upon the capture by Pizarro and his pathetically small force of the Inca Sun-king, Atahuallpa. The play is notable for its music, spectacle, narrative by the chorus – like Old Martin – in short for an example of 'total theatre' carried through. One scene is called The Mime of the Great Ascent, another, The Mime of the Great Massacre, and the play is full of theatrical interest and relevant action. Dramatic irony is achieved by the Narrator, who from the future, and in a state of wisdom and understanding, views his idealistic young self, as he blindly follows his 'hero' Pizarro, without fully understanding the nature of warfare or conquest.

OTHER MODERN PLAYWRIGHTS

Of John Osborne's plays, *Look Back in Anger*, *The Entertainer* and *Epitaph for George Dillon* have all appeared on A-level syllabuses. He excels in the eloquent tirade. Other notable modern playwrights include: David Mercer (*Let's Murder Vivaldi*); John Arden (*Sergeant Musgrave's Dance*); John Whiting (*A Penny For a Song*); Tom Stoppard (*Rosencrantz and Guildenstern Are Dead*); John Mortimer (*The Lunch Hour, A Shot in the Dark*); Joe Orton (*Loot, What the Butler Saw*). Orton contains many of the elements of modern theatre: black humour, outrageous wit and irreverence (the tradition of Oscar Wilde), violence and savage protest, often of a satirical nature such as that directed against policemen. He shows in his plays a firm grasp of traditional stagecraft and structure.

Many European dramatists of the first order have injected new life into twentieth- century drama, and frequently their best plays are translated and staged in this country; these include Ibsen, Chekov, Alfred Jarry – the father of Absurd drama, Wedekind, Anouilh, Brecht, Pirandello, Giradoux, Max Frisch and Eugene Ionesco, to name but a few. These playwrights have influenced the course of modern drama and some have been set in A-level exams. One may add to these the Americans and Irish, whose plays are more commonly set than the translated ones. Eugene O'Neill, the American tragedian (*The Emperor Jones, The Iceman Cometh*); Arthur Miller (*The Crucible, Death of a Salesman*), and Tennessee Williams (*The Glass Menagerie*) are all noteworthy. Of the Irish drama, you should note particularly great plays written by John Synge (*The Playboy of the Western World*), Sean O'Casey (*The Plough and the Stars, Juno and the Paycock*) and WB Yeats (*The Words upon the Window-pane, Purgatory*).

Besides the leading dramatists of the age, there is a host of lesser lights, many of whom give great pleasure and good service to the playgoing public. There are comedians, farce writers, thriller writers, tragedians, all of which could be cited in A-level answers as examples of various sorts of drama. The field is very wide and there is no need to be exclusive or narrow while the plays are there to be enjoyed in all our many theatres throughout the country.

Question bank

BEN JONSON: *Every Man in His Humour*

1 Either, (a) Discuss the comic and dramatic qualities of this extract.

Or, (b) How characteristic is this episode of the humour in the play as a whole?

> *Cob* [*Knocking*] What Tib, Tib, I say!
>
> *Tib* [*From within*] How now, what cuckold is that knocks so hard? [*She opens the door*]
>   Oh, husband, is't you? What's the news?
>
> *Cob* Nay, you have stunned me, i' faith! You ha' gi'en me a knock o' the forehead,
> 5   will stick by me! Cuckold? 'Slid, cuckold?
>
> *Tib* Away, you fool, did I know it was you, that knocked? Come, come, you may call
>   me as bad, when you list.
>
> *Cob* May I? Tib, you are a whore.
>
> *Tib* You lie in your throat, husband.

10 *Cob* How, the lie? And in my throat too? Do you long to be stabbed, ha?

Tib Why, you are no soldier, I hope?

Cob Oh, must you be stabbed by a soldier? Mass, that's true! When was Bobadill here? Your captain? That rogue, that foist, that fencing Burgullian? I'll tickle him, i' faith.

Tib Why, what's the matter? Trow!

15 *Cob* Oh, he has basted me, rarely, sumptuously! But I have it here in black and white: [*Pulls out his warrant*] for his black, and blue: shall pay him. Oh, the Justice! The honestest old brave Trojan in London! I do honour the very flea of his dog. A plague on him though, he put me once in a villainous filthy fear; marry, it vanished away, like the smoke of tobacco; but I was smoked soundly first. I thank the devil,

20 and his good angel, my guest. Well, wife, or Tib – which you will – get you in, and lock the door, I charge you, let nobody in to you; wife, no body in, to you: those are my words. Not Captain Bob himself, nor the fiend, in his likeness; you are a woman; you have flesh and blood enough in you, to be tempted; therefore, keep the door, shut, upon all comers.

25 *Tib* I warrant you, there shall nobody enter here, without my consent.

Cob Nor with your consent, sweet Tib, and so I leave you.

Tib It's more, than you know, whether you leave me so.

Cob How?

Tib Why, sweet.

30 *Cob* Tut, sweet, or sour, thou art a flower, [*Kissing her*] Keep closed thy door, I ask no more.   [*Exeunt*]

(Act 4, Scene 2)
Cambridge 1994

BEN JONSON: *Volpone*

2 Either, (a) 'The only person we feel any sympathy for is Celia.' Discuss.

Or, (b) What contribution does the foreign setting make to the play?

AEB 1994

WEBSTER: *The Duchess of Malfi*

3 Either, (a) Who is worse, the Cardinal or Ferdinand?

Or, (b) Do you find the horrors of Act 4 dramatically effective?

Cambridge 1994

JOHN FORD: *'Tis Pity She's A Whore*

4 Either, (a) 'It were more ease to stop the ocean.'
How appropriate is it to claim that the disasters of the play are inevitable?

Or, (b) 'Grimaldi is a particularly obnoxious creature.' Discuss the character and role of Grimaldi in the light of this criticism.

AEB 1994

WILLIAM CONGREVE: *The Way of The World*

5 Either, (a) 'Sir Wilfull Witwoud is not quite the country bumpkin he is at first made out to be.' Discuss the character and role of Sir Wilfull Witwoud in the play.

Or, (b) What is 'The Way of the World' as defined by this play?

AEB 1994

APHRA BEHN: *The Rover*

6 Either, (a) What do you think Aphra Behn has to say about prostitution?

Or, (b) How does Aphra Behn reveal the characters of Angellica and Willmore at their first meeting? (This is scene vii in the RSC edition, Act II sc II in the Methuen Student edition.) In what ways do you find the scene to be dramatically effective?

RICHARD SHERIDAN: *The Rivals*

Or, (c) Examine the different ways in which Sheridan creates comedy in Act IV, scene ii, the scene in Mrs Malaprop's lodgings.

Or, (d) Do you agree that it is 'love' which triumphs at the end of the play?

JOHN MARSTON: *The Malcontent*

Or, (e) How are the contrasts between Malevole and Mendoza presented in the play, and for what purposes?

Or, (f) Having studied the text carefully, what do you think would be the particular challenges and difficulties in directing the play for performance?

AEB 1994

SYNGE: *The Playboy of the Western World*

7 Either, (a) Christy Mahon has been described as growing 'in stature and in poetry' during the course of the play until, at the end, he has gained 'a new certainty of himself'. Is this how you see him? Whatever line of argument you follow, refer closely to the play in order to illustrate and support it.

Or, (b) Turn to Act 1, approximately 5 pages from the end of the Act, beginning with the stage direction [Someone knocks] CHRISTY [Clinging to Pegeen] 'Oh glory! it's late for knocking...'. (This may be found on page 59 of the Methuen edition.) Remind yourself of this section, ending with the curtain at the close of the Act. Consider the insight into character given here, the way in which the nature of the dialogue contributes to the total effect and the way in which the Act builds up to a dramatic climax.

ULEAC 1994

TENNESSEE WILLIAMS: *A Streetcar Named Desire*

8 Either, (a) 'Blanche cannot see that life has its impossibilities.' Discuss.

Or, (b) 'And so it was I entered the broken world.'
How 'broken' is the world of this play?

AEB 1994

MILLER: *Death of a Salesman*

9 Either, (a) Does *Death of a Salesman* seem to you both to judge the society it portrays and to offer any hope for its improvement?

Or, (b) Look at the conversation between Willy and Biff in Boston in Act II from 'BIFF: Why didn't you answer' to 'WILLY: But we were supposed to have dinner together' (pages 92–6 of the Penguin edition). Show how Miller presents the father-son relationship in this extract at the same time as guiding the audience's reaction to the events.

ULEAC 1994

2.5 SHAKESPEARE

INTRODUCTION

All examination boards include questions on the plays of William Shakespeare (1564–1616). Most syllabuses require candidates to study two plays, and, looking at the papers over a number of years, the favoured texts for A-Level study are: *Antony and Cleopatra, Hamlet, Henry IV pt. 2, King Lear, Macbeth, Much Ado About Nothing, The Tempest, Troilus and Cressida, Twelfth Night* and *The Winter's Tale.* Of these, the current 'chart-toppers' are *Antony and Cleopatra, King Lear* and *The Winter's Tale* (having recently displaced *Hamlet* and *Othello*) and *As You Like It* and *Love's Labours Lost* are now being favoured by a number of boards. There are variations. On two occasions the Oxford Examination Board has set *The Sonnets* on its optional paper 2 and the Cambridge Local Examination Board has featured *Coriolanus.* Recently the Northern Examinations and Assessment Board has set *King Lear, Antony and Cleopatra* and, more unusually, *Henry V, Measure for Measure,* and *Cymbeline* for study.

In this part of the book, dealing with the study of Shakespeare, we give you a little general advice, a brief outline of Shakespeare's theatre, the sources used for the stories of some of Shakespeare's plays and some general comments on Shakespeare's use of imagery. This is only the tip of the iceberg. There is much more for you to find out.

We will continue by giving practical advice on tackling a two-year course of study of a Shakespeare play and go on to discuss general points on settings, poetry, characterisation and so on, as applicable to any Shakespeare play, but with special reference to *The Winter's Tale, Othello* and *Measure for Measure.* In conclusion, there is a passage from Hamlet to show you how you should handle difficult Shakespearian language and advice on reading examination questions and writing examination answers.

Using the correct text and the correct notes

Make sure that you are studying the play in a form recommended by your examination board, i.e. that you have the correct version of the text prescribed by the recommended publisher. Read any introductory notes on Shakespeare's life, the Elizabethan theatre, the verse form Shakespeare uses, the historical background to the play, the sources of the play, the characters, and so on.

Use all the textual notes

These may be at the foot or the side of the page, or at the back of the book. They will be numbered – this is the line reference which you will find alongside the text of the play.

Do not be tempted to guess at the meaning of the Shakespearian language. Unless you are very familiar already with the study of Shakespeare's plays you ought to treat it almost like a foreign language at first and use all the 'translation aids' you can. Only when you fully understand the meaning can you appreciate the poetry of the language.

Annotate your text freely. Your teacher would probably prefer you to do this in pencil! Remember this text will be referred to again and again over the two-year period and it is for *your use and your benefit.* Do not be lazy when your teacher is explaining the meaning of words and phrases; WRITE THEM IN. Do *not* rely on 'crib notes'. They are no substitute for detailed study of the text.

SHAKESPEARE'S THEATRE

Shakespeare spent most of his working life writing plays for the Globe Theatre, which was situated on the South Bank of the Thames at Southwark. The actors and shareholders included Richard Burbage, the tragic actor; Kemp, the comic actor, and Shakespeare himself who was the resident playwright.

We know very little of the theatre itself; what we do know is conjecture as the historical documentation is practically non-existent. It is thought that it was probably shaped like a cylinder, constructed of wood and plaster, and on top of it was what looked like a squat wooden tower. Round the inner wall were three tiers of galleries which extended round the sides of the stage and these were the most expensive seats. The top gallery was covered with a roof of thatch. The platform stage was 40 feet in width and surrounded by the audience on three sides, meaning that most of the audience were exposed. On the fourth side was a room called the tiring house where the prompter sat and costumes, furniture and properties were kept here. This is where the actors made their entrances and exits between the doors, the alcove and the curtain. It is here that Polonius is stabbed by Hamlet as he hides behind the arras and here where Juliet is discovered supposedly dead in bed by her nurse. Higher still was the place where the trumpeter announced the start of a performance and on the very top was the flag which announced the beginning of a play. It depicted Hercules carrying the Globe.

The audience capacity of the theatre was large, about 2,500. The audience itself was made up of a cross-section of social classes including noblemen, tradesmen, serving men and tourists. The theatre audiences were often criticised as unruly by the Puritans, who were particularly scathing of the women in the audience. The Puritans called these women low and like prostitutes 'plying a convenient trade', but as the Puritans never went inside a theatre, these reports could only be hearsay, and there is also much contemporary literature which testifies to the audience's sobriety.

The way the theatres were constructed bore direct relation to the way the plays were performed. There was close contact between the actors and the audience as there was no curtain and the audience could touch the actors. The actor could establish personal contact with the audience and could look the audience in the eye during speeches and soliloquies, such as Mark Anthony's oration to the Romans in *Julius Caesar*. The acoustics were very good which made the dialogue easy to hear; essential when a play lasted in full between $2\,^1/_2$ and $2\,^3/_4$ hours.

PLOT IN SHAKESPEARIAN DRAMA

Shakespeare used a wide range of narrative materials for his plays. For his histories and tragedies he used Roman history, legendary British history and contemporary English and Scottish history. For his comedies he used a rich assortment of prose romances, narrative poems and plays ranging from the Roman dramatist, Plautus, to contemporary dramatists of the sixteenth century.

Shakespeare had an insatiable interest in human nature and experience and people's dilemmas and problems. His range of subject is far greater than any comparable contemporary playwright, Ben Jonson for instance. Shakespeare does not merely tell a story, he creates and discovers dramatic possibilities. He deepens the narrative, makes it more coherent and more descriptive of human behaviour. For instance, he took the story *The Moor of Venice* by Giraldi Cinthio, which was a slight, sordid tale of jealousy and revenge, and transformed it into a major tragedy, *Othello*. He transformed *Romeo and Juliet* from a light romance tragedy to a dramatic narrative. He took the famous story of the Trojan war in *Troilus and Cressida* and enriched it by his dialogue. The play never fails in the theatre, though critics cannot decide whether the play is comedy, tragedy or satire.

The tragedy *Antony and Cleopatra* is taken from Plutarch's life of Antony, but a lot of the events could not be shown on the stage because of their scale – events like the sea battle of Actium. Instead, Shakespeare develops a brilliant technique of short scenes which concentrate on behaviour rather than action.

Shakespeare's dramatic form is characterised by being larger than life. For instance, in *King Lear*, the father, Lear, loses his daughter, Cordelia; brother and sister, Sebastian and Viola, are reunited in *Twelfth Night*; Leontes, in *The Winter's Tale*, recovers his lost wife. This sense of pushing things to the extreme until the worst happens heightens the feeling of tragedy. He also invents characters who have no equivalent in the source; Enobarbus in *Antony and Cleopatra*, Queen Margaret in *Richard III*, Mercutio in *Romeo and Juliet* and Lucio in *Measure for Measure*. These extra characters make significant contributions to the plays. Enobarbus is a spokesman for scepticism, irreverence and humour; qualities which enlist audience participation. He creates a sense of reality in the play. In much the same way, Lucio contributes to the plot of *Measure for Measure* and Thersites to the plot of *Troilus and Cressida*.

Shakespeare often combines more than one story or plot into his plays, particularly his comedies. In *Twelfth Night* he combines the story of the girl who adopts male disguise (Viola) with the Malvolio story. Shakespeare felt that he needed two actions that were not incongruous, so the two plots are linked in various ways. Viola is involved in a duel with Sir Andrew Aguecheek; Malvolio acts as a rival to Orsino for Olivia's hand; Feste, the jester, wanders from one household to the other. Shakespeare's preference for two or more stories gives the plays much of their fascination as the intrigues develop.

IMAGERY IN SHAKESPEARIAN DRAMA

To study Shakespeare's imagery was an accepted critical approach in the first half of the twentieth century. Previous to this there had been very little study of imagery which was surprising, as Shakespeare, of all writers, is much given to using imagery. The revival of interest in the imagery of Shakespeare's plays is simultaneous with the interest in the Metaphysical poets and is one way, but not the only way, of analysing his works.

An **image** should always help the reader to understand the writer's work better, by describing something in terms of something else (see Glossary). This can take the form of a **metaphor** or a **simile**. A writer always uses imagery to achieve vividness. For example, in *Richard III*, when Hastings is proclaimed a traitor and condemned to immediate death, Shakespeare uses the simile of a sailor about to topple into the sea to convey his feelings of dizziness and vertigo:

> (*Hastings*) lives like a drunken sailor on a mast
> Ready with every nod to tumble down
> into the fatal bowels of the deep.

The image of falling here suggests something essential about Hastings's feelings. It is not always easy to decide what an image is doing. In this case it appeals to our visual sense and conveys Hastings's feelings with precision and speed.

Images, therefore, are word pictures which are essentially visual. In *Macbeth*, many of the speeches of the main characters are densely metaphorical. Lady Macbeth, early on in the play at the murder of Duncan, delivers a speech full of imagery:

> Come, thick night,
> And pall thee in the dullest smoke of hell
> That my keen knife see not the wound it make
> Nor heaven peep through the blanket of the dark
> To cry, "Hold" "Hold".

This speech is full of metaphors, 'pall thee in the dullest smoke of hell', 'my keen knife see not the wound it makes', 'nor heaven peep through the blanket of the dark'. None of these metaphors requires any great effort on our part to picture the processes involved; the metaphors are bold enough. When Macbeth describes the murder of Duncan he talks of:

> his gashed stabs looked like a breach in nature
> For ruin's wasteful entrance.

This metaphor evokes the destruction of the entire universe and allows chaos and ruin to rush in and upset the natural order of nature. This violent imagery stimulates us and startles us into thought. It makes us entertain possibilities too remote from our experience and gives the dramatist a degree of control over the feelings of his audience.

Paradox is used in *Measure for Measure*, in which Claudio is taken to prison for having unlawful sexual intercourse with an unmarried girl. When Lucio asks why he is in chains, he replies:

> From too much liberty, my Lucio, liberty.

He has been too free, so now he has lost his freedom.

Troilus and Cressida contains a whole stream of metaphors. For example, in his speech on time, Ulysses tries to describe the way in which time is only interested in present achievements and tries to forget what human beings have achieved:

> For time is like a fashionable host
> That slightly shakes his parting guest by the hand
> And with his arms outstretched as he would fly
> Grasps in the comer: welcome ever smiles
> And farewell goes out sighing.

Imagery criticism is not as important now in literary criticism as it used to be. It is just one of the aspects of the larger study of Shakespeare's language and style.

STUDYING A SHAKESPEARE PLAY OVER TWO YEARS

First year

Experience the play as a whole before you begin the study to see *how* Shakespeare achieved his effects. The best way, of course, is to see a good production or, failing this, a film or television video. Schools and colleges often have video facilities, so that a tape of a play can be used over and over again. It can also be switched off and discussed, and thus is a most versatile visual aid. A record or tape can be used in a similar way, or you can stage a play-reading with fellow students, but one does miss the visual stimulus. In all of these ways, dramatic experience will precede dramatic analysis.

Look at the overall structure of the play and the dramatic movements within the play; for instance, the importance of the opening scene, the dramatic excitement, the introduction of the main issues and protagonists, the early impressions of character (remembering that characters develop during the course of the play), the dramatic climaxes and how Shakespeare handles build-ups and subsequent anti-climaxes. Such structure can sometimes be rendered in the form of a chart or graph summarising the narrative sequence of the play and the peaks of the action.

Some knowledge of other Shakepeare plays of a similar kind is useful in year one of study. This can be achieved by play-reading in class or video sessions. Similar plays could be linked together – for instance *Macbeth* with *Othello* or *The Tempest* with *The Winter's Tale*.

Then begin to study the play, noticing some of the topics already mentioned, paying particular attention to how things happen as well as to what happens. Always use the text to illustrate your points. A series of notes with cross references to Act, Scene and line number are very useful here. Short, relevant quotations are better than long, memorised speeches which show nothing except that they have been memorised.

Second year and exam revision

Re-work and re-read your notes and essays, and re-read the play. *Keep asking yourself questions.* For instance, if you are studying *Othello*, you may ask why is Cassio in the play? Why does Shakespeare give him the kind of character he does? Why does Desdemona go to such lengths to help him?

> He hath a daily beauty in his life
> that makes me ugly.

Is this an important comment by Iago about Cassio? What does it tell us about both men? Always go back to the text to answer any of these questions.

Use of critics

Use critics who provide useful background information, but be careful of the way-out opinion designed mainly to show how clever the critic is and to find something new (however outrageous). It is useful to know such criticism exists, but it is dangerous to follow it slavishly and to reproduce it as if it were your own. You may well have only half understood a complicated or tortuous argument.

Go back to central issues, such as the two-play structure of *The Winter's Tale*, and ensure that you are thinking clearly about them and that you have appropriate textual references to support your views. Establish your own key words as memory links but, above all, know the play and *do not* try to devise an all-purpose answer suitable for all questions. This leads to the slightly off-focus answer that creates so many problems for examiners. *If you know the play well and understand the basic issues, there is nothing that an examiner can ask that you will be unable to answer.*

THE STUDY OF *OTHELLO* AND *THE WINTER'S TALE*

(NB These are general points, applicable to any plays.)

Detailed study implies close study, but do not get so involved in textual detail that you lose your grasp on the play as a whole. Always see any speech in the context of the play. Useful divisions for study (there may be others) are:

- **Language** – understand the difficulties. Always make sure that you know the basic meaning, using footnotes from the text. Some boards test this knowledge by the use of italicised phrases in extracts.

- **Poetry** – understand the function of dramatic verse and the nature of the poetry Shakespeare uses. For instance, he uses poetry to build up character and the facets of character in *Othello*. In *The Winter's Tale* we see the tortured, broken syntax of the jealousy-ridden Leontes and the different rhythms and imagery in Act IV of the same play. Therefore you need to consider the function of poetry in the plays. Does it interfere with the action in such plays as *Richard II* or *Romeo and Juliet*, or does it enhance it?

- **Dramatic structure** – the limitations and opportunities of drama imposing their own restrictions. You should note the particular features of structure for individual plays; for instance the double time scheme and dramatic compression of *Othello*, the two-part structure of *The Winter's Tale* and the usefulness of comparing *The Winter's Tale* with *The Tempest* where the dramatist faces similar problems, but solves them in different ways.

- **Character** – character always relates to dramatic function and importance. The 'psychological character study' can be more hindrance than help to a candidate. A play is not a psychological novel, though many candidates approach it as if it were. Thus Leontes's immediate jealousy is a dramatic necessity in *The Winter's Tale* and has to be dramatically convincing. The rapidity of Othello's jealousy has to be dramatically as well as psychologically prepared for. Certain traits indicated in Othello's character, position, status and situation make it psychologically credible, but it has to be rapid because of dramatic necessity.

- **Relationship of character to plot** – this is linked with the section on character but this relationship is of particular importance with such a character as Iago, who begins by controlling the plot, but later becomes controlled by it, in that events move away from him, and also with reference to the character of Cassio. Candidates should always consider the dramatic importance of any character and his role in the play. For instance, why bring Autolycus into *The Winter's Tale*?

- **How the dramatist creates character** – the word 'how' is often ignored in A-level study.

  The dramatist creates characters by the following means:
  1. the style in which they speak;
  2. how they respond to events;
  3. if and how they initiate action;
  4. what others say about them (bearing in mind the nature and circumstances of those who speak);

  and – importantly – *the relationship between characters* – what such relationships contribute dramatically and what they tell us about each character, e.g. Iago and Emilia, Cassio and Desdemona, Iago and Roderigo as well as the obvious Othello/Desdemona, Iago/Othello relationships, parents/children, Hermione/Paulina and Florizel/Perdita relationships.

  Study the permutations of these relationships within a play. The characters will show different aspects in different situations and in different company. But this will always be for a common dramatic purpose.

- **Theme** – A play will be *about* something – but be careful not to over-simplify and force the play into a neat box, e.g. *Othello* – jealousy theme, *Macbeth* – ambition, *Hamlet* – delay, *The Winter's Tale* – forgiveness. The plays, of course, contain such themes, but they are more than this. Look for unifying themes, dramatically handled in a play but always go back to the text to see how these are worked out in dramatic terms – the interplay of character with character and character with event.

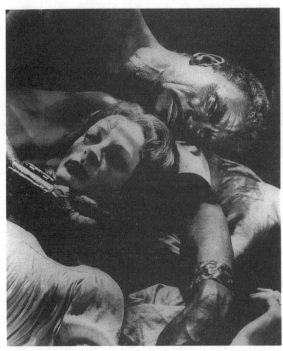

Othello and Desdemona

STUDY NOTES ON *MEASURE FOR MEASURE*

Measure For Measure

General points It is perhaps a play of which much can be taken in at a first reading, though it is hardly necessary to say that it cannot be fully understood without an awareness from the outset of its moral and religious assumptions. Further study as the exam approaches should be directed to deepening this awareness and noting how these assumptions are illustrated in the play.

Position in the canon of Shakespeare's works It was written in 1604 not long after *Hamlet*, with whose moral and religious background it has affinities. Therefore, in the middle of the tragic period, it belongs with the other 'problem' plays. Why are they so called? Not just because they pose ethical problems, though they certainly do, but also because it is difficult to fit them into any neat category. *Measure For Measure* may be considered a 'comedy' in the sense that, after intrigue and confusion all is cleared up and ends with wedding bells (like *All's Well That Ends Well*, though not *Troilus and Cressida*). But the road to the happy ending is not (as in, say *Twelfth Night*) necessarily a particularly merry one. The play is pervaded by **satire** and cynicism. Its view of life, while allowing that there is good in human nature, is often pessimistic, approaching **tragic**, but without the elevation of feeling and tone that redeems the tragedies from sourness.

Structure The low-life scenes have hardly any bearing on the main action and exist chiefly to illustrate the depravity of Vienna and the disregard for law, as well as providing something for the groundlings to guffaw at. Lucio serves as a 'link' character with the weightier matter. Once the sequence of events is firmly grasped, it will be seen that the action develops in a straightforward 'linear' fashion with successive crises clearly identified. Note how tension is maintained by the unexpected twist given to events by Angelo ordering Claudio's immediate execution. Also in Act V we know Angelo is going to be unmasked. He repeatedly avoids exposure; we wonder just how and when it will come.

Atmosphere and ideology The play's institutions and morality are nominally Catholic – this may be largely for dramatic convenience as nunneries and friar's hoods are useful for practical purposes. Claudio's apparent belief in the doctrine of Purgatory adds force to his fear of death. On the other hand, the acceptability of the bed-trick (also used in *All's Well That Ends Well*) to a supposedly severe moralist and near nun-like Isabella has been questioned. Death for fornication smacks more of Calvin's Geneva than any Catholic state and the Duke's impersonation of a friar, purporting to confess and give absolution, is surely a mortal sin. In all this, Shakespeare probably reflects the state of mind of many contemporaries who had a considerable hangover of ideas from pre-Reformation times.

The play is constructed around sexual behaviour and motives which links it with *Hamlet*, *Othello* and *Lear*, especially in its concentration on the sleazier physical aspects of life. There is an obsession with female virginity which may seem strange to many young people today. The brothel-life of *Measure For Measure* and the jokes about venereal diseases are quite brutal. The prison scenes are also very typical of Shakespeare's age in the mixture of brutality with easy-going informality.

Characterisation presents difficulties, especially with the Duke and Isabella. The Duke, despite individual touches such as a dislike of popularity which he shared with James I, is more of a symbol than an individual. What looks like his personal busy-bodying must be related to the preoccupation with the position and duties of a ruler. In a hierarchical society, thought of as reflecting universal order, the ruler is the counterpart of God; his highest duty is to incarnate and dispense justice. The Duke puts himself into disguise so that, like God, he may see into men's hearts and so do perfect justice, tempered with mercy, at the end. It looks like an almost malicious cat-and-mouse game; spinning out Claudio's and Isabella's distress and letting Angelo think he is going to get away with his misdeeds, may be compared with the mysterious ways of God to man. Heaven punishes the bad and proves the best. But the suggestion that the Duke is almost a representation of God must not be pressed too far; after all, if he didn't behave as he does there would be no play.

Isabella is an **ambiguous** character. Apart from her connivance in the bed-trick already mentioned, 'the lady doth protest her chastity too much'. Note how readily she hurries off to virtuous sheets at the end; we hear no more of her vocation to a nunnery.

Angelo is in many ways more credible, as a picture of the man who has but slenderly known himself, having never before been tempted. He incarnates the old theme of the punishment of 'hubris' without becoming in any way a lay figure and enables Shakespeare to **satirise** the abuse of power.

The other main characters – Lucio, Claudio, Pompey – are more 'natural', though Lucio is a mass of contradictions. He is cynical and debauched, a liar and a slanderer who shops his associates for no apparent reason, seems genuinely fond of Claudio and does what he can to help him.

The play as Art rather than Nature Even this brief run-through of the characters shows that they are not very easy to grasp. To a large extent 'natural' behaviour is subordinated to the demand of the **fable**. The same point can be made about many of the situations and events. Isabella is just about to take the veil when she is recalled to contend with the Flesh and the Devil. Her calling as a nun seems rather a patent device to heighten the interest of her situation. The parallels between the Claudio/Juliet and Angelo/Mariana relationships seem a remarkably happy coincidence (though the impediment to each marriage is one typical of the age – a matter of dowry). Angelo heaps damnation on himself from the very beginning – as soon as he utters

> When I, that censure him, do so offend
> Let mine own judgement pattern out my death
> and nothing come in partial

We sense the Infernal Machine creaking into action (Act II, Sc1); the bed-trick substitution seems improbable even if all cats are grey in the dark; the convenient death of Ragozine and his resemblance to Claudio are almost perfunctory solutions to the problem of avoiding violent death in a comedy. *But* we are not meant to apply the test of 'could it all really have happened?' Take account of these improbabilities, by all means, but recognise that the play is a kind of fable in which they are to be accepted to heighten dramatic impact and underline moral issues.

Language As always, the power of Shakespeare's language carries us along and suspends our disbelief. The flexible and superbly articulated style of the two great debates between Angelo and Isabella, touching deep matters, and Angelo's self-probing soliloquies, with their blend of passion and reasoning, take us into the world of the great tragedies. On the other hand, apart from Lucio's witty sallies in the 'smart young man' vein, the prose is rather undistinguished. The comic malapropisms of Elbow and the vulgar loquacity of Pompey (who is given his name so that jokes may be made about it) are unambitious popular stuff. Much of the prose is devoted to giving practical information, e.g. for the bed-trick and the description of Angelo.

ANALYSIS AND COMMENTARY

The following passage should help you analyse the difficult language of Shakespeare's plays. Although there is probably far more detail here than you would need in an examination answer, if you absorb most of the information you will give yourself a good chance of giving the examiner what he is looking for.

Hamlet, **Act I, Sc. IV, lines 23–38** (Hamlet's father, the King of Denmark, has recently died and been succeeded by his brother Claudius, who has married the widowed Queen, Hamlet's mother. Much grieved by these events, Hamlet has been further distressed to learn that his father's ghost has appeared to the sentries on the ramparts of the castle of Elsinore.)

```
 1    So, oft it chances in particular men,
      That, for some vicious mole of nature in them,
      As, in their birth, – wherein they are not guilty,
      Since nature cannot choose his origin, –
 5    By the o'ergrowth of some complexion,
      Oft breaking down the pales and forts of reason,
      Or by some habit that too much o'er-leavens
      The form of plausive manners; that these men,
      Carrying, I say, the stamp of one defect,
10    Being nature's livery, or fortune's star,
      Their virtues else, be they as pure as grace,
      As infinite as man may undergo,
      Shall in the general censure take corruption
      From that particular fault: the dram of evil
15    Doth all the noble substance of a doubt,
      To his own scandal.
```

Context It is night. Hamlet is keeping watch with the soldiers to see if the ghost will appear again. There has just been a burst of noisy revelry from the castle hall where the King 'drains his draughts of Rhenish down'. Hamlet remarks to his friend Horatio that this Danish delight in drinking is a fault which tarnishes the country's reputation, and goes on to speak the lines above. Immediately afterwards, the ghost appears.

Meaning and expression The whole passage is an extended comparison in which the speaker draws a parallel between the consequences of a defect in national character and of one in individuals ('particular men'). The language makes considerable use of **metaphor**. The weakness, of whatever kind, is compared with a physical blemish (a 'mole'), and the first example we are given is illegitimacy, for which, as Hamlet charitably observes, the bastard child is not responsible - he 'cannot choose his origin'. (Note here our ancestors' view of bastardy as an indelible taint, very possibly fitting one to play a villain's part – think of Edmund in *King Lear*, or Don John in *Much Ado About Nothing*.) Next comes disturbance of the mind. Here the individual's sanity is compared with a beseiged garrison protected by palisades ('pales') and fortifications set up by reason, but battered down by a combination of physical and temperamental factors ('complexion') grown too strong to resist. Lastly comes outward eccentricity, working too powerfully ('o'er-leavens' – like too much yeast producing excessive fermentation) on a normally pleasing ('plausive') manner and behaviour. Here we can see reflected the preoccupation of Shakespeare's age, especially in the drama, with 'humour', i.e. extreme oddity of dress, behaviour, and ideas arising from an obsessive ruling passion. Any of these defects is stamped on a man as an impression is stamped on a coin; it is like a badge ('livery') bestowed on him by nature as noblemen gave badges to be worn by their servants, or like a star which, according to astrology, controls his life as fate ('fortune') decrees.

We find in these lines a number of words still used in modern English, but with a change of meaning, e.g. 'complexion'. Another example not yet mentioned is 'censure', in line 13, which means, not 'blame', as it always does today, but simply 'judgment' or 'opinion'.

If you have paid some attention – as you should – to what is called 'textual criticism', you will know that lines 14–15 present editors with considerable difficulty. Some have chosen to follow the version of

> the dram of eale
> Doth all the noble substance of a doubt,

which seems meaningless. 'Eale' is probably a misprint. The version we have printed makes better sense: 'the small drop of evil often quenches ('douts') a man's noble qualities.'

(**Note** Examining boards generally announce which edition of Shakespeare, and sometimes of other older writers, they will use for setting passage-based questions. You should check that your edition is the same as your board's, or that you can refer to the nominated edition when textual problems arise.)

The whole of this passage down to 'particular fault' (line 13) is one long sentence. It is not incoherent, but Hamlet does seem to feel the need to remind himself of what he is talking about in

> … that these men,
> Carrying, I say, the stamp… (lines 8–9)

This slight tendency to ramble and lose one's thread contrasts with, and is possibly restrained by the comparative strictness of the verse. Differing in this respect from Shakespeare's later plays, the lines are fairly regular, although many have an extra syllable which gives variety to the **metre**, and most of them are **end-stopped**.

Character Though Hamlet begins the speech from which these lines are taken by addressing Horatio, it could be argued that in the part of it quoted he is really talking to himself, meditating on an aspect of human life. As we learn elsewhere, though some thirty years old, he has until very lately been a student at the University of Wittenberg, and he exhibits here some of the features of a certain kind of scholarly mind – systematic up to a point, inclined to digression and elaboration, but never quite losing his thread. If we think of him as continuing to speak to Horatio throughout, then indeed his words have a good deal of the tone we might expect in a teacher or a lecturer.

Importance to the plot The passage does not contribute to the development of the action. Events stand still while we are offered comment and reflection.

Stage effect, atmosphere The suspension of action certainly does not mean that interest is lost. On the contrary, if the full context of the speech is called to mind, or if, better still, we are seeing the play in performance, we experience a feeling of uneasy suspense. There is a contrast between the King's noisy revelry in the lighted hall and the silence, cold, and darkness of the ramparts of Elsinore. Among the little group of soldiers, Hamlet is already an isolated, preoccupied figure. We are instinctively prepared for something strange to happen at any moment – as indeed it does ('Look, my lord, it comes') – to interrupt his musings.

In a modern production in an indoor theatre we would expect much use to be made of lighting to help create the eerie midnight atmosphere. In Shakespeare's theatre, of course, the performance would take place in daylight, but there would be plenty of sound effects – kettledrums and trumpets are specifically called for a little earlier – and the actors in this scene would be in the gallery or upper stage.

Themes In this respect the importance of the passage is considerable. It is often cited to support the view that a tragic hero is a man with great qualities destroyed by a fatal flaw. Hamlet, it is argued, is really thinking of himself, and already conscious of that weakness he repeatedly accuses himself of throughout the play – excessive introspection, reluctance to act, 'thinking too precisely on the event', all of which seems to him to carry with it the taint of cowardice. Whether his self-accusation is justified, whether the 'fatal flaw' theory of tragic character is sound, are matters for discussion.

The lines also show beyond question an acceptance of the influence of factors they cannot control upon men's lives, an awareness of the way character and fate work hand in hand, which is felt in *Hamlet* as in all great tragedy.

Finally, in lines 5–8 we can see foreshadowed two important elements in the later course of the play: Hamlet's fears for his own sanity, and his assumption of an 'antic disposition' which disguises his normally 'plausive manners'.

COMMON ERRORS TO BE AVOIDED IN ANSWERING SHAKESPEARE QUESTIONS

Context-type questions

• Candidates spend much too long placing passages in context, often virtually telling the whole story of what has gone before, while still omitting points relevant to the passage.

- Asked to comment on language and style, too many take refuge in paraphrase. Others seem to believe that identification is enough and reel off lists of metaphors without explanation of meaning or suggestions about effect.
- There is too much use of technical terms – caesura, onomatopoeia and so on – usually without understanding.
- Many believe that punctuation in itself has some kind of magical power – to quote from a recent report, 'Punctuation is a mere indicator of *syntax*. Lots of commas do not show emotion, but disturbed syntax and short phrases marked off by commas *can* do in certain cases.'

How to use quotation in drama essays

- Always integrate quotation into the text you are writing.
- Don't destroy the syntax of your sentence.
- Avoid quoting large chunks pointlessly or quoting verse as if it was prose, with no attention to where one line ends and one begins.
- Always distinguish verse from prose, by ear and typographically.
- Don't mistake *Othello* (the play) for Othello the character – this goes for *King Lear*, *Julius Caesar* and many other Shakespeare plays – and other plays, poems and novels!
- Bear in mind this extract from a recent examiners' report: 'Candidates waste their energies when the page becomes a series of verse passage punctuated by the odd line of literally pointless prose. A line or two, or a phrase, often from the second soldier rather than from the set speech of a major character, can be (and in the best scripts is) far more valuable. Quotations easily become clichés, and candidates should be advised firmly and clearly that the examination is *not* a test of mechanical memorisation. Clear allusion is often as effective as quotation in providing argued proof, unless linguistic or poetic matters are involved. Then, indeed, quotation is obligatory, and must be accurate if it is to have any value.'

Essay questions

- Here the major fault is the belief that every question can be answered by lengthy narrative. Candidates do not address themselves closely enough to the requirements of the question and are weak in constructing logically argued answers.
- Prepared answers rarely fit the questions. Genuine personal response is what the examiner is looking for.
- In general, candidates lack understanding of critical terms. 'Plot' is generally taken to mean no more than 'story', 'action' and 'drama' are too often equated with sensational events.
- Introductions to answers are often excessively long, and conclusions are pointlessly repetitive.

CHOOSING AND READING EXAMINATION QUESTIONS ON SHAKESPEARE

It is useful to look at the ways in which candidates in English examinations choose examination questions and how they read them when they have chosen them.

We will begin with the choice. The results of a survey over a number of years have demonstrated that, given the choice of two questions on a text, most candidates, in the approximate proportion of 60/40 will choose the first, and, given the choice between a long question and a short question, most candidates, in the approximate proportion of 70/30, will choose the short question. If, therefore, there is a short first question, and a long alternative. it does not take a computer to work out the odds. The reason for this would seem to be that, for many candidates, if the first question seems not impossible (or even, at first sight, easy) then many candidates do not go on to read the alternative at all, even though in retrospect they may come to see that it was even more to their liking. Long questions seem to put some students off by their mere appearance on the page, although, by their very nature, they often give the candidate important and useful information and are therefore, in that sense, 'easier' than shorter, more open-ended questions of the 'is *King Lear* a tragedy?' variety.

Choice is given by examiners in order to try to give opportunities of as wide a range of interest and ability as possible. Examiners are trying to create opportunities to reward the hardworking, possibly rather limited candidate as well as the perceptive, talented individual who might even make something of the daunting *King Lear* question. Many of the more limited candidates ignore questions that would be very suitable for them, possibly for the reasons already given, and embark on more perilous seas. All A-level Shakespeare questions demand some discussion and analysis and not merely 're-telling the story' but some questions, by their very nature, demand a more discursive approach than others. It will repay students, therefore, to decide what kind of questions they are more competent to deal with and then to spend a little time in making their choice.

Once the choice has been made, of course, the great problem, familiar to all teachers of English, is irrelevance. The reasons are, no doubt, complex, but we are convinced that one major reason is that the questions are read as words and not as sentences. If we may explain this a little further: in the very understandable moment of nervous panic when a candidate first sees the examination paper, he or she is likely to be immensely reassured by two things – firstly, that the books studied are those appearing on the paper and their English teacher has not misread the syllabus and, secondly, that the characters' names are familiar. It is at this stage that mistakes occur. Seeing the name 'Ophelia' in the question, the candidate jumps to the conclusion that a character-sketch of Ophelia is required and promptly supplies one, whereas the question might have read 'Discuss the view that not Ophelia but Gertrude is the real victim in Hamlet'. This is an extreme example (and an appalling question) but it will serve as an illustration. If the candidate reads the question as a sentence and notes its sense and progression, there is a fair chance that he or she will answer it. It is also useful to remind the examiner from time to time that the question is being dealt with – e.g. 'having considered X we now turn to Y' – provided that this technique is not carried to absurd lengths.

The most depressing thing in examining Shakespeare is seeing young people misapplying knowledge that they have acquired by conscientious application and hard work over two years. No examiner should ever set out to 'fail' anyone; the effort should always be to mark positively and to reward knowledge, perception and understanding wherever it appears. Unfortunately, many candidates make it difficult for themselves and for examiners by not writing on the subject, and a few extra minutes spent over the choice of question and then a careful reading of exactly what is being asked, can help to ensure that the student's hard work and that of the English staff over the two years of the course is not thrown away at the first fence.

Illustrative question and answer

1 Discuss the extract below, concentrating on
    (i)   revelation of Isabella's character;
    (ii)   Claudio's developing response to the dilemma;
    (iii) how language and style reflect the dramatic tension

Isabella Dost thou think, Claudio,
    If I would yield him my virginity
    Thou mightst be freed?
Claudio O heavens, it cannot be!
Isabella Yes, he would give't thee, from this rank offence,
    So to offend him still. This night's the time
    That I should do what I abhor to name,
    Or else thou diest tomorrow.
Claudio Thou shalt not do't.
Isabella O, were it but my life,
    I'd throw it down for your deliverance
    As frankly as a pin.
Claudio Thanks, dear Isabel.
Isabella Be ready, Claudio, for your death tomorrow.
Claudio Yes. Has he affections in him
    That thus can make him bite the law by the nose
    When he would force it? Sure it is not sin,
    Or of the deadly seven it is the least.

Isabella Which is the least?

Claudio If it were damnable, he being so wise,
　　Why would he for the momentary trick
　　Be perdurably fined? O Isabel –

Isabella What says my brother?

Claudio Death is a fearful thing.

Isabella And shaméd life a hateful.

Claudio Ay, but to die, and go we know not where,
　　To line in cold obstruction, and to rot,
　　This sensible warm motion to become
　　A kneaded clod; and the delighted spirit
　　To bathe in fiery floods or to reside
　　In thrilling region of thick-ribbéd ice,
　　To be imprisoned in the viewless winds
　　And blown with restless violence round about
　　The pendent world, or to be worse than worst
　　Of those that lawless and incertain thought
　　Imagine howling – 'tis too horrible!
　　The weariest and most loathéd worldly life
　　That age, ache, penury, and imprisonment
　　Can lay on nature is a paradise
　　To what we fear of death.

Isabella Alas, alas!

Claudio Sweet sister, let me live.
　　What sin you do to save a brother's life,
　　Nature dispenses with the deed so far
　　That it becomes a virtue.

Isabella O you beast!
　　O faithless coward, O dishonest wretch!
　　Wilt thou be made a man out of my vice?
　　Is't not a kind of incest to take life
　　From thine own sister's shame? What should I think?
　　Heaven shield my mother played my father fair,
　　For such a warpéd slip of wilderness
　　Ne'er issued from his blood. Take my defiance,
　　Die, perish! Might but my bending down
　　Reprieve thee from thy fate, it should proceed.
　　I'll pray a thousand prayers for thy death,
　　No word to save thee.

Claudio Nay, hear me, Isabel –

Isabella O fie, fie, fie!
　　Thy sin's not accidental, but a trade.
　　Mercy to thee would prove itself a bawd,
　　'Tis best that thou diest quickly.

Claudio O hear me, Isabella –　　　　　　　　*Enter Duke as a Friar*

Specimen answer

(i) The extract begins with Isabella finally telling Claudio the conditions for his release. Her cruelness prior to this in letting her brother believe that he might merely incur life imprisonment is important in establishing the mood of the audience. Isabella has not spoken plainly, and indeed displayed cruelty in that she did not recognise how her actions would be received by a man condemned to death. This is an important facet of her personality in the extract. Isabella displays a certain righteousness that the only possible way forward is through the course of action she suggests. Her response to Claudio's 'Death is a fearful thing' is 'And shaméd life a hateful' and this reveals what would appear to be a selfishness in her cold refusal to bend even slightly from her course. 'Fearful' shows a humanity in Claudio that Isabella's response does not match. This is a theme running through the extract. Isabella thinks she is right, that no other dilemma that is being faced could equal what she is feeling. By stating:

'O, were it but my life,
I'd throw it down for your deliverance'

Isabella is recognising the fact that death is easier than the loss of chastity and therein lies the tacit assumption that Claudio will also feel this way.

Isabella's reaction to Claudio's changing responses actually seems to make her more human, and not enforce her righteous image.

'...O you beast!
O faithless coward, O dishonest wretch!'

is the hysterical reaction of someone not getting their own way, and this begins to make Isabella's reactions actually appear natural.

However, the nature of her response, the reason behind it, shows again her total belief in her cause. She reacts heavily against Claudio, even to the point of suggesting:

'Is't not a kind of incest to take life
From thine own sister's shame'

because he has challenged what she perceived as the natural way forward. Isabella does not accept a viewpoint different from her own. The strength of language she uses, for example, 'Die, perish!' illustrates the hysteria she feels at the suggestion of challenge to her chastity. This illustrates an innocence, almost naïvety about Isabella. Her reaction to a point of view suggesting a different course than what she wants shows that Claudio's viewpoint was totally unexpected, and that, naively, she expected him not to want to take a way out that would enable him to live. She does not mean it when she renounces the fact that they shared the same father – 'Heaven shield my mother played my father fair' but it is the immediate reaction of one receiving a totally unexpected shock.

(ii) Claudio's first response is that of a martyr. He tells Isabella 'Thou shalt not do't', as this is the way he feels he should behave. For example, his previous meeting with the friar displayed the same emotion. During their dialogue he responded positively to the Friar's message of welcoming death, and indeed he states that he will 'hug it [death] as my bride.' This is the first response of someone not thinking through the implications. Claudio did not expect a reprieve and so the only course of action open was to be reconciled to death. It is this reaction that governs his initial response to Isabella. Of course she should not surrender her chastity to save his life.

However, Isabella makes him realise the punishment to which he has agreed. In l.14 she tells Claudio to 'Be ready, Claudio, for your death tomorrow' and this must concentrate his mind on the fact that he is to die. Claudio's response is a very human reaction. He does not want to die, and as he thinks about the alternative he realises that there is actually a way of cheating death. His statement that if Angelo is prepared to sin, then it must be the 'least' of sins, is one of a desperate man clutching at life. He follows this with 'Death is a fearful thing' and by this recognises the truth which he has been fighting against. Claudio is scared, and does not want to die. His speech of l.26–40 illustrates his feeling which, since his imprisonment, he has been attempting to suppress. Claudio feels that any form of life is better than '...what we fear of death' and it is this that prompts his changing response.

Indeed, as Claudio realises what he wants to argue, his language becomes more impassioned and eloquent. His life literally depends on being able to convince Isabella to sleep with Angelo and it is because of this that he implores Isabella, 'Sweet sister, let me live.'

(iii) Isabella begins the extract occupying what she feels to be the high moral ground, and this is illustrated by her use of rhetoric – 'Dost thou think, Claudio...'. Claudio's response is significant in its shortness. He gives one-line answers to the explanation by Isabella of what Angelo has proposed. This is because Claudio's response is governed by a sense of duty of how he feels he should react. He injects no passion because deep in his heart he does not believe his own response. However, as the realisation of the proposal becomes apparent, Claudio's speech becomes more eloquent and impassioned. His answers change from being short, to himself posing questions to Isabella in long, persuasive verse. His life literally depends on Isabella and therefore his art of persuasion must be great.

The rise in Claudio's art of language is marched by a deterioration in Isabella's. Her high moral position has been challenged, and she begins to crumble. Her response to his impassioned plea shows a degeneration into hysteria. Isabella was unprepared to face a plea from Claudio, and she cannot take the strain of being asked to change her moral ground. This is illustrated by her use of overblown argument:

'Is't not a kind of incest to take life
From thine own sister's shame?'

This is not literal, can't possibly be answered as such, but Claudio has penetrated her moral armour and her only response can be this. She is unable to listen to the arguments that Claudio puts to her in persuasive language, for example she interrupts his 'Nay, hear me, Isabel' because this would challenge the security she feels by the possession of her principles.

The dialogue has to be interrupted by a third character because of the impasse that they have arrived at. Isabella's refusal means Claudio must die, but for true self-learning to be enacted, this cannot be allowed. Therefore the Duke, disguised as the Friar, provides the third party which will enable the problems to be solved.

Question bank: context questions

1 Choose one of the following passages and:
   (i) State briefly where your chosen passage occurs in the action of the play.
   (ii) Write a detailed commentary on the extract. Remember that your discussion should concentrate on such matters as content, including the characterisation, and style. You should not simply retell the story.

KING LEAR: Passage one

Regan How dost, my lord?
Gloucester O! madam, my old heart is crack'd, it's crack'd.
Regan What! did my father's godson seek your life?
  He whom my father nam'd? your Edgar?
5 *Gloucester* O! Lady, Lady, shame would have it hid.
Regan Was he not companion with the riotous knights
  That tended upon my father?
Gloucester I know not, madam; 'tis too bad, too bad.
Edmund Yes, madam, he was of that consort.
10 *Regan* No marvel then though he were ill affected;
  'Tis they have put him on the old man's death,
  To have the expense and waste of his revenues.
  I have this present evening from my sister
  Been well-inform'd of them, and with such cautions
15   That if they come to sojourn at my house,
  I'll not be there.
Cornwall Nor I, assure thee, Regan.
  Edmund, I hear that you have shown your father
  A child-like office.
Edmund 'Twas my duty, sir.
Gloucester He did bewray his practice; and receiv'd
20   This hurt you see, striving to apprehend him.
Cornwall Is he pursu'd?
Gloucester Ay, my good lord.
Cornwall If he be taken he shall never more
  Be fear'd of doing harm; make your own purpose,
  How in my strength you please. For you, Edmund,
25   Whose virtue and obedience doth this instant
  So much commend itself, you shall be ours:

KING LEAR: Passage two

1 *Lear* Poor naked wretches, wheresoe'er you are,
  That bide the pelting of this pitiless storm,
  How shall your houseless heads and unfed sides,
  Your loop'd and window'd raggedness, defend you
5   From seasons such as these? O! I have ta'en

Too little care of this. Take physic, pomp;
Expose thyself to feel what wretches feel,
That thou mayst shake the superflux to them,
And show the heavens more just.

10 *Edgar* [*Within.*] Fathom and half, fathom and half! Poor Tom!
[*The Fool runs out from the hovel*]

Fool Come not in here, Nuncle; here's a spirit.
Help me! help me!

Kent: Give me thy hand. Who's there?

Fool: A spirit, a spirit: he says his name's poor Tom.

Kent: What art thou that dost grumble there i' th' straw?
Come forth
Enter Edgar disguised as a madman

15 *Edgar* Away! the foul fiend follows me!
Through the sharp hawthorn blow the winds.
Humh! go to thy cold bed and warm thee.

Lear Didst thou give all to thy two daughters?
And art thou come to this?

20 *Edgar* Who gives anything to poor Tom?

AEB 1994

2 Another Shakespeare context

HAMLET

King But now, my cousin Hamlet, and my son –

Hamlet [*Aside*] A little more than kin, and less than kind.

King How is it that the clouds still hang on you?

Hamlet Not so, my lord; I am too much in the sun.

5 *Queen* Good Hamlet, cast thy nighted colour off,
And let thine eye look like a friend on Denmark.
Do not for ever with thy vailed lids
Seek for thy noble father in the dust.
Thou know'st 'tis common: all that lives must die,

10 Passing through nature to eternity.

Hamlet Ay, madam, it is common.

Queen If it be,
Why seems it so particular with thee?

Hamlet Seems, madam! Nay, it is; I know not 'seems'.
'Tis not alone my inky cloak, good mother,

15 Nor customary suits of solemn black,
Nor windy suspiration of forc'd breath,
No, nor the fruitful river in the eye,
Nor the dejected haviour of the visage,
Together with all forms, moods, shapes of grief,

20 That can denote me truly. These, indeed, seem;
For they are actions that a man might play;
But I have that within which passes show,
These but the trappings and the suits of woe.

King 'Tis sweet and commendable in your nature, Hamlet,

25 To give these mourning duties to your father;
But you must know your father lost a father;
That father lost lost his; and the survivor bound,
In filial obligation, for some term
To do obsequious sorrow. But to persever

30 In obstinate condolement is a course
Of impious stubbornness; 'tis unmanly grief;
It shows a will most incorrect to heaven,
A heart unfortified, a mind impatient,
An understanding simple and unschool'd;

35 For what we know must be, and is as common
As any the most vulgar thing to sense,
Why should we in our peevish opposition
Take it to heart? Fie! 'tis a fault to heaven,
A fault against the dead, a fault to nature,

40 To reason most absurd; whose common theme
Is death of fathers, and who still hath cried,
From the first corse till he that died to-day,
'This must be so'.

(Act 1, Scene 2, lines 64–106)

What impressions of Hamlet's domestic situation are created here and by what means?

Cambridge 1994

Question bank: essay questions

King Lear

1 Compare and contrast the personalities of Goneril and Regan, and show their different contributions to the play.

AEB 1994

2 Some see grotesque comedy in this play. Do you?

AEB 1994

Much Ado About Nothing

3 Consider the differing contributions to the play made by, on the one hand, Borachio and Conrade, and, on the other, Margaret and Ursula.

AEB 1994

Timon of Athens

4   *Timon* My hand to thee; mine honour on my promise. (Act I, sc. 1)

    Apemantus Grant I may never prove so fond,
        To trust man on his oath or bond. (Act I, sc. 2)

How close to the play's central concerns do you consider these quotations?

AEB 1994

5 Examine the character, and particularly the function, of Alcibiades in the play.

AEB 1994

The Tempest

6 How does the Stephano-Trinculo-Caliban sub-plot reinforce the thematic concerns of the play?

AEB 1994

7 Examine the relevance to *The Tempest* of its title.

AEB 1994

A Midsummer Night's Dream

8 **Either**, (a) Look again at the end of *A Midsummer Night's Dream*, from Act 5 Scene 1, line 360 ('Puck: Now the hungry lion roars') until the curtain.

How effective do you find these speeches of the fairies as a conclusion to the play? Try to comment on Shakespeare's poetic and dramatic technique as well as theme and character.

Or, (b) Remind yourself of the love scenes between Hermia and Lysander (Act 1, Scene 1, lines 128–179, from 'Lysander: How now, my love?' up to 'Enter Helena') and between Titania and Bottom (Act 4, Scene 1, lines 1–44, from 'Titania: Come, sit thee down...' up to 'They sleep. Enter Puck').

By examining both scenes, compare their different presentations of love and relate them to Shakespeare's treatment of love in the play as a whole.

WJEC 1994

Antony and Cleopatra

9 Either, (a) 'Notwithstanding the title of the play and the complex portrayal of Cleopatra, it is Antony's situation which most engages our interest.' How far do you agree?

Or, (b) The play has recently been criticised for 'defective construction, geographical restlessness, the use of rhetoric to glorify sexual obsession'. Consider your own response to the play *Antony and Cleopatra* in the light of these comments.

Cambridge 1994

The Merchant of Venice

10 Either, (a) 'Who chooseth me must give and hazard all he hath.' How important is the idea of hazard (chance or risk) to what you take *The Merchant of Venice* to be about?

Or, (b) To what extent do you agree that the audience's greatest difficulty with the play *The Merchant of Venice* is that there is no character with whom one can sympathise?

Cambridge 1994

Hamlet

11 Either, (a) Discuss the importance of images of acting and the theatre in the play *Hamlet*.

Or, (b) To Horatio, Hamlet describes himself and Claudius as 'mighty opposites'. How far do you see the relationship between Hamlet and Claudius as the central conflict of the play?

Cambridge 1994

Richard II

12 Either, (a) How, and with what dramatic effect, is the idea of England – its land and people – presented in the play *Richard II*?

Or, (b) 'He is that most dangerous of climbing politicians, the man who will go further than his rivals because he never allows himself to know where he is going.' Consider the characterisation of Bolingbroke in the light of this statement.

Cambridge 1994

SHAKESPEARE BIBLIOGRAPHY

Bassnett, Susan	*Shakespeare: The Elizabethan*
Brooks, Jean R	*Hamlet by William Shakespeare*
Colie, Rosalie	*Some Facets of King Lear*
Cooke, Katharine	*A C Bradley and His Influence*
Dean, Leonard	*Shakespeare: Modern Essays*
Honigmann, E A J	*Shakespeare: The Lost Years*
Leggatt, Alexander	*English Drama: Shakespeare*
Lloyd Evans	*Shakespeare in the Limelight*
Morgann, Maurice	*Shakespearian Critics*
Poole, Adrian	*Tragedy: Shakespeare*
Powell, Raymond	*Shakespeare and the Critics*
Talbert, Ernest W	*Elizabethan Drama and Shakespeare*

THE NOVEL AND OTHER PROSE WORKS

Units in this chapter

3.1 *Approaches to prose*
3.2 *Nonfiction*
3.3 *The novel*

Chapter objectives

Questions on prose works, which in most cases means novels, but also includes collections of short stories, essays and good examples of other genres, such as letters or biography, take up about a third of those asked by all the examining boards; the other questions consist of those on poetry and drama.

Several boards illustrate this proportion well enough in their two papers, of which the first, besides Shakespeare and Chaucer or Milton, offers a major (usually Victorian) novel as an option instead of either Chaucer or Milton. The second paper may be chosen from five periods of literary history, in which approximately a third are prose works, though the proportion varies according to the period. Some periods are more productive of good prose than others, which may be strongest in poetry or drama. The modern period is well represented by all three main categories of literature.

It is not usually possible, and in any case inadvisable, to miss entirely preparation for texts in any one of these categories. You should read carefully the rubric of your board to ascertain what the exact requirements are. For example, you should find out how far candidates are encouraged to read parallel literature, what proportion and what types of questions are asked on such, and what choice is allowed on the prescribed texts.

The majority of examination boards set two types of question on prose works. The first is the general essay question and the second the critical appreciation question on an unseen passage or passages.

Several Boards also set questions which ask for comment on a printed passage or passages from a prescribed work. (The relevant syllabuses give details.) In tackling this type of question you should follow the general guidelines on critical appraisal in Unit 2.1. You will also be expected to show evidence of your knowledge of the work as a whole. For example, if characters are involved in the passage chosen, you should be able to analyse them more effectively because of your study of their development throughout the work. You should be very careful to confine yourself to remarks that are relevant to the printed passage.

3.1 APPROACHES TO PROSE

Critical appraisal of prose means the close and detailed analysis of relatively short pieces of writing, extracts from novels, short stories and essays, in order to determine how the writer obtains certain effects. These effects include the selection of language and the arrangement and structuring of ideas in order to achieve his or her purpose most effectively in writing.

It is very important to know how to evaluate prose writing, as much writing today is carefully designed to manipulate our minds and condition us to the writer's way of thinking. A critical mind may help to develop a healthy critical awareness of the written word.

Critical appraisal of prose, even literary prose, is in many ways more difficult than poetry. Novelists, through use of language in the creation of characters, description of events and so on, manipulate our responses just as effectively as poets, but, because their effects tend to be large-scale effects, we are not immediately aware of them. If a novel is successful, we are usually so absorbed in the action that we only notice techniques used by the author at the second or third reading. Do not worry if you are not consciously noting the author's technique in the first reading. Subsequent readings are for detailed study.

METHOD OF APPROACH

When you are faced with a prose passage for appraisal, read the passage through carefully twice, aiming to comprehend fully the meaning of what is said.

Read thoroughly the part of this chapter beginning 'Aspects of character drawing' and see which of the criteria of **style** given apply to your passage. Although not all these aspects of style will be found, some will certainly be relevant and you must find illustrations of their use and discuss why the author has chosen them as I have done.

Examples from A-level set books are given for each of the aspects of style, which illustrate clearly what each is showing.

At the end of the chapter are two passages, one with a detailed model commentary and questions, the other just with questions for you to try. The answers you give will help to clarify your further reading of the passage. Then, to write your commentary, you must scrutinise the passage in great detail, noting all the devices of writing the writer has employed and estimating why he or she has employed them and how successfully. Before you write your commentary, read the passage slowly, trying to 'feel' the tone and the quality of the writing. You should then be in a position to write an informed critical appreciation of the passage.

ASPECTS OF CHARACTER DRAWING

Character can be revealed by the following methods:

1. **Action** (A character performing an action typical of him or her.) In *Wuthering Heights* by Emily Brontë, there are many examples of characters revealing themselves through their actions. At the beginning of the novel, when Mr Lockwood meets Heathcliff, his coarse manner betrays his rough nature.

> I took a seat at the end of the hearthstone opposite that towards which my landlord advanced, and filled up an interval of silence by attempting to caress the canine mother, who had left her nursery, and was sneaking wolfishly to the back of my legs, her lip curled up, and her white teeth watering for a snatch. My caress provoked a long, guttural gnarl.
>
> 'You'd better let the dog alone,' growled Mr Heathcliff in unison, checking fiercer demonstrations with a punch of his foot. 'She's not accustomed to be spoiled – not kept for a pet.' Then, striding to a side door, he shouted again, 'Joseph!'

Another example of Heathcliff's frighteningly violent behaviour is when Mr Lockwood has a terrifying nightmare and Heathcliff's reaction is equally aggressive. Notice the phrases 'crushing his nails into his palms' and 'grinding his teeth'.

> Heathcliff stood near the entrance, in his shirt and trousers; with a candle dripping over his fingers, and his face as white as the wall behind him. The first creak of the oak startled him like an electric shock: the light leaped from his hold to a distance of some feet, and his agitation was so extreme,

that he could hardly pick it up.

'It is only your guest, sir,' I called out, desirous to spare him the humiliation of exposing his cowardice further. 'I had the misfortune to scream in my sleep, owing to a frightful nightmare. I'm sorry I disturbed you.'

'Oh, God confound you, Mr Lockwood! I wish you were at the....' commenced my host, setting the candle on a chair. because he found it impossible to hold it steady. ' And who showed you up to this room?' he continued, crushing his nails into his palms, and grinding his teeth to subdue the maxillary convulsions. 'Who was it? I've a good mind to turn them out of the house this moment!'

An example of the spoilt childhoods of Edgar and Isabella Linton at Thrushcross Grange is found in Chapter 5 of *Wuthering Heights* when Heathcliff and Catherine see the two children squabbling over a little dog.

Both of us were able to look in by standing on the basement, and clinging to the ledge, and we saw – ah! it was beautiful – a splendid place carpeted with crimson, and crimson-covered chairs and tables, and a pure white ceiling bordered by gold, a shower of glass-drops hanging in silver chains from the centre, and shimmering with little soft tapers. Old Mr and Mrs Linton were not there; Edgar and his sister had it entirely to themselves. Shouldn't they have been happy? We should have thought ourselves in heaven! And now, guess what your good children were doing? Isabella – I believe she is eleven, a year younger than Cathy – lay screaming at the farther end of the room, shrieking as if witches were running red-hot needles into her. Edgar stood on the hearth weeping silently, and in the middle of the table sat a little dog, shaking its paw and yelping; which, from their mutual accusations, we understood they had nearly pulled in two between them. The idiots! That was their pleasure! To quarrel who should hold a heap of warm hair, and each begin to cry because both, after struggling to get it, refused to take it. We laughed outright at the petted things; we did despise them!

❷ **The way the characters reveal themselves in their speech** In the first chapter of *Pride and Prejudice* by Jane Austen, Mr and Mrs Bennet are discussing the arrival of Mr Bingley, an eligible and wealthy bachelor. Mrs Bennet is desperate that he will marry one of their daughters. Mr Bennet feigns indifference. Note the length of Mrs Bennet's sentences compared with those of her husband.

It is a truth universally acknowledged, that a single man in possession of a good fortune must be in want of a wife. However little known the feeling or views of such a man may be on his first entering a neighborhood, this truth is so well fixed in the minds of the surrounding families, that he is considered as the rightful property of some one or other of their daughters.

'My dear Mr Bennet,' said his lady to him one day, 'have you heard that Netherfield Park is let at last?'
Mr Bennet replied that he had not.
'But it is,' returned she; 'for Mrs Long has just been here and she told me all about it.'
Mr Bennet made no answer.
'Do not you want to know who has taken it?' cried his wife impatiently.
'You want to tell me, and I have no objection to hearing it.'
This was invitation enough.
'Why, my dear, you must know, Mrs Long says Netherfield is taken by a young man of large fortune from the North of England; that he came down on Monday in a chaise and four to see the place, and was so much delighted with it, that he agreed with Mr Morris immediately; that he is to take possession before Michaelmas, and some of his servants are to be in the house by the end of next week.'
'What is his name?'
'Bingley.'
'Is he married or single?'
'Oh! single, my dear, to be sure! A single man of large fortune; four or five thousand a-year. What a fine thing for our girls!'
'How so! how can it affect them?'
'My dear Mr Bennet,' replied his wife, 'how can you be so tiresome! you must know that I am thinking of his marrying one of them.'
'Is that his design in settling here?'
'Design! nonsense, how can you talk so! But it is very likely that he may fall in love with one of them, and therefore you must visit him as soon as he comes.'
'I see no occasion for that. You and the girls may go, or you may send them by themselves, which perhaps will be still better, for as you are as handsome as any of them, Mr Bingley might like you the best of the party.'
'My dear, you flatter me. I certainly have had my share of beauty, but I do not pretend to be anything extraordinary now. When a woman has five grown-up daughters, she ought to give over

thinking of her own beauty.'

'In such cases, a woman has not often much beauty to think of.'

'But, my dear, you must indeed go and see Mr Bingley when he comes into the neighborhood.

'It is more than I engage for, I assure you.'

'But consider your daughters. Only think what an establishment it would be for one of them. Sir William and Lady Lucas are determined to go, merely on that account, for in general, you know, they visit no newcomers. Indeed you must go, for it will be impossible for us to visit him if you do not.'

'You are over-scrupulous, surely. I dare say Mr Bingley will be very glad to see you; and I will send a few lines by you to assure him of my hearty consent to his marrying whichever he chooses of the girls; though I must throw in a good word for my little Lizzy.'

'I desire you will do no such thing. Lizzy is not a bit better than the others; and I am sure she is not half so handsome as Jane, nor half so good-humoured as Lydia. But you are always giving her the preference.'

'They have none of them much to recommend them,' replied he; 'they are all silly and ignorant, like other girls; but Lizzy has something more of quickness than her sisters.'

'Mr Bennet, how can you abuse your own children in such a way! You take delight in vexing me. You have no compassion on my poor nerves!'

'You mistake me, my dear. I have a high respect for your nerves. They are my old friends. I have heard you mention them with consideration these twenty years at least.'

'Ah! You do not know what I suffer.'

'But I hope you will get over it, and live to see many young men of four thousand a-year come into the neighborhood.'

'It will be no use to us, if twenty such should come, since you will not visit them.'

'Depend upon it, my dear, that when there are twenty, I will visit them all.'

Mr Bennet was so odd a mixture of quick parts, sarcastic humor, reserve, and caprice, that the experience of three-and-twenty years had been insufficient to make his wife understand his character. Her mind was less difficult to develop. She was a woman of mean understanding, little information, and uncertain temper. When she was discontented, she fancied herself nervous. The business of her life was to get her daughters married; its solace was visiting and news.

❸ By direct statement of the author on the character Where the author tells you directly his or her opinion and what you ought to think of the character at this particular time in the novel.

In *Washington Square* by Henry James, the passage I have chosen appears at a crucial point where Morris Townsend knows he could marry Catherine, but has to weigh up whether he could do better. The following passage is an interesting example because of the double-edged nature of James's address to the reader.

He had slightly misrepresented the matter in saying that Catherine had consented to take the great step. We left her just now declaring that she would burn her ships behind her; but Morris, after having elicited this declaration, had become conscious of good reasons for not taking it up. He avoided, gracefully enough, fixing a day, though he left her under the impression that he had his eye on one. Catherine may have had her difficulties; but those of her circumspect suitor are also worthy of consideration. The prize was certainly great; but it was only to be won by striking the happy mean between precipitancy and caution. It would be all very well to take one's jump and trust to Providence; Providence was more especially on the side of clever people, and clever people were known by an indisposition to risk their bones.

The ultimate reward of a union with a young woman who was both unattractive and impoverished ought to be connected with immediate disadvantages by some very palpable chain. Between the fear of losing Catherine and her possible fortune altogether, and the fear of taking her too soon and finding this possible fortune as void of actuality as a collection of emptied bottles, it was not comfortable for Morris Townsend to choose – a fact that should be remembered by readers disposed to judge harshly of a young man who may have struck them as making but an indifferently successful use of fine natural parts. He had not forgotten that in any event Catherine had her own ten thousand a year; he had devoted an abundance of meditation to this circumstance. But with his fine parts he rated himself high, and he had a perfectly definite appreciation of his value, which seemed to him inadequately represented by the sum I have mentioned. At the same time he reminded himself that this sum was considerable, that everything is relative, and that if a modest income is less desirable than a large one, the complete absence of revenue is nowhere accounted an advantage.

These reflections gave him plenty of occupation, and made it necessary that he should trim his sail. Doctor Sloper's opposition was the unknown quantity in the problem he had to work out. The natural way to work it out was by marrying Catherine; but in mathematics there are many short cuts, and Morris was not without a hope that he should yet discover one. When Catherine took him at his word, and consented to renounce the attempt to mollify her father, he drew back skilfully enough, as I have said, and kept the wedding-day still an open question. Her faith in his sincerity was so complete that she was incapable of suspecting that he was playing with her; her trouble just now was of another kind. The poor girl had an admirable sense of honour, and from the moment she had brought herself to the point of violating her father's wish, it seemed to her that she had no right to enjoy his protection.

❹ Description of characters in a novel by an omniscient narrator In novels like Fitzgerald's *The Great Gatsby*, and Evelyn Waugh's *Brideshead Revisited*, the personalities of characters are revealed by the narrator, who is also one of the characters.

Charles, in *Brideshead Revisited*, gives us clear and amusing character studies of two of his contemporaries at Oxford, Anthony Blanche and Sebastian Flyte.

He was tall, slim, rather swarthy, with large saucy eyes. The rest of us wore rough tweeds and brogues. He had on a smooth chocolate-brown suit with loud white stripes, suede shoes, a large bow-tie and he drew off yellow, wash-leather gloves as he came into the room; part Gallic, part Yankee, part, perhaps, Jew; wholly exotic.

This, I did not need telling, was Anthony Blanche, the 'aesthete' par excellence, a byword of iniquity from Cherwell Edge to Somerville. He had been pointed out to me often in the streets, as he pranced along with his high peacock tread; I had heard his voice in 'The George' challenging the conventions; and now meeting him, under the spell of Sebastian, I found myself enjoying him voraciously.

I knew Sebastian by sight long before I met him. That was unavoidable for, from his first week, he was the most conspicuous man of his year by reason of his beauty, which was arresting, and his eccentricities of behaviour, which seemed to know no bounds. My first sight of him was in the door of Germer's, and, on that occasion, I was struck less by his looks than by the fact that he was carrying a large teddy-bear.

'That,' said the barber, as I took his chair, 'was Lord Sebastian Flyte. A most amusing young gentleman.'

'Apparently,' I said coldly.

'The Marquis of Marchmain's second boy. His brother the Earl of Brideshead, went down last term. Now he was very different, a very quiet gentleman, quite like an old man. What do you suppose Lord Sebastian wanted? A hair brush for his teddy-bear; it had to have very stiff bristles, not, Lord Sebastian said, to brush him with, but to threaten him with a spanking when he was sulky. He bought a very nice one with an ivory back and he's having "Aloysius" engraved on it – that's the bear's name.' The man, who, in his time, had had ample chance to tire of undergraduate fantasy, was plainly captivated. I, however, remained censorious, and subsequent glimpses of him, driving in a hansom cab and dining at the George in false whiskers, did not soften me, although Collins, who was reading Freud, had a number of technical terms to cover everything.

❺ By association of one character with a recurrent image In DH Lawrence's novel, *The Rainbow*, the Brangwen men have for generations farmed the land between Derbyshire and Nottinghamshire. Lawrence vividly suggests the closeness of the Brangwen men to the soil in the following passage.

The Brangwens had lived for generations on the Marsh Farm, in the meadows where the Erewash twisted sluggishly through alder trees, separating Derbyshire from Nottinghamshire. Two miles away, a church-tower stood on a hill, the houses of the little country town climbing assiduously up to it. Whenever one of the Brangwens in the fields lifted his head from his work, he saw the church-tower at Ilkeston in the empty sky. So that as he turned again to the horizontal land, he was aware of something standing above him and beyond him in the distance.

There was a look in the eyes of the Brangwens as if they were expecting something unknown, about which they were eager. They had that air of readiness for what would come to them, a kind of surety, an expectancy, the look of an inheritor.

They were fresh, blond, slow-speaking people, revealing themselves plainly, but slowly, so that one could watch the change in their eyes from laughter to anger, blue, lit-up laughter, to a hard blue-staring anger; through all the irresolute stages of the sky when the weather is changing.

Living on rich land, on their own land, near to a growing town, they had forgotten what it was to be in straitened circumstances. They had never become rich, because there were always children, and the patrimony was divided every time. But always, at the Marsh, there was ample.

So the Brangwens came and went without fear of necessity, working hard because of the life that was in them, not for want of the money. Neither were they thriftless. They were aware of the last halfpenny, and instinct made them not waste the peeling of their apple, for it would help to feed the cattle. But heaven and earth was teeming around them, and how should this cease? They felt the rush of the sap in spring, they knew the wave which cannot halt, but every year throws forward the seed to begetting, and, falling back, leaves the young-born on the earth. They knew the intercourse between heaven and earth, sunshine drawn into the breast and bowels, the rain sucked up in the daytime, nakedness that comes under the wind in autumn, showing the birds' nests no longer worth hiding. Their life and inter-relations were such; feeling the pulse and body of the soil, that opened to their furrow for the grain, and became smooth and supple after their ploughing, and clung to their feet with a weight that pulled like desire, lying hard and unresponsive when the crops were to be shorn away. The young corn waved and was silken, and the lustre slid along the limbs of the men who saw it. They took the udder of the cows, the cows yielded milk and pulsed against the hands of the men, the pulse of the blood of the teats of the cows beat into the pulse of the hands of the men. They mounted their horses, and held life between the grip of their knees, they harnessed their horses at the wagon, and, with hand on the bridle-rings, drew the heaving of the horses after their will.

Another example of the use of recurrent imagery is found in *Dombey and Son* by Charles Dickens where the river, sea and ebbing tide imagery is linked with the child Paul Dombey.

Another time, in the same place, he fell asleep and slept quietly for a long time. Awaking suddenly, he listened, started up and sat listening. Florence asked him what he thought he heard.

'I want to know what it says,' he answered, looking steadily in her face. 'The sea, Floy, what is it that it keeps on saying?'

She told him that it was only the noise of the rolling waves.

'Yes, yes,' he said, 'But I know that they are always saying something. Always the same thing. What place is over there?' He rose up, looking eagerly at the horizon.

She told him there was another country opposite, but he said he didn't mean that; he meant farther away – farther away!

Very often afterwards, in the midst of their talk, he would break off, to try to understand what it was that the waves were always saying; and would rise up in his couch to look towards that invisible region, far away.

George Eliot uses reptile imagery a good deal in *Middlemarch* and in Chapter 41 she compares Mr Rigg Featherstone with a frog, who may appeal to certain lowly people, but not to people of any intelligence.

Having made this rather lofty comparison I am less uneasy in calling attention to the existence of low people by whose interference, however little we may like it, the course of the world is very much determined. It would be well, certainly, if we could help to reduce their number, and something might perhaps be done by not lightly giving occasion to their existence. Socially speaking, Joshua Rigg would have been generally pronounced a superfluity. But those who like Peter Featherstone never had a copy of themselves demanded, are the very last to wait for such a request either in prose or verse. The copy in this case bore more of outside resemblance to the mother, in whose sex frog-features, accompanied with fresh-coloured cheeks and well-rounded figure, are compatible with much charm for a certain order of admirers. The result is sometimes a frog-faced male, desirable, surely, to no order of intelligent beings. Especially when he is suddenly brought into evidence to frustrate other people's expectations – the very lowest aspect in which a social superfluity can present himself.

6 **By associating a character with one particular point of view or action with which he can be easily identified** In *The History Man*, a new A-level set book in which Malcolm Bradbury satirises the intermeshings of human relationships between academics on the campus of a new university, Henry Beamish, a member of the Sociology Department, is lampooned by Bradbury for his complete clumsiness and ineptitude in every direction. In this passage, having damaged his wrist in an 'accident' at Howard Kirk's party, he tries to negotiate his tray through the queue at the university cafeteria. His public humiliation symbolises his unlucky life.

A very loud crash comes from the direction of the self-service line. The sociologists' heads all turn; in the line, someone, a bandaged person, has dropped an entire tray and its contents. 'Oh, God,' says Flora, 'it's Henry.' Henry Beamish stands transfixed in the line, with yoghurt all over his trousers…

7 **By choice of words and picking out a particular feature or detail which calls a character vividly to mind** In Flaubert's novel, *Madame Bovary*, Emma Bovary, married to a country doctor, is totally bored and dissatisfied with her marriage. An incurable romantic, she longs for a lover who can satisfy her desires. In the following passage Flaubert uses the imagery of the sea and the shipwrecked sailor to suggest her isolation.

And all the time, deep within her, she was waiting for something to happen. Like a shipwrecked sailor she scanned her solitude with desperate eyes for the sight of a white sail far off on the misty horizon. She had no idea what that chance would be, what wind would waft it to her, where it would set her ashore, whether it was a launch or a three-decker, laden with anguish or filled to the portholes with happiness. But every morning when she woke she hoped to find it there. She listened to every sound, started out of bed, and was surprised when nothing came. Then at sunset, sadder every day, she longed for the morrow.

Dickens uses the image of an engine to describe vividly Pancks in *Little Dorrit*, Chapter XIII.

He had scarcely left the room, and allowed the ticking to become audible again, when a quick hand turned a latchkey in the house-door, opened it, and shut it. Immediately afterwards, a quick and eager short dark man came into the room with so much way upon him, that he was within a foot of Clennam before he could stop.

'Halloa!' he said.

Clennam saw no reason why he should not say 'Halloa!' too.

'What's the matter?' said the short dark man.

'I have not heard that anything is the matter,' returned Clennam.

'Where's Mr Casby?' asked the short dark man, looking about.

'He will be here directly, if you want him.'

'I want him?' said the short dark man. 'Don't you?'

This elicited a word or two of explanation from Clennam, during the delivery of which the short dark man held his breath and looked at him. He was dressed in black and rusty iron grey; had jet black beads of eyes; a scrubby little black chin; wiry black hair striking out from his head in prongs, like forks or hair-pins; and a complexion that was very dingy by nature, or very dirty by art, or a compound of nature and art. He had dirty hands and dirty broken nails, and looked as if he had been in the coals; he was in a perspiration, and snorted and sniffed and puffed and blew, like a little labouring steam-engine.

'Oh!' said he, when Arthur had told him how he came to be there. 'Very well. That's right. If he should ask for Pancks, will you be so good as to say that Pancks is come in?' And so, with a snort and a puff, he walked out by another door.

Note how the layers of images are built up with the idea of a steam engine developing from earlier metallic imagery: 'black and rusty', 'forks or hair-pins'.

Descriptive prose

The background against which the characters in a novel operate can either be merely a place in which they happen to live or can be inextricably linked with their characters. In novels the author often deliberately chooses the setting to illustrate or underline some aspect of his characters. For instance, in Hardy's novels, much use is made of the wild, inhospitable heathland to reflect the author's notion that man lives in an environment often hostile to him. The following methods can be used to form a detailed description:

❶ selected detail to build up a complete picture;
❷ concrete detail to make the reader feel the reality of the description;
❸ comparisons to make the descriptions more vivid and easy to imagine;
❹ the use of words to appeal to our senses so that we see, feel and hear objects more precisely;
❺ the use of words as images to give us a good picture of what the author is trying to describe.

An excellent illustration of a building being used to highlight an integral part of a character is the description of the lighthouse in *To The Lighthouse* by Virginia Woolf. The lighthouse is used both as a setting and a symbol, highlighting fears and hopes within different characters.

He was an awful prig – oh yes, an insufferable bore. For, though they had reached the town now and were in the main street, with carts grinding past on the cobbles, still he went on talking, about settlements, and teaching, and working-men, and helping our own class, and lectures, till she gathered that he had got back entire self-confidence, had recovered from the circus, and was about (and now again she liked him warmly) to tell her – but here, the houses falling away on both sides, they came out on the quay, and the whole bay spread before them and Mrs Ramsey could not help exclaiming, 'Oh, how beautiful!' For the great plateful of blue water was before her; the hoary Lighthouse, distant, austere, in the midst; and on the right, as far as the eye could see, fading and falling, in soft low pleats, the green sand dunes with the wild flowing grasses on them, which always seemed to be running away into some moon country, uninhabited of men.

That was the view, she said, stopping, growing greyer-eyed, that her husband loved.

She paused a moment. But now, she said, artists had come here. There indeed, only a few paces off, stood one of them, in Panama hat and yellow boots, seriously, softly, absorbedly, for all that he was watched by ten little boys, with an air of profound contentment on his round red face, gazing, and then, when he had gazed, dipping; imbuing the tip of his brush in some soft mound of green or pink.

Another example of how settings are used as symbols for the emotions of the different characters is found in the descriptions of the Marabar Caves in EM Forster's novel *A Passage to India:*

The caves are readily described. A tunnel eight feet long, five feet high, three feet wide, leads to a circular chamber about twenty feet in diameter. This arrangement occurs again and again throughout the group of hills, and this is all, this is a Marabar Cave. Having seen one such cave, having seen two, having seen three, four, fourteen, twenty-four, the visitor returns to Chandrapore uncertain whether he has had an interesting experience or a dull one or any experience at all. He finds it difficult to discuss the caves, or to keep them apart in his mind, for the pattern never varies, and no carving, not even a bees' nest or a bat, distinguishes one from another. Nothing, nothing attaches to them and their reputation – for they have one – does not depend upon human speech. It is as if the surrounding plain or the passing birds have taken upon themselves to exclaim 'extraordinary', and the word has taken root in the air, and been inhaled by mankind.

They are dark caves. Even when they open towards the sun, very little light penetrates down the entrance tunnel into the circular chamber. There is little to see, and no eye to see it, until the visitor arrives for his five minutes, and strikes a match.* Immediately another flame rises in the depths of the rock and moves towards the surface like an imprisoned spirit: the walls of the circular chamber have been most marvellously polished. The two flames approach and strive to unite, but cannot, because one of them breathes air, the other stone. A mirror inlaid with lovely colours divides the lovers, delicate stars of pink and grey interpose, exquisite nebulae, shading fainter than the tail of a comet or the midday moon, all the evanescent life of the granite, only here visible. Fists and fingers thrust above the advancing soil – here at last is their skin, finer than any covering acquired by the animals, smoother than windless water, more voluptuous than love. The radiance increases, the flames touch one another, kiss, expire. The cave is dark again, like all the caves.

Only the wall of the circular chamber has been polished thus. The sides of the tunnel are left rough, they impinge as an afterthought upon the internal perfection. An entrance was necessary, so mankind made one. But elsewhere, deeper in the granite, are there certain chambers that have no entrance? Chambers never unsealed since the arrival of the gods. Local report declares that these exceed in number those that can be visited, as the dead exceed the living – four hundred of them, four thousand or million. Nothing is inside them, they were sealed up before the creation of pestilence or treasure; if mankind grew curious and excavated, nothing, nothing would be added to the sum of good or evil. One of them is rumoured within the boulder that swings on the summit of the highest of the hills; a bubble-shaped cave that has neither ceiling nor floor, and mirrors its own darkness in every direction infinitely. If the boulder falls and smashes, the cave will smash too – empty as an Easter egg. The boulder because of its hollowness sways in the wind, and even moves when a crow perches upon it; hence its name and the name of its stupendous pedestal: the Kawa Dol.

* Note how the passage changes dramatically at this point. Boredom and confusion give way to delight when light is introduced into the cave.

THE WRITER'S OPINION

Often a novelist is strongly committed to a certain character or cause in the novel. The student should try to show how he reveals his opinions. Does he use rhetoric, emotional prose or calm reasoned argument? Does he make it clear that he sympathises with one character more than another? If so, how does he do this – by the character's speech and actions or by direct comment by the author in his role of omniscient narrator?

In *Animal Farm* George Orwell shows his contempt of both the Communist and autocratic methods of government. The pigs overthrow the cruel farmer, Mr Jones, and replace his rule with a supposedly Utopian situation. They make Seven Commandments which are the moral rules for the guidance of all the animals. However, the corrupt pigs, led by Napoleon, with Squealer as his propaganda agent, soon turn the farm back to an almost exact replica of how it was under Mr Jones:

It was just after the sheep had returned, on a pleasant evening when the animals had finished work and were making their way back to the farm buildings, that the terrified neighing of a horse sounded from the yard. Startled, the animals stopped in their tracks. It was Clover's voice. She neighed again, and all the animals broke into a gallop and rushed into the yard. Then they saw what Clover had seen.

It was a pig walking on his hind legs.

Yes, it was Squealer. A little awkwardly, as though not quite used to supporting his considerable bulk in that position, but with perfect balance, he was strolling across the yard. And a moment later, out from the door of the farmhouse came a long file of pigs, all walking on their hind legs. Some did it better than others, one or two were even a trifle unsteady and looked as though they would have liked the support of a stick, but every one of them made his way right round the yard successfully. And finally there was a tremendous baying of dogs and a shrill crowing from the black cockerel, and out came Napoleon himself, majestically upright, casting haughty glances from side to side, and with his dogs gambolling round him.

He carried a whip in his trotter.

There was a deadly silence. Amazed, terrified, huddling together, the animals watched the long line of pigs march slowly round the yard. It was as though the world had turned upside-down. Then there came a moment when the first shock had worn off and when, in spite of everything – in spite of their terror of the dogs, and of the habit, developed through long years, of never complaining, never criticising, no matter what happened – they might have uttered some word of protest. But just at that moment, as though at a signal, all the sheep burst out into a tremendous bleating of –

'Four legs good, two legs better! Four legs good, two legs better! Four legs good, two legs better!'

It went on for five minutes without stopping. And by the time the sheep had quieted down, the chance to utter any protest had passed, for the pigs had marched back into the farmhouse.

Benjamin felt a nose nuzzling at his shoulder. He looked round. It was Clover. Her old eyes looked dimmer than ever. Without saying anything, she tugged gently at his mane and led him round to the end of the big barn, where the Seven Commandments were written. For a minute or two they stood gazing at the tarred wall with its white lettering.

'My sight is failing,' she said finally. 'Even when I was young I could not have read what was written there. But it appears to me that that wall looks different. Are the Seven Commandments the same as they used to be Benjamin?'

For once Benjamin consented to break his rule, and he read out to her what was written on the wall. There was nothing there now except a single Commandment. It ran:

> **ALL ANIMALS ARE EQUAL**
> **BUT SOME ANIMALS ARE MORE**
> **EQUAL THAN OTHERS**

TONE

The words an author actually uses gives us the most obvious indication of the tone of voice the writer is employing.

The tone may be:

1. formal or informal;
2. sympathetic or unsympathetic;
3. serious or comic;
4. emotional or restrained;
5. cynical or sentimental;
6. biased or impartial.

You must imagine the author reading the passage and try to hear the intonation he would put into his words. This should let you know what tone the author intends to adopt.

Although examples of all different kinds of tone are too numerous to mention, I have tried to choose some of the main ones and give illustrations of them from passages of A-level set texts.

Pessimistic tone

Thomas Hardy in his novels reveals a fatalistic and pessimistic view of life. He feels that however his characters struggle against their fates, their movements and destinies are controlled by an arbitrary and sometimes malevolent being who seems often to conspire against them.

In *Tess of the D'Urbervilles* Tess is used and manipulated by Alec d'Urberville, whom she eventually kills. One might feel justice had been done but the courts find her guilty and she is hanged. Angel Clare, her true love, views her death from a distance.

> Upon the cornice of the tower a tall staff was fixed. Their eyes were riveted on it. A few minutes after the hour had struck something moved slowly up the staff, and extended itself upon the breeze. It was a black flag.
>
> 'Justice' was done, and the President of the Immortals, in Aeschylean phrase, had ended his sport with Tess. And the D'Urberville knights and dames slept on in their tombs unknowing. The two speechless gazers bent themselves down to the earth, as if in prayer, and remained thus a long time, absolutely motionless; the flag continued to wave silently. As soon as they had strength they arose, joined hands again, and went on.

Hardy's exploration of the human condition of his society certainly had melancholy overtones. This attitude of his met with severe critical comment when his novels were published. When *Jude the Obscure* was published as a complete novel in 1895, the *New York Bookman* said of it, 'It is simply one of the most objectionable books that we have ever read in any language whatsoever'; and a reviewer in *The World*, betraying the characteristic Victorian middle-class opinion that gloom is somehow socially undesirable, remarked that 'None but a writer of exceptional talent indeed could have produced so gruesome and gloomy a book'.

At the end of the fifth chapter of *The Return of the Native*, the returning native, Clym Yeobright, expresses his feelings that anything hopeful in his life has come too late for him.

> Yeobright's manner had been so quiet, he had uttered so few syllables since his reappearance, that Venn imagined him resigned. It was only when they had left the room and stood upon the landing that the true state of his mind was apparent. Here he said, with a wild smile, inclining his head towards the chamber in which Eustacia lay, 'She is the second woman I have killed this year. I was a great cause of my mother's death; and I am the chief cause of hers.'
>
> 'I spoke cruel words to her, and she left my house. I did not invite her back till it was too late. It is I who ought to have drowned myself. It would have been a charity to the living had the river overwhelmed me and borne her up. But I cannot die. Those who ought to have lived lie dead; and here am I alive!'
>
> 'But you can't charge yourself with crimes in that way,' said Venn. 'You may as well say that the parents be the cause of a murder by the child, for without the parents the child would never have been begot.'
>
> 'Yes, Venn, that is very true; but you don't know all the circumstances. If it had pleased God to put an end to me it would have been a good thing for all. But I am getting used to the horror of my existence. They say that a time comes when men laugh at misery through long acquaintance with it. Surely that time will soon come to me!'
>
> 'Your aim has always been good,' said Venn. 'Why should you say such desperate things?'
>
> 'No, they're not desperate. They are only hopeless; and my great regret is that for what I have done no man or law can punish me!'

Cynical tone

The whole tone of *The History Man* expresses cynicism about human relationships. The main character, Howard Kirk, is a totally selfish individual who manipulates others both politically and sexually in the single-minded pursuit of his goals. He becomes involved with one of his students, Felicity Phee, but tries to convince one of his other lady friends that he was acting totally unselfishly as she needed his help. Note how Miss Callendar treats Kirk briskly as if he were a tiresome child.

> 'The key question is now my relationship with Miss Phee. You remember Miss Phee.'
>
> 'Do I?' says Miss Callendar. 'Yes,' says Howard, 'you saw me with her in my downstairs study, when you were leaving the party.' 'Then that was one of your episodes,' says Miss Callendar, 'I did rather think so.' 'It's a pity you don't know her better,' says Howard, 'then perhaps, instead of supporting Carmody's crazy story, you'd understand what repressed, evil nonsense it is.' 'I don't support his story,' says Miss Callendar, 'I don't know whether his interpretation of what he saw is right at all. I just have some reason, don't I, for thinking he saw what he saw.'
>
> 'But he saw nothing,' says Howard, 'he just looked in on me from outside and made corrupt deductions. Miss Phee's one of my advisees. She's a very sad creature. She's been through everything. Boy trouble, girl trouble, an abortion, the identity crisis, a breakdown....' 'The menopause,' says Miss Callendar. 'Not yet,' says Howard. 'Well, you've something to come,' says Miss Callendar, 'A scone? I made them myself.' 'Thanks,' says Howard. 'She had a crisis that night. A lesbian affair she was having was breaking up.' 'Isn't she rather hogging the problems?' asks Miss Callendar. 'She was in trouble,' says Howard, 'she went down there into my study, and started raking through my papers. She wanted to be caught, I think; anyway, I caught her.' 'The instinct of

curiosity,' says Miss Callendar, 'Mr Carmody has that too.' 'Of course I was angry. But the meaning of the situation was obvious. She was crying out for attention.' 'So you laid her down and gave her some,' says Miss Callendar. 'No,' says Howard, 'it was very much the other way around.' 'Oh, God, how awful,' says Miss Callendar, 'did she attack you? Were you hurt?' 'I'm explaining to you that she has no attraction for me,' says Howard, 'I didn't want her at all. I wanted someone else. In fact, you. Out there beyond the window.' 'But in my absence you settled for her instead,' says Miss Callendar.

Sympathetic or unsympathetic tone

The author can either remain neutral or let you know which of his characters his sympathies are with. In *The Sandcastle*, Iris Murdoch seems to have mixed feelings about the matrimonial difficulties of the two main characters, Nan and Mor. Nan is a somewhat cold and unsympathetic character, but she wins in the end as she makes a speech putting forward her husband, Mor, as a political candidate. This makes it virtually impossible for him to continue his affair with Rain Carter as he now has to appear totally respectable.

'It has been for many years,' Nan went on, 'the dear wish and ambition of my husband, myself, and our children that he should serve his country in the highest role to which a democratic society can call its citizens – that of a Member of Parliament. After a long period of patient work, my husband has now the great happiness of being able to realise his lifelong ambition. The nearby borough of Marsington has decided to adopt him as their Labour candidate – and as we know, Marsington, with all respect to those present who are of the other party, is a safe Labour seat.'

Amazement, horror, and anger struggled within him; Mor could scarcely believe his ears. He turned his head to where Demoyte and Rain were sitting. Demoyte looked completely stunned; he was half turned towards Nan, his hand raised to his mouth. Then he turned sharply back towards Mor, a look of surprise, dismay, and accusation. But it was the face of Rain that made Mor almost cry out aloud. He had told her nothing of his political plans. She was hearing of them now for the first time. She looked towards him, her lips parting as if to question him, her eyes expressing astonishment and sheer horror, her whole face working in an agony of interrogation. Mor shook his head violently.

Nan was going on. 'As Shakespeare says, there is a tide in the affairs of men that taken at the flood leads on to fortune. This tide now runs for my husband, and for myself, and for our children. We have discussed the matter fully, and we are at last agreed that there is no other bond or tie which can prevent us from adventuring forward together. Courage is needed to make the great step. To delay would be fatal. Such a chance comes but once in a lifetime. Courage he has never lacked – nor is it likely that he will hesitate now when all his deepest and most cherished wishes are about to find so complete a fulfilment.'

Mor was breathing deeply. He was still almost deprived of breath by the shock. Who would have thought that Nan would be so ingenious – or so desperate? He knew that something vital, perhaps final, was happening to him, but he did not fully see what it was. He tried to keep Rain's eyes, but she turned away from him, grimacing with distress. Mor told himself that what he ought to do now, now this very minute, was to get up from his seat and lead Rain out of the room. Nan had attempted to corner him by a public gesture. She should be answered in the same way. To rise now and go out with Rain would set the seal on all his intentions. At last Nan had raised the storm. It was for him to ride it. But Rain had turned away her eyes – and although Mor struggled in his seat he could not bring himself to get up. A lifetime of conformity was too much for him. He stayed where he was.

Emotional and restrained tone

Often the author becomes very emotionally involved with the characters, especially when they are going through some crisis or traumatic event in their lives. In *The Millstone* by Margaret Drabble, Rosamund Stacey is the unmarried mother of a baby girl. Her baby becomes ill and is taken to hospital. Margaret Drabble, herself a mother, emotively narrates the scene where Rosamund confronts an irate Sister who is determined not to let her see her baby. This whole episode is told through the eyes of Rosamund. Mr Protheroe is the specialist paediatrician involved in the case.

'I told you this morning,' said Sister, 'that visiting is quite out of the question.'

'I don't care what you told me,' I said. 'I want to see my baby. If you don't take me straight there, I shall walk round until I find the way myself. She's not kept under lock and key, I assume?'

'Miss Stacy,' said Sister, 'you are behaving most foolishly, and I must ask you to leave at once.'

'I won't leave,' I said. 'You'd much better take me straight there, I don't want to be compelled to wander round upsetting the whole of your hospital until I find my baby.'

'Now then, now then,' said Sister, 'this is neither the time nor the place for hysterical talk like that. We must all be grateful that your child is ….'

'Grateful,' I said. 'I am grateful. I admire your hospital, I admire your work, I am devoted to the National Health Service. Now I want to see my baby.'

She came over to me and took my arm and started to push me gently towards the door; I have spent so much of my life in intelligent, superior effort to understand ignorance that I recognised her look at once. She pitied me and she was amazed. I let her get me as far as the door, being unable at first to resist the physical sense of propulsion, but when we got to the door I stopped and said, 'No, I'm not going to leave. I'm going to stay here until you change your mind.'

'I have no intention of changing my mind,' she said, and once more took hold of my elbow and started to push. I resisted. We stood there for a moment; I could not believe that physical violence could possibly take place, but on the other hand I did not see what else I could do. So when she started to push, I started to scream. I screamed very loudly, shutting my eyes to do it, and listening in amazement to the deafening shindy that filled my head. Once I started, I could not stop; I stood there, motionless, screaming, whilst they shook me and yelled at me and told me that I was upsetting everybody in earshot. 'I don't care,' I yelled, finding words for my inarticulate passion, 'I don't care, I don't care, I don't care about anyone, I don't care, I don't care, I don't care.'

Eventually they got me to sit down, but I went on screaming and moaning and keeping my eyes shut; through the noise I could hear things happening, people coming and going, someone slapped my face, someone tried to put a wet flannel on my head, and all the time I was thinking I must go on doing this until they let me see her. Inside my head it was red and black and very hot, I remember, and I remember also the clearness of my consciousness and the ferocity of my emotion, and myself enduring them, myself neither one nor the other, but enduring them, and not breaking in two. After a while I heard someone shouting above the din, 'For God's sake tell her she can see the baby, someone try and tell her,' and I heard these words and instantly stopped and opened my eyes and beheld the stricken, confused silence around me.

'Did you say I could see the baby?' I said.

'Of course you can see the baby,' said Mr Protheroe. 'Of course you can see the baby. I cannot imagine why you should ever have been prevented from seeing the baby.'

A humorous or a serious tone

Different authors adopt or present different attitudes to an institution like marriage. The attitude to marriage presented by Jane Austen is a paradoxical mixture of the romantic and the mercenary. Nowhere is this more apparent than in *Pride and Prejudice*, where there is a spectrum of attitudes:

Wholly mercenary	Partly mercenary	Romantic
Mrs Bennet	Charlotte Lucas	Jane Bennet
Miss Bingley	Mr Wickham	Lydia Bennet
		Mr Bingley

In this episode, Charlotte is explaining how she can contemplate marriage to a man she does not love, namely Mr Collins, to her horrified friend, Elizabeth Bennet.

Miss Lucas called soon after breakfast, and in a private conference with Elizabeth related the event of the day before.

The possibility of Mr Collins' fancying himself in love with her friend had once occurred to Elizabeth within the last day or two; but that Charlotte could encourage him seemed almost as far from possibility as she could encourage him herself, and her astonishment was consequently so great as to overcome at first the bounds of decorum, and she could not help crying out –

'Engaged to Mr Collins! my dear Charlotte, – impossible!'

The steady countenance which Miss Lucas had commanded in telling her story, gave way to a momentary confusion here on receiving so direct a reproach; though, as it was no more than she expected, she soon regained her composure, and calmly replied –

'Why should you be surprised, my dear Eliza? – Do you think it incredible that Mr Collins should be able to procure any woman's good opinion, because he was not so happy as to succeed with you?'

But Elizabeth had now recollected herself, and making a strong effort for it, was able to assure her with tolerable firmness that the prospect of their relationship was highly grateful to her, and that she wished her all imaginable happiness.

'I see what you are feeling,' replied Charlotte, – 'you must be surprised, very much surprised – so lately as Mr Collins was wishing to marry you. But when you have had time to think it all over, I hope you will be satisfied with what I have done. I am not romantic, you know; I never was. I ask only a comfortable home; and considering Mr Collins' character, connections, and situation in life. I am convinced that my chance of happiness with him is as fair as most people can boast on entering the marriage state.'

Elizabeth quietly answered, 'Undoubtedly'; – and after an awkward pause, they returned to the rest of the family. Charlotte did not stay much longer and Elizabeth was left to reflect on what she had heard. It was a long time before she became at all reconciled to the idea of so unsuitable a match. The strangeness of Mr Collins' making two offers of marriage within three days was nothing in comparison of his being now accepted. She had always felt that Charlotte's opinion of matrimony was not exactly like her own, but she could not have supposed it possible that, when called into action, she would have sacrificed every better feeling to worldly advantage. Charlotte the wife of Mr Collins, was a most humiliating picture! – And to the pang of a friend disgracing herself and sunk in her esteem, was added the distressing conviction that it was impossible for that friend to be tolerably happy in the lot she had chosen.

A much more cynical but vastly amusing view of marriage is presented in *Tristram Shandy* by Lawrence Sterne. This extract shows Widow Wadman's pursuit of Uncle Toby in Chapter XXIV.

– I am half distracted, captain Shandy, said Mrs Wadman, holding up her cambrick handkerchief to her left eye, as she approach'd the door of my uncle Toby's sentry-box – a mote – or sand – or something – I know not what, has got into this eye of mine – do look into it – it is not in the white–

In saying which, Mrs Wadman edged herself close in beside my uncle Toby, and squeezing herself down upon the corner of his bench, she gave him an opportunity of doing it without rising up – Do look into it – said she.

Honest soul! thou didst look into it with as much innocency of heart, as ever child look'd into a raree-shew-box; and 'twere as much a sin to have hurt thee.

– If a man will be peeping of his own accord into things of that nature – I've nothing to say to it –

My uncle Toby never did; and I will answer for him, that he would have sat quietly upon a sofa from June to January (which, you know, takes in both the hot and cold months), with an eye as fine as the Thracian Rodope's beside him, without being able to tell, whether it was a black or blue one.

The difficulty was to get my uncle Toby to look at one at all.

'Tis surmounted. And

I see him yonder with his pipe pendulous in his hand, and the ashes falling out of it looking and looking – then rubbing his eyes – and looking again, with twice the good nature that ever Gallileo look'd for a spot in the sun.

– In vain! for by all the powers which animate the organ – Widow Wadman's left eye shines this moment as lucid as her right – there is neither mote, or sand, or dust, or chaff, or speck, or particle of opake matter floating in it – There is nothing, my dear paternal uncle! but one lambent delicious fire, furtively shooting out from every part of it, in all directions, into thine –

– If thou lookest, uncle Toby, in search of this mote one moment longer – thou art undone.

STYLE

You may be asked to comment on the style of a passage. These are the main areas that need to be examined:

Sentence structure

You must decide what effect the sentence structure has and whether this effect is appropriate to the subject matter.

Language and imagery

Is the language and imagery suitable to the subject? Whether the subject be comic, serious or poetical, the language and imagery should echo the subject.

Tone

Although this has been dealt with in greater detail in an earlier part of the chapter, an integral part of any discussion on style must contain a discussion of whether the tone is suitable to the passage; for instance, is the tone ironical, comic or serious?

DIFFERENT TYPES OF STYLE AND EXAMPLES

Colloquial style

This is used when the author wishes to suggest a certain class, or create a regional atmosphere. Lawrence is a master of Nottingham dialect, as is Alan Sillitoe in *Saturday Night and Sunday Morning*.

In *Billy Liar*, Billy and his friend, Arthur, mockingly imitate the Yorkshire dialect of Councillor Duxbury. Billy mocks everything to do with his home background as he is trying desperately to leave the North and become a scriptwriter in London. The author, Keith Waterhouse, uses this passage to show Billy's quick and intelligent mind and his ability to see the comic and grotesque side of any situation. It also shows his immaturity in fighting against his home background when he has neither the money nor the talent to leave it.

> The door-bell tinkled and we put on our funeral faces but it was nobody, only Councillor Duxbury. He crossed the floor to his own office with an old man's shuffle, putting all his thought into the grip of his stick and the pattern of the faded, broken lino. A thick, good coat sat heavily on his bowed back, and there were enamelled medallions on his watch-chain. At the door of his room he half-turned, moving his whole body like an old robot, and muttered: 'Morning lads'.
>
> We chanted, half-dutifully, half-ironically: 'Good morning, Councillor Duxbury,' and directly the door was closed, began our imitation of him. 'It's Councillor Duxbury, lad, Councillor Duxbury. Tha wun't call Lord Harewood mister, would tha? Councillor, that's mah title. Now think on.'
>
> 'Ah'm just about thraiped,' said Arthur in broad dialect. The word was one we had made up to use in the Yorkshire dialect routine, where we took the Michael out of Councillor Duxbury and people like him. Duxbury prided himself on his dialect, which was practically unintelligible even to seasoned Yorkshiremen.
>
> 'Tha's getten more bracken ivvery day, lad,' I said.
>
> 'Aye, an' fair scritten anall,' said Arthur.
>
> 'Tha mun wi't' gangling-iron.'
>
> 'Aye.'
>
> We swung into the other half of the routine, which was Councillor Duxbury remembering, as he did every birthday in an interview with the *Stradhoughton Echo*. Arthur screwed up his face into the lined old man's wrinkles and said:
>
> 'Course, all this were fields when I were a lad.'
>
> '– and course, ah'd nobbut one clog to mah feet when ah come to Stradhoughton,' I said in the wheezing voice.
>
> 'Tha could get a meat pie and change out o'fourpence –'
>
> 'Aye, an' a box at t'Empire and cab home at t' end on it.'
>
> 'Ah had to tak' a cab home because ah only had one clog.' said Arthur.

Didactic style

Didactic means 'fitted or intended to teach.' An author who writes didactically is intending to instruct his readers in the way they ought to think either about the ideas he is putting forward or his characters.

George Eliot is an ideal example of an author using didactic style. The passage represented here from *The Mill on the Floss*, where she criticises the narrowness of society, shows how George Eliot felt her own isolation from a narrow-minded society because of her relationship with GH Lewes. To understand much of George Eliot's writing we have to go back to the facts of her life.

In order to reach a position where she could deploy her capacities to the full, she had to live unconventionally, to leave Coventry and set up as a journalist alone in London. There was nothing all that unusual in this – many intelligent women of her time had done as much, but George Eliot chose to link her life with that of a married man. For 25 years until his death in 1879 she lived with the scientific populariser and scholar George Henry Lewes. Again this wouldn't have mattered if she had chosen to stay in that part of society where it did not matter, but in the more respectable intellectual social circles in which she wanted to move, it did matter, at least before her professional reputation was established. By the conventions of the time, Lewes could be received anywhere: she could not. In later years, nobody could be more readily respectable than the Leweses, as they were known, and hardly anyone would be but honoured to receive George Eliot. But for her lack of respectability as well as for her plain appearance she had known many years of rejection and pain.

Perhaps something akin to this oppressive feeling may have weighed upon you in watching this old-fashioned family life on the banks of the Floss, which even sorrow hardly suffices to lift above the level of the tragi-comic. It is a sordid life, you say, this of the Tullivers and Dodsons – irradiated by no sublime principles, no romantic visions, no active, self-renouncing faith – moved by none of those wild, uncontrollable passions which create the dark shadows of misery and crime – without that primitive rough simplicity of wants, that hard, submissive ill-paid toil, that childlike spelling-out of what nature has written, which gives its poetry to peasant life. Here one has conventional wordly notions and habits without instruction and without polish – surely the most prosaic form of human life – proud respectability in a gig of unfashionable build, worldliness without side-dishes. Observing these people narrowly, even when the iron hand of misfortune has shaken them from their unquestioning hold on the world, one sees little trace of religion, still less of a distinctively Christian creed. Their belief in the Unseen, so far as it manifests itself at all, seems to be rather of a pagan kind; their moral notions, though held with strong tenacity, seem to have no standard beyond hereditary custom. You could not live among such people; you are stifled for want of an outlet towards something beautiful, great, or noble; you are irritated with these dull men and women, as a kind of population out of keeping with the earth on which they live – with this rich plain where the great river flows for ever onward, and links the small pulse of the old English town with the beatings of the world's mighty heart. A vigorous superstition, that lashes its gods or lashes its own back, seems to be more congruous with the mystery of the human lot than the mental condition of these emmet-like Dodsons and Tullivers.

I share with you this sense of oppressive narrowness; but it is necessary that we should feel it, if we care to understand how it acted on the lives of Tom and Maggie – how it has acted on young natures in many generations, that in the onward tendency of human things have risen above the mental level of the generation before them, to which they have been nevertheless tied by the strongest fibres of their hearts. The suffering, whether martyr or victim, which belongs to every historical advance of mankind is represented in this way in every town and by hundreds of obscure hearths. And we need not shrink from this comparison of small things with great; for does not science tell us that its highest striving is after the ascertainment of a unity which shall bind the smallest things with the greatest? In natural science, I have understood, there is nothing petty to the mind that has a large vision of relations, and to which every single object suggests a vast sum of conditions. It is surely the same with the observation of human life.

Dramatic style

Dramatic style is often the most difficult to achieve, as it can be overdone and appear melodramatic and false. Often the most effective dramatic writing is understated. On rare occasions, a truly skilful writer can use all the exigences of high drama, such as exclamation, emotive words and onomatopoeia and succeed.

Such an example is found in the powerful writing of Joseph Conrad in *The Secret Agent* where Ossipon attacks Mrs Verloc:

He leaped a foot high. Unexpectedly Mrs Verloc had desecrated the unbroken, reserved decency of her home by a shrill and terrible shriek.

'Help, Tom! Save me. I won't be hanged!'

He rushed forward, groping for her mouth with a silencing hand, and the shriek died out. But in his rush he had knocked her over. He felt her now clinging round his legs, and his terror reached its culminating point, became a sort of intoxication, entertained delusions, acquired the characteristics of delirium tremens. He positively saw snakes now. He saw the woman twined round him like a snake, not to be shaken off. She was not deadly. She was death itself – the companion of life.

Mrs Verloc, as if relieved by the outburst, was very far from behaving noisily now. She was pitiful.

'Tom, you can't throw me off now,' she murmured from the floor. 'Not unless you crush my head under your heel. I won't leave you.'

'Get up,' said Ossipon.

His face was so pale as to be quite visible in the profound black darkness of the shop; while Mrs Verloc, veiled, had no face, almost no discernible form. The trembling of something small and white, a flower in her hat, marked her place, her movements.

It rose in the blackness. She had got up from the floor, and Ossipon regretted not having run out at once into the street. But he perceived easily that it would not do. It would not do. She would run after him. She would pursue him shrieking till she sent every policeman within hearing in chase. And then goodness only knew what she would say of him. He was so frightened that for a moment the insane notion of strangling her in the dark passed through his mind. And he became more frightened than ever! She had him. He saw himself living in abject terror in some obscure hamlet in Spain or Italy; till some fine morning they found him dead, too, with a knife in his breast – like Mr Verloc. He sighed deeply. He dared not move. And Mrs Verloc waited in silence the good pleasure of her saviour, deriving comfort from his reflective silence.

Comic style

It is difficult to analyse what makes people laugh and what constitutes a comic style, but an A-level student ought to be able to pick out the comic elements in a passage and say why they are humorous.

Simple humour which can stem from the childish misinterpretation of a situation is found in *Cider with Rosie* by Laurie Lee. It is one of the most vividly drawn scenes of the novel – the village school. The writing is humorous but always quietly controlled and the ending of the passage is amusing, but understated.

> The village school at that time provided all the instruction we were likely to ask for. It was a small stone barn divided by a wooden partition into two rooms – The Infants and The Big Ones. There was one dame teacher, and perhaps a young girl assistant. Every child in the valley crowding there, remained till he was fourteen years old, then was presented to the working field or factory with nothing in his head more burdensome than a few mnemonics, a jumbled list of wars, and a dreamy image of the world's geography. It seemed enough to get by with, in any case; and was one up on our poor old grandparents.
>
> This school, when I came to it, was at its peak. Universal education and unusual fertility had packed it to the walls with pupils. Wild boys and girls from miles around – from the outlying farms and half-hidden hovels way up at the ends of the valley – swept down each day to add to our numbers, bringing with them strange oaths and odours, quaint garments and curious pies. They were my first amazed vision of any world outside the womanly warmth of my family; I didn't expect to survive it for long, and I was confronted with it at the age of four.
>
> The morning came, without any warning, when my sisters surrounded me, wrapped me in scarves, tied up my bootlaces, thrust a cap on my head, and stuffed a baked potato in my pocket.
>
> 'What's this?' I said.
>
> 'You're starting school today.'
>
> 'I ain't. I'm stopping 'ome.'
>
> 'Now, come on Loll. You're a big boy now.'
>
> 'I ain't.'
>
> 'You are.'
>
> 'Boo-hoo.'
>
> They picked me up bodily, kicking and bawling, and carried me up to the road.
>
> 'Boys who don't go to school get put into boxes, and turn into rabbits, and get chopped up Sundays.'
>
> I felt this was overdoing it rather, but I said no more after that. I arrived at the school just three feet tall and fatly wrapped in my scarves. The playground roared like a rodeo, and the potato burned through my thigh. Old boots, ragged stockings, torn trousers and skirts, went skating and skidding around me. The rabble closed in; I was encircled; grit flew in my face like shrapnel. Tall girls with frizzled hair, and huge boys with sharp elbows, began to prod me with hideous interest. They plucked at my scarves, spun me round like a top, screwed my nose, and stole my potato.
>
> I was rescued at last by a gracious lady – the sixteen-year-old junior-teacher – who boxed a few ears and dried my face and led me off to The Infants. I spent that first day picking holes in paper, then went home in a smouldering temper.
>
> 'What's the matter, Loll ? Didn't he like it at school, then?'
>
> 'They never gave me the present!'
>
> 'Present? What present?'
>
> 'They said they'd give me a present.'
>
> 'Well, now, I'm sure they didn't.'
>
> 'They did! They said: "You're Laurie Lee, ain't you? Well, just you sit there for the present." I sat there all day but I never got it. I ain't going back there again!'

Another example of language being used as a source of humour is in 'the foreign visitor' episode of *Our Mutual Friend* by Charles Dickens. In this extract we have the humorous situation of lack of communication between Mr Podsnap and the foreign gentleman.

> The majority of the guests were like the plate, and included several heavy articles weighing ever so much. But there was a foreign gentleman among them: whom Mr Podsnap had invited after much debate with himself – believing the whole European continent to be in mortal alliance against the young person – and there was a droll disposition, not only on the part of Mr Podsnap, but of everybody else, to treat him as if he were a child who was hard of hearing.
>
> As a delicate concession to this unfortunately-born foreigner, Mr Podsnap, in receiving him, had presented his wife as 'Madame Podsnap'; also his daughter as 'Mademoiselle Podsnap', with some inclination to add 'ma fille', in which bold venture, however, he checked himself. The Veneerings being at that time the only other arrivals, he had added (in a condescendingly explanatory

manner), 'Monsieur Vey-nair-reeng', and had then subsided into English.

'How do you like London?' Mr Podsnap now inquired from his station of host, as if he were administering something in the nature of a powder or potion to the deaf child; 'London, Londres, London?'

The foreign gentleman admired it.

'You find it Very Large?' said Mr Podsnap, spaciously.

The foreign gentleman found it very large.

'And Very Rich?'

The foreign gentleman found it, without doubt énormément riche.

'Enormously Rich, we say,' returned Mr Podsnap, in a condescending manner. 'Our English adverbs do Not terminate in Mong, and we Pronounce the "ch" as if there were a "t" before it. We Say Ritch.'

'Reetch,' remarked the foreign gentleman.

'And Do You Find, Sir,' pursued Mr Podsnap, with dignity, 'Many Evidences that Strike You, of our British Constitution in the Streets of The World's Metropolis, London, Londres, London?'

The foreign gentleman begged to be pardoned, but did not altogether understand.

'The Constitution Britannique,' Mr Podsnap explained, as if he were teaching in an infant school. 'We Say British, But You Say Britannique, You Know' (forgivingly, as if that were not his fault). 'The Constitution, Sir.'

The foreign gentleman said, 'Mais, yees; I know eem.'

A youngish sallowish gentleman in spectacles, with a lumpy forehead, seated in a supplementary chair at a corner of the table, here caused a profound sensation by saying, in a raised voice, 'Esker,' and then stopping dead.

'Mais oui,' said the foreign gentleman, turning towards him. 'Est-ce que? Quoi donc?'

But the gentleman with the lumpy forehead having for the time delivered himself of all that he found behind his lumps, spake for the time no more.

'I Was Enquiring,' said Mr Podsnap, resuming the thread of his discourse, 'Whether You Have Observed in our Streets as We should say, Upon Our Pavvy as you would say, any Tokens –'

The foreign gentleman with patient courtesy entreated pardon; 'But what was tokenz?'

Marks,' said Mr Podsnap; 'Signs, you know, Appearances – Traces.'

'Ah! Of a Orse?' inquired the foreign gentleman.

'We call it Horse,' said Mr Podsnap, with forbearance. 'In England, Angleterre, England, We Aspirate the "H", and We Say "Horse". Only our Lower Classes Say "Orse"?'

'Pardon,' said the foreign gentleman; 'I am alwiz wrong!'

'Our Language,' said Mr Podsnap, with a gracious consciousness of being always right, 'is Difficult. Ours is a Copious Language, and Trying to Strangers. I will not Pursue my Question.'

MODEL PASSAGE AND COMMENTARY

Passage A

'O, Angel – I am almost glad – because now you can forgive me! I have not made my confession. I have a confession, too – remember, I said so.'

'Ah, to be sure! Now then for it, wicked little one.'

'Perhaps, although you smile, it is as serious as yours, or more so.'

'It can hardly be more serious, dearest.'

'It cannot – O no, it cannot!' She jumped up joyfully at the hope. 'No, it cannot be more serious, certainly,' she cried, 'because 'tis just the same! I will tell you now.'

She sat down again.

Their hands were still joined. The ashes under the grate were lit by the fire vertically, like a torrid waste. Imagination might have beheld a Last Day luridity in this red-coaled glow, which fell on his face and hand, and on hers, peering into the loose hair about her brow, and firing the delicate skin underneath. A large shadow of her shape rose upon the wall and ceiling. She bent forward, at which each diamond on her neck gave a sinister wink like a toad's; and pressing her forehead against his temple she entered on her story of her acquaintance with Alec d'Urberville and its results, murmuring the words without flinching, and with her eyelids drooping down.

Her narrative ended; even its re-assertions and secondary explanations were done. Tess's voice throughout had hardly risen higher than its opening tone; there had been no exculpatory phrase of any kind, and she had not wept.

But the complexion even of external things seemed to suffer transmutation as her announcement progressed. The fire in the grate looked impish – demonically funny, as if it did not care in the least about her strait. The fender grinned idly, as if it too did not care. The light from the water-bottle was merely engaged in a chromatic problem. All material objects around announced their irresponsibility with terrible iteration. And yet nothing had changed since the moments when he had been kissing her; or rather, nothing in the substance of things. But the essence of things had changed.

When she ceased, the auricular impressions from their previous endearments seemed to hustle away into the corner of their brains, repeating themselves as echoes from a time of supremely purblind foolishness.

Clare performed the irrelevant act of stirring the fire; the intelligence had not even yet got to the bottom of him. After stirring the embers he rose to his feet, all the force of her disclosure had imparted itself now. His face had withered. In the strenuousness of his concentration he treadled fitfully on the floor. He could not, by any contrivance, think closely enough; that was the meaning of his vague movement. When he spoke it was in the most inadequate, commonplace voice of the many varied tones she had heard from him.

'Tess!'

'Yes, dearest.'

'Am I to believe this? From your manner I am to take it as true. O you cannot be out of your mind! You ought to be! Yet you are not... . My wife, my Tess – nothing in you warrants such a supposition as that?'

'I am not out of my mind,' she said.

'And yet –' He looked vacantly at her, to resume with dazed senses: 'Why didn't you tell me before? Ah, yes, you would have told me, in a way – but I hindered you, I remember!' These and other of his words were nothing but the perfunctory babble of the surface while the depths remained paralyzed. He turned away, and bent over a chair. Tess followed him to the middle of the room where he was, and stood there staring at him with eyes that did not weep. Presently she slid down upon her knees beside his foot, and from this position she crouched in a heap.

'In the name of our love, forgive me!' she whispered with a dry mouth. 'I have forgiven you for the same!'

(The end of Chapter XXXIV and the beginning of Chapter XXXV, *Tess of the D'Urbervilles*.)

Commentary on Passage A

This passage is taken from the novel *Tess of the D' Urbervilles*, by Thomas Hardy. Tess has been seduced by Alec d'Urberville, a distant relation, and she has had his child. This child has subsequently died. Tess falls in love with Angel Clare, who is undergoing practical experience of dairy farming at Talbothay's Dairy. He is the youngest son of a poor parson; he has to learn a practical skill to make his way in the world. Tess at first resists Angel's advances as she feels tainted by her relationship with d'Urberville, but because of the depth of her feelings she agrees to marry him. On their wedding night they agree to confess their past misdeeds. Clare confesses to having a sexual relationship with another woman prior to his marriage. Tess is just about to confess her relationship with Alec d'Urberville.

Tess's modest and unassuming nature is shown clearly in this passage. She uses phrases like 'forgive me', 'make my confession', as though she regards Angel as her Father Confessor and she definitely sees him as a superior being to herself. When she tells the story of Alec d'Urberville and herself she 'murmurs the words without flinching, and with her eyelids drooping down'.

Her total charm is demonstrated by descriptions of her physical beauty. The fire 'peered into the loose hair about her brow and fired the delicate skin underneath'. Her movements are light and graceful, 'she jumped joyfully up at the hope', her hesitancy and slight stumbling in her speech reflect her anxiety and her naivety. 'O, Angel – I am almost glad – because now you can forgive me! I have not made my confession, I have a confession, too – remember, I said so.'

Tess starts her confession with complete faith that Angel will forgive her. The sentence 'Their hands were still joined' shows their transitory united state which is soon to be shattered. She is so confident that she will be pardoned that she does not attempt to offer any excuses for her behaviour. 'Tess's voice throughout had hardly risen higher than its opening tone: there had been no exculpatory phrase of any kind, and she had not wept.' She does not realise until her confession is over that a double standard operates in Angel's mind over his sins and hers: his is judged as normal masculine behaviour, hers is unpardonable.

Although Angel's character has been hinted at when talking of Tess, a detailed analysis of his personality is needed in any commentary on this passage. At the beginning of the passage, he treats her confession as trivial – something which he cannot take seriously.

'Ah, to be sure! Now then for it, wicked little one.'

'Perhaps, although you smile, it is as serious as yours, or more so.'

'It can hardly be more serious, dearest.'

After she has confessed, although the surroundings are unaltered, everything will never be the same, 'the essence of things had changed'. Their previous idyllic state of happiness now seems 'supremely purblind foolishness'.

Hardy shows Angel's shocked state of mind in a series of short, staccato-like statements. His face and voice betray his complete loss of faith and feeling for his wife. 'His face had withered. In the strenuousness of his concentration he treadled fitfully on the floor. He could not, by any contrivance, think closely enough;'...

> 'Tess!'
> 'Yes, dearest.'
> 'Am I to believe this? From your manner I am to take it to be true. O you cannot be out of your mind! You ought to be! Yet you are not.... My wife, my Tess – nothing in you warrants such a supposition as that?'

The **melodramatic** tone of his speech shows his shocked mind. He knows that she has tried to tell him before when she wrote him a letter, but the letter was lost and so this attempt failed.

Angel is an unbending character who cannot vary his opinions once they are formed, 'These and other of his words were nothing but the perfunctory babble of the surface while the depths remained paralyzed.' He is beyond any emotion and beyond any human feeling. The double standard of morality has operated against Tess and 'she stood there staring at him with eyes that did not weep'. Her last words illustrate the desperation and hopelessness of her plight –

> 'In the name of our love, forgive me!' she whispered with a dry mouth. 'I have forgiven you for the same!'

The main features of the style of this passage are the short, melodramatic sentence structure and the use of household objects to suggest foreboding. The melodramatic style of speech has already been discussed, but the other **imagery** needs further explanation. Household objects which would normally appear friendly and comforting take on a sinister appearance and seem to be conspiring against Tess. 'The ashes under the grate were lit by the fire vertically, like a torrid waste. Imagination might have beheld a Last Day luridness in this red-coaled glow.' The image evoked is one which is reminiscent of Milton's *Paradise Lost* and the depths of hell where sinners suffer eternal damnation. The firelight makes things of beauty appear full of evil – 'A large shadow of her shape rose upon the wall and ceiling. She bent forward, at which each diamond on her neck gave a sinister wink like a toad's.'

After her story has ended, the household objects seem to gloat at her misery.

> The fire in the grate looked impish – demoniacally funny, as if it did not care in the least about her strait. The fender grinned idly... The light from the water-bottle was merely engaged in a chromatic problem. All material objects around announced their irresponsibility with terrible iteration.'

Hardy's pessimistic feeling that virtue and honesty go unrewarded is well shown in this passage. Tess is an innocent who suffers at the hands of a bigoted and unbending husband and when his forgiveness comes, it comes too late.

MODEL PASSAGE WITH QUESTIONS FOR PRACTICE

Passage B

> The rains having passed the uplands were dry. The wheels of the dairyman's spring cart, as he sped home from market, licked up the pulverised surface of the highway, and were followed by white ribands of dust, as if they had set a thin powder-train on fire. The cows jumped wildly over the five-barred barton-gate, maddened by the gad-fly; Dairyman Crick kept his shirt-sleeves permanently rolled up from Monday to Saturday: open windows had no effect in ventilation without open doors, and in the dairy-garden the blackbirds and thrushes crept about under the currant-bushes, rather in the manner of quadrupeds than of winged creatures. The flies in the kitchen were lazy, teasing, and familiar, crawling about in unwonted places, on the floors, into drawers, and over the

backs of the milkmaids' hands. Conversations were concerning sunstroke; while butter-making, and still more butter-keeping, was a despair.

They milked entirely in the meads for coolness and convenience, without driving in the cows. During the day the animals obsequiously followed the shadow of the smallest tree as it moved round the stem with the diurnal roll; and when the milkers came they could hardly stand still for the flies.

On one of these afternoons four or five unmilked cows chanced to stand apart from the general herd, behind the corner of a hedge, among them being Dumpling and Old Pretty, who loved Tess's hands above those of any other maid. When she rose from her stool under a finished cow Angel Clare, who had been observing her for some time, asked her if she would take the aforesaid creatures next. She silently assented, and with her stool at arm's length, and the pail against her knee, went round to where they stood. Soon the sound of Old Pretty's milk fizzing into the pail came through the hedge, and then Angel felt inclined to go round the corner also, to finish off a hard-yielding milcher who had strayed there, he being now as capable of this as the dairyman himself.

All the men, and some of the women, when milking, dug their foreheads into the cows and gazed into the pail. But a few – mainly the younger ones – rested their heads sideways. This was Tess Durbeyfield's habit. Her temple pressing the milcher's flank, her eyes fixed on the far end of the meadow with the quiet of one lost in meditation. She was milking Old Pretty thus, and the sun chancing to be on the milking-side it shone flat upon her pink gowned form and her white curtain-bonnet, and upon her profile, rendering it keen as a cameo cut from the dun background of the cow.

She did not know that Clare had followed her round, and that he sat under his cow watching her. The stillness of her head and features was remarkable: she might have been in a trance, her eyes open, yet unseeing. Nothing in the picture moved but Old Pretty's tail and Tess's pink hands, the latter so gently as to be a rhythmic pulsation only, as if they were obeying a reflex stimulus, like a beating heart.

How very lovable her face was to him. Yet there was nothing ethereal about it; all was real vitality, real warmth, real incarnation. And it was in her mouth that this culminated. Eyes almost as deep and speaking he had seen before, and cheeks perhaps as fair; brows as arched, a chin and throat almost as shapely; her mouth he had seen nothing to equal on the face of the earth. To a young man with the least fire in him, that little upward lift in the middle of her red top lip was distracting, infatuating, maddening. He had never before seen a woman's lips and teeth which forced upon his mind with such persistant iteration the old Elizabethan simile of roses filled with snow. Perfect, he, as a lover, might have called them off-hand. But no – they were not perfect. And it was the touch of the imperfect upon the would-be perfect that gave the sweetness, because it was that which gave the humanity.

(Chapter XXIV, *Tess of the D'Urbervilles*)

Passage B, *Tess of the D'Urbervilles*

Answer the following short questions on the passage and then use the information you have written to write a commentary on the passage along the lines suggested for Passage A.

1 How does Hardy suggest the heat in the passage?

2 What do you learn of the character and appearance of Tess? Use your own words and quote extracts from the passage.

3 What do you learn of the character and appearance of Angel Clare? Use your own words and quote from the passage.

4 How does Hardy suggest the attractiveness of the country setting?

5 How does Hardy suggest the relationship between Tess and Angel Clare?

6 Explain the following phrases:
   (a) line 2 'pulverized surface of the highway'
   (b) line 3 'as if they had set a thin powder-train on fire'
   (c) line 7 'rather in the manner of quadrupeds than of winged creatures'
   (d) lines 13–14 'the animals obsequiously followed the shadow of the smallest tree and moved round the stem with the diurnal roll'
   (e) lines 30–31 'rendering it as a cameo cut from the dun background of the cow'

(f) lines 35–36 'the latter so gently as to be a rhythmic pulsation only, as if they were obeying a reflex stimulus, like a beating heart.'

(g) lines 37–38 'Yet there was nothing ethereal about it; all was real vitality, real warmth, real incarnation.'

(h) lines 42–46 'He had never before seen a woman's lips and teeth which forced upon his mind with such persistent iteration the old Elizabethan simile of roses filled with snow. Perfect, he as a lover, might have called them off-hand. But no – they were not perfect. And it was the touch of the imperfect upon the would–be perfect that gave the sweetness, because it was that which gave the humanity.'

7 Comment on the sentence structure of the passage.

Now, using all this information and reading the model commentary on Passage A, write your own commentary.

Question bank

VIRGINIA WOOLF: *To the Lighthouse*

1 Either (a) Write an appreciation of the passage below, paying particular attention to its narrative and stylistic features.

Or (b) The next section of the novel begins:
'So with the house empty and the doors locked and the mattresses rolled round, those stray airs, advance guards of great armies, blustered in, brushed bare boards, nibbled and fanned...'
(i) Continue the section in your own words but in the same style, for another paragraph or two; then
(ii) Write a brief commentary on what you have written. Comment on any difficulties you may have experienced in imitating Virginia Woolf's style. How far did writing your own version help you to identify and appreciate the characteristic features of the original?

But what after all is one night? A short space, especially when the darkness dims so soon, and so soon a bird sings, a cock crows, or a faint green quickens, like a turning leaf, in the hollow of the wave. Night, however, succeeds to night. The winter holds a pack of them in store and deals them equally, evenly, with indefatigable
5 fingers. They lengthen; they darken. Some of them hold aloft clear planets, plates of brightness. The autumn trees, ravaged as they are, take on the flash of tattered flags kindling in the gloom of cool cathedral caves where gold letters on marble pages describe death in battle and how bones bleach and burn far away in Indian sands. The autumn trees gleam in the yellow moonlight, in the light of the harvest
10 moons, the light which mellows the energy of labour, and smooths the stubble, and brings the wave lapping blue to the shore.
    It seemed now as if, touched by human penitence and all its toil, divine goodness had parted the curtain and displayed behind it, single, distinct, the hare erect; the wave falling; the boat rocking, which, did we deserve them, should be ours always.
15 But alas, divine goodness, twitching the cord, draws the curtain; it does not please him; he covers his treasures in a drench of hail, and so breaks them, so confuses them that it seems impossible that their calm should ever return or that we should ever compose from their fragments a perfect whole or read in the littered pieces the clear words of truth. For our penitence deserves a glimpse only; our toil respite only.
20   The nights now are full of wind and destruction; the trees plunge and bend and their leaves fly helter skelter until the lawn is plastered with them and they lie packed in gutters and choke rain pipes and scatter damp paths. Also the sea tosses itself and breaks itself, and should any sleeper fancying that he might find on the beach an answer to his doubts, a sharer of his solitude, throw off his bedclothes and go down
25 by himself to walk on the sand, no image with semblance of serving and divine

promptitude comes readily to hand bringing the night to order and making the world
reflect the compass of the soul. The hand dwindles in his hand; the voice bellows in
his ear. Almost it would appear that it is useless in such confusion to ask the night
those questions as to what, and why, and wherefore, which tempt the sleeper from
30   his bed to seek an answer.
      [Mr Ramsay stumbling along a passage stretched his arms out one dark morning,
but, Mrs Ramsay having died rather suddenly the night before, he stretched his
arms out. They remained empty.]

Cambridge 1994

JANE AUSTEN: *Pride and Prejudice*

2 Either (a) In what ways is this passage characteristic of Jane Austen's narrative
style in *Pride and Prejudice*?

Or (b) How far does this discussion of Jane and the Bingley family foreshadow the
major themes of the novel?

The ladies of Longbourn soon waited on those of Netherfield. The visit was returned
in due form, Miss Bennet's pleasing manners grew on the good will of Mrs Hurst
and Miss Bingley; and though the mother was found to be intolerable and the
younger sisters not worth speaking to, a wish of being better acquainted with them,
5   was expressed towards the two eldest. By Jane this attention was received with the
greatest pleasure; but Elizabeth still saw superciliousness in their treatment of every
body, hardly excepting even her sister, and could not like them; though their
kindness to Jane, such as it was, had a value as arising in all probability from the
influence of their brother's admiration. It was generally evident whenever they met,
10   that he did admire her, and to her it was equally evident that Jane was yielding to
the preference which she had begun to entertain for him from the first, and was in a
way to be very much in love; but she considered with pleasure that it was not likely
to be discovered by the world in general, since Jane united with great strength of
feeling, a composure of temper and a uniform cheerfulness of manner, which would
15   guard her from the suspicions of the impertinent. She mentioned this to her friend
Miss Lucas.
      'It may perhaps be pleasant', replied Charlotte, 'to be able to impose on the public
in such a case; but it is sometimes a disadvantage to be so very guarded. If a
woman conceals her affection with the same skill from the object of it, she may lose
20   the opportunity of fixing him; and it will then be but poor consolation to believe the
world equally in the dark. There is so much of gratitude or vanity in almost every
attachment, that it is not safe to leave any to itself. We can all begin freely – a slight
preference is natural enough; but there are very few of us who have heart enough to
be really in love without encouragement. In nine cases out of ten, a woman had
25   better shew more affection than she feels. Bingley likes your sister undoubtedly; but
he may never do more than like her, if she does not help him on.'
      'But she does help him on, as much as her nature will allow. If I can perceive her
regard for him, he must be a simpleton indeed not to discover it too.'
      'Remember, Eliza, that he does not know Jane's disposition as you do.'
30   'But if a woman is partial to a man, and does not endeavour to conceal it, he must
find it out.'
      'Perhaps he must, if he sees enough of her. But though Bingley and Jane meet
tolerably often, it is never for many hours together; and as they always see each
other in large mixed parties, it is impossible that every moment should be employed
35   in conversing together. Jane should therefore make the most of every half hour in
which she can command his attention. When she is secure of him, there will be
leisure for falling in love as much as she chooses.'

(Chapter 6)

Cambridge 1994

NOVEL CRITICISM BIBLIOGRAPHY

Allen, Walter	*Reading a Novel*
	English Novel: Developments
Gilmour, Robin	*The Novel in the Victorian Times*
Graham, Kenneth	*English Criticism of the Novel*
Hardy, Barbara	*The Appropriate Form*
Hawthorn, Jeremy	*Studying the Novel: An Introduction*
Liddell, Robert	*A Treatise on the Novel*
Lodge, David	*Language of Fiction: Essays*
MacCarthy, B G	*Women Writers: Their Contribution*
Matthews, J H	*Surrealism and the Novel*
Miller, Stuart	*The Picaresque Novel*
Stubbs, Patricia	*Women and Fiction: Feminism*
	The Novel Today
Watt, Ian	*The Victorian Novel*

3.2 NONFICTION

NOTE ON NONFICTION TEXTS

Although the novel from Defoe to William Golding holds, rightly, the pride of place in sections devoted to prose on the syllabuses, works from other genres may conveniently be noted here as they appear among the prose texts set:

Essays (Bacon, Milton, Addison, Johnson, Lamb, Hazlitt);

Biographies and autobiographies (De Quincey, Boswell, Gibbon, Johnson, Charles Darwin, Gosse);

Diaries (Pepys and John Evelyn);

Letters (of many good collections of these the one normally found is a selection of Keats's and even this usually in conjunction with the poetry);

Criticism Prescribed for its own excellence of style and the light thrown upon the thought of the critics themselves, since those chosen for A-level study are usually great writers in other genres too: Dryden's Prefaces and *Essay on Dramatic Poetry*, Addison on Milton, Johnson, Wordsworth, Coleridge, Matthew Arnold, Shaw, Lawrence, Eliot and Auden;

Occasional works in other genres, specially chosen for their intrinsic merit or special interest with regard to English language or literature: philosophy (Browne, Bacon, Hobbes); natural history or sociology (Gilbert White, Richard Jefferies, Flora Thompson's *Lark Rise to Candleford*); linguistics (Sir Ernest Gowers' *Complete Plain Words*). This list is not exhaustive but will give an indication of the range of works set.

3.3 THE NOVEL

INTRODUCTION

Depending on the sort of novel prescribed (and for convenience I will include other kinds of prose work under this head in future) there are likely to be certain common features in the questions. The candidate must know the principal features of the book he or she has chosen, for it is usually these features that are singled out for the questions, not more peripheral concerns. You must therefore grasp firmly and thoroughly whichever of the following (points 1–9) forms one or more of the main features of the novel you are studying.

1 Satirical, polemical or didactic elements

Nearly every great novel, to a greater or lesser degree, or more or less profoundly, bears examination on the following points:

❶ Is the author trying to change, reform or attack anything?

❷ Is the author holding anything up for ridicule, or even harmless amusement?

❸ Is the author bitter about any social abuses or other forms of folly or wickedness?

If you decide the novel you are studying does have satirical, polemical or didactic elements, you should analyse how such elements can be identified and the manner of their expression.

If the novel you are studying is not contemporary and satirises a political or social situation of its own time, you should ask yourself:

❶ How effective was the satire? Did it change anything?

❷ What proportion of the novel is devoted to such elements? Is the novel still valuable if the cause or motive for the satire is now past?

❸ If the cause is not yet dead, is the satire still relevant?

❹ Does the satire take on new significance in the light of events that have occurred since the work was written?

With regard to the continuing relevance of satirical works, you should note that political satire may be regenerated if history repeats itself. Much moral satire is, of course, perennial. For instance, vanity may present itself in different guises, but the underlying vice is the same.

It should be remembered that even in the case of a primarily satirical novel or essay, other elements may play a very important part. You should decide whether the characters survive the burden of their satiric intent, as do many of Dickens's characters, for example. Are they credible and 'solid' or are they mere 'types'? Are they intended as 'types' (for this, their names may give a clue, for example, 'Hypocrisy' in *The Pilgrim's Progress*).

2 Character

It is important to remember that characters are not 'persons' who can be detached from their books as people can be taken from their normal lives; they are a part of their story and very often closely interrelated with several other characters of the book. Even Hemingway's lonely old man (*The Old Man and the Sea*) owes much of his character to the people of his memories and daydreams, as well as to the boy through whose eyes we see him. He is the centre of a parable created by the author to make a certain point about human endeavour, and man's place and state in life. You may find it useful to prepare 'character studies' of all the main characters in the novels you are studying as an exercise in preliminary memorising or foundation work. However, while at GCSE such preparation can form a basis for examination answers, A-level questions require more subtle treatment. The isolated character study is likely to prove too mechanical for the questions that are asked. They will require a more selective treatment, with more assessment and comparison of aspects of character based upon an overall close understanding of the whole work. One cannot dispense with close reference, examples and supporting details to illustrate generalisations and therefore you cannot afford to despise the sort of information gathered in character studies. You should, however, be able to transcend the method, and without knowing substantially less, know how to arrange the material more sensitively, because it is better digested and related to other characters, themes and subject matter.

A more useful preparation on character would almost certainly be intelligent and well-informed discussion with other students, perhaps led by an instructor with special knowledge of the book. (Sixth-form conferences can be very helpful in this.) Such discussions should include considerations such as the comparison of one character with another, the motives of their actions, their characteristic outlook and thinking, their values and their special foibles or traits.

You should examine not only how the characters operate but also in what manner they are operated upon and with what result. (Tess in Hardy's novel *Tess of the D'Urbervilles* is a good example of the fruitfulness of this line of thinking.) A good light upon character is thrown by examining a character's reactions to events. For example, in Hardy's *Far From the Madding Crowd*, Bathsheba's vanity and frivolity cause her to write Mr Boldwood a valentine; his stern, humourless and intense nature causes him to take it seriously. These small beginnings, mixed with the extraordinary personality of Sergeant Troy, lead to murder and suicide. Again, in Jane Austen's *Northanger Abbey*, Catherine's earlier predilection for the ridiculous 'Gothic horror' novels – an affected fashion of the time – leads directly to her unfortunate misunderstandings in the country mansion, her head being full of romantic nonsense. This aberration, of course, can be and is dispelled, making her a maturer, wiser woman. Similar romantic delusions, derived from reading, pervert the behaviour and thought of characters as diverse as DH Lawrence's Miriam Leivers (*Sons and Lovers*), and Joseph Conrad's Lord Jim.

You should consider a character's role in the novel: Mrs Ramsay's centrality in Virginia Woolf's *To the Lighthouse* for example, or Nostromo's in Conrad's novel of that name. A-level questions often ask for comment on a character's achievement or failure in some endeavour, or on how far a character or a set of characters express their nature in a certain key chapter or scene.

Characters may also be assessed as to how far they are realistic, credible, natural, or heightened for special purpose such as satire, humour or tragic grandeur. They may range from cardboard stereotypes, or mere personifications of qualities as in an allegory; through grotesqueness or exaggeration of traits to heroically idealised or deliberately demeaned persons, such as are often found in moralities like some Victorian novels and twentieth-century books such as *The Lord of the Flies* by William Golding. There is, for example, the interesting trio of Angel Clare, Tess and Alec d'Urberville in Hardy's *Tess of the D'Urbervilles*.

It is worth remembering that a first-person narrator in a novel is not the novelist but a character who sees things only in the light of his or her own point of view, and coloured by his or her personality. Thus in Conrad's *Lord Jim*, after some pages of authorial third-person narration, we begin to view things as Marlow saw them, and later as did the girl Jewel in Patusan, and even (since Marlow was not present at the later scenes) as did Gentleman Brown, a biased villain. Conrad gains variety and depth by the use of these different viewpoints. Conrad's *Nostromo* is far more complex in the use of the same technique, and Henry James's *What Maisie Knew* and *The Ambassadors* are remarkable in their application of this principle. You should resist the temptation to assume that the author's main character is synonymous with the author. For example, Stephen Dedalus in Joyce's *A Portrait of the Artist as a Young Man* and *Ulysses* is not necessarily representing Joyce himself. Autobiographical knowledge of an author can be enlightening but should be handled with caution. Identification of any fictional character with a prototype in real life is a bad practice; many characters are combinations of different people, not to mention the author's creative additions. An autobiographical persona such as Dedalus in Joyce's *A Portrait of the Artist as a Young Man* or *Ulysses*, Birkin in Lawrence's *Women in Love*, or David Copperfield or Pip in Dickens, are not to be taken as complete or even accurate portraits of their authors – they are often no more than studies in self-criticism. In the same way, the innumerable portraits by artists of their friends, enemies or acquaintances are notoriously one-sided, exaggerated and even, on occasion, libellous. Hence the familiar disclaimer on many novels' title pages.

To summarise on character in novels, students should ask themselves these elementary questions:

1. Is what other characters say or think about this character true?
2. Is what the character says or thinks about him- or herself true?
3. Is his or her character revealed in action or in suffering of events?
4. How is his or her character revealed by what he or she says and thinks, and in what terms does he or she express his or her thoughts?
5. Does the author use 'all knowing' privilege to throw any light upon the character?
6. Does the character undergo any significant change in the story?

You should also ask yourself more subtle questions:

1. Does the character carry conviction?
2. Is the character consistent? Is he or she played off against another/other character(s)?
3. Does the character come to life or remain as a stereotype – if the latter, is this for a special purpose?
4. Do we ever care what is happening to the character?

5 Do we wonder how the character will behave – are we ever suprised by his or her behaviour?

6 Does the character play a brief or minor role, if so how necessary is he or she to the action?

7 What is his or her role if a major character – do his or her words or actions carry themes?

8 Does he or she influence events and lives – if so, how far?

9 Is he or she used as a mouthpiece for authorial ideas or opinion?

It is by these and similar investigations that one may prepare for questions on character.

3 Theme

Care must be taken not to confuse the theme and plot as sometimes happens in the case of strongly plotted novels such as George Eliot's *Silas Marner* and Dickens's *A Christmas Carol*.

A *combination* of plot, characters and language may form the vehicle for whatever themes the novel has. A simple (and simplified) definition would be that the novel's theme is what it is about and its plot is what happens in it. It is very common, of course, for novels to have no themes at all and yet still display wonderful plots (e.g. *Tarzan of the Apes*, Edgar Rice Burroughs; *Enter the Saint*, Leslie Charteris). A vast flood of such works is released on to the market in every generation to enable people to pass otherwise unoccupied time agreeably and to make money for their authors.

Important themes, that is, those that advance or restate in satisfying new ways our understanding of ourselves and our world, are 'hallmarks' of good literature. The book of trivial or no theme, unfortunately, is the one often acclaimed and widely read, although it will not be found on A-level syllabuses.

Many fine, even great novels, though they cannot be such without themes, can and do dispense with any recognisable plot. Short stories exemplify this; many are little more than 'studies' or situations. Where there is no real plot the theme must necessarily be carried by character and/or language; but if such are the heart, the theme is the soul of the work.

Novels that are thematic rather than plotted, such as Virginia Woolf's *The Waves* are often considered 'difficult'. The attitude reflected in EM Forster's resigned dictum 'yes – oh dear – yes – the novel tells a story' is still common. Chapter 2 of EM Forster's *Aspects of the Novel* is stimulating reading on this subject and has been used as a basis for A-level questions.

The importance placed on themes in A-level questions may be illustrated by a paper where only one alternative was set on Lawrence's *The Rainbow*. The first option was 'What do you think Lawrence is trying to tell us about marriage and parenthood in *The Rainbow*?'; the second 'Why do you think Lawrence called his novel *The Rainbow*'?

It is not uncommon for a novel's major theme to be suggested by its title. Other examples of this include *To the Lighthouse* (Virginia Woolf), *The Way of All Flesh* (Samuel Butler), *The Lord of the Flies* and *The Inheritors* (William Golding), *Heart of Darkness* (Joseph Conrad). The titles of a novel's parts may also be used in this way, as: 'The Mosque', 'The Caves', 'The Temple' (*A Passage to India*, EM Forster), 'The Silver of the Mine', 'The Isabels', 'The Lighthouse' (*Nostromo*, Joseph Conrad).

It is necessary to identify themes from whatever element in the novel is enlisted to express them, whether story, character or language. For example *A Portrait of the Artist as a Young Man* by James Joyce may, at first reading and at a first level, seem not much more than just that – a neutral if faithful exercise in autobiography with the character Stephen Dedalus representing Joyce himself. However, as the book develops, if you like at a second level, there is growing evidence that what it is really about at least includes the imperative need to escape from all that Dublin contains: family, religion, friends and academicism, to be free to be his creative self. One of the characteristic motifs of the novel is 'I will not serve'. It is about the growing awareness of Stephen of his genius and what threatens to destroy it. It is therefore, at a third level, also about how the human spirit may be enslaved by the dead, corrupt and sham elements of its environment and in that sense the novel is of universal application and embodies a theme as old as Exodus. Thus in order to get to the heart of a novel's theme you should learn to look and then look again.

An interesting example of the use of images or 'motifs' to help convey the essential themes of a novel, is to be found in *The Inheritors* by William Golding. As the title indicates and as is expanded in the book, the overall theme is the supercession of the old – comfortable as it may be – by the new, because more technically advanced and intellectually vigorous. In the clash and interplay of these two worlds lies all the tension and interest of the book. For example, the Old People hate water, but the New Ones have mastered it, and the presence and sound of the roaring waterfall is intermittently referred to throughout the book: the New People cross the river on canoes never seen before by the Old, who can scarcely cross a creek as their log bridge has been removed.

When deciding on a novel's major themes, it is a useful procedure to begin with the most obvious and work down to the smallest details and incidents, noting how these fit in and build up the picture. If details are taken irrespective of any overall theme, it is easier to be irrelevant and waste time over less important aspects.

By dovetailing the small pieces into the larger ones, the selection or pursuit of irrelevancies may be avoided. The thematic reasons for placing Gulliver (*Gulliver's Travels*, Jonathan Swift) first in Lilliput, then in Brobdingnag, then Laputa and other places and lastly the country of the Houyhnhnms and Yahoos, should be well grasped before any of the lesser activities in any place may be well understood. The broader gradations and differing emphases of satire should be noted in the whole work, the better to understand local episodes. In the first two, betrayals by royalty ('of so little weight are the greatest Services to Princes, when put into the balance with a Refusal to gratify their Passions') are set against services and kindnesses, while in 'Laputa' Swift gives freer reign to his attacks on pedantic folly, and in the last part he achieves the greatest power of the famous 'saeva indignatio' in the contrast between the two kinds of creature. Gulliver, as the 'normal' man, moves through these scenes as a foil for the ways of life of the creatures in them, expressing the likely reaction of the reader rather like a Greek chorus. Our moral or political positions are shown up in various lights, although of course the eighteenth-century context makes a good deal of this special to that time and in some cases peculiar to Swift. Presumably the Royal Society would not agree with all of his attitudes to scientific research, nor would modern scientists who have descended from them. (It should be observed here that very often, perhaps due to the length of the novel, Parts I and II only of this novel are set for A level.)

Similarly the content and thematic contributions of each of the three sections of *Nostromo* and *A Passage to India* must be balanced and assessed for their place in the whole work; indeed, in the case of the latter, to appreciate why the third part was added to it at all. This is a good example of a book which, if read for the story only, seems to be all over by the end of the 'Caves'. Unless the transcending yet also immanent theme of communication or its failure between men, between races and between men and their land, or men and God, is deduced from the characters, incidents and language of all three parts, there is little value in criticising any one part or paragraph of *A Passage to India*.

Finally it must be said that for much the same reason, other novels, poems or essays by, and good biographies about, these and other great novelists whose work is prescribed, most emphatically repay attention. You can then trace themes and give weight to your opinions.

4 Plot

Although A-level questions seldom, if ever, require straightforward plot narration, the student should know thoroughly every stage of development of the plot, especially every stage of the development of the relationships of the leading characters with their attendant circumstances. It is helpful to draw diagrammatic plot plans to bring out more clearly circumstances on a time-line. These emphasise the significant 'turns' and advances, the main crises and clarify complications such as time-shifts or changes of scene. Time-shifts include gaps or leaps of time forward as well as backward, and simultaneous action in other scenes.

An obvious warning should be recorded here: candidates should be particularly on their guard against being drawn into an irrelevant parade of such knowledge; questions always require you to judge, select and make new rearrangements of the prepared material, rarely to trot it straight out, unless by a happy coincidence a particular question has been fully prepared in advance. This warning holds good for lengthy quotations; these should not be uncritically or unselectively quoted simply because known. You should only quote the relevant lines, and not too many of them. For example, no question is likely to ask a candidate to reproduce in full any particular episode of, say, *Middlemarch* by George Eliot, but in answer to a question on how far Dorothea, its heroine, gains in self-knowledge, the candidate is called upon to refer to such episodes and incidents of the novel as properly illustrate circumstances in which she becomes aware of her strengths, her limitations, in short, aware of herself. Here, the art is to be as comprehensive as possible: the examiner is likely to have as a guide a list of the possible areas of reference relevant to this question, and it behoves candidates aspiring to full marks to be as complete as possible, and not to dwell too long on one or two episodes they perhaps know better than others. This requires a period of steady and concentrated thinking in advance, with possibly a few notes jotted down as memory aids.

If the question is actually based on the plot, as for example, 'Show how the separate strands of *Middlemarch* are blended into a unified whole' then the same principle applies: large sketches of each 'strand' including the leading story should be left in favour of consideration of the actual manner in which such 'strands' are linked one with the other by character, cross-over of thematic or narrative material, or symmetry of structure. Notice how closely the need for actual knowledge of the material goes hand in hand with the successful answering of such questions. It cannot be denied that a judicious and discriminating intelligence is necessary for tackling A-level questions; fortunately the pomposity and jargon of the old phrasing of questions in which simple and straightforward ideas were wrapped up in obscurity, are no longer inflicted on the candidate.

A further illustration of comprehensiveness in the selection of relevant plot material can be given by a question which requires an examination of Walter Morel's status in and popularity with his family in DH Lawrence's *Son and Lovers*. The times when he is accepted by the children should be cited as well as the more immediately obvious drunken bullying and loss of sympathy; the special relationship with Mrs Morel should be noted and distinguished from the implacable hatred of the sick Paul, and the latter's uncompromising rejection of Walter's clumsy attempts at sympathy and communication. In a consideration of the attitudes of the parents to their children, Walter's reception of the news of William's death may be usefully compared or contrasted with Gertrude's where the only thing that brings her back to life is the near death of her youngest son and next object of possessive love, Paul.

The following examination question on Joyce's *A Portrait of the Artist as a Young Man* is a thematic question but required selection from the plot may demonstrate the reverse process: thus, 'What chiefly motivates Stephen is an increasing desire for freedom. Discuss', necessitates the survey of the novel with a view to writing on this subject. The candidate might turn over in his or her mind all the respects in which Stephen is restricted or cramped or frustrated; as he grows up, he is hampered by conditions in his home, by the schools he attends, by his ignorant and insensitive companions, by hidebound teachers, by his mother's religion and Jesuitical indoctrination, by sexual frustration and the terror of damnation springing from sermons and by artistic narrowness and Philistinism, and by the 'dear dirty' city of Dublin itself. Growing impatience and restiveness under it all leads in the end to self-appointed exile – a complete break with his entire background. He gains freedom from all previous shackles as he applies his 'Non serviam' to each one. Relevant quotation may be made; in particular, remarks about Stephen's mother; his refusal of her dying entreaty that he should make his communion. But as the question invites one to 'discuss' this proposition, it should be noticed that it is quite relevant to consider, more briefly because less significantly, the other possible motivations for Stephen's actions in his early life – that is the period covered by this book (he appears again in *Ulysses*). We have examined what 'chiefly' motivates Stephen, but there are such drives as his desire for intellectual supereminence; his desire for others' recognition of this and his desire to be an artist. These things are more positive than his urgent need for freedom – he needs to be free for something, and gaining his freedom is the prerequisite for his larger ambitions. His 'epiphanies', especially the one of the girl on the beach, give him some of the evidence to justify these motives.

There are two main types of plot found in novels: the first is the highly structured, architectonic story, with artfully arranged parallels, contrasts, discoveries, shifts of scene and time, character groupings or major character establishment (e.g. the parallel or contrasting pairs in Conrad's *Victory*, the police and anarchist groups in *The Secret Agent*, and Nostromo and Decoud in *Nostromo*), the engineering of coincidences, concealed with varying success so as to appear natural or inevitable. It may be that the structure of this type may be loose, or full of unresolved beginnings or dead ends, but the principal test of such plots is that they may be easily paraphrased or told as stories. Time shifts may be rearranged to be chronological as the film of *Lord Jim* did for that novel and generally speaking there is a strong air of 'what happens next' in such plots.

The second type may be called 'episodic' or 'organic': there is less concern with 'a story' and more with the growth and development of affairs, or the progress of events, as in life.

The progress through time of a character or set of characters, merely to see where they will arrive, is one of the examples of this type such as in *War and Peace*, *The Rainbow*, *Mrs Dalloway*, *The Forsyte Saga*, *Tristram Shandy*: usually only parts, if anything, of such novels can be related as 'stories'. Events grow naturally from prior events, with no obvious plan (though of course with unifying themes).

A third type of novel may be considered to have scarcely any plot, but since the content of such novels may be described, and as this type includes very good novels, I mention them here: they are the 'poetical' novels, almost prose poems; the action subsists in character and language, in some extreme cases in language alone. This is a type which not so long ago would not have been regarded as a novel at all, but with the work of Woolf (*The Waves*), Joyce (*Finnegans Wake*) and Beckett (*Watt*, *The Unnameable*, *How It Is*), the definition or boundaries of the novel have to be redrawn to accommodate them: there is a decided and firm, even formal, structure to such novels, but it is a structure of their material and language rather than a plot structure.

5 Setting and background in novels

The geographical and social background of most novels is significant and should be studied for itself, whether it be the Victorian London of Dickens's *Our Mutual Friend*, the Mexico of Graham Green's *The Power and Glory*, or, should it ever be set, Lawrence's *The Plumed Serpent* or the lovely Wessex of nearly all of Hardy. Most authors of such novels, of course, know their country very well at first hand. However, it is not necessarily the authenticity that makes the setting so important, but its use in many novels not only as a background but actually as a force in the novel, for thematic or other purposes. Whether it was poets or novelists who first consciously conceived the idea of turning backgrounds into active partners is hard to say: the honour may even be Shakespeare's; it is sufficient to be aware of their employment as such.

Hardy's settings, for example, often of several distinct kinds in one novel, are as vital to the understanding of his themes as the deliberately exploited landscape features of the poet WH Auden's *Bucolics*. Certainly an imaginative power akin to that of fine nature poetry is achieved by such novels as Hardy's *The Return of the Native*. Here, the famous first chapter which develops the atmosphere of Egdon Heath establishes a mood that prevails over the book, and which the characters seem to share. This conscious handling of scenery is a kind of Wordsworthian alchemy, in which moral, sensuous, spiritual or even intellectual concepts may be established. At its plainest we find this in open allegory such as Spenser's epic *The Faerie Queene* which is a set of narrations in verse, and Bunyan's *The Pilgrim's Progress*, or in concealed allegory such as *The Spire* or *The Lord of the Flies*, both by William Golding. The allegory may become very subtle in works such as *The Rainbow* or *Women in Love* by DH Lawrence, in Hardy's *Far from the Madding Crowd* and *Tess of the D'Urbervilles*, in Emily Brontë's *Wuthering Heights* or Conrad's *Heart of Darkness*.

A fine example of the suggestive painting of a setting is the first chapter of *The Rainbow* with its delicate allusions to the pressures and impulses in the lives of the inhabitants of the environs of Cossethay, from which the characters of the ensuing novel are to be drawn from one generation to another. See also the treatment of *The Man Who Loved Islands* by Lawrence, where the theme is paralleled by the successive series of diminishing islands in which the man hopes, self-deludingly, to be happy. In Conrad's *Victory* there is a supposedly paradisal island, but its derelict coal mine, black jetty and abandoned rails, offices and bungalows unmistakably suggest the vanity of trying to escape, and the violent storm, as so often in Conrad, heralds the catastrophe. Axel Heyst is forcibly returned to the evil realities of existence, as the setting so ominously suggests he will be.

To summarise: the ordinary function of the setting is to provide realism of context to plot and character; it gives them a historical, social and geographical background which enhances their authenticity; it adds atmosphere, colour and interest; as a side-effect it can provide documentary knowledge of place rather in the manner of a travel guide and this can also add interest, verisimilitude and satisfaction to our normal curiosity about our world and its affairs. Many novelists have first-hand experience or do careful research on their settings (e.g. Conrad for *Nostromo*, as he had never experienced life on a Caribbean island). Novels, even bad ones, may therefore be mines of information but the main and organic function of setting remains the provision of a living and cooperative medium for the better understanding of character, plot and, above all, themes.

6 Comparison of the novel with other genres

Occasionally questions are set at A level which touch on the similarity of a novel to a work or works of another genre, either in its structure or its method. Such questions presuppose a good knowledge of, and ability to define at least competently, the genre for comparison. For example, medieval morality and allegory lie behind Bunyan's *The Pilgrim's Progress* and social history behind Dickens's *A Tale of Two Cities* and Elizabeth Gaskell's *North and South*.

Tragedy It is particularly necessary to be able to define and know some good examples of tragedy, as this has a large body of theory and practice built up over the centuries. Some ages in history tend to produce tragic novels rather than tragedies: *Tess of the D'Urbervilles*, *Jude the Obscure* and *The Mayor of Casterbridge* are examples from the nineteenth century. For generally dramatic treatment in the eighteenth century there are Henry Fielding's *Joseph Andrews* and Oliver Goldsmith's *The Vicar of Wakefield*.

Journalism diaries and letters Documentary journalism may be referred to in connection with novels such as Daniel Defoe's *Moll Flanders* and the journal or diary in connection with, for example, the same author's *Journal of the Plague Year*.

Biography and autobiography Biography and autobiography are very closely linked to the novel, so that different kinds of prose work as set may be required to be compared with kinds not set. As for novels, the features and elements of the genre not prescribed have to be recognised in the work that is prescribed: if the work is in any way similar to another genre, such features need to be analysed in advance of probable questions. Although it is not normally expected, for autobiographical novels, that the candidate be conversant with the life of the author and where the parallels lie, it is useful and certainly often very interesting to read a good biography of those novelists who are particularly strong in autobiographical material in their work, or some of it. A short list here should include:

Compton Mackenzie (*Sinister Street*)
Somerset Maugham (*The Razor's Edge*)
Orwell (*Burmese Days*, *A Clergyman's Daughter* – others of his books are frankly autobiographical, such as *Down and Out in Paris and London*, *Homage to Catalonia*)
Lawrence (*Sons and Lovers*)
Scott Fitzgerald (*Tender is the Night*)
Hemingway (*A Farewell to Arms*)
Conrad (*Youth*, *The Heart of Darkness*)

In the nineteenth century:

Dickens (*David Copperfield*)
Hardy (*A Pair of Blue Eyes*)
George Eliot (*Scenes from Clerical Life*, *The Mill on the Floss*)
Melville (*Bartleby*)
Samuel Butler (*The Way of All Flesh*)
Kipling (*Kim*, *Stalky and Co.*)

Autobiographies occasionally seen on the syllabuses may be noted here: Johnson's *Journey to the Western Islands of Scotland*, which should be read in conjunction with Boswell's *Journal of a Tour to the Hebrides*; Edmund Goss's *Father and Son*, Darwin's *The Voyage of the Beagle*; Conrad's *A Personal Record* and *The Mirror of the Sea*; Sassoon's *Memoirs of an Infantry Officer*; Graves's *Goodbye to All That*; Cyril Connolly's *Enemies of Promise*; T E Lawrence's *The Mint*; Koestler's *Darkness at Noon*; Ford Madox Ford's *Memories and Impressions* read in conjunction with *The Good Soldier*. In the same way Graves, Lawrence, Hardy and Sassoon should be read with their related poetry, and Keith Douglas's *Alamein to Zem Zem* with his Second World War poems. Many poets have written at least one novel, and beside Hardy's double achievement should be read his autobiography published under the name of a biography by his second wife and secretary, Florence Emily Hardy.

Political theory Behind George Orwell's *1984*, stemming from the political allegory of *Animal Farm*, for example, may be noted the political theory directly embodied in *Goldstein's Book* and elsewhere implicit in the ideas and action of the novel.

Useful reading A useful book which relates the theory of tragedy to its foundation in Aristotle's *Poetics* is F L Lucas's *Tragedy*. Other studies of the different genres include an interesting series of essays published by Martin Secker, – titled *The Art and Craft of Letters*:

Comedy, Parody, Satire, Ballad, Epic, Short Story and History are described. However, the best examples of the major practitioners remain the most useful frames of reference and comparison.

7 Humour

If the novel or a large part of it is meant to be humorous, it is to be hoped that we still find it so, even if the novel is 'dated'. Or if the novel is of our own age, we hope we shall find funny that which the author intended to be so. By far the best initial response to comic material is genuine amusement. This is true for texts as old as Apuleius, as well as those as recent as Evelyn Waugh.

With this in mind, readers should do their part by trying to appreciate exactly what sort of humorous effects the author intended, and what special conditions pertained in his or her time which gave the humour its point. Much humour, for instance, depends on satire and therefore relies for its effect on an appreciation of this and an understanding of what is being satirised.

Some kinds of humour wear better than others. In general, if the humour is derived from universally applicable and perennially relevant sources, it should survive. If it derives from topicalities, special fashions or tastes, or concerns limited by the circumstances common to the author and his contemporary readers, but not to those of a later age, it will fail unless historical research revives it.

On the whole, if you have been unable to react appropriately and genuinely to the humour of a particular novel, you will find it difficult to write convincingly about it, whether it be on character, situation or dialogue. In some questions, for example, the candidate is asked to comment on the humorous elements, and these will not be evident if he or she has not been amused by anything. As preparation, however, it would be worth noting as you read through the book where the humorous elements occur and how a humorous effect is gained.

Humorous effects may be achieved by a combination of the following: incongruity, absurdity, sudden surprise accompanied by relief of tension, anticlimax, abrupt contrast or disappointed expectation. Better humour also involves the development of a sympathetic (i.e. credible) humorous character, whose behaviour or speech specially provokes laughter. Wit, clever neatness of expression, the 'epigrammatic' or brilliantly incisive turn of phrase also heighten the humorous atmosphere or help develop a humorous character.

Cruel humour Much humour works by cruelty, perhaps in the psychological sense 'Thank God I'm not the one to be made ridiculous' (or even hurt). 'Slapstick' and other forms of humorous cruelty are funny usually precisely because not intended as serious: the actions are grotesque and they involve 'opposite' behaviour to that which is normally accepted. This is also partly how people can contemplate any work representing suffering: it is known not to be real. The pleasure and appreciation of all art in this sense is a form of broad and calm humour, 'good humour' as distinct from the sudden intense effect. This is why humorous novels may be less realistic than others; those with subordinate humorous parts (like the peasant scenes in Hardy's novels), may be less realistic in these parts than in the 'straight' scenes because of their dependence on increased incongruity or caricature. In plays, such scenes are often used as 'comic relief' to scenes of intense tragedy or high tension. When human foibles or weaknesses are exaggerated, humour joins hands with satire to create even greater opportunities for comic effect, as for instance in *The Secret Lives of Walter Mitty* (James Thurber) or *The Village Cricket Match* (A G Macdonald).

Sadistic or sexual humour, both being grotesque distortions of themes of unfailing interest, are also a good deal 'softened' by being presented in the form and framework of traditional conventions, such as stage farce, elements of which often appear in novels, for example, *My Family and Other Animals* (Gerald Durrell) passes itself off as autobiography and thus increases the surprise that humour thrives on. If meant to be funny, violence or sex is usually endowed with more than usual absurdity to escape causing offence.

Incongruity Another convention often employed by humorous writers, but expecially dramatists, from whose domain they originate, is the use of the 'unmatched pair', normally a 'straight man' (serious, pompous, slow witted, earnest, trying to maintain standards of ordinary morality) and a 'fall guy' (zany, outrageous, unserious, sharp, playful, deflating, etc). The process is most obviously seen in stage comedy but it is found also in many books of humour: in Mark Twain's two great novels, *Tom Sawyer* and *Huckleberry Finn*, in *Barchester*

Towers (Mrs Proudie and Slope or Signora Neroni) and in most of the 'anti hero' novels (e.g. Kingsley Amis's Lucky Jim and his professor; Billy Liar and the majority of the adults he encounters in the real world). There is something of the 'David and Goliath' satisfaction as depicted by these pairings, since the 'straight man' is usually proud and powerful in some respect. When pride and powers are affected by a personality defect and are confronted by humility and a lively mind, the ingredients for comedy are present. A comic scene worthy of close attention for the manner of Victorian fictional humour, is the Rainbow Inn chapter of George Eliot's *Silas Marner*. The individualisation of the villagers, their controversies and tensions, and the motives of these, Macey's ghost story culminating in an apparently genuine apparition with the sudden irruption of Silas, repay analysis. Most of the ingredients of good comedy are to be found here.

8 Morality

Questions such as the following might be asked and discussed on the novel:

1. What is its moral tone?
2. What is the accepted norm of its morality? (Although in Western literature this is usually more or less Christian or humanist, one should be aware that this is not necessarily so.)
3. Are the standards of what is good or bad, right or wrong, those of our society now, or the society of the novel's author, or both?
4. Is the novel especially concerned with the moral problems (as are those of Henry James and Conrad)?
5. If the hero's or any leading character's morality is perverted, or deviant from the norm of the author's background, does the author, or do the other characters approve?

If the author appears to condone lines of action of whose morality the reader disapproves, then such morality becomes at once debatable, but such debates are rarely relevant in written answers; the book is to be treated *per se*. Only differences in morality between the characters themselves are admissible subjects for written debate.

In a picaresque novel, such as Fielding's *Tom Jones*, or its twentieth-century counterparts, such as *The Loneliness of the Long Distance Runner* (Allan Sillitoe) or *Autobiography of a Super Tramp* (WH Davies), we should ask whether the deeper layers of morality underlying the roguery or delinquency of the hero are more moral than those of 'respectable' or establishment characters with whom he is at odds, and whose laws he breaks? In this connection the misfortunes of Moll Flanders are also relevant; her prostitution being an angry indictment of the factors that lead her to this. The same thing applies a century and half later to the Artful Dodger, and Oliver Twist. In novels of more subtle morality there is greater ambiguity (although to be sure Moll Flanders is nothing if not a recognisable character drawn from life): in *The Secret Agent* for example, if Winnie the murderess is clearly as 'right' as Tess, and Ossipon and 'the Professor' clearly vile, what are we to make of the well-meaning but disastrous Verloc, or the equally double game-playing Chief Inspector Heat?

Great passion and intensity of purpose may override ordinary morality, or at least rise above it, as for Heathcliffe in Emily Brontë's *Wuthering Heights* or Captain Ahab in Melville's *Moby Dick* or Jocelyn in William Golding's *The Spire*. Sometimes morality is almost externalised or allegorised as in a medieval morality play; for example, Golding's *The Lord of the Flies* or Melville's *Billy Budd*. Very seldom in our accepted great novels do we feel that the morality is bad to the core, as we do sometimes in the case of weak books which, apart from their failure as artistic works, may embody immoral concepts in their very values, e.g. some science fiction in which battles are enjoyed merely as battles, Tarzan books which make monsters out of ordinary animals, books which extol black magic, the great number of pornographic books which make a virtue of lust. Perhaps worse, because they are accepted and more widely regarded as harmless, are the mass of sentimentalised love stories which dangerously pervert reality with no hint of authorial criticism or irony, if indeed the author be capable of such.

Most English novels have as their reference point Christian ethics. Works that do not spring from Christian morality at all include those that may be termed 'existentialist' such as a French example *L'Etranger* (*The Outsider*, Camus), nihilistic (Beckett's *No's Knife*, especially *Texts for Nothing*), amoral and agnostic (*The Great Gatsby*, Scott Fitzgerald), fatalistic or pessimistic (*Jude the Obscure*, Hardy), Satanistic or superstitious in other ways – a host of novels probably specially churned out for the ready market (e.g. *The Exorcist*). Some oddities include experiments in surrealism (short stories in Dylan Thomas's *The Map of Love*) and mere verbal game-playing. Some experiments have yet to be properly accepted as authentic, yet are surely worthy of suspended judgement e.g. Joyce's *Finnegans Wake*.

9 Style and language

The style and language in each novel you study need separate and sustained analysis. Vocabulary, diction and modes of sentence structure often vary from one generation to another and can give clear clues to the period of their composition, like music. In the next unit we discuss practical criticism of individual passages. You should apply also these critical techniques in your own preparation of your set novels.

Different styles may be deliberately employed in one work, apart from the varieties of dialogue, which suit their speakers' characters. There may be 'quasi-dialogue' or prose that is not dialogue as such, but which is in the style of a character's speech, commentating upon his or her actions or thoughts. 'Stream of consciousness' writing, as found in Virginia Woolf's *Mrs Dalloway*, is an example of this.

The way characters express themselves can also be used in 'point of view' writing, or when they are employed as narrators. Such styles may subtly change when the characters come to write letters, as they do in Emily Brontë's *Wuthering Heights*, Hardy's *Tess of the D'Urbervilles*, Conrad's *Nostromo* and many others. Mrs Durbeyfield, for instance, writes in an appropriately garrulous and illiterate manner, worse than her speech. There is, in ordinary narration, an extraordinary change of style near the end of *The Inheritors* (William Golding) to mark the sudden transition from a Neanderthal to New People's outlook. In *Ulysses* James Joyce employs a selective variety of styles in one chapter to indicate the evolution of prose over the centuries, as an analogue to the development during gestation of Mrs Purefoy's baby as she comes to childbed. However, the *tour de force* remains partly a verbal game. Hemingway in *A Farewell to Arms* manipulates style to parallel meaning, as for example in the impressionistic passage when a shell nearly kills the Lieutenant, and its actual effect on him as he loses consciousness is conveyed by mimetic prose:

> I ate the end of my piece of cheese and took a swallow of wine. Through the other noise I heard a cough, then came the chuh-chuh-chuh-chuch – then there was a flash, as a blast-furnace door is swung open, and a roar that started white and went red and on and on in a rushing wind. I tried to breathe but my breath would not come and I felt myself rush bodily out of myself and out and out and out and all the time bodily in the wind.

Conrad uses a rapturous tone in *Youth* and a sardonic, consistently ironic style in *The Secret Agent*, in keeping with their themes: boyhood's glowing, optimistic expectation, idealism and romantic sensibility in the first; the shady scheming and terrible betrayals in the second.

Seventeenth century We have cited below examples from the seventeenth century. Many would maintain that this is the age in which the literary prose of the modern English was founded and perfected.

• Milton habitually employs the colours of high rhetoric (on false leaders in the Church):

> O let them not bring about their damned designs that stand now at the entrance of the bottomless pit expecting the Watchword to open and let out those dreadful Locusts and Scorpions, to re-involve us in that pitchy Cloud of infernal darkness, where we shall never more see the Sun of thy Truth again, never hope for the cheerful dawn, never more hear the Bird of Morning sing.

• Dryden affects a similar style, though not with such an exalted tone (on the plots of Roman comedy):

> These are plots built after the Italian mode of houses, you see through them all at once; the characters are indeed the imitations of nature, but so narrow as if they had imitated only an eye or a hand, and did not dare to venture on the lines of a face or the proportion of a body.

There is a slightly looser structure, but an increase of wit such as the use of the 'see through' and 'narrow'. The same interest in extended metaphor is evident, however.

• Sir Thomas Browne favoured a balanced, antithetical style, highly polished and with a love of exact Latinate words (on funeral customs):

> Though the Funeral pyre of Patroclus took up a hundred foot, a piece of an old boat burnt Pompey,
> And if the burthen of Isaac were sufficient for an holocaust, a man may carry his own pyre.

• Bacon's style is similar to this, though much pithier and more terse, his words carry a greater load of the content and thought, without much embroidery:

> In the youth of a state arms do flourish; in the middle age of a state, learning; and then both of them together for a time; in the declining age of a state, mechanical arts and merchandise.

Eighteenth century In the eighteenth century we still find great influence of the Ciceronian style, shown with great power and vigour by Dr Samuel Johnson. Note there is a suppleness and fluency that renders it agreeable to the modern ear:

> As there are none more ambitious of fame, than those who are conversant in poetry it is very natural for such as have not succeeded in it to depreciate the works of those who have.
>
> (Addison from The Spectator, Dec 1711)

> Among the various methods of consolation to which the miseries inseparable from our present state have given occasion it has been, as I have already remarked, recommended by some writers to put the sufferer in mind of heavier pressures and more excruciating calamities than those of which he has himself reason to complain.
>
> (from The Rambler, September 1750)

This gives a fair example of Johnson's love of full phrasing well weighed and balanced, and drawing to an unhurried finish. There is less employment of fanciful images here – the influence represented by Sprat, and the Royal Society now having taken effect. Sprat declared to the Society that it was necessary for their Fellows 'to separate the knowledge of nature from the colours of Rhetorick, the devices of Fancy, or the delightful deceit of Fables.'

Nineteenth century Even more translucence is added to the precision and rhythm of the phrases, by Jane Austen. This, from *Emma*:

> She felt all the honest pride and complacency which her alliance with the present and future proprietor could fairly warrant, as she viewed the respectable size and style of the building, its suitable, becoming, characteristic situation, low and sheltered – its ample gardens stretching down to meadows washed by a stream, of which the Abbey, with all the old neglect of prospect, had scarcely a sight – and its abundance of timber in rows and avenues, which neither fashion nor extravagance had rooted up.

This well-carpentered sentence leads the proud and complacent eye of Emma all over the estate to which she has so strong a link. The novel was published in 1816, the great Romantic poets had already brought out much of their main work, Keats was soon to be adding almost the last word with *Poems* of 1821; prose was soon to be allowed to recapture some of its old colours. With Charles Lamb, born in 1775, the effects are still subdued, the tone easy, the content light:

> Do you remember the brown suit, which you made to hang upon you, till all your friends cried in shame upon you, it grew so thread-bare – and all because of that folio Beaumont and Fletcher, which you dragged home late at night from Barker's in Covent Garden?

But before long, style is to resume most of all its old finery, and yet retain the perfect lucidity learned from Johnson and Austen. Writes Robert Louis Stevenson in *Virginibus Puerisque* of 1884:

> For we are all so busy and have so many far-off projects to realise, and castles in the fire to turn into solid habitable mansions on a gravel soil, that we can find no time for pleasure trips into the Land of Thought and among the Hills of Vanity.

We must turn to the novels of the middle to late nineteenth century to see the new imagination working at its fullest, and only two brief examples must be made to serve the purpose: they have a continuing progeny among the novels of this century and even this present age. This then of 1874, Hardy's first widely acclaimed novel, *Far From the Madding Crowd*:

> The sheep-washing pool was a perfectly circular basin of brickwork in the meadows, full of the clearest water. To birds on the wing its glassy surface, reflecting the light sky, must have been visible for miles around as a glistening Cyclops' eye in a green face.

– the first master of the cinematographic technique, with the bonus of a beautiful simile (as well as apposite, in its reference to sheep, a hero and a monster)! The aerial view is put to good service later in Hardy, notably in *The Dynasts*.

Our other example, from Dickens's *Bleak House* published twenty years earlier, illustrates the energy of Victorian novels allied to their mythopoeic (myth-making) quality:

> We looked at one another, half laughing at our being like the children in the wood, when a curious little old woman in a squeezed bonnet, and carrying a reticule, came curtseying and smiling up to us, with an air of great ceremony.
>
> 'O!' said she. 'The wards in Jarndyce! Ve-ry happy, I am sure, to have the honour! It is a good omen for youth and hope and beauty, when they find themselves in this place and don't know what's to come of it.'
>
> 'Mad!' whispered Richard, not thinking she could hear him.
>
> 'Right! Mad, young gentleman,' she returned so quickly that he was quite abashed.

The Brothers Grimm would have admired this, especially as it goes the logical step further and uses the whole machinery of the folk tale for the purpose of adding colour to the real jungle of Chancery, and the real innocence of two victims of it, meeting the mad decrepitude of one long snared in its coils.

Ironic style Some notable features of style may be due to some special purpose of the novelist, such as satire. Irony is one of the chief stylistic weapons of the satirist, and is used by nearly all great authors, though not necessarily as a prevailing mode. Both passages from Victorian novels quoted above are ironical, the first through the implications of the chosen image, the second through the words of the old woman, who is knowingly being ironical, and whose 'Right! Mad...' contains the consequent irony of her present state as the result of what the innocent pair are about to plunge into.

Much of the plainest irony is achieved by the author's initial establishment of a certain situation or set of circumstances, against the background of which, since these are present in the mind of the reader, he or she may 'play off' speeches of characters themselves ignorant of such circumstances, and which nevertheless refer to them in various ways that contain significance for us, but not the the speakers. The old woman from *Bleak House* quoted above herself uses the technique on Richard Carstone and Esther Summerson, though she soon begins to indicate what she really means.

A good sustained example of dramatic irony (working in plot and action rather than in character development or narrative comment), is to be found in Conrad's *Under Western Eyes*.

We are shown the revolutionary Russian student Haldin desperately applying to a friend for help and asylum, after assassinating a political enemy. Haldin believes the views of his friend, Razumov, to be identical to his own, and has good reason to think so. But Razumov, from fear and a sense of outrage – the futility of such violence – refuses to grant what he begs, so Haldin tries to get out by himself, is betrayed by Razumov, arrested, and breathing no word of his interview with his friend, he is executed. His devoted mother and sister having been placed in Geneva for safety, meet Razumov who has been set by the police to spy on them and other political troublemakers. The subsequent scenes between Razumov and these women, particularly Miss Haldin, are promising ground for irony of which Conrad does not fail to take advantage.

Irony pervades Conrad's previous book *The Secret Agent* and reaches one of its peaks in the famous remark of Mr Verloc to his wife Winnie, when she has just discovered that her husband has caused the death of the one person she loves above all others, her 'simple-minded' brother:

> Do be reasonable, Winnie. What would it have been if you had lost me?

Beyond doubt, if Verloc had been killed she not only would have had her brother but been saved from an egocentric, vastly lethargic and completely deceitful husband, whom she shortly murders, thereby damning herself to a miserable suicide. There are many shades and facets of irony, and the reader simply has to be alert and responsive to all the strands of the web that is being unfolded before him. We will conclude with a typical but subtle example from the greatest exponent of delicate, usually humorously gentle, but always penetrating irony, Jane Austen. In *Mansfield Park* Lady Bertram has learned of her daughters' escape from their parents and home, one to elope, the other (unhappily married), with a lover. Lady Bertram is a person whose main characteristic is never to stir herself, or upset herself, unnecessarily – which for her practically means never at all. The irony of the following makes its effect by innuendo and understatement:

> Lady Bertram did not think deeply, but, guided by Sir Thomas, she thought justly on all important points, and she saw therefore in all its enormity, what had happened, and neither endeavoured herself, nor required Fanny to advise her, to think little of guilt and infamy.

Bertram just manages in these circumstances to stir on her sofa and unsettle her lap-dog.

Twentieth century

We approach now the enormous variety of style and stylistic devices to be encountered among novels of our century. There was plenty of variety before, but since Henry James ushered in the modern novel, for those who took notice of him, there can be found in English and American – not to mention Irish and lately Australian, South African and even West Indian novels – every conceivable style except the stiffly formal. There are also the experiments – not all of them likely to prove dead-ends, of Woolf, Joyce, James Merrill in *The (Diblos) Notebook*, Salinger, Beckett, Anthony Burgess and others. None of the old facilities and felicities of rhetoric has been dispensed with. An example from Updike's *A Month of Sundays* can be quoted (a book which may one day appear on an A-level syllabus):

> The silence of this room m'effraie. It is not one silence but many; The lampshade is silent, the bulb silently burns, the bed in silence waits for my next oblivion, the bathroom mirror silently plays catch with a corner of my bathrobe, the carpeting is a hungry populace of individual acrylic silences, even the air-conditioning, today, is silent. Has the power failed? Has the desert cooled? Has the beautiful last beseeching of the Bible ('Even so, come, Lord Jesus'– *Rev* 22.20) been at last answered, and Man's two millennia of Inbetweentimes ended? No, my clock says an hour to noon remains.

There are more than enough rhetorical devices applied to this passage, and yet the whole is unquestionably of our era. The desert and Biblical reference may be explained by the situation in which a priest has been defrocked and banished to a 'rest home' in the Arizona desert.

Some styles are flat 'reporting', to convey realism in scenes of horror or unusually violent action (Crane's *The Red Badge of Courage*, Hemingway's *A Farewell to Arms*, Greene's *The Power and the Glory*). Other novels favour a highly subjective, 'committed', style (Lawrence's *Kangaroo* and novellas); others may be emotive, suggestive or impressionistic rather than directly descriptive (*To the Lighthouse*, Virginia Woolf, *Dubliners*, James Joyce). Henry James's last four novels have taken the exploration of the possibilities of style far in the direction of refinement of sensibility, but all his splitting and resplitting of hairs are justified by the world such writing opens to us.

Conclusion

Faced with an essay question, the student must think: What are its implications? All relevant matter connected with the novel under question must be turned over, sifted, selected for use and arranged into a reasonable order for composition.

Broad, obvious ideas should occur at once: these, even after further thought, will probably form the backbone of the answer, but you should not take them straight into the essay without longer and deeper thought. Pursuit of the less obvious is just as necessary for completeness. Are all the possibilities exhausted? Minor points may well turn out to be quite vital to a satisfactory answer.

In any discussion, both sides of the case should be aired before judgement is made, even if the topic for discussion clearly seems a correct comment; e.g. 'Is *The Eustace Diamonds* a detective thriller?' – do not assume that it is not, nor assume that it is. Cast your mind over all the evidence that points to its being so, and welcome as equally useful any reservations that may lead eventually to the conclusion that the novel is not of the 'detective' or 'thriller' school. It is this 'pro' and 'con' discussion which gives essay-writers the meat of their answers.

Above all, the candidate needs to maintain a firm control of what is relevant to the answer and what is not. Many good students begin an essay well and proceed to forget or ignore the actual requirements of a particular question. Others go to the opposite (and worse) extreme, and in every paragraph reassert the terms of the question in their answer, as if the latter were revolving round the former like a moth round a candle. The first fault is often because good knowledge is not made to serve the limited requirement and specified field of thought; the second is due to insufficient knowledge. The first is, therefore, that which may result in an injustice to the candidate.

Question bank

AUSTEN: *Mansfield Park*

1 Either, (a) Write an essay on the roles of Henry and Mary Crawford in the novel *Mansfield Park*.

Or, (b) Write a commentary on the following passage suggesting what it reveals of the characters involved.

> Mrs Norris fetched breath, and went on again.
> 'The nonsense and folly of people's stepping out of their rank and trying to appear above themselves makes me think it right to give you a hint, Fanny, now that you are going into company without any of us; and I do beseech and
> 5 entreat you not to be putting yourself forward, and talking and giving your opinion as if you were one of your cousins – as if you were dear Mrs Rushworth or Julia.
> 'That will never do, believe me. Remember, wherever you are, you must be the lowest and last; and though Miss Crawford is in a manner at home at the
> 10 parsonage, you are not to be taking place of her. And as to coming away at night, you are to stay just as long as Edmund chooses. Leave him to settle that.'
> 'Yes, ma'am; I should not think of anything else.'
> 'And if it should rain – which I think exceedingly likely, for I never saw it more threatening for a wet evening in my life – you must manage as well as you can,
> 15 and not be expecting the carriage to be sent for you. I certainly do not go home tonight, and, therefore, the carriage will not be out on my account; so you must make up your mind to what may happen, and take your things accordingly.'
> Her niece thought it perfectly reasonable. She rated her own claims to comfort as low even as Mrs Norris could; and when Sir Thomas soon afterwards just
> 20 opening the door, said, 'Fanny, at what time would you have the carriage come round?' she felt a degree of astonishment which made it impossible for her to speak.
> 'My dear Sir Thomas,' cried Mrs Norris, red with anger, 'Fanny can walk!'
> 'Walk!' repeated Sir Thomas, in a tone of most unanswerable dignity, and
> 25 coming farther into the room – 'my niece walk to a dinner engagement at this time of the year! – Will twenty minutes after four suit you?'
> 'Yes, sir', was Fanny's humble answer, given with the feelings almost of a criminal towards Mrs Norris; and not bearing to remain with her in what might seem a state of triumph, she followed her uncle out of the room, having stayed
> 30 behind him only long enough to hear these words spoken in angry agitation, –
> 'Quite unnecessary! – a great deal too kind! But Edmund goes too. True, it is upon Edmund's account. I observed he was hoarse on Thursday night.'

Cambridge 1994

DICKENS: *David Copperfield*

2 Either, (a) Examine Dickens' portrayal of Uriah Heep in *David Copperfield*. What role does he play in the novel?

Or, (b) Look again at Chapter XLIV (44) ' Our Housekeeping'.
Comment on the ways Dickens portrays Dora and David's life together.
Consider Dickens' narrative technique as well as plot and character.

WJEC 1994

DICKENS: *Bleak House*

3 In *Bleak House* Dickens places the stress on common involvement and common responsibility. How far do you agree?

Cambridge 1994

HARDY: *The Mayor of Casterbridge*

4 Either, (a) Explore some of the attitudes to women which Hardy reveals in *The Mayor of Casterbridge*.

Or, (b) Remind yourself of Chapter 39.
By analysing this chapter in detail show its significance to the novel as a whole.

WJEC 1994

HARDY: *The Distracted Preacher and Other Tales*

5 Write an essay on Hardy's use of irony in these stories.

Cambridge 1994

JAMES JOYCE: *A Portrait of the Artist as a Young Man*

6 Either, (a) 'Stephen's inner experience is constantly contrasted with the reality of his external circumstances.' Consider in what ways such contrasts contribute to Joyce's presentation of Stephen Dedalus.

Or, (b) How far and in what ways does Joyce succeed in convincing us that Stephen Dedalus has the potential to become an artist?

Cambridge 1994

VIRGINIA WOOLF: *Mrs Dalloway*

7 Either, (a) Virginia Woolf's style has often been described as 'stream of consciousness'. Choose one section of the novel and explain in detail how her method of writing works.

Or, (b) How much empathy does Virginia Woolf allow you to have with the men in *Mrs Dalloway*?

D H LAWRENCE: *Sons and Lovers*

Or, (c) Why do you think Lawrence called the novel *Sons and Lovers* rather than *Son and Lovers*?

Or, (d) What different aspects of Paul's character attract him to Miriam and to Clara?

AEB 1994

ENGLISH LANGUAGE

Units in this chapter

Chapter objectives

Many new and exciting courses are now combining the study of English Literature with that of Language. In this chapter we look at some of the skills needed to tackle an English Language examination at A and AS level. Although this section does not pretend to cover all aspects of language study fully, it will act as a useful resource regardless of the specific syllabus that you are following.

An excellent idea is to clarify which course you are studying and attempt to obtain relevant past papers from the board. The Chief Examiner's Reports, issued annually for all examinations, also repay study.

There are obvious similarities between the study of language and literature, but the difference lies in the amount of specialist, factual knowledge you are expected to acquire about linguistic theory, stylistic analysis, grammar and phonetics.

The types of questions asked by the examination boards vary considerably. Most offer opportunities for you to put theory into practice by analysing language and its functions (both spoken and written). Questions also test how effectively you have developed your own use of English by asking you to demonstrate advanced expertise in a variety of writing tasks and styles.

Language examinations may include several of the following types of questions in a variety of combinations.
- Essays on controversial topics – extended writing.
- Essays on areas of linguistic theory (the use of language – languages issues).
- Comprehension skills.
- The précis or summary.
- Close analysis of spoken or written texts.
- Rewriting material for a specific audience and purpose.

4.1   THE ESSAY

The essays set are nearly always argumentative in nature, requiring some ability to organise abstract thought. They are not likely to be narrative or simple description.

For example, a likely topic might well be *Liberty or Law – is there a conflict?* rather than *A description of a town you like* or *Tell a story dealing with the detection of crime*. This means that they need to be thought about and organised carefully.

Advice on planning and writing an essay on a controversial subject

There are two main types of controversial essay. One asks for the points for and against a particular subject; the other asks you to concentrate on one side only, either presenting a case for a particular point of view or condemning it. Whichever type of essay you attempt, find out whether you have enough facts and ideas on which to build an argument. The second stage is to mull over the facts and ideas you have and to start to organise them into some kind of plan.

After considering the material at your disposal, your own point of view should become clearer and this will help you in the organisation of your material. However, if your point of view is divided, you may wish to present a fair and unbiased account of the evidence on both sides, leaving the reader to make up his or her mind. You may decide that one side of the argument is stronger and gains your support and you will come out on this side in your conclusion. You must know where you stand before you start writing the essay. You cannot start a discursive essay supporting one side and then find, when you are halfway through that you have changed your mind.

Clarity is obviously important if a reader is to be expected to follow your point of view. State your arguments clearly and simply and make sure you leave out no essential steps in the argument. Remember a short, pithy sentence is often useful, particularly at the beginning of a paragraph, to establish a point which can be elaborated in greater detail later.

Cultivate the technique of writing persuasively. If there are arguments against your standpoint, treat them fairly and balance them against your own points which, of course, you consider more important. One way of being persuasive is to give plenty of examples to support your point of view. Such examples should be pertinent and woven into the essay naturally so as to illumine the points made, not simply cited in a list and tacked on for effect.

Quotation can be used to add humour or vitality to your essay. For instance, an essay on *The Problems of an Aging Population* could include this quotation from Thackeray, 'Next to the very young, I suppose the very old are the most selfish,' whilst an essay on *Following Trends in Fashion* could include this observation by Smollet, 'Fashion – ridiculous modes, invented by ignorance and adopted by folly'. A quotation can be used as an effective opening to your essay, provided it is apt. It is a good idea to collect quotations from your general reading which might prove useful in examination essays.

Make your beginnings and endings interesting. Do not merely repeat the question or say things like 'In conclusion I would like to say' or 'To sum up, my point of view is'. These are almost certain to be boring and repetitive. Try to move on to new ground, leaving the reader with a new angle on what has already been said in the rest of the essay, and perhaps leaving him or her questioning former assumptions. You should therefore adopt a positive approach throughout your essay. Use an arresting opening and after an interesting discussion leave a good impression by ending convincingly rather than simply petering out.

General advice

1. Read all the possible titles and choose the one where you have most information (not necessarily the one where you have the strongest views).
2. Plan your approach in note form. Remember you need some sense of shape – introduction: development: conclusion. Assemble arguments carefully, using as many examples as illustration of your argument as possible.
3. Try to adopt a balanced approach, considering both sides of an argument rather than indulging in shrill propaganda.

④ Write careful, accurate English, paying particular attention to punctuation, spelling and sentence construction – give yourself time, at the end of the examination, to check this.

⑤ Above all – practise the technique of writing this kind of essay to this length (800–900 words – 3 to 4 sides) throughout the course and do not leave it until the day of the examination.

You will be marked on the quality of what you say and how you say it and, of course, these two influence one another – opinions, as all politicians know, look more convincing if they are presented in an attractive way.

A summary of what Chief Examiners have singled out as faults from past papers is given below:
* persistent use of the comma where a full-stop or semi-colon is needed;
* poor sentence construction – e.g. no main verb;
* limited range of vocabulary;
* vocabulary frequently badly chosen and inappropriate – e.g. slang. (Examiners do not demand a pretentious 'literary style' and welcome lively, vivid English but often candidates, trying to be off-hand and 'with-it', present views in an ugly, slip-shod and inaccurate way.);
* lack of planning – the essay becomes merely a number of thoughts as they occurred to the writer whilst in the act of writing, with no links between them and no coherent developing argument;
* no illustration of assertions;
* no link between one paragraph and the next;
* dullness – little evidence of any ideas at all.

In short, candidates who read sensibly, keep their eyes and ears open, and have some interest in life and some ideas of their own, who have learnt the basic structure of an English sentence and how to organise an argument clearly and effectively, score well on the essay. Mature candidates (20+ in particular) may find that this question appeals to them, provided they have practised the technique of writing the 900-word essay.

Suggested reading

* 'Quality' newspapers – *The Times*, *The Guardian*
* Sunday papers – *The Sunday Times*, *The Observer*, *The Sunday Telegraph*
* Weekly journals such as *New Statesman and Society*, *Spectator*

4.2 THE PRÉCIS

Read the passage carefully several times before writing. It will be about 600 words long and you will be required to reduce it to about one-third of its length.
* Don't start writing your own version before you have fully understood the original.
* Don't spend great time and effort getting the piece to exactly one-third (or the number of words stipulated) but do try not to exceed the number.
* Don't reproduce great chunks of the original in your own version, but use your own words as far as possible. At the same time, don't go to ridiculous lengths to avoid using words from the original – it is complete phrases and sentences you should try to avoid. It will often be necessary, for example, to use key words from the original in your own version.

Practice You cannot expect to write a good précis in the examination if you have not written one during the course. It is a technique which is learnt by practice and experience.

Example of précis

Write a summary of the following passage in not more than 240 words (the passage contains 701 words). Your summary, in clear, connected English, should be given a brief title and the number of words used should be indicated at the end.

There is a sense, of course, in which there has always been a war of the generations among men, although it is more conspicuous in some other animals – among deer, elephants and seals. Young bucks displace old bulls. In this sense the war of generations is akin to the war of the sexes: there has always been a struggle for dominance, or for relative placings, and sheer force has not always been more important than subtlety in the process. But the war of generations has now ceased to be a private war, in herds, families or local communities. It has become war in the public arena, in which significant segments of the younger generation identify themselves as something set over against the rest of society. That they use contrasting styles as a way of subdividing themselves does not eclipse the fact that at least these styles have a certain relevance for each other: those of the older generation have none. And the styles are not local styles, nor the language a local argot – they are presented as appropriate for a whole generation, and only for that generation.

The agency that has provided a style appropriate to the whole youth culture is of course the entertainment industry acting through the mass-media, which are themselves increasingly devoted to entertainment. The most expensive entertainment, and hence the most prestigious, is that provided for the section of the public with the largest uncommitted incomes, which, being the young, is also the section with the least cultivated taste, and the highest vulnerability to whatever will arouse animal passions. Whereas community recreation in the past used to bring the generations together, commercial entertainment now drives them apart. We pass from a society in which we had films that were unsuitable for adolescents to one with coffee bars unsuitable for adults. The mass-media are not merely the providers of entertainment, but for the young they are also the disseminators of styles, postures and patterns of behaviour.

Television has been particularly important since, in a way that has not been true of earlier agencies of communication, it completely rejects any moral stance. Even radio, in pre-television days, had a philosophy of public responsibility, and, as an agency the goals of which were neither profit nor mere popularity ratings, its directors, conspicuously Lord Reith, saw themselves as participating in the guardianship and dissemination of particular cultural and moral values. Television, operated for profits or popularity (or both), proceeds in a completely amoral way. It has tested the market, escaped the conventions governing printed matter and the theatre and has steadily grown more daring about levels of public decency. It presents all types of attitudes and values without adopting any firm moral stance of its own. It disavows positive values and accepts the yardstick of the market, which, on moral issues, is an invitation to viewers to abandon their own standards of propriety which – because television is technical, prestigious and clearly identified with the metropolis – suddenly are made to seem provincial if not parochial. Without exerting or seeking to exert direct, didactic authority, television has managed to convey the impression that men who are outside the advanced circles of the semi-literary entertainment people who run television are somehow antiquated in their moral senses. In consequence many people, and particularly young people, who are least sure of their values, and least socialised, have aped the manners and styles of television, which is the new authority on acceptable, prestige-conferring behaviour.

Competition for audiences between channels has been the principal factor behind this development, and entertainment has been its principal genre. But this effect has also been brought about because television has adopted the impersonal, detached style of an agency that merely 'holds the ring', 'provides the facilities' for 'all points of view'. Everything is put across with the same sort of authority. An inevitable result ensues, given what is offered, given the ease with which men readily prefer to indulge gross sensations rather than engage in elevating experiences, or wrestle with subtleties. Letting things find their own level with a mass audience is to invite the steady deterioration in standards, to let the salacious and the sensational displace or infect other material.

Bryan Wilson

Suggested answer to précis

The generation war and the media

There has always been a struggle for dominance between the generations. This struggle is most obvious in animals but also occurs in humans where cunning is as important for success as mere brute force. This conflict is now no longer fought in small groups but in large sections of society and, in particular, between the younger generation and the rest. Although there are groups within the younger generation, there are enough common characteristics in attitude and behaviour to unite them.

These unifying elements are, to a large degree, in the attitudes directed at the young by the entertainments industry. The taste of the young is undeveloped and susceptible to the sensational. Entertainment can therefore influence young people's ideas and values and this, in turn, alienates them from the values of an older generation.

Although early radio was very conscious of morality, television today is largely amoral, being dominated purely by commercial success and adopting an attitude which suggests its own sophisticated superiority. By suggesting that others have old-fashioned and outdated principles, it encourages moral laxity. Young people, with unformed views, all too easily accept the authority and values of television. Therefore, because popular taste inevitably tends towards the sensational and because the mass media give no rules for guidance, traditional standards or morality are undermined and more beneficial material excluded purely because it would not be able to sustain a mass audience. Thus there is an inevitable decline of standards.

239 words

Commentary on the précis

There is no such thing as the one perfect answer to a précis. A number of different versions can be written which can all achieve high marks . They must, however, have certain things in common:

1. **Length** The instructions gave 240 words as the required length. Do not become neurotic about length but do not exceed the required amount by more than ten. You may well be able to write a sound précis 20 words under; there is no need to search around for another 20 words. This version happens to be 239.

2. **Information** You must get all the essential information from the passage and render this information in your own words and in a clear, concise way. This version does contain all the important information and does not reproduce the style of the original passage by lifting out whole chunks verbatim. There is some repetition and the passage might have been pruned back even further. You might like to see where this occurs.

3. **Style** The précis must read as a piece of connected, coherent English in its own right. The reader should not be able to guess that it is a shortened version of another passage.

4. **The Title** The title should summarise, as briefly as possible, the essential contents of the passage.

4.3 A-LEVEL COMPREHENSION

Answers to comprehension exercises need to be as crisp and accurate as possible. They also need to be simply and clearly expressed in your own words. Where a mark allocation is given, as in this case, this provides a clear guide to the number of points that you will need to make in your answer. For example, in **(a)** five marks are allocated and the answer gives five pieces of information. Check this out for yourself in the remaining points of the answer.

Write the answers in connected English prose. The only exception to this is in **(h)** where the one-word equivalent can be used. (For the purposes of this specimen answer, all five words have been explained; a candidate, of course, should do as he or she is told and only give explanations for four. If all five are answered the examiner will probably only credit the first four.)

Read the following passage and answer the questions below it.

1   Study and the pursuit of knowledge is generally pleasurable. The efficient exercise of any function is normally pleasurable. If the practice of study is painful, something is almost certainly wrong – an unfortunate choice of subjects, defective methods of work, or faulty working conditions. The best results are never secured by feverish energy born of the fear
5   of failure. Most commonly, perhaps, the student is worried by the 'difficulty' of his subject; but difficulties looked at the right way up may be a source of pleasure. The sense of difficulty is by no means always to be attributed to personal limitations. In fact, all our studies should be 'difficult', full of problems, and the process of solving them the normal source of pleasure in intellectual pursuits. Perhaps the reason why students do not more frequently take their
10   pleasures in this way is partly because they are apt to be harassed by an overcrowded syllabus which leaves no time for thought, and partly because the sense of difficulty has come through faulty educational methods to be associated with a sense of subjective limitation. There are, however, intrinsically difficult subjects – subjects essentially consisting of a set of problems.

15 These never can and never should be easy. They are inherently difficult, not only to the student but also to the teacher. If the novice thinks he understands a work on the first casual reading, this in itself is sufficient proof that he hasn't. He is only beginning to understand it when he finds it difficult. This applies to some parts of most subjects. It is a misunderstanding of the situation when difficulty of this kind is introjected as a sense of personal incompetence. The trouble is aggravated by the application of inappropriate

20 standards of progress and by the pursuit of inappropriate ideals. Commonly, the student expects to progress at the same rate in these subjects as in easy subjects, and failing to do so blames himself or complains of the limitations of his powers. But there is a fundamental difference between progress in 'easy' and progress in 'difficult' subjects. The characteristic of an 'easy' subject is that its facts, individually, are not difficult of comprehension. The

25 only problem is to assimilate, organise, and apply. Under such conditions progress may be perceptibly rapid, and this engenders confidence. In the 'difficult' subject (and the difficult parts of an easy subject) the facts themselves, through the abstractness of their complexity, require an effort of thought merely to be understood. The process of mere assimilation is slow and gradual. The student, obsessed by the ideal of erudition, is discouraged by his

30 apparent lack of progress, even where progress may be all the greater by reason of being slow. In such subjects independent judgments are almost certain to be wrong. He is accustomed to being told what he should believe, and to the arbitration of authority. What 'it says' in the book tends to be taken as final. That the book was written by some human and fallible hand is a late and devastating revelation. Apart from the special stimulus of

35 encouragement, the measure of independence appropriate to intellectual maturity is liable to be delayed. Ultimately self-confidence requires a rational foundation. Non-rational suggestions may be useful in countering equally non-rational causes of diffidence; but in the last resort it is desirable that we should face our tasks with confidence based upon a dispassionate appreciation of attested merits. It is something gained if we at least escape the

40 domination of inhibiting ideas. There has been a tendency in recent years to underestimate the influence of mere ideas upon the emotional life. It is true that we cannot awaken idealism merely by preaching abstract principles. Nevertheless, there are some ideas which are naturally congruent with enthusiasm, and there are some that stultify. The remedy is to make the most of powers with which we are endowed, to find rational grounds for self-

45 confidence by doing as well as we can what we can do best. Moreover, we might be a little more exacting in our demand for proof of our own incompetence. Incidentally it may be noted that the proof of the absence of ability is always longer than the proof that it is present. If we have once performed a task, that is sufficient proof that we can do it. A single failure, on the other hand, is not sufficient proof that we cannot.

CA Mace, *The Psychology of Study*

(**Note** Your answers should be in your own words as far as possible)

1 Say what might lead to a 'painful' practice of study with poor results. (5)

2 Why might some students fail to find pleasure in 'difficult' studies? (3)

3 In what ways might a student misjudge an 'intrinsically difficult' subject? (4)

4 Explain in your own words the writer's comments on the study of 'easy' subjects. (6)

5 What are the problems of a student faced with a 'difficult' subject? (7)

6 What reasons are offered for lack of self-assurance in a student? (4)

7 What remedies are suggested for a lack of confidence? (7)

8 Give the meaning of four of the following as they appear in the passage:
   (i) inherently – (line 14)
   (ii) introjected – (line 18)
   (iii) assimilate – (line 25)
   (iv) fallible – (line 34)
   (v) stultify – (line 43)

(4)

Total: 40 marks

Model answer to the comprehension passage

1 There are a number of reasons why study may be painful for the student and why the results achieved may be poor. A student may have chosen the wrong subject. He may not have learnt to study most effectively or he may have to study in unsatisfactory conditions. He may worry when faced with the subject's inevitable difficulties and this may lead to panic over possible failure.

2 Students may fail to find pleasure in difficult subjects because they are under pressure through lack of time. This is probably the main reason, but poor teaching may have contributed to a lack of confidence.

3 A student may misjudge an 'intrinsically difficult subject' if he thinks that the difficulties are only there for him, arising from his own inadequacies. Some students may not even see that there are any difficulties and others may not focus their efforts correctly on the right targets even if they realise that there are difficulties. Other students may get confused because they are unable to judge their own progress.

4 An 'easy' subject, according to the writer, is one where basic facts can be quickly and easily understood. These facts are quickly absorbed, ordered into a coherent pattern and then used by the student. This leads to rapid progress in the mastery of the subject and therefore to an equally rapid increase in confidence by the student.

5 With a 'difficult subject' a student is faced with complicated facts which need to be carefully examined before they can be fully understood. It is a slow process and the effort involved can destroy confidence. It is a great temptation to become vague and imprecise or superficial and this can result in more confusion.

6 Many students lack self-assurance because they have never had to rely on their own powers of thought. They are used to merely accepting instruction and regarding opinions in books as the final truth. They may have made mistakes when attempting to solve problems on their own.

7 The remedies suggested by the writer for improving a student's self-confidence are mainly linked with positive encouragement. Students should learn to make the most of their own ability by looking at problems objectively, trying to understand where mistakes have been made (and realising that these are inevitable) and, above all, ignoring the occasional failure, building on the occasional success. Any success is a proof of ability.

8
inherently	innately or naturally
introjected	taken personally
assimilate	absorb
fallible	likely to make mistakes
stultify	to deaden the mind

4.4 LANGUAGE ISSUES

Many language components now focus on one or more of the four main areas of linguistic theory. Here is a suggested check list of some topics which may be covered during your A-level or AS-level course.

Language and society

- Language in relation to issues such as – gender, class, generation and peer groups.
- The effect of language on society and social attitudes towards language, e.g. the debate on Standard English.
- How language works in social interaction – paralinguistics discourse analysis.
- The relationship between purpose and contact in language use.

Language acquisition

- The growth of language structures, e.g. sound systems, morphology, grammar and meanings.
- Development of language functions.
- Theories of language acquisition – Chomsky, Piaget, etc.

Language varieties

- Formal and informal use of language.
- Spoken and written language.
- Variety of textual functions and styles, e.g. the language of advertising; the language of the law; the language of politics, etc.
- Accent and dialect.
- Register.

Language change

- Historical 'overview' of the major changes in the English language.
- Changes in words and meanings (semantics).
- Changes in written English and its sound system (the great vowel shift).
- Changes in grammar and social contexts.

It would be impossible to cover these areas in this chapter but having listed them you may now have a clearer idea as to the breadth of most courses. Secondary reading forms a vital part of any A- or AS-level course. Complement the ideas discussed in tutorial sessions with private research and independent linguistic study.

Most boards test your knowledge of these issues in essay questions and passages offered for stylistic analysis or more general critical comment.

ESSAY ON STANDARD ENGLISH

Here is a suggested answer to a theory question set by the NEAB. It relates to both language and society and language varieties.

The following statement is from a report on English teaching in the UK.

'All pupils should learn, and if necessary be explicitly taught, Standard English.'
(English for ages 5 to 16, HMSO, 1989).

Explain what you understand by the term Standard English, and discuss the social implications of the requirement that all school pupils should learn Standard English.

Specimen answer

Most languages have many dialects within that language. A dialect is a variety of language which differs syntactically and lexically from other varieties. 'Standard English' is one such variety. It is frequently spoken with a specific accent – known as Received Pronunciation – but is distinct from accent: it is possible to speak Standard English with, for example, a Yorkshire or Cumbrian accent. Standard English then is a particular set of rules for word order and vocabulary adopted by a certain group of people.

The 'standard' in any language is the variety used in most forms of writing and is taught to non-native speakers. It is the form in which most education takes place. In effect, it is the prestige dialect; it holds social power. However, the word 'standard' has within it connotations of conformity and a certain level of performance. As a consequence, many people see the 'standard' as the 'correct' version of the language. Take for example 'I ain't done nothing'. This is a non-standard version of 'I haven't done anything'. The latter is considered by many to be a superior form – dismissing the former as a 'double negative' and therefore illogical. However, when 'I ain't done nothing' is spoken, people are not confused as to the meaning. So why did one version become thought of as 'superior'?

There seems to be a trend in the history of English to standardise the language. When the Romans withdrew from the island 'Britannia' as they called it, the Celts were left to defend themselves against attacks from the north of the country. To help in their defence, they invited the Angles – from across the North Sea. The Angles came, but not to their aid. Instead they attacked the Celts. The Celts, who spoke dialects of Celtish, were driven to the west of the country. The invaders, who named the country Angle Land (England) spoke dialects of a language family now known as West Germanic. There was no particular 'standard' as such, and the dialects were geographically based. The language was later affected by Old Norse, with the Viking invasion, and likewise by Northern French, with the Norman Conquest.

However, in the tenth and eleventh centuries, West Saxon was becoming the standard written language – this was a dialect of West Saxon spoken in the south and south-west of the country. West Saxon spelling was used in writing in the other dialect areas of England and changes in pronunciation even in West Saxon itself, were not always recorded. With the Norman Conquest however, French-speaking scribes when writing in English tended to write what they heard. This period in language use is known today as 'Middle English'.

So far, any real attempts at standardisation had been thwarted due to the nature of language change. However, with Caxton's invention of the printing press in the fifteenth century a new 'standard' was established. William Caxton spoke a variety of English occurring in the centres of political and economic power: London, Oxford and Cambridge – and Standard English today derives from this variety. It was not that Caxton's English was essentially 'better' in any way, but rather that the people who spoke it held the power. The dialect was therefore imitated and established by others who wanted a stake in that power, a process known as upward convergence.

Standard English therefore is merely another dialect of English which, through circumstance, has gained greater social prestige than others.

There still remains the attitude that non-standard dialects are not rational; the double negative is often claimed to be an illogical use of language. Taking 'haven't got none' as an example, the reasoning is as follows: since 'haven't' indicates an absence, when nothing is absent, then something must be present. However, by looking carefully at the function of grammar it becomes clear that this way of thinking is misguided. Grammar involves the verification of meaning through inflection and word order: 'Two man walk yesterday.' The meaning is clear without the use of inflection. However, in Standard English 'man' turns to 'men', to show that there was more than one of them, and the –ed inflection for 'walked' supports the meaning of 'yesterday' – it happened in the past. So the 'none' of 'I haven't got none' merely verifies the zero quantity. It does not 'cancel out' the absence to make a positive in the same way that 'walked' does not cancel out the past to make the present. Those who claim that the double negative is 'illogical' are simply imposing the rules of one specific dialect – Standard English – onto other dialects.

The use of the double negative occurred frequently in Old English; Standard English merely dropped the form whilst other dialects retained it. People who use the form are often thought of as attempting to imitate the standard, but failing. It is also often associated with ignorance, poverty and even hooliganism (Norman Tebbitt in the '80s on 'Grammar and Hooliganism'). Yet because of the social disadvantages that do occur, should Standard English therefore be taught to all school pupils in this country? The educational establishment uses this form in writing and in most speech. If schools are to offer equal opportunity to all their students, it would seem that teaching the standard is necessary – both to aid learning and for future career opportunities – as the HMSO recommends.

Attempting to replace one dialect with another, however, is likely to be met with resistance. Teaching Standard English as a replacement would reinforce the idea of this dialect being 'better'. The result could be one of downward divergence, where the speakers of the non-standard dialects strengthen their language in order to distance themselves from their Standard English interlocutors. There is also the possibility of parent and child feeling that barriers have been inflicted between them.

However, this is not the only route. It is possible to create equality by retaining the variety of dialects we have and removing prejudice, rather than the other way round.

A further alternative would involve code-switching. This is the process whereby bi-dialectal speakers are able to switch from one dialect to another, according to the context. This would enable speakers of a non-standard variety to use the standard in a business – or likewise appropriate – situation, and to return to their own dialect at home and with friends: in informal contexts. This resolution allows for the social empowering of individuals whilst preventing estrangement from family and friends.

4.5   PHONETICS

Before we learn how to read and write we all learn how to talk (if we are able). To understand a language we must recognise both its sounds and its written symbols. Listening to a language you do not speak is a confusing experience. The confusion arises because we are unable to discern where one word ends and the other begins. Even if you could somehow segment the sounds you would still remain ignorant of their meaning.

To know a language we must first learn its specific sounds, reproduce them with our own vocal tracts, and then grasp how to segment and sequence them. The formal study of these 'speech sounds' used by language to represent meaning is called Phonetics.

During the course of your studies you may well find that a basic knowledge of phonetics proves invaluable when considering the nature, function and uses of language. Many excellent books have been written about this subject and you would be advised to acquaint yourself with some of them.

Here is a quick diagrammatic 'check list' of some of the basic terms and aspects you should be conversant with, if phonetics is included as a topic in your course.

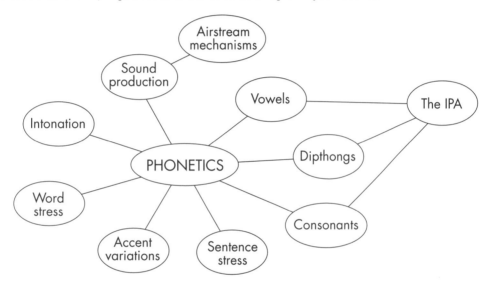

How might phonetics fit in with the rest of your course?

PHONETICS AND LANGUAGE ACQUISITION

A good working knowledge of the International Phonetic Alphabet (IPA) might prove invaluable when investigating an issue such as – How does a child learn/construct phonological rules? Having collected your data you may address yourself to questions such as:
- Do children generalise word patterns?
- Do they construct rules of their own?
- How do they distinguish between voiced and voiceless consonants?
- How do children begin to distinguish between phonological segments? Do they simply imitate?

Don't panic – this is just an example. Make sure that you are certain how much knowledge of this area your course requires.

4.6   GRAMMAR

Your course may not include direct questions on grammatical structures but most language syllabuses require candidates to comment (with differing levels of complexity) on grammatical features of texts. It is therefore extremely important that you become conversant with at least the basic principles of grammar (including spelling and punctuation).

Attitudes to grammar differ and terminology can be inconsistent. Most boards support a hierarchical structure known as systematic grammar. This represents the English Language as being a system of units where each level consists of one or more units from the level below it.

The standard hierarchy agreed is:

1. Sentence
2. Clause
3. Phrase
4. Word
5. Morpheme

What is a sentence?

Attempting to define a sentence is a difficult task but it is useful to think of it as the largest unit of grammar – standing, as it does, at the head of a hierarchy of other smaller grammatical units.

The logic of this pattern would then dictate that a sentence consists of one or more clauses. A clause consists of one or more phrases. A phrase consists of one or more words and a word (or lexical item) consists of one or more morphemes.

ANALYSIS OF GRAMMAR

Most examinations ask you to apply your knowledge of grammar through analysis (see suggested answer to stylistic analysis question on Frankenstein pp.178–81). Once you have grasped the basics, attempt to use your knowledge of studying the structure of a variety of texts in detail, e.g.:

• Newspaper articles
• Letters
• Extracts from novels
• Poems

The diagrams below and overleaf outline some of the basic terms you should acquaint yourself with. You can do this by referring to the many excellent books which discuss the structure of the English Language in much greater depth. It is in these specialist texts that you will find full descriptions of the functions of such lexical categories as nouns, verbs, adjectives, etc.

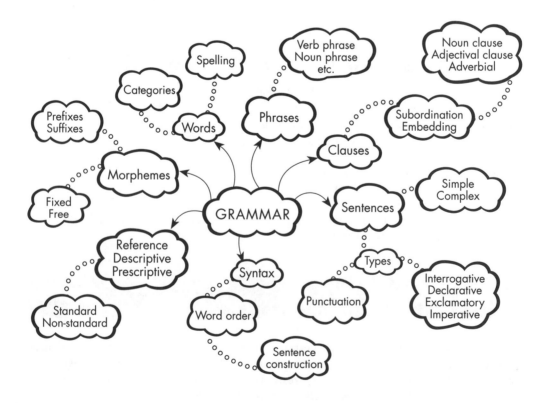

4.7 STYLISTIC ANALYSIS

What do texts mean? – this is a question you will be familiar with and is the central concern of most students of literature. How do texts mean? – is a question intrinsic to this part of linguistics and distinguishes the focus of a language-based response to both literary and non-literary texts.

'We know what language is and we also know that it varies according to circumstances.'
(G W Turner – *Stylistics*)

In Stylistic Analysis we make use of linguistic description to investigate how spoken or written language communicates meaning in a variety of contexts.

By the time you reach A level you will already be a competent user of the English Language. You will possess your own personal style. Stylistics should not be a new set of concepts for you (a new set of labels, maybe) – rather an opportunity to make your implicit knowledge explicit. In other words, it should enable you to articulate 'how' you recognise certain types of speech and writing such as:

• a tabloid newspaper
• an advert
• a text book
• a car manual
• a poem

Words, when we hear or read them, affect us. Close analysis of lexis, syntax and phonological or graphological features of a text can explain how they are able to do this. This links stylistics with theories related to language use, e.g. language and gender, etc.

Here is a framework of terms related to this type of analysis. You, as a candidate, would be advised to read one of the many excellent books written about this topic and familiarise yourself with the basic terms.

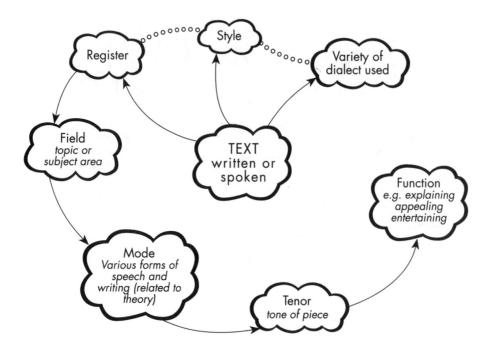

Most stylistic questions in examinations are worded as follows:

Comment on how language is used to...

In your answer you might refer to overall structure dialogue, figurative language, vocabulary and meanings, grammar and other linguistic matters you think are relevant.

General advice

- Read the question very carefully – make sure you are clear about what is being asked.
- Read the extract(s) carefully. What kind of text is it? Where would you expect to find it? And so on.
- What is its function? What is it trying to do?
- What is its tone? (Bias?)
- Is there an implied audience; field-specific vocabulary, etc.
- What is the pattern of the text? How is it structured?
- Is there anything different or unusual about the language used? What has been used for specific 'effect'?
- Remember your focus is how the texts work – this does not exclude you from discussing meaning, it simply requires a shift of perspective.

Illustrative question and answer

Stylistic analysis is a complex process. What follows is a suggested answer to a literary stylistics question.

Extract from *Frankenstein*.

It was on a dreary night of November that I beheld the accomplishment of my toils. With an anxiety that almost amounted to agony, I collected the instruments of life around me, that I might infuse a spark of being into the lifeless thing that lay at my feet. It was already one in the morning: the rain pattered dismally against the panes, and my candle was nearly burnt out, when, by the glimmer of the half-extinguished light, I saw the dull yellow eye of the creature open: it breathed hard, and a convulsive motion agitated its limbs.

How can I describe my emotions at this catastrophe, or how delineate the wretch whom with such infinite pains and care I had endeavoured to form? His limbs were in proportion, and I had selected his features as beautiful. Beautiful! Great God! His yellow skin scarcely covered the work of muscles and arteries beneath: his hair was of a lustrous black, and flowing: his teeth of pearly whiteness: but these luxuriances only formed a more horrid contrast with his watery eyes, that seemed almost of the same colour as the dun-white sockets in which they were set, his shrivelled complexion and straight black lips.

The different accidents of life are not so changeable as the feelings of human nature. I had worked hard for nearly two years, for the sole purpose of infusing life into an inanimate body. For this I had deprived myself of rest and health. I had desired it with an ardour that far exceeded moderation: but now that I had finished, the beauty of the dream vanished, and breathless horror and disgust filled my heart. Unable to endure the aspect of the being I had created, I rushed out of the room and continued a long time traversing my bedchamber, unable to compose my mind to sleep. At length lassitude succeeded to the tumult I had before endured, and I threw myself on the bed in my clothes, endeavouring to seek a few moments of forgetfulness. But it was in vain; I slept, indeed, but I was disturbed by the wildest dreams. I thought I saw Elizabeth, in the bloom of health, walking in the streets of Ingolstadt. Delighted and surprised, I embraced her, but as I imprinted the first kiss on her lips, they became livid with the hue of death; her features appeared to change and I thought that I held the corpse of my dead mother in my arms; a shroud enveloped her form, and I saw the grave-worms crawling in the folds of the flannel. I started from my sleep with horror; a cold dew covered my forehead, my teeth chattered, and every limb became convulsed; when, by the dim and yellow light of the moon, as it forced its way through the window shutters, I beheld the wretch – the miserable monster whom I had created. He held up the curtain of the bed; and his eyes, if eyes they may be called, were fixed on me. His jaws opened, and he muttered some inarticulate sounds, while a grin wrinkled his cheeks. He might have spoken, but I did not hear; one hand was stretched out, seemingly to detain me, but I escaped and rushed downstairs. I took refuge in the courtyard belonging to the house which I inhabited, where I remained during the rest of the night, walking up and down in the greatest agitation, listening attentively, catching and fearing each sound as if it were to announce the approach of the daemoniacal corpse to which I had so miserably given life.

Oh! No mortal could support the horror of that countenance. A mummy again endued with animation could not be so hideous as that wretch. I had gazed on him while unfinished; he was ugly then, but when those muscles and joints were rendered capable of motion, it became a thing such as even Dante could not have conceived.

I passed the night wretchedly. Sometimes my pulse beat so quickly and hardly that I felt the palpitation of every artery; at others, I nearly sank to the ground through languor and extreme weakness. Mingled with this horror, I felt the bitterness of disappointment; dreams that had been my food and pleasant rest for so long a space were now become a hell to me; and the change was so rapid, the overthrow so complete!

How is language used to create an atmosphere of horror? In your answer you should refer to vocabulary and meanings, grammar, tone and any other linguistic feature(s) you consider relevant.

Specimen answer

The extract from Mary Shelley's *Frankenstein* is a narrative account by Frankenstein of the animation of his creation. An atmosphere of horror is created in a variety of ways by Shelley – the contrasts of life and death, the use of setting, first person narration and the immaculate use of detail to describe Frankenstein's situation and his reaction to it.

Frankenstein's aim is to 'infuse a spark of being into the lifeless thing'. The principal lexical sets of the piece, I believe, fall into categories implied therein – the body, life, and death. The term 'being' implies not only life, but a human aspect. Throughout the piece our attention is relentlessly drawn to physical attributes of the 'thing', with references to 'limbs', 'eyes', 'form', 'skin', 'teeth', 'hair', 'lips', 'grin', and 'on hand... stretched out, seemingly to detain'. The anatomical 'field-specific' vocabulary used to describe the creature, 'his yellow skin scarcely covered the work of muscles and arteries beneath', has a cold, detached tone which creates horror. The graphic description is distasteful. (It is interesting to note that these terms, used later in reference to Frankenstein himself when 'sometimes [his] pulse beat so quickly and hardly that [he] felt the palpitation of every artery', emphasise the connection between creator and creation.) The theme of 'life' is also apparent in the more 'active' vocabulary of human emotion, with 'desired', 'endure', 'delighted', and 'ardour'.

Frankenstein has created this 'thing' from the 'lifeless', and notions of death prevail – 'inanimate body', 'shroud', 'grave-worms', 'corpse'. The proximity of these lexical sets throughout creates horror as it keeps to the forefront of our minds the unnatural aspect of the creature – a life created from death. 'Evil' is also associated with the adjective 'daemoniacal' being attributed to 'corpse'.

The setting of the piece creates atmosphere. Adjectives and adverbs are used effectively in establishing mood – the night was 'dreary', the rain pattered 'dismally', the candle was 'nearly burnt out', the light 'half extinguished'. The aspects of these are negative and so build an appropriate forum for 'darkness' and horror to prevail. Superlatives occur – his dreams are the 'wildest', qualifying terror. Intensifiers serve the same purpose – 'the change was so rapid, the overthrow so complete'.

Senses govern our emotions and are played upon to provoke horror. Visually, we are given images, with the use of colour – 'lustrous black' hair, 'teeth of pearly white-ness'. These colours are symbolically imbued with extended meanings of death/life, evil/innocence. To create paradox, these 'luxuriances' are juxtaposed with 'watery eyes', 'shrivelled complexion' and 'straight black lips' to disconcert the reader. The features selected by Frankenstein as 'beautiful' are referred to ironically through the repetitive exclamatory 'Beautiful!' followed by the expletive 'Good God!' The structural positioning of references to the creature's 'dull yellow eye' and the 'dim and yellow light of the moon' draws a deliberate parallel. The vocabulary of movement is almost visual, and has a 'jarring', unsettling effect: 'convulsive', 'agitated', 'traversing', 'threw', 'disturbed'.

The extract operates not only visually, but on a phonological level. Onomatopoeic qualities in certain words ensure we 'hear' the situation – 'breathless horror', 'lassi-tude', 'crawling', 'my teeth chattered', 'rushed downstairs', 'catching and fearing'. When the creature opened its jaws 'he muttered some inarticulate sounds'. Confusion is apparent, preceded by reference to Frankenstein's 'tumult'. Alliteration, in my opin-ion, not only makes for phonological impact, but increases the pace of the piece in some places – 'an anxiety that almost amounted to agony', by creating a fluency. It emphasises certain features in the text, such as 'breathless horror and disgust' (sibi-lance), 'cold dew covered my forehead, my teeth chattered, and every limb became convulsed'. (Once more it is apparent that Shelley uses the same vocabulary for both Frankenstein and his creation to indicate correspondences.)

The pace of the extract is also affected by complex syntax structures – subordination of clauses, 'his eyes, if eyes they may be called, were fixed on me', are reminiscent of asides in conversation, augmenting the immediacy of the piece created throughout the use of a first person 'voice'. The rhetorical question reflects the depth of despair felt by Frankenstein – 'How can I describe...?' whilst engaging us as readers – we became involved in his 'dialogue' and therefore respond more to the horror he feels. Within complex sentences, punctuation is effectively used to dictate pace, 'I saw the dull yellow eye of the creature open: it breathed hard, and a convulsive motion agitated its limbs', and to lend emphasis and impact.

The use of tense, in my opinion, adds to the atmosphere of horror. Past perfect is used – 'I had worked hard', 'I had desired', creating a time phase which makes the simple past more immediate/recent – 'I escaped and rushed downstairs', 'I took refuge'. The conditional tense – 'as if it were to announce the approach...', 'he might have spoken...' creates an element of uncertainty – a key factor in any 'horror'.

Syntax affects the tone of the piece by foregrounding certain notions, for example '...the sole purpose of infusing life into an inanimate body', 'the miserable monster whom I had created'. There is irony in the reference to the creature being 'a thing such as even Dante could not have conceived'. Frankenstein 'passed the night wretchedly'.

Some of the vocabulary of the extract is no longer commonly used in modern English, yet is typical of the Gothic novel era and thereby helps create an atmosphere of horror due to style – 'I beheld the accomplishment of my toils', 'how to delineate the wretch, whom with such infinite pains and care, I had endeavoured to form', 'the courtyard belonging to the house which I inhabited'. The formality of style might be seen to create horror through a certain 'detachment'.

The metaphor in the final section of the extract – 'dreams that had been my food and pleasant rest for so long a space were now become a hell for me' – indicates how the insubstantial sustained – the unrealised motivated reality. The irony is tangible through the juxtaposition of 'dreams' and 'pleasant' with 'hell' – the essential oppositional elements of creation and destruction are joined in the same breath, emphasising the horror of Frankenstein. Once 'alive', that which had been 'beautiful' was 'ugly' and horrific to him.

4.8 CASE STUDIES

Rewriting in a different style for a specified audience and purpose

This is an exercise, usually under examination conditions, designed to call upon the individual skills relevant to other parts of your course. You, as a candidate, are asked to combine the analytical skills required for investigative purpose (linked to theory) with the creative ability needed for the original writing component of the course.

Shortly before the examination, usually 48 hours, you will be issued with a series of 'packages' or range of articles which contain information from a variety of sources. Recent topics have included:
- Baseball
- Volcanoes
- Multiple Sclerosis
- Child Care
- Study Skills
- Brass Bands

In the examination, you will be asked to undertake a specific task related to the source material provided. A certain amount of 'cutting and shrinking' is permitted in the composition of your piece but guidelines on this vary.

Sometimes material might provide clues as to the type of task you might be set – but a word of warning – do not waste time guessing! Positive tasks set may include:
- a magazine or newspaper article
- a leaflet or pamphlet
- a report or survey
- a programme or tourist guide
- a radio documentary
- an historical or narrative reconstruction based on factual material

What do you need to know?

In preparation:
- Read the pack(s) thoroughly – just once is not enough.
- Read to distinguish fact from opinion – is a bias view stated as fact, etc.
- Establish links/connections between the material and decide what different aspects of the subject are being dealt with.
- Summary and annotation skills (see earlier sections) prove useful in preparing the texts for the examination.
- Attempt to gain a sense of order and feel confident that you 'know' the material.

In the Exam:
- If there is a choice – choose carefully. An unwise decision could cost you dearly.
- Once again be certain (see coursework chapter – original writing p. 206) that your purpose and intended audience are clear in your mind.
- Plan your response. Keep an eye on time.
- Remember style (tone of voice) is related to purpose and audience so select appropriately and remain consistent. Use an appropriate format.
- Use your own words – have you constructed a new text or a 'pick and mix' monster?
- Presentation is important.
- For further guidance refer to the section on general exam techniques (pp. 33–7) which also apply here.

This type of examination is creative and active, try to have fun but never underestimate its complexity.

Illustrative question and answer

Multiple Sclerosis

Sponsored by a well known firm of audio tape manufacturers, the Multiple Sclerosis Society wishes to produce a recorded cassette for relatives, friends and acquaintances of MS sufferers, as part of its new information campaign. The cassette will be available free, not only to individuals but also through organisations and public libraries.

You have been asked to write a script based upon the material in the file. The Society believes that knowledge about the disease will promote sympathetic understanding of the problems associated with it, and a willingness to help sufferers and their families. Your task is not to appeal directly for money, but to inform listeners about MS in the most telling way possible. Available medical knowledge should be made clear but the script should focus on everyday human experience. For a long time MS has mystified both doctors and lay persons. Your script should above all capture interest and help to reduce anxiety.

Choose your own title and style of presentation. The tape should run for about 12 to 15 minutes. You may suggest sound effects but remember that it is your text that is of prime importance.

You have also been asked to write a liner note to slip inside the cassette box. It should be no more than 100 words, and may contain an illustration if you wish.

Case study – specimen answer

Multiple Sclerosis   Vivienne Lowthian-Wells

My tape will be recorded by several people with different voices, for variation. One female reader with RP will read the main script. Quotes, and some other sections will be read by three other people: one a male with a northern dialect, one female with a Scottish dialect and one male with a southern, perhaps London, dialect. I feel that this will make the stories more relevant to normal people who may be suffering from multiple sclerosis. In my script, I will indicate where the various people will speak by using the following:

RPF   Main Reader (female)
SF   Scottish female reader
LM   Southern/London male reader
NM   Northern male reader

v clear

TITLE:

MULTIPLE SCLEROSIS:
A HOPE IN HELL?

an excellent choice

Music will be played at the beginning and end of the tape, the music will be the end of Elgar's Cello Concerto, played by Jacqueline du Pré, who had MS.

good title

NM: MULTIPLE SCLEROSIS:
A HOPE IN HELL?

RPF

shd you stress the spoken nature

This tape is produced by the Multiple Sclerosis Society, to help relatives, friends and acquaintances of multiple sclerosis sufferers. The extracts on this tape have been written by real-life sufferers and their relatives.

SF

My father, who is disabled, has had many problems, me being one of them. In the year of 1984 he was involved in a car accident. Luckily, he just suffered a concussion (the others involved suffered from minor injuries). Although it wasn't his fault he was shocked and slowly started to go downhill and had problems walking. Many tests were done and it was later found that my father, of all people, had got multiple sclerosis.

RPF

is this a little too hard hitting

Many people misunderstand multiple sclerosis. It is a disease which has baffled scientists and doctors; a disease for which there is no cure. It affects 60 to 100 in every 100,000 people. Treatment is available, but is at present very limited. It includes the use of pulses of steroids or ACTH. Pain relievers and muscle relaxants are used, as are occupational and physiotherapy. Multiple sclerosis is a long and painful disease. Sufferers can have long remissions, sometimes decades long, but the relapses will be longer and more severe. Symptoms often start with 'pins and needles' sensations in parts of the body, for example, the legs. 'Sophie', a teacher, experienced these symptoms, at first unaware of what they were:

SF

Well done – a suitably 'spoken extract'

On 17th November 1987, I made an appointment to see my doctor because I'd had a strange sort of sensation in my feet, a bit like 'pins and needles' actually and not unlike a condition I had suffered from 18 months previously. Then, it had affected the area around my waist and I had gone to see a neurologist who told me it was a 'virus of the spine' and would no doubt be out of my system within a year. I was curiously naive; I accepted it all without question and didn't make any real connection between all that and these 'pins and needles' in my feet.

SLEEVE NOTES

clear and straightforward – a little repetitive

The Multiple Sclerosis Society was founded to promote and fund research into finding the cause and cure for multiple sclerosis. It provides a welfare and support service for families with a member suffering from MS. The society also aims to educate people about the disease.

This tape aims to help friends, family and acquaintances of MS sufferers, to tell them about the disease and its consequences and how they can offer support and help to the sufferer.

Examiners' comments

Text – is cohesive with a definite introduction and conclusion.

Instructions about readings etc. are generally good although a few other voices might have been necessary. Excellent design of tape cover, liner insert, etc.

Tenor – good selection of material, establishing personal stories of generally reassuring natures.

Good control over and fluency of your own language use.

40/50

4.9 AEB ENGLISH LANGUAGE

The AEB offers an A-level examination in which English Language provides a substantial element. This examination is called merely English and consists of three papers:

Paper 1 (2 hrs 30 mins) contains an essay for which 60 marks are allocated and a précis for which 40 marks are allocated. Total 100.

Paper 2 (3 hrs) contains a prose passage with questions mainly on content but also occasionally on style and opinion, for which 40 marks are allocated. There are then two further sections each containing three set books. Candidates must answer one question from each section and a third question chosen from either of the two sections or an alternative question dealing with an aspect of language. Each of these questions is given 20 marks. Total 100.

Paper 3 (3 hrs) is literature only and is divided into two sections. Candidates must answer two questions from each section. Marks are given as 4 × 25. Section 1 usually contains literature pre-1800.

It is therefore possible, if the optional language question on Paper 2 is answered, to have 160 of the possible 300 marks allocated on what might be called English Language; if this question is not taken, then 140 marks are in this area; the examination is therefore on an approximately equal division between language and literature.

FURTHER READING

Aitchison, J	*Language Change: Progress or Decay?* (Fontana, 1981)
Crystal, D & Davy, D	*Investigating English Style* (Longman, 1969)
Crystal, D	*Child Language, Learning and Linguistics* (E Arnold, 1976)
Crystal, D	*Rediscovering English Grammar* (Longman, 1992)
Fowler, R	*Linguistic Criticism* (OUP, 1986)
Freeburn, D *et al*	*Varieties of English* (Macmillan, 1987)
Fromkin, V & Rodman, R	*An Introduction to Language* (Holt, Rinehart & Winston, 1988)
Hughes, A & Trudgill, P	*English Accents and Dialects* (E Arnold, 1979)
Ladefaged, P	*A Course in Phonetics* (Harcourt Brace, 1982)
Leech, G & Short, M	*Style in Fiction* (Longman, 1981)
Montgomery, M	*An Introduction to Language and Society* (Mathews)
O'Donnell, W R & Todd, L	*Variety in Contemporary English* (Allen & Unwin, 1980)
Smith, P M	*Language, the Sexes and Society* (Blackwell, 1988)
Stubbs, M	*Discursive Analysis* (Blackwell, 1988)
Turner, C W	*Stylistics* (Peluni, 1973)

Question bank

1 Answer both parts (a) and (b) of this question.

(a) Using the five passages below as supporting evidence, argue for or against the view that the English Language has remained virtually unchanged over the last 400 years. (15)

A Why, this is hell, nor am I out of it:
Think'st thou that I, who saw the face of God,
And tasted the eternal joys of heaven,
Am not tormented with ten thousand hells,
In being depriv'd of everlasting bliss?

(Christopher Marlowe, c.1589)

B Wherefore are these things hid? Wherefore have these gifts a curtain before
em? Are they like to take dust, like Mistress Mall's picture? Why dost
thou not go to church in a galliard and come home in a coranto? My very
walk should be a jig...

(William Shakespeare, c.1601)

C As I walk'd through the wilderness of this world, I lighted on a certain place,
where was a den; And I laid me down in that place to sleep: And as I slept I
dreamed a dream. I dreamed, and behold I saw a man clothed with rags,
standing in a certain place, with his face from his own house, a book in his
hand, and a great burden upon his back. I looked, and saw him open the
book, and read therein; and as he read, he wept and trembled: and not being
able to contain, he brake out with a lamentable cry: saying, *what shall I do?*

(John Bunyan, 1678)

D 'Nay, nay,' said Mr Poyser, 'thee musn't judge Hetty too hard. Them
young gells are like the unripe grain; they'll make a good meal by-and-by,
but they're squashy as yet'.

(George Eliot, 1859)

E ...Well I dinnae know how ti'describe it – it was that dark – it was pitch – an'
I couldnae see hide nor hair of anither body – I was that scared – I could feel
the heart thumpin' in me – I run on – not knowin' where I run – but hopin'
I'd see a light or hear a sound – an' then – I got my wish – I seen two wee
yellow lights about six inches off the groun' – an' they lights were comin'
straight for me – Some wise man once said that the biggest misfortune that
could happen a body would be to get their heart's desire – an' that night I
learnt the truth o' what he said – one minute I was lookin' to see a light – an'
the next minute I would a give anythin' to see the wee lights go away – for
slowly but unmistakably they were comin' straight at me...

(Mrs X, 1989)

(b) Look carefully again at passage E and answer the following questions.
 Where, in your judgement, does the speaker come from? (1)
 Select and comment on the linguistic features that have helped you to decide. (2)
 What devices are used by the narrator to gain and hold the listener's interest? (2)

Oxford

2 Continuous Writing

You are advised to spend about 1½ hours on this question and to revise your
writing carefully. Choose one of the following topics. Credit will be given for skilled
planning, quality of information, clarity and accuracy of expression.

(a) Do comic book versions and animated films of Shakespeare's plays and other
classics insult the authors of the original texts, or are they welcome additions to
contemporary popular culture?

(b) Should the press be prevented from exposing the follies of the famous? If so,
what limitations should there be to the freedom of journalists to pursue stories,
and newspaper publishers to print them? If not, why not?

(c) Which books would you recommend parents to give to their children to stimulate
an interest in reading, and why?

(d) A young boy was heard to suggest that the voting age should be lowered to ten,
because by the time they are eighteen people have been exposed to too much

brainwashing to make independent decisions. Do you feel that eighteen is an appropriate age at which to be given the vote, and do first-time voters receive sufficient unbiased information to make their own rational choices?

(e) Write the talk you would give to students at the start of their A-level studies if you were asked to advise them about how to approach their work.

(f) Write a short story or a poem under the title 'I was a stranger in a strange land'. If you choose to write a poem, it need not be longer than twenty lines.

(g) Is employment a right or a privilege?

(h) Which three persons, no longer living, would you like to meet, and why?

AEB 1994

3 Test of skills of Summary Writing (40 marks)

THE GUARDIAN
Friday June 26 1992

Jenny Bryan says sensible snacking could make the difference between winning at Wimbledon and losing

Yes, do have those bananas

AS TENNIS stars unpacked their bags by the umpire's chair at Wimbledon this week you'd be forgiven for thinking that some had come for a picnic. Under the favourite racquets and lucky sweatbands were the bananas, biscuits and muesli bars that players increasingly rely on to boost their flagging energy levels at the end of tough matches. And, as the pace hots up next week, the snack boxes will begin to bulge.

"I can show you players at the end of a five set match who have lost because they didn't eat and drink sensibly during the game," says Iona Smeaton, state registered dietician to the Lawn Tennis Association. "At the US Open last year so many players dropped out because of heat stress that a nine point advice sheet was put up in the men's changing room to remind them how to avoid getting ill during matches," she adds.

Dehydration is a tennis player's biggest enemy. A few years ago players could be seen drinking all manner of magic potions brewed in the secrecy of their hotel rooms. But most now recognise that you can't do much better than plain water, perhaps with a pinch of salt.

Trained athletes sweat twice as much as unfit people. Men sweat more than women, who rely on radiation to get rid of excess heat. That's why women players tend to get redder in the face than men. But both need to preload their stomach with 1/2 to 3/4 pint of water before they go on court and then top that up with a cupful of liquid every 10 to 15 minutes during their match.

It's important to keep drinking even during the warm-up and the first few nervy opening games because dehydration quickly dulls the concentration and slows the legs. Athletes don't need to add much salt to their drinks because their sweat is remarkably dilute, says Dr Craig Sharp, chief physiologist at the British Olympic Medical Centre in Middlesex.

They conserve salt much better than someone who is unfit because their sweat glands work differently, he explains.

He believes the various commercial drinks designed for sportsmen and women have little or no advantage over water and he knows of no special ingredient in orange or lemon barley water that could be responsible for its appeal at Wimbledon.

Making drinks very sweet would be counter-productive, says Iona Smeaton, because this actually slows the rate at which water is absorbed.

"A drink that contains more than 12 per cent sugar can actually make you dehydrated. It would have so much sugar in it that the body would need to pull back some water into the intestines to help the sugar get absorbed," she points out.

So a tennis player may take a swig or two of cola but they'll quickly follow it with several gulps of water to dilute it.

They do need glucose for energy though and that's where bananas come in. The American player Michael Chang was one of the first to popularise bananas and he's been known to get through three or four in a match. There's no magic ingredient to a banana but about a fifth of its weight is carbohydrate. It contains a good mixture of sugars, some of which will slip quickly into the muscles to boost energy levels and some more slowly to give a prolonged effect. It also tastes good and is easy to digest.

Tennis players rely on bursts of speed so their muscles run on glucose. In the days before a competition they will bolster the fuel supply in their muscles by eating a carbohydrate-rich diet of bread, pasta and rice.

For a straight sets match under a dull sky, the energy stores they have built up pre-match will probably be enough to see them through. But there's no predicting when they will come up against a player who is determined to upset the seedings and put even the Boris Beckers and Steffi Graffs of the championships through an unexpectedly long and gruelling match.

The picnic basket is especially important for the players who compete in the doubles and mixed doubles as well as the singles during the Wimbledon fortnight. They may have to play twice in a day and their energy stores will almost certainly run low.

Iona Smeaton advises young British hopefuls to replenish their energy supplies as soon as they come off court. "There is evidence that in the first half an hour to an hour after exercise the muscles are most geared to refuelling. So players should eat immediately after they come off court. People who refuel most effectively can start their next match with 20 to 30 per cent more energy in their muscles than their opponent," she says.

In the last painful minutes of a three or four hour match, that could mean the difference between posing with the famous Wimbledon trophy and going down in the record books as a gallant loser.

Your task is to use the information contained in the above article to produce an information sheet for competitors in a junior tennis tournament, advising them about what they should eat and drink during the course of the event.

Work on the assumption that the average age of your readers is fifteen.

Your presentation should be appropriate to the task and to the intended readership.

Your writing must not exceed 200 words.

AEB 1994

4 Over a decade ago, the Plain English Campaign began campaigning to improve the quality of informative writing. The campaign objected to 'gobbledygook' such as that used in the extract from a letter reprinted below. The extract sparked off correspondence in a daily newspaper on the question of 'Plain English'.

> **Letter from Local Council Concerning Library Posters**
> Your enquiry about the use of the entrance area of the library for displaying posters about income support rights gives rise to the question of the provenance and authoritativeness of the material to be displayed. Items of a disputatious or polemic kind, whilst not necessarily excluded, are considered individually.

Write a letter to a national daily broadsheet newspaper outlining some of the features which the Plain English Campaigners complain about. You may use illustrations from the above extract if you wish. Give your own views about whether 'plain English' is always appropriate.

ULEAC

5 Robert McCrum, in an article in *The Listener* of October 2nd 1986 about the BBC's role in establishing RP as the socially acceptable accent for the radio, writes:

> The Scots broadcaster Susan Rae describes how 'people write to me and say "please don't take this personally", then they proceed to say how much they hate me and how much they hate my accent, and then tell me to get back to the hills and the heather'.

Write a short article for *The Radio Times* explaining this attitude to accents, giving your own views about the opinions expressed to Susan Rae and suggesting what BBC policy on accents should be.

ULEAC

6 The following paragraphs appeared in a newspaper article in the *Daily Telegraph* on 27th October 1989:

> A list of 'sexist' terms such as snowman, tomboy, man overboard and masterpiece was put before city councillors yesterday after a 'slightly tongue-in-cheek' motion went too far.
> Liberal Democrats in Liverpool called for a glossary of unacceptable racist and sexist words to be issued to councillors and officials after a Labour member took offence to 'denigrate' because it stems from 'niger', Latin for black.

(i) What do some people object to in the terms *snowman, tomboy, man overboard* and *masterpiece*?
(ii) Make a list of six other racist and sexist words about which complaints might be made. For each word, explain what is being objected to.
(iii) Briefly give your views on racist and sexist words.

ULEAC

7 Describe some of the attitudes held towards regional and other accents, and the effects of these attitudes on speakers' language behaviour.

NEAB

8 Discuss some of the ways in which the language of speakers and/or writers may be influenced by their intended audience.

NEAB

9 Discuss some of the ways in which ideas about the functions of language contribute to our understanding of how children acquire English as their first language.

NEAB

10 Explain some of the ways in which variations in people's use of English might be influenced by social class.

NEAB

11 Describe and comment on some of the changes which have taken place in English spelling, vocabulary and grammar since the late sixteenth century.

Make close reference to the following edited letter written by Queen Elizabeth I to her successor at that time, James VI of Scotland. Elizabeth is replying to James's plea for a reversal of her decision to have Mary Queen of Scots, his mother, executed.

> To my deare brother and cousin,
> the kinge of Skotz.
>
> Be not caried away, my deare brother, with the lewd perswations of suche, as insteade of infowrming you of my to nideful and helples cause of defending the brethe that God hath given
> 5 me, to be better spent than spilt by the bloudy invention of traitors handz, may perhaps make you belive, that ether the offense was not so great, or if that cannot serue them, for the over-manifest triall wiche in publik and by the greatest and most in this land hathe bine manifestly proved, yet the wyl make that her life may be saved and myne safe.
>
> Your commissionars telz me, that I may trust her in the hande of some indifferent prince, and have
> 10 all her cousins and allies promis she wil no more seake my ruine. Deare brother and cousin, way in true and equal balance wither the lak not muche good ground when suche stuf serves for ther bilding. Suppose you I am so mad to truste my life in anothers hand and send hit out of my owne?
>
> Make account, I pray you, of my firme frindship loue and care, from wiche, my deare brother, let no sinistar whisperars, nor busy troblars of princis states, persuade to leave your surest, and stike
> 15 to vnstable staies. And so, God hold you ever in his blessed kiping, and make you see your tru frinds. Excuse my not writing sonar, for paine in one of my yees was only the cause.
>
> Your most assured lovinge sistar and cousin,
> ELIZABETH R.

(Letters of Queen Elizabeth and King James VI of Scotland, edited Bruce)

NEAB

12 Discuss some of the factors which create different kinds of language interaction.

If you wish, you may focus on the following exchanges for comment and illustration. The transcripts are extracts from exchanges within two different groups of 15-year-olds.

Exchange 1

Anne Would you be able to look after a handicapped child...?

Mandy No, I think it'd probably get you down.

Jane I'd probably need some help.

Anne Probably yeah you'd need some help, but do you think you'd
5   be able to cope with looking after one?

Jane I would...

Mandy Did you see that programme...

Jane ...if they showed me what to do...

Mandy ...last year, where he went and got all them little things for
10   the kids; that really upset me to think that he tried to do them things and he hurt himself, you know what I mean?

Sue That, that programme we watched last year?

Jane Yeah, he had no legs.

Mandy Oh...

15 *Sue* Yeah and no arms.

Jane Yeah. Yeah. But he had the good side about it didn't he?

Sue He did...

Anne He got a chance to live.

Mandy Yeah, I wasn't meaning not having his legs on. That's all right
20   ... it's what ... it's when they just don't understand you.

Sue At least he's got a good brain...

Exchange 2

Stuart Barry Drive...That's in Kirby, innit?

Dave What?

Ian That's where Edmonds lives, innit?

Dave What?

5   *Ian* Barry Drive.

Stuart Is that the rich part?

Dave No idea (indistinct) Barry Drive's got £80,000 houses on it.

Ian Flippin' eck.

(*Twenty seconds' pause*)

10   *Ian* Leicester Forest East.

Stuart It's rich up there, innit?

Ian Yes, near LFE, some of the places…because they've got that
massive hotel there, haven't they?

Dave Yeah, because I know of that hotel because we always take a short

15   cut through.

Ian Everybody says you shouldn't go down there, but we used to go right
through. Takes about an extra 15 miles. I mean you can cut straight
through there…you'd save about ten miles.

(*Lipservice*, Jones, 1988)
NEAB 1994

13 Discuss and illustrate some of the ways in which it may be possible to distinguish between a *dialect* and a *register*.

NEAB 1994

14 The first of the following extracts is from *Uncertain Summer* by Betty Neels, published in 1972. Serena, who works in London as a nurse, is at home with her family, including her younger sister Susan. Laurens, a Dutch doctor, whom Serena has recently met, has strongly hinted that he wishes to marry her. Gijs van Amstel is a friend of Laurens.

The second extract is from *Jane Eyre* by Charlotte Brontë, published in 1847. The narrator, Jane Eyre, has recently accepted a proposal of marriage from Mr Rochester, in whose house she is employed as a governess.

Comment on how the two extracts use language to express the thoughts, feelings, points of view and values of Serena and Jane.

In your answer you may refer to vocabulary, grammar, overall structure, figurative language and any other linguistic matters you think are relevant to meaning.

Extract I

Serena stood at the old-fashioned kitchen sink and as she worked she thought about Laurens, trying to make herself think sensibly. No one in their right minds fell in love like this, to the exclusion of everything and everyone else. She was, she reminded herself over and over again, a sensible girl, no longer young and silly like little Susan; she saw also that

5   there was a lot more to marriage than falling in love. Besides, Laurens, even though he had told her so delightfully and surprisingly that she was going to marry him—for surely that was what he had meant—might be in the habit of falling in love with any girl who chanced to take his fancy. She began to dry the dishes, resolving that, whatever her feelings, she would not allow herself to be hurried into any situation, however wonderful it might seem.

10   She had put the china and silver away and was on her way upstairs to make the beds when she remembered the strange intent look Gijs van Amstel had given her when Laurens had suggested she should go out with him. There had been no reason for it and it puzzled her that the small episode should stick so firmly in her memory. She shook it free from her thoughts and joined her mother, already busy in the boys' room.

15   The day passed pleasantly so that she forgot her impatience for Monday's arrival. When she had finished her chores she duly visited the sexton's* wife, admired the baby—the sixth and surely the last?—presented the proud mother with a small gift for the tiny creature, and turned her attention to the sexton's other five children, who had arrived with an almost monotonous regularity every eighteen months or so. They all bore a marked resemblance

20   to each other and, Serena had to admit, they all looked remarkably healthy. She asked tentatively: 'Do you find it a bit much—six, Mrs Snow?'

Her hostess smiled broadly. 'Lor' no, Miss Serena, they'm good as gold and proper little

loves, we wouldn't be without 'em. You'll see, when you'm wed and 'as little 'uns to rear.'
Serena tried to imagine herself with six small children, and somehow the picture was
25 blurred because deep in her bones some-thing told her that Laurens wouldn't want to be
bothered with a houseful of children to absorb her time—and his. He would want her for
himself.... The thought sent a small doubt niggling at the back of her mind, for she loved
children; provided she had help she was quite sure she could cope with half a dozen, but
only if their father did his share too, and Laurens, she was sure, even though she knew very
little about him, wasn't that kind of man.

* sexton – a caretaker of a church   (*Uncertain Summer*, Betty Neels, 1972)

Extract 2

As I rose and dressed, I thought over what had happened, and wondered if it were a dream.
I could not be certain of the reality till I had seen Mr Rochester again, and heard him renew
his words of love and promise.
    While arranging my hair, I looked at my face in the glass, and felt it was no longer plain:
5   there was hope in its aspect, and life in its colour: and my eyes seemed as if they had beheld
the fount of fruition, and borrowed beams from the lustrous ripple. I had often been
unwilling to look at my master, because I feared he could not be pleased at my look; but
I was sure I might lift my face to his now, and not cool his affection by its expression. I
took a plain but clean and light summer dress from my drawer and put it on: it seemed
10 no attire had ever so well become me; because none had I ever worn in so blissful a mood.
    I was not surprised, when I ran down into the hall, to see that a brilliant June morning
had succeeded to the tempest of the night; and to feel, through the open glass door, the
breathing of a fresh and fragrant breeze. Nature must be gladsome when I was so happy.
A beggar-woman and her little boy—pale, ragged objects both—were coming up the walk,
15 and I ran down and gave them all the money I happened to have in my purse—some three
or four shillings: good or bad, they must partake of my jubilee. The rooks cawed, and blither
birds sang; but nothing was so merry or so musical as my own rejoicing heart.

(*Jane Eyre*, Charlotte Brontë, 1847)

NEAB 1994

CHAPTER 5

COURSEWORK

Units in this chapter

Chapter objectives

The most striking difference over recent years has been the inclusion of coursework in A-level language and literature syllabuses. This appeals to many candidates who have written essays under coursework conditions at GCSE and who prefer to give a more considered and well researched approach to their work. They can either set the task themselves or negotiate it with their teacher and there is considerable room for change until the final draft is given in. Coursework also gives considerable freedom of choice in the books chosen and the task set and appeals to candidates who like to research their essays thoroughly.

One consequence of including coursework in the syllabuses has been the acceleration of the trend towards giving greater emphasis on writers of the late 20th Century. Whilst the core syllabus insists that at least one pre-20th Century writer, other than Shakespeare, be included as a minimum, many candidates choose modern authors to examine.

5.1 LITERATURE COURSEWORK

The exam boards vary in the type of coursework they set, but generally it is of the following type:
- A group of essays between 800–1200 words long
- Longer essays (2000 words)
- Extended essay of 3000+ words
- A creative writing option
- Occasionally a short test of oral proficiency

Do remember that choosing the coursework option isn't easy. You have to work hard over a long period of time and must not let things slide. You have to show initiative in carrying out original research and seeking out advice from your teacher. You must set yourself a realistic task for the time available and organise your notes and other materials carefully.

Here are some pointers given by an English Literature Chief Examiner:
- Bear in mind the importance of the task set. So much coursework is slackly written, lacking in argument, shape or direction because the tasks set have not been sufficiently demanding. Often candidates choose their own titles; they need to make sure that

what they set out to do will allow them to demonstrate the sort of skills needed at A-level (listed below).

- Candidates need to be concise, to stick to word limits, to cut down on extraneous material such as biography, historical background and narrative and must not mistake quantity for quality.
- Use the unique opportunity coursework gives candidates for restructuring and revising their work. Only when you submit your essay for assessment in its final form must the process of redrafting stop.
- It is an enormous help to use word processing facilities which can be used in the re-drafting process. You should take the opportunity of using them if available.

Please study the core objectives listed below, taken from AEB 1994 syllabus support material. Although these may not be common to all boards, they contain skills which all candidates should try to cover.

Coursework assignments will continue to offer considerable opportunities in the choice of texts and tasks, and for student autonomy. The assessment objectives of the examination part of the syllabus will be reflected in the assessment of coursework. These objectives include:

- To show first-hand knowledge and understanding of a text and, where appropriate, of the personal and historical context in which it was written.
- To see meanings below the surface of a text.
- To understand and appreciate a writer's use of structure and language, and particular features of a text – for example, character, argument, imagery.
- To make a well considered personal response to a text.
- To show how a text may excite emotions in readers or audiences.
- To make engaged and informed conjectures about the purpose of a text.
- To make meaningful connections and comparisons between texts.
- To explore works written for a different kind of society and in a different idiom from the candidate's own.
- To write effectively and appropriately in response to texts studied.
- (Optional) – oral component. To show skill in presenting an oral response to a text.

GUIDANCE GIVEN BY EXAM BOARDS FOR COMPLETION OF COURSEWORK

Again this may vary from Board to Board, but the following guidelines would seem common to all:

- Assessment and marking will be by whole folder criteria – according to the assessment grid – see below.
- It should be remembered that all coursework assignments should be of A-level standard. Whilst the format of standard A-level examination questions may not be appropriate for the particular conditions of coursework assignments, centres should ensure – well before the stage of trial moderation – that all assignments are of comparable challenge.
- It is recommended that a bibliography of references, apart from set texts, should be included in the coursework folder.
- The pieces of work must be filed in chronological order (if more than one piece is produced) and listed on the sheet supplied by the Board.
- Each piece must be dated, with an explanation of the conditions under which it was produced, clearly written at the top of the first page. Failure to comply with this regulation may result in work not being accepted for moderation.
- Revised work may be included, but once a piece of work has been submitted for formal assessment it may not be further revised.
- The selection of work is to be determined by the teacher and the candidate in consultation. However, in the unlikely event of any disagreement, the candidate's choice should take precedence.
- Incomplete folders will be assessed on a pro-rata basis (that is, they will be treated in the same way as an incomplete examination script).

HOW SCRIPTS ARE ASSESSED

The following grid, again from the AEB Handbook, gives an idea of the four levels of assessment the AEB examiners employ and the criteria attached to these levels. Obviously all candidates will aim for level two and above, so this should give them a clear idea of what is required. Although all Exam Boards vary slightly, this grid should be helpful to all students.

English literature marking grid

Level	Marks	Textual grasp and appreciation	Conveying the text (and answering relevantly)	Quality of expression
Level 1	1–3	Narrative approach with frequent misreadings.	Mere assertion of points of view. Often irrelevant answer.	Frequent weakness of expression. Excessive, aimless quotation. Misunderstood technical terms.
	4–5	Merely accurate storytelling. Skimpy readings.	Difficulty in engaging with question. Assertive comments largely undeveloped and unsupported.	Simple expression. Flawed but conveying basic ideas. Paraphrase plus lengthy quotation. Unassimilated notes.
Level 2	6–8	Response to surface features of text. Basic and generalised but usually accurate response.	Some awareness of effect of text on selves. An attempt to use specific details to support points made.	Expression generally able to convey ideas. Greater variety of vocabulary and sentence structure. Paraphrase with some embedded ideas. Quotation often overlong. Technical terms or unassimilated notes may be intrusive.
	9–10	Some awareness of implicit meaning. Straightforward approach. Response to obvious contrasts and comparisons.	Can explain moods and feelings in text. Becoming aware of effect on reader of scene or events. At least implicit relevance to question.	Adequate expression matching understanding. More sophisticated vocabulary, structure of response can be identified. Quotation probably over-long but sometimes analysed. Fair grasp of technical terms and some ability to use notes.
Level 3	11–15	Beginnings of appreciation of language and style. Secure knowledge and understanding of text. Awareness of subtlety. Closer reading becomes obvious.	Can see alternative interpretations and/or pursue strong personal response. Analysing. Exploring. Clearly aware of effect on reader of scene or event. Coherent, shaped and relevant response.	Expression is clear and controlled. Paraphrase rare. Well structured with links between sentences and paragraphs. Wide vocabulary. Neat and purposeful use of short quotation as part of structured argument. Technical terms and assimilated notes become integral part of informed personal response.

Answers in the category below will have some of the following characteristics in addition to all of those in Level 3.

Level	Marks	Textual grasp and appreciation	Conveying the text (and answering relevantly)	Quality of expression
Level 4	16–20	Insight. Conceptualised response. Confident exploration of ideas, language, style. Autonomy as reader.	Overview. Mastery of detail of text. Originality.	Mastery of structure. Confidence in expression. Rarely at a loss for the right word. Skilful use of quotation and close analysis of it. Technical terms and secondary sources enhance response to text.

COURSEWORK ESSAY PLANS

The following coursework essay plan shows what could be the skeleton of an extended essay. Note the detailed bibliography at the end.

'Much of Sylvia Plath's writing is concerned with women's lives and the choices they make.' (Wagner-Martin) Write a close essay plan on the subject.

Specimen answer

- Women – their role in life – relationships with other women
- Children
- Husbands

Relationships with other women

Bell Jar: 'If Mrs Nolan, an English woman, felt herself a stranger in Devon after six years, what hope had I, an American, of infiltrating that rooted society?'

The Bee Meeting
Women are very concerned with people, esp. other women. The surroundings do not seem to matter. A woman asks 'Who are these people at the bridge to meet me?' She observes in great detail how they dress, what their positions are, constantly comparing them to herself. 'In my sleeveless summery dress I have no protection, And they are all gloved and covered, why did nobody tell me?' This also shows how women can be greatly disturbed at being different from their counterparts, leading to great introspection. 'I am nude as a chicken neck, does nobody love me?'

Yet she feels that despite all this, she must continue to try, or she will never get to know anyone 'I could not run without having to run forever.' Yet, still, community is like a white hive: 'The white hive is snug as a virgin, Sealing off her brood cells, her honey, and quietly humming' just like the village community.

All the time, the villagers are trying to root out a member of another community: the queen bee. They have the collective power to decide who should be accepted and who should not.

Wintering
Sees a very different relationship between women. This time it is all women who have refused to live under the constraints and barriers placed by a male-orientated society. 'The bees are all women...They have got rid of the men...' Here they are all sticking together as a community whose common ground is that they share a past of dominance of others over them, and now they have broken free.

The women in the poem 'Stings': 'These women who only scurry Whose news is the open cherry, the open clover' are also part of this community. They only hate those who have broken the barriers they dared not challenge. Here we see two sets of women emerging. The 'enlightened ones', and 'the oppressed ones'.

A Birthday Present
There is one other relationship found in Plath's poetry: that between the wife and the invisible mistress. The presence of this 'other woman' greatly unbalances the wife. She is constantly wondering what she has done to fail her husband. Is the mistress better than her? 'has it breasts, has it edges?' 'Is this the one I am to appear for'? Creates great introspection.

Relationships with children

Morning Song
Plath obviously finds children, esp. younger ones, a great deal more favourable than her female counterparts. The child is a 'fat gold watch.' Full of potential and life. Full of fitness. She is also very touched by how naked, bare, unprotected and defenceless the child is. She obviously feels a great responsibility for it.

'I'm no more your mother Than the cloud that distills a mirror to reflect its own slow Effacement at the wind's hand.' She obviously feels that she has no right, or is not worthy to have claim on the child. Children's rights! She sees children as being free, 'The clear vowels rise like balloons.' Nothing holds balloons down. The child also asserts rather an extreme form of freedom of speech.

Children also occupy almost all the parents' time. She is 'cow-heavy and floral In my Victorian nightgown'. Her body is geared up to look after the child, her breasts being full of milk, and she seems to have no time to do her own thing, to keep her own identity or to assert her own sexuality, thus the reference to the Victorian nightgown.

Balloons
Here we see the balloons representing illusions, half-truths – contorting the picture of life. Obviously there is nothing she can do to see past them, as she has lived among them too long. However, the baby is able to question, and then reject, these illusions. He is left with 'A red Shred in his little fist.' The baby represents truth, clarity, and true reality to her. In 'Kindness' Plath asks 'What is so real as the cry of a child?' A baby is the true form of innocent perfection.

The Munich Mannequins
In this poem, we see the other side of her attitude to children: the choices made before a child is formed. Apparently, 'Perfection is terrible, it cannot have children...it tramps the womb.' She obviously feels that having children is a sign of weakness, a sign that women cannot go against their own emotions in order to stay perfect.

She also feels that women have a choice between remaining celibate and untarnished in order to be perfect, and giving up perfection in order to enjoy life. This highlights an interesting paradox, that she feels that sexual intercourse makes one imperfect, yet the result of the act is the production of a perfect creature glorified in so many of her poems.

This is possibly meant to highlight the different pressures experienced by women. On the one hand, women want to be the best they can, as perfect as is possible, and are told that to lead their own lives is better than being tied down by marriage and babies. On the other hand, the hormones, the brain and other sections of society are pushing women to have children, to lead a family life and to prove their sexuality.

It is also interesting that she feels that sex, even within marriage, means that you cannot be perfect. She obviously does not feel that it plays any part in helping couples to love each other more and therefore become the 'perfect couple'.

You're
This poem best highlights the love she has for children. She sees it as 'clownlike', simple, perfect, full of potential and other such things. It is a 'clean slate'. It plays a big part in her life and she wants to model herself around it. The child is not surrounded by any 'Bell Jar' and is simply free to be, something she always wanted to be. Children obviously play a large part in women's lives.

Relationships with husbands

It is quite obvious from her poetry that Plath had a big problem with men. In 'Daddy' she even refers to her own father as a 'bastard'. In 'The Applicant' her opinion is not much better.

The Applicant

This is a conversation between two men, one an older, supposedly wiser person and one a younger person who has come to a point in his life where he feels something is missing, his 'hand is empty'. It is obvious that she feels that both men, and men in general, look upon women as an expendable commodity, a thing which comes in useful for occasional enjoyment or for making home life more comfortable. The woman is referred to impersonally using the words 'it', 'ticket', 'sweetie' rather than 'her', 'woman' or even 'female' at least 25 times throughout the poem. Naturally, she is not very happy about this attitude, and through the poem shows how stupid the two actually are.

Generally, it shows that women have to face a life of dominance and misuse by men and a life where their qualities and gifts are used to keep men happy. Whether or not Plath's opinion is correct is, of course, debatable, but the poem is very good at putting across her opinion.

The poem also throws into confusion the choices women must make. I have already discussed how they are torn between the two traditional values of either being 'home makers' or having their own identity and exerting their own sexuality. Now another factor enters the equation. If women want to start a family and exert their own sexuality by producing children, then they are ultimately going to have to marry or at least become emotionally involved with a member of the dreaded male species. Therefore, women will lose their identity in the act of asserting their sexuality.

Bibliography

The Bell Jar, by Sylvia Plath

Ariel, by Sylvia Plath

Script of '*Sylvia Plath*' – a play performed by Royal Shakespeare Theatre in 1973, directed by Barry Kyle

Biographies by Lynda Wagner-Martin, Alan Alverez, Susan Bassnett, Anne Stevenson

EXAMPLES OF COURSEWORK ESSAYS

The following two pieces of coursework, one about a pre-20th Century author, one about a modern writer, show how coursework is assessed by teachers and moderators.

Text: Shakespeare, *The Merchant of Venice*

Unit 1: Examine a production of the play that you have seen, and explain how far its interpretation can, in your view, be justified by the text.

You may if you wish, confine yourself to detailed analysis of a character or scene that interests you.   *AEB*

Conditions of study and writing

The play was read in class, with brief discussion of each scene. The class saw and discussed the production by the English Shakespeare Company.

A choice of essay titles was offered, based on students' interests.

A class discussion followed on Portia.

The piece was written in private study; three weeks were given for draft and final version.

Word count – c1000 words (one-third of the whole folder).

Teacher's comments

An effective essay, in which you engage with the text and argue skilfully. You present your case well and with care, using apt illustration; but on occasions you do not interpret the text precisely (see page 1), which weakens your point rather. What I particularly like is that you are prepared to think for yourself.

The quality of this writing indicates high level 3 work; if this is typical of the whole folder of work, the overall mark is likely to be 15/20.

Moderator's comments

Agreed; an attentive, well engaged account, with promise of even higher level work in evidence.

Specimen answer

In the recent production of *The Merchant of Venice* performed by the English Shakespeare Company the character of Portia was presented, on numerous occasions, as a stereotypical 'rich bitch'. This was strongly illustrated to the audience in Act 1 scene ii when Portia, accompanied by Nerissa, makes her first physical appearance in the play. In this scene the director chose to endow Portia with an almost overpowering sense of confidence, and flippancy. These feelings and senses were conveyed to the audience through Portia's actions and mannerisms, which in this particular scene included the carefree tossing aside of a fur-lined cape, and the repeated tasting of expensive chocolates. During the course of my essay I intend to show that the text does not fully support this interpretation, and as a consequence alters one of the most fundamental ideas that Shakespeare puts forward regarding Portia's character and position, and that of women in general.

Bassanio's speech about Portia, which serves as an introduction to the character, seems to contradict the image that was presented on the stage, as although he states that she has great wealth before he mentions her beauty, he compares her to a goddess.

'Her name is Portia – nothing undervalu'd to Cato's daughter, Brutus' Portia.' Here Bassanio uses repeated references to Greek gods in order to describe her, this helps to give the audience the feeling that Portia is a 'forbidden fruit' character that is out of Bassanio's reach, as he confesses himself when he states that if 'he had the means' he would join the others in seeking to marry her. This feeling that she is, one way or another, out of Bassanio's reach is again stressed at the beginning of his description, when he clearly states that she is 'In Belmont'. This feeling of separation and detachment is stressed by Shakespeare in the way that the audience discover that she is actually physically out of reach before they find out about her character.

However, if Portia was a prominent figure within the popular 'cafe' society, as suggested in the stage production, then this captive isolation on the island of Belmont seems less likely.

I believe that Shakespeare wanted the audience to receive this information about Portia's public image in this way as it gives the character a reputation, and the audience, as Bassanio himself, believe that they know her before they actually see her.

In the scene where both Nerissa and Portia discuss and comment on her various visiting suitors, her tone seems to contradict both the sophisticated and the goddess images. In this light-hearted scene both Portia and Nerissa are portrayed in an immature light, as she continually makes fun of the various suitors who have been to see her. But this defamation of character is not carried out in a malicious way, as would be expected from the kind of character presented in the production, but is jovial and to some degree petty: 'Portia, Ay, that's a colt indeed, for he doth nothing but talk of his horse; and he makes it a great appropriation to his own good parts that he can shoe himself; I am much afear'd my lady his mother play'd false with a smith.'

These small cosmetic criticisms, which also include the inability to speak Italian, portray Portia in an almost girlish light, as she appears to be poking fun at them for no real concrete reason. Also these complaints are only aired behind the men's backs, when she is safely alone, which suggests a weakness in her character, as it appears that she is not confident enough to tell the suitors her true feelings towards them. A weakness that would not be apparent in a ruthless and callous character, like the one presented on the stage.

But also in this scene Portia shows a more serious and self-conscious side to her character which is also in conflict with the director's, and Bassanio's, view of her: 'I can easier teach twenty what were good to be done than be one of the twenty to follow mine own teaching.' In this passage she displays a sense of self-doubt, as she questions her actions, but also the audience discover that she believes that she is neither a sophisticated heiress or a faultless goddess, but is humble enough to recognise her faults. Here Portia also illustrates her concern for doing good. Throughout this scene both Portia and Nerissa display a certain degree of self-confidence, shown in the ways they discuss the suitors, but I believe this in no way would support the interpretation described above, as throughout this scene she is in a very safe environment, isolated on her island, with no intruders, such as the male suitors.

Later in the play when Bassanio comes to Belmont, and is about to select a casket, Portia displays another aspect of her complex character, and becomes very insecure and emotional, indicating the strength of her love for Bassanio as she is deeply worried that he may choose the wrong casket. This worry, which is conveyed to the audience in Portia's visible emotion, something that would never be displayed if, as the stage production suggested, Portia was cold and calculating, seems to transform Portia, as she is filled with insecurity: 'I pray you tarry; pause a day or two before you hazard; for in choosing wrong, I lose your company; therefore forebear a while.'

Here the weakness of her character, displayed in her opening scene, surfaces again, as she has not the will to carry on with the process, as she is so afraid that he may choose the wrong casket. She would prefer Bassanio to wait a few more days as she can't face losing him. Also in this scene, both before and after the choice has been made, she continually questions the strength of Bassanio's love for her, as Cleopatra in 'Antony and Cleopatra', this phenomenon illustrates to the audience how worried Portia actually is. Also in this scene she expresses her belief that she is an innocent girl: 'But the full sum of me is the sum of something which, to term in gross, is an unlesson'd girl, unschool'd, unpractis'd'.

Here Portia 'warns' Bassanio that she has no sexual experience of men, this innocent statement would be very hard to believe if Portia was a 'rich bitch' as she was presented in the stage production. Also in this scene, after she discovers the content of Antonio's letter, she again becomes very concerned for Bassanio, and her reaction is almost immediate: 'What! no more? Pay him six thousand, and deface the bond; double six, and then treble that, before a friend of this description.' This instantaneous reply suggests that Portia still feels insecure in her brief relationship with Bassanio, that it is her belief that she must please him by doing this in order to keep him loving her. Also as she asks him to marry her before he goes back, this suggests that she fears that he may stay in Venice and forget about her, something that would not be feared by a confident headstrong woman. Her concern for doing good is again expressed which further destroys the image portrayed in the recent production.

Only when she is dressed as a man, in the Venice courtroom does her other side come to the surface, which in the production was evident from the beginning, so the dramatic effect was lost on the audience. If Shakespeare had intended her to be a simple hard character he would not have had to use the court scene in the way he did. The way that both Portia and Nerissa dressed as men was used to illustrate to the audience that women can also be intelligent and strong-willed. This did not have the same dramatic impact on the audience as Portia had been strong from her opening scene. After the court scene she appears, in the eyes of the audience, to have changed. This is because they are aware of all the sides of her complex character and not people's perceptions of her and what she should be.

COMPARATIVE SKILLS

Texts: Orwell, *Animal Farm*
McPherson, *What Went Wrong?*
Atwood, *The Handmaid's Tale*

Unit 5: Revolution. A comparison of the portrayal of revolution in fiction and non-fiction texts   (with reference to cited texts).   *AEB*

Conditions of study and writing

Having opted to prepare a longer piece of writing (representing three-quarters of the whole coursework) the candidate added McPherson's *What Went Wrong?* to two texts that were already set and studied for coursework.

The work was completed in one term and one holiday under teacher-supervisor guidance (three sessions plus planning session).

Word count – c2800 words (three-quarters of whole folder).

Teacher's comments

There is a good, sophisticated argument hidden in here. It emerges on occasion but is not quite developed. You relate the texts to each other within the framework you have chosen, and point to many structural and thematic similarities. You clearly know the texts well, and you consider preferred readings, alternative interpretations, and the use of point of view. I felt that your analysis could be more detailed, and could have focused more on the use of language; but you do consider the oppressor, the revolution and the revolutionaries in each, and make perceptive points.

Provisional level/marks

The quality of this writing indicates the middle range of level 3 work; if this is typical of the whole folder, the overall mark would be 12/20.

Moderator's comments

Agreed; while the study is clearly within 'level 3' attainment, the quality tends to be inconsistent, within that level. Whole folder assessment will, it is hoped, do more clear justice to this coursework.

Specimen answer

Throughout all three texts I eventually used I found one definite recurring theme, that is of things not really changing. Although on the surface a revolution had occurred, underneath the 'old ways' were still being practised. A quote from William McPherson's book seems to capture this idea very well: 'The wolves have changed their fur but not their habits'. This gives the impression that they have changed simply to save their own skin, that they have changed perhaps because some groups of people in the country are pushing for reform and fear if they do not respond they will have a rebellion against them. So by encouraging perhaps a 'revolution' on the surface they calm the groups of people but stay in power themselves. This relates to *What Went Wrong?* the idea of a false revolution that has only happened on the surface because many Communist practices are still evident in Romania. The alternative explanation is that the 'revolutionaries' simply want power for themselves and have no intention of listening to people once they have got their own way. They may simply use the people and their grievances to help them get rid of the institution they want, and then once power is achieved simply ignore the needs of the people they claim to serve and represent. Alternatively it could be that when the 'revolutionaries' finally get into power it goes straight to their heads and they start acting like the people they have just ousted from power. It shows that for all the good will in the world you can't change the attitudes of some people, particularly those of politicians. The third alternative best relates to *Animal Farm* and the idea that power corrupts the pigs. *The Handmaid's Tale* does not fit as clearly into any category although perhaps fits the first part of the second explanation that the revolutionaries simply want power for themselves but had no intention of listening to the people. This though does not mean to say these texts have to fit these explanations, they all contain elements of each other and it would be hard to fit each one into a definite niche. The three texts approach the revolutions in different ways. *What Went Wrong?* gives a more personalised view of the revolution whereas *Animal Farm* is more of a narrative of the events. This may be because *Animal Farm* is a fictional text, but my third text, also a fictional text, *The Handmaid's Tale,* gives a personalised view in the style of a personal journal similar to that of *What Went Wrong?*.

First of all I want to deal with how each text characterises the revolution. McPherson's book *What Went Wrong?* is a piece of journalism, a first-hand account of the revolution in Romania. McPherson uses his preconceived western notions to explore the revolution. He sees the revolution in theory as good for the Romanian people because they are escaping from Communism into a 'democratic' western style society. McPherson appears not quite to believe though in the revolution that has occurred, partly through the title suggesting that this revolution has gone wrong and also in the way he concentrates on the people still protesting, the people who are not satisfied with the new government.

Although he reports the events as others see them he is bound to have influenced those ideas with his own so what you end up with is a portrayal of the revolution as McPherson thinks the Romanian people see it. This text gives an 'insider' view, what could be said to be a 'truthful' account of what was happening. McPherson's text explores the parts of the revolution as he himself discovers them. Journalists have to make the events they report into a news story to create an interesting piece of journalism. They often, to save time, fit the events into an established generalised view of the subject. For example the revolution in Romania as McPherson reports it, fits very well into the framework of *Animal Farm*. In this way the journalist will have to manipulate the facts and add or miss parts out that don't agree with the storyline.

Animal Farm is 'primarily a satire on the Russian Revolution' says Orwell himself, although it can also have wider reference to revolutions in general, in particular the theme of corruption within the new government. Orwell suggests that the new powers manipulate and mislead the people deliberately to gain what they can from the situation. For example in *Animal Farm* Napoleon starts to deal with other local farmers after saying he will not have anything to do with humans. To achieve this he changes the original 'Seven Commandments' to suit himself.

Orwell, like McPherson, characterises the revolution primarily as good for the animals, escaping the dictatorship of Mr Jones and enjoying their new found 'freedom' in a democracy. Being a satire of the Russian Revolution one gets the idea that Orwell does not believe in the revolution that has occurred and sees it only as a 'surface' revolution, that underneath the corruption still carries on but under different leadership. Again in a quote from the introduction Orwell himself characterises the revolution as a 'violent conspiratorial revolution, led by unconsciously power-hungry people'. The animals had to use violence to overcome Mr Jones. They plotted against him and then by using violence frightened the Jones and their farm hands away. The revolution is seen as a step in the right direction for the animals.

Margaret Atwood's book, *The Handmaid's Tale,* is written around a revolution although not specifically about one. She tackles the issue by writing the book from the point of view of an ordinary person after the revolution and how they cope with the new regime. In some ways Margaret Atwood's book is opposite to the two others, her book is written from a female perspective – both the others are written by men and are mainly involved with men. *The Handmaid's Tale* is also a reversal of a 'normal' revolution (if there is such a thing). Her revolution goes from a 'capitalist' and 'developed' country to one that is oppressed, it turns from being democratic, to being strictly ruled by a non-elected governing body. With both the other revolutions they change from a bad government to one that is better in theory at least.

Again this may have something to do with the way it is written. Margaret Atwood through 'Offred' gives the impression that this revolution was not for the good of woman in particular, as Offred and the other 'Handmaids' are simply used in 'breeding programmes'. Offred remembers back to when she was free and eventually starts breaking the rules and planning how she could either kill herself or escape. This only really gives the point of view of the people against the revolution, the people who are also breaking the rules, the Commander, Nick, and her friend Ofglen who teaches her of the 'underground' movement 'Mayday'. Occasionally opinions of the 'devout' believers are voiced through the Commander's wife Serena Joy, and the new Ofglen.

The Handmaids Tale is different from the other two texts in that it explores the revolution as a participant. The others are written with an outsider's viewpoint as a narrative. In this way Atwood's book is perhaps more concerned with the technicalities of the revolution. Margaret Atwood explores the revolution personally in her book. There is no lead up, it starts after the revolution has occurred. The reader learns what life was like before from the 'flashbacks' Offred has. The time you assume is the twentieth century and from the place references learn it is based in America. This is the sort of democratic society the other books are striving to achieve, the society the founders of the 'Republic of Gilead' are trying to wipe out in *The Handmaid's Tale*.

The next part of the revolution I want to look at are the actual oppressors that have been a cause for a revolution. William McPherson's book hardly mentions Ceausescu and his government, he is more interested in the actual revolutionaries. He does mention slightly more often the 'securitate', the old Communist security force. When he talks to Ion he discovers that he was an informer for the 'securitate'. When he originally refused to become an informer they took his identity card which meant he could not collect his wages. Ion was forced into doing what the 'securitate' wanted against his wishes. Some of the people in Romania still believe that the new government under Iliescu is equally oppressive. William McPherson quotes some marchers as chanting 'Sound asleep you voted in a dictator'. He hardly reports the march and dismisses the people as opportunists. This perhaps suggests he does not see the new government as oppressive. In this report the old Communists not the new 'democratic' government are the oppressors. Although because of some of the interviews and quotes in the book I think that Iliescu's government appears just as oppressive. When the students voice an opinion against him he puts them down as 'counter-revolutionary' and tries to dismiss them, because they do not agree with his viewpoint they are covered up and labelled 'deviant'. It appears that many parts of the old Communist state of Romania have seeped into the 'new' Romania. This reinforces the idea of a false or surface revolution as the students protest about former 'securitate' members joining the new National Guard. Communism seen under the disguise of a new regime.

In *Animal Farm* the oppressor is clearly Mr Jones. The animals see humans as oppressors signified by Mr Jones. The animals believe humans are undeserving of leadership – they don't see any reason why they should serve humans as they do not give anything. They say humans have no useful qualities, they cannot lay eggs, pull a plough and such. They complain that they labour for another's profit. Mr Jones is a 'typical' oppressor – he is cruel, he abuses the animals after he has been drinking and is a hard master and sometimes forgets to feed them. The animals are totally dependent on Mr Jones, they are under his dictatorship and they have no say in what happens to them until they overthrow Mr Jones and the other humans on the farm. Napoleon emerges as the new leader and although is not as oppressive as Mr Jones, his rule does start to have oppressive overtones. While the ordinary animals work he doesn't, he lives in the farmhouse with plenty of warmth and food while the other animals suffer the cold in the barn and don't always get enough food to live on. Napoleon starts to abuse his leadership and manipulates the 'Seven Commandments' to suit himself. He abuses his power by starting to live in Mr Jones' farmhouse, wear clothes, and drink alcohol. This shows how the power eventually corrupts the pigs. They start out with good intentions but as they realise what this new found power lets them do they start to become more oppressive and like Mr Jones.

The oppressors in *The Handmaid's Tale* are not the old government but the new. This was a very oppressive movement that took over America, they forbade reading and writing and anything that may lead people in the country to become subversive and disagree with what was happening. The laws and rituals in *The Handmaid's Tale* are oppressive and very strict. They are given no space to think for themselves and by not being allowed to read and write are encouraged not to think. The 'Handmaids' have no choices, they are put with a Commander for 'breeding' purposes and have no choice about it. They could choose suicide but that was increasingly difficult as anything they could use was taken away. Everything in the 'Republic of Gilead' is uniform, everything conforms to the rules and regulations set out. Life carries on in a uniform way – that is the way it happens. Everything is done the same way, they perform rituals all the time – everything they do is government ordained. For example the way their life is carried out, the 'Handmaids' can only go shopping in pairs. They are told what to wear. They are issued with summer and winter clothes. When Offred first arrives she is allowed through the front door but after that she must use the back. Everything they do has been decided for them already so there is no need to think for themselves. The oppressors are those who institute these laws and rituals; at the 'Red Centre' it is the Aunts who teach the 'Handmaids' the way to live and behave. The Eyes are the security force of sorts, they are the spies that check these laws and rituals are not being broken. Offred seems wary that everyone could be an Eye, the doctor who offers to help her become pregnant, and Nick one of the Commander's Guardians who she begins sleeping with at first to become pregnant but later because of both their needs. In a way the Commanders' wives are also oppressors because if the 'Handmaids' deviate from the acceptable way of life it is the wife that has the authority to deal out the punishment, unless it is so serious that the Eyes deal with it first. They are all portrayed in a bad light because Offred resents this oppression and dislikes the way the Gileadean society functions. It shows in the way Offred writes about these oppressors and how much she hates them. Aunt Lydia from the 'Red Centre' comes under direct attack. When Offred sees her again at a salvaging, she says, 'Hatred fills my mouth like spit'. These are strong sentiments and perhaps deep down they are the feelings she has for the whole Gileadean society and Aunt Lydia simply signifies this hatred.

'Everyone was a revolutionary, no one wanted Communism' proclaims William McPherson of the Romanians. He supports the 'respectable' revolutionaries not the opportunists. In Romania then he believes everyone to be a revolutionary. He interviews Savu, the president of the Front, in his enterprise he is a hero of the revolution. He interviews Savu on a train and gains some interesting quotes. Savu tells him he 'fought for real democracy', he 'fought with all my being for the rights of the people'. He also says, 'I do not want power, I have no interest in power'. He seems to believe what Savu is saying. Perhaps McPherson has found in Savu his perfect revolutionary who does not want power compared to some of the less respectable opportunists, like the marchers he dismisses earlier. Another revolutionary he talks to is Petru, a reporter for the local student newspaper. He is portrayed as quite naive about the way things happen in a revolution. Petru has a list of informers for the 'securitate' that he found on a former 'securitate' member's desk after he quickly fled. McPherson believes it has been planted there for someone to find, but Petru will not believe him and carries on arguing that it is authentic. The other revolutionaries, according to George a fellow journalist, are 'gypsies, vagabonds and rubbish people' who along with some 'good people' formed the first post-revolutionary government of the country. McPherson appears to favour all the revolutionaries providing they do not simply want power for themselves for the wrong reasons.

Old Major is the original revolutionary in *Animal Farm*. He puts forward the idea of man being the animals' enemy and the idea of a rebellion. When Old Major dies, Napoleon comes to the forefront with Snowball and Squealer, who were generally regarded by the other animals as the most intelligent, they saw it as their duty to prepare everyone for the revolution whenever it happened. They are all portrayed as having the power of persuasive speech, they could all argue their cases well, much like politicians. The revolution finally happened after Mr Jones had been drinking and left the animals unfed, this led to their uprising. The animals were very organised and united in the hate of all mankind. You start to see slight divisions occurring as the pigs break off to form the leadership of *Animal Farm*, they being the more intelligent ones on the farm. In this way the animals are quite naive about the way Napoleon manipulates power. They trust Napoleon, Snowball and the others and it is this trust that enables Napoleon to abuse his power and get away with it. When the apples are collected solely for the pigs and the animals complain, Squealer tells them that the pigs do not in fact enjoy the apples but eat them because they are essential for their health. The animals accept this with no more questioning. Napoleon and his 'council' begin to take more power, Napoleon claiming that it is a burden and if he didn't have to take the leadership he wouldn't. In a way he is like Savu, who also claims he doesn't want power in *What Went Wrong?*. The animals are portrayed as naive like Petru in *What Went Wrong?*.

In *The Handmaid's Tale* the revolutionaries are actually the oppressors and so the revolutionaries are in fact counter-revolutionaries and in this respect differ from those in the other texts. The revolutionaries are the underground movement 'Mayday'. They are seen as good as they help Offred out by saving her from her fate under Serena Joy. They are the people who do not believe in the new 'Republic of Gilead' and through a network of 'safe houses' help people escape the regime. They are not really revolution-aries but rebels: people who are breaking the rules, people like Offred, Nick and Moira, who finds a way out of what she hated, i.e. being a 'Handmaid', and after escaping is recaptured and given the choice of the colonies or 'Jezebels'. She prefers 'Jezebels' as she has food, drink, drugs, all the things she has been denied as a 'Handmaid'. These people are seen in a favourable light because of how much Offred hates her way of life and the fact that they appear to rescue her in her time of need after Serena Joy discovers she has been seeing the Commander privately.

What Went Wrong? and *Animal Farm* appear very similar in storyline – you can see some very strong links between 'characters' and ideas. Napoleon could relate to Iliescu, the leaders that perhaps want more power than they admit. They both take over as leaders and begin to take over themselves. Napoleon starts out as leader then president, he builds around him a committee of pigs ('all animals are equal but some are more equal than others') like Iliescu's new Front. Furthermore Napoleon's security force of dogs is like the new National Guard in Romania. *The Handmaid's Tale* is really quite different, it does not relate to either but it does still show the idea of power corrupting.

Looking more closely at the three texts it still appears that 'The wolves have changed their fur but not their habits'. In McPherson's text this is demonstrated by the amount of former Communists still in control. This revolution started because the ruling govern-ment was not serving some of the people's needs in the country. After the Ceausescus were overthrown and executed, the first 'seeds of doubt' are sown as to the real motives of the new government. The first local election is held, although voting is 'orderly', it seems the 'people's' candidates were chosen by this new government. 'The wolves have changed their fur but not their habits' perhaps? The next event is the 'landslide' victory of the National Salvation Front in the elections, later allegations of electoral malpractice are made against the Front. Another sign that the old Communist ways are 'seeping' into the running of the country is that former members of the 'securitate' joined the new National Guard.

Animal Farm is similar to this in that humanity starts to 'seep' slowly into 'animalism' taking small steps until it is so powerful it is not animalism anymore. Napoleon moves into the farmhouse, sleeps in the beds, drinks alcohol, and wears Mr Jones' clothes. The animals accept this for the time being. This shows how the power eventually corrupts the pigs. They start out with good intentions but as they realise how much power they have and what it allows them to do, they start to become more oppressive than Mr Jones. What is most shocking is when the pigs start walking on their hind legs, this undermines the original idea that 'four legs are good, two legs are bad' replacing it with 'two legs are better'. This is signified in Orwell's final statement when the local farmers have been invited to dinner and the animals are watching at the window. 'Twelve voices were shouting in anger, and they were all alike. No question, now, what had happened to the faces of the pigs. The creatures outside looked from man to pig, and from pig to man again: but already it was impossible to say which was which'.

In *The Handmaid's Tale* this going back to the 'old ways' is signified mainly by the Commander. It starts in a small way by her seeing the Commander privately then he takes her to 'Jezebels' the officers' club full of 'government issue' prostitutes. 'Jezebels' perhaps signifies again this going back to 'old ways' because it is in effect one of the things that the 'Republic of Gilead' is trying to get away from, but it doesn't stop the officers as they can still get whatever they want. Again 'The wolves have changed their fur but not their habits'.

FINAL ADVICE

After you have read these two essays, you will no doubt have ideas buzzing in your mind on how to tackle an essay of this length. Do remember this checklist of words of wisdom:
• Discuss your work all the way through with your teacher
• Think carefully about the subject
• Bring in wider reading
• Be flexible in your title
• Keep notes in an efficient way, e.g. on cue cards

- Always acknowledge your sources
- Give a comprehensive bibliography at the end
- Never copy or pass off other writing as your own – this is called plagiarism

Above all

- Start planning early
- Discuss
- Negotiate
- Be organised
- Show personal and lively interest
- Be proud of the finished product

5.2 LANGUAGE COURSEWORK

The English Language exam component of the combined syllabuses is covered in Chapter 4. Most combined courses now include an element of language-based coursework. Each board makes different demands on candidates by asking them to produce assignments such as:
- Extended essays on aspects of language issues/use.
- Individual 'project' investigations into an area of language which interests you.
- Original writing for a variety of audiences and specific purposes (with commentaries).

WRITING AN ESSAY ON A LANGUAGE TOPIC

All the advice offered in 'planning and writing an essay on a controversial subject' p.167 is also important here. In addition to your written submission you might also wish to include graphic or taped material, where appropriate.

The major difference when writing a language essay lies in research techniques. You, the candidate, are expected to collect ideas and data in a scientific and systematic way. Remember to set up a question or hypothesis (aim) regarding the topic under consideration and carry out your analysis in a detailed and open-minded way. Work closely with secondary texts if appropriate and always acknowledge your sources. Plan your essays carefully and use the time provided wisely. Possible topics include:
- The aims and achievements of the Plain English movement.
- The language of computing.
- British Sign Language.

If possible try to choose an area which interests you otherwise you could soon find yourself becoming 'bogged down' by the whole experience.

AN INVESTIGATION INTO LANGUAGE USE

Areas of theory and skills related to stylistic analysis, if relevant to your syllabus, will have been covered thoroughly by your tutor. You might also have an excellent working knowledge of grammar and phonetics. Now, armed with all this information, you are provided with an opportunity to set off alone and explore a 'small' area of language use which interests you. This particular coursework component is not an essay but a carefully constructed piece of linguistic analysis.

Choosing a topic for investigation

Most candidates find this problematic. This can be a time-consuming piece of work, collecting and analysing data cannot be done successfully 'overnight'. The sooner you get started the more organised you will be.

Once again, as in the essay, the most important piece of advice is to choose a topic that really interests you. This may sound like common sense but many candidates embark upon investigations without sufficient thought and end up 'changing tack', losing precious time as a result.

The range of choice is initially divided into two main areas (or a comparison of both):

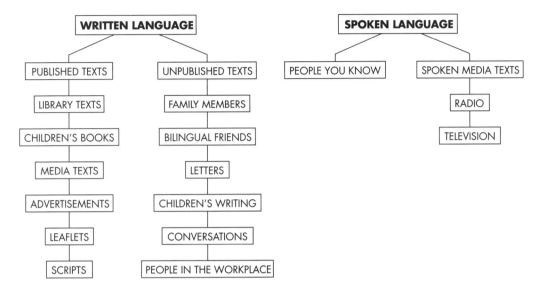

The list goes on....

Written language

What skills might you need?
If, for instance, you wished to investigate an area of language in advertising:
- The area is wide – be selective and specific, e.g. the language of Bovril adverts through the decades.
- Your task is to investigate how the language is being used to produce deliberate effects – e.g. to persuade a target group, etc.
- Make sure the data you gather is compatible, if it is not you will soon run into difficulty.
- Do not overreach the scope of the investigation. It is always a temptation to take on far too much material leading to a fragmented and superficial analysis. Be selective – limit the amount of data you gather to a manageable quantity and analyse it in detail.
- Be realistic in your aims.

What should you focus your study on?
Remember that simply listing features is not enough. Always comment on what effect specific language use has in the data you are analysing – e.g. Why are concrete nouns used? How is bias created (transitivity – gender of pronouns, etc).

Here are some ideas for 'pegs' to hang your analysis of written language on:
Layout and graphics; sentence types; syntax; lexis (slang, archaisms, jargon) phonology, overall structure, figurative use of language (metaphor, similes, metonyms, etc).

Spoken language

What skills might you need?
If you wish to examine and investigate an aspect of spoken language you may focus on language acquisition – What have they learnt at a particular stage? Given a particular situation what functions are used, e.g. reasoning, controlling, inquiring, etc?

To study any aspect of spoken language in detail (and the list of possible areas is very long indeed) you must tape your subject(s). This can prove much more difficult than you might think:
- Avoid situations with distracting background noise (transcription can be a nightmare from an infant class).
- Always make sure that you are patient and persevere.
- A transcription, using appropriate symbols, should then be written.
- Ensure that your transcript is accurate.
- All tapes and transcripts should be submitted with the completed investigation in the appendices.

Other topics which involve an analysis of spoken language might include:
- The language of chat show hosts
- Political speeches
- Soaps
- Comedy
- Quiz programmes
- Lyrics

Areas to focus on are –
- The structure of utterances
- Lexis
- Modes of address
- Phonological features (stress/intonation)
- Fillers
- Questions
- Turn taking

Writing the investigation

Here is a suggested framework as recommended by the NEAB.

Aims and Objectives – What you intend to do!

Methodology – How you did it.

Introduction – General discussion of area of study.

Main Body of analysis – Have a clear plan – use sub-headings – use tables, graphs, diagrams, if relevant.

Conclusions – Make sure you come to some! Your project will be incomplete without this section.

Bibliography/Appendices – Acknowledge all sources and include data, letters and any other relevant material collected.

The investigation should be enjoyable and display your ability to put theory into practice. Whilst presentation is important, it is content that counts.

ORIGINAL WRITING: WITH COMMENTARIES
(Writing for a variety of specific purposes)

This kind of coursework assignment, once again, allows you to develop and apply insights gained in other areas of the course.

The main aim in creating an original piece of writing is to recognise the relationship between intended audience and purpose, and to understand this relationship.

❶ Purpose: to entertain; to persuade; to inform; to instruct (there is overlapping).

❷ Audience: children, teenagers, students, adults, specific interest groups...
the list goes on.

Always attempt to try out your writing on its intended audience. You can act on the 'feedback' you receive and include their written responses in your commentary.

Style

Once you have decided upon audience and purpose you need to establish (and maintain) an appropriate tone and format.

Think about the context of your piece – where would it be published, etc. Once you have decided where it might appear, read as many examples of the kind of 'thing' you are writing.

Drafts

The board may well require these as 'proof' of process, therefore do not throw them away.

The commentary

Once you have completed your piece(s) you need to write a commentary (some boards do not require this – check the syllabus you are following).

In a commentary you must:

• Clearly state your aims and intentions, explain the purpose of your piece and outline who the intended audience is.

- Include factual information about the origins of the material, adaptations, secondary sources, etc.
- Comment on the drafting process – include accounts of significant deletions, additions, revisions and so on, as this reveals the conscious decisions you have made about language use.
- Delineate decisions made regarding specific linguistic features such as vocabulary (lexis), syntax, layout and general presentation.
- Reflect on any problems encountered during the process of writing. Do you believe the finished product achieves what it set out to do? Are you pleased with it?

Extracts from commentaries

Purpose: to entertain

Vocabulary employed within the piece takes on a simple nature with attention to detail. The use of the adverb 'just' in the opening sentence indicates immediacy and helps to set the scene of a peaceful and sunny morning. I have used the rhythmical phrase 'today was the day', to produce a light-hearted feel and to emphasise the happy and exciting circumstances with which the badgers set off. The use of the colloquial phrase 'fast asleep' again allows there to be a familiar essence towards a homely image. The employment of the adjective 'only', is one that should be stressed by the reader. I have used it as an example of typical child exaggeration and to emphasise to the audience the earliness at which the badgers rise.

The employment of inverted syntax in the clause 'so up they got' produces a poetic line which in turn suggests vitality and which emphasises the excitement of getting up so early. I hope that this will appeal to the audience, as excitement and adventure forms a large part of a child's life. The use of the adverb 'all' to describe how many flowers Mrs Badger smelt within the wood, suggests peace and tranquility which emphasises the beauty of the countryside and provides security for the audience by placing weight upon the natural and unharmful elements within the countryside.

My use of the colloquial phrase, 'They had this great game', was to produce greater intimacy between the reader and the audience, which is most often familiar within informal speech. I used the noun 'Bang' as it is extremely familiar with a child audience as it is often used within cartoons and suggests unserious harm.

The use of the adverb 'very' in the line where Mrs Badger is cross with her children for knocking into her, emphasises her feelings and also the severity of the action. My employment of the contracted form 'didn't' again serves the purpose of producing an informal and intimate air between the reader and the audience. The use of the third person singular of the verb 'to tumble', was employed to emphasise that the badgers were falling but also that no serious harm was caused.

Purpose: to persuade

'Facts are all I care about. I have no time for lies. I hate being conned.'

Most who read this felt that they were immediately distanced from the speaker and were less prepared to listen to an argument written in this style. They felt using the personal pronoun 'I' did not make them feel the speaker wanted to address them and talk truthfully and honestly. They also felt the variable noun 'Facts' was too harsh and unfeeling. Changing 'Facts' to 'Truth' expressed better the context of the following argument.

The first paragraph now reads: 'The truth is all we are concerned about. We have no time...' This gets the speaker's audience 'on side' which is a powerful weapon in a debate speech.

There are many similarities between original writing in language coursework and creative writing in literature. The important thing is that you become more aware of the process involved in original composition.

TEST RUN

In this section:

Mock Exam

Examiners' Report on Critical Appreciation Paper

Mock Exam Answers

- This section should be tackled towards the end of your revision programme, when you have covered all your syllabus topics, and attempted some practice questions.

- The Mock Exam is set out like a real exam paper. It contains a wide spread of question styles and topics, drawn from various examination boards. You should attempt this paper under examination conditions. Read the instructions carefully. Attempt the paper in the time allowed, and without reference to the text.

- Use the Examiners' Report to gain valuable insight into what examiners are looking for in candidates' responses to unseen passages of prose and poetry.

- Compare your answers to our Mock Exam Answers. These answers were written by students under exam conditions. We have printed the examiners' comments to each answer, indicating where it might have been improved, and giving the mark awarded by the examiner.

The set texts for **Paper 1** are:

> Shakespeare's *Hamlet*
> Shakespeare's *The Winter's Tale*
> TS Eliot's *The Waste Land*
> Poems of Wilfred Owen

for **Paper 2**:

> Chaucer: *The Pardoner's Tale*
> Forster: *Howards End*
> Conrad: *Heart of Darkness*
> Plath: *Ariel*

Paper 3 consists of two passages for critical appreciation

PAPER 1 3 Hours

Section A

1 Three passages are printed below, one from *Hamlet* and two from *The Winter's Tale*. Select one passage and answer the questions about it.

(a) *Hamlet*

Elsinore. The guard-platform of the Castle. FRANCISCO *at his post. Enter to him* BARNARDO.

Bar. Who's there?

Fran. Nay, answer me. Stand and unfold yourself.

Bar. Long live the King!

Fran. Barnardo?

Bar. He.

Fran. You come most carefully upon your hour.

Bar. 'Tis now struck twelve; get thee to bed, Francisco.

Fran. For this relief much thanks. 'Tis bitter cold,
    And I am sick at heart.

Bar. Have you had quiet guard?

Fran. Not a mouse stirring.

Bar. Well, good night.
    If you do meet Horatio and Marcellus,
    The rivals of my watch, bid them make haste.

(*Enter* HORATIO *and* MARCELLUS.)

Fran. I think I hear them. Stand, ho! Who is there?

Hor. Friends to this ground.

Mar. And liegemen to the Dane.

Fran. Give you good night.

Mar. O, farewell, honest soldier! Who hath reliev'd you?

Fran. Barnardo hath my place. Give you good night.   (*Exit.*)

Mar. Holla, Barnardo!

Bar. Say—What, is Horatio there?

Hor. A piece of him.

Bar. Welcome, Horatio; welcome good Marcellus.

Hor. What, has this thing appear'd again to-night?

Bar. I have seen nothing.

Mar. Horatio says 'tis but our fantasy,
    And will not let belief take hold of him,
    Touching this dreaded sight, twice seen of us;
    Therefore I have entreated him along
    With us to watch the minutes of this night,
    That if again this apparition come,
    He may approve our eyes and speak to it.

Hor. Tush, tush, 'twill not appear.

Bar. Sit down awhile,
  And let us once again assail your ears,
  That are so fortified against our story,
  What we have two nights seen.

Hor. Well, sit we down,
  And let us hear Barnardo speak of this.

Bar. Last night of all,
  When yond same star that's westward from the pole
  Had made his course t'illume that part of heaven
  Where now it burns, Marcellus and myself,
  The bell then beating one—

(*Enter* GHOST)

Mar. Peace, break thee off; look where it comes again.

Bar. In the same figure, like the King that's dead.

Mar. Thou art a scholar; speak to it, Horatio.

Bar. Looks 'a not like the King? Mark it, Horatio.

Hor. Most like. It harrows me with fear and wonder.

Bar. It would be spoke to.

Mar. Question it, Horatio.

Hor. What art thou that usurp'st this time of night,
  Together with that fair and warlike form
  In which the majesty of buried Denmark
  Did sometimes march? By heaven I charge thee, speak!

Mar. It is offended.

Bar. See, it stalks away.

Hor. Stay! speak, speak! I charge thee, speak!

(*Exit* GHOST)

Mar. 'Tis gone, and will not answer.

Bar. How now, Horatio! You tremble and look pale.
  Is not this something more than fantasy?
  What think you on't?

Hor. Before my God, I might not this believe
  Without the sensible and true avouch
  Of mine own eyes.

Mar. Is it not like the King?

Hor. As thou art to thyself:
  Such was the very armour he had on
  When he the ambitious Norway combated;
  So frown'd he once when, in an angry parle,
  He smote the sledded Polacks on the ice.
  'Tis strange.

Mar. Thus twice before, and jump at this dead hour,
  With martial stalk hath he gone by our watch.

Hor. In what particular thought to work I know not;
  But in the gross and scope of mine opinion,
  This bodes some strange eruption to our state.

Discuss the above extract, focusing on:
(i) the revelation of character
(ii) the bringing out of themes
(iii) the use of language and verse
(iv) stage action

20

(b) *The Winter's Tale*

Either,

The following passage occurs just after Hermione has been successful in persuading Polixenes to extend the length of his visit to Sicilia.

Read the passage carefully and answer the questions below it.

Leon. (*Aside*) Too hot, too hot!
  To mingle friendship far is mingling bloods.

I have *tremor cordis* on me: my heart dances,
But not for joy – not joy. This entertainment
May a free face put on, derive a liberty
From heartiness, from bounty, fertile bosom,
And well become the agent: 't may, I grant:
But to be paddling palms and pinching fingers,
As now they are, and making practis'd smiles
As in a looking-glass; and then to sigh, as 'twere
The mort o' th' deer – O! that is entertainment
My bosom likes not, nor my brows. Mamillius,
Art thou my boy?

Mam. Ay, my good lord.

Leon. I' fecks:
Why that's my bawcock. What! hast smutch'd thy nose?
They say it is a copy out of mine. Come, captain,
We must be neat; not neat, but cleanly, captain:
And yet the steer, the heifer, and the calf
Are all call'd neat. Still virginalling
Upon his palm – How now, you wanton calf!
Art thou my calf?

Mam. Yes, if you will, my lord.

Leon. Thou want'st a rough pash and the shoots that I have
To be full like me: yet they say we are
Almost as like as eggs; women say so,
(That will say anything): but were they false
As o'er-dy'd blacks, as wind, as waters; false
As dice are to be wish'd by one that fixes
No bourn 'twixt his and mine, yet were it true
To say this boy were like me. Come, sir page,
Look on me with your welkin eye: sweet villain!
Most dear'st! my collop! Can thy dam?—may't be?—
Affection! thy intention stabs the centre:
Thou dost make possible things not so held,
Communicat'st with dreams;—how can this be?—
With what's unreal thou co-active art,
And fellow'st nothing: then, 'tis very credent
Thou mayst co-join with something; and thou dost,
(And that beyond commission), and I find it,
(And that to the infection of my brains
And hard'ning of my brows).

Pol. What means Sicilia?

Her. He something seems unsettled.

Pol. How, my lord?
What cheer? how is't with you, best brother?

Her. You look
As if you held a brow of much distraction:
Are you mov'd, my lord?

Leon. No, in good earnest.
How sometimes nature will betray its folly,
Its tenderness, and make itself a pastime
To harder bosoms! Looking on the lines
Of my boy's face, methoughts I did recoil
Twenty-three years, and saw myself unbreech'd,
In my green velvet coat, my dagger muzzl'd,
Lest it should bite its master, and so prove,
As ornaments oft do, too dangerous:
How like, methought, I then was to this kernel,
This squash, this gentleman. Mine honest friend,
Will you take eggs for money?

Mam. No my lord, I'll fight.

(i) What does the extract reveal about Leontes' personality and his state of mind at this time?   **10**

(ii) How dramatically convincing, in your opinion, are the means by which the effects of Leontes' jealousy are resolved in the course of the play?   **10**

NICCEA 1994

or, *The Winter's Tale*

Her. Come, I'll question you
    Of my lord's tricks, and yours, when you were boys.
    You were pretty lordings then?

Pol. We were, fair queen,
    Two lads that thought there was no more behind,
    But such a day to-morrow as to-day,
    And to be boy eternal.

Her. Was not my lord
    The verier wag o' th' two?

Pol. We were as twinn'd lambs that did frisk i' th' sun,
    And bleat the one at th' other: what we chang'd
    Was innocence for innocence: we knew not
    The doctrine of ill-doing, nor dream'd
    That any did. Had we pursu'd that life,
    And our weak spirits ne'er been higher rear'd
    With stronger blood, we should have answer'd heaven
    Boldly 'not guilty', the imposition clear'd
    Hereditary ours.

Her. By this we gather
    You have tripp'd since.

Pol. O my most sacred lady,
    Temptations have since then been born to 's: for
    In those unfledg'd days was my wife a girl;
    Your precious self had then not cross'd the eyes
    Of my young play-fellow.

Her. Grace to boot!
    Of this make no conclusion, lest you say
    Your queen and I are devils. Yet go on;
    Th' offences we have made you do, we'll answer,
    If you first sinn'd with us, and that with us
    You did continue fault, and that you slipp'd not
    With any but with us.

Leon. Is he won yet?

Her. He'll stay, my lord.

Leon. At my request he would not.
    Hermione, my dearest, thou never spok'st
    To better purpose.

Her. Never?

Leon. Never but once.

Her. What! have I twice said well? when was't before?
    I prithee tell me: cram 's with praise, and make 's
    As fat as tame things: one good deed, dying tongueless,
    Slaughters a thousand, waiting upon that.
    Our praises are our wages. You may ride 's
    With one soft kiss a thousand furlongs ere
    With spur we heat an acre. But to th' goal:
    My last good deed was to entreat his stay:
    What was my first? It has an elder sister,
    Or I mistake you: O, would her name were Grace!
    But once before I spoke to th' purpose? when?
    Nay, let me have't: I long!

Leon. Why, that was when
    Three crabbed months had sour'd themselves to death,
    Ere I could make thee open thy white hand,
    And clap thyself my love; then didst thou utter
    'I am yours for ever.'

Her. 'Tis Grace indeed.
    Why lo you now; I have spoke to th' purpose twice:
    The one, for ever earn'd a royal husband;
    Th' other, for some while a friend. *(Giving her hand to Pol.)*

Leon. (Aside) Too hot, too hot!
    To mingle friendship far, is mingling bloods.

I have *tremor cordis* on me: my heart dances,
But not for joy—not joy. This entertainment
May a free face put on, derive a liberty
From heartiness, from bounty, fertile bosom,
And well become the agent: 't may, I grant:
But to be paddling palms, and pinching fingers,
As now they are, and making practis'd smiles
As in a looking-glass; and then to sigh, as 'twere
The mort o' th' deer—O, that is entertainment
My bosom likes not, nor my brows. Mamillius,
Art thou my boy?

Mam. Ay, my good lord.

Leon. I' fecks:
Why that's my bawcock. What! hast smutch'd thy nose?
They say it is a copy out of mine. Come, captain,
We must be neat; not neat, but cleanly, captain:
And yet the steer, the heifer and the calf
Are all call'd neat.—Still virginalling
Upon his palm!—How now, you wanton calf!
Art thou my calf?

Discuss the above extract, considering presentation of character, development of themes, imagery and dramatic significance. **20**

Section B: Answer *two* questions — one on each play — from this section.

2 Either, (a) Is Hamlet mad? Illustrate your answer with close reference to the text. **20**

Or, (b) 'Frailty, thy name is woman'. How far is this judgement reflected in the presentation of the characters of Ophelia and Gertrude in Hamlet? **20**

3 Either, (a) 'No play of Shakespeare's boasts three such women as Hermione, Perdita and Paulina'. What are the strengths of these three characters? **20**

Or, *(b)* 'It is not a subtle play; it is obvious, careless and flawed'. Can you defend *The Winter's Tale* against this charge? **20**

Section C: Answer *one* question from this section.

4 Either, (a) In what ways is Wilfred Owen's contribution to twentieth-century war poetry unique? Give detailed examples from at least *three* poems to support your answer. **20**

Or, (b) How effectively does Owen present individual soldiers to us in his war poetry? Answer with reference to three characters from different poems. **20**

5 Either, (a) Illustrate the range and nature of some of the emotions expressed in *The Waste Land*. **20**

Or, (b) 'Poetry can communicate before it is understood'. Do you agree with T S Eliot's comment about *The Waste Land*? **20**

PAPER 2   2½ hours

Answer *three* questions, each on a different text.

1 CHAUCER: *The Pardoner's Tale*

Either, (a) From a detailed examination of the passage below, and with
appropriate reference to other parts of the Tale, discuss and illustrate the
Pardoner's storytelling techniques.   **20**

> The apostel wepyng seith ful pitously,
> "Ther walken manye of whiche yow toold have I—
> I seye it now wepyng, with pitous voys—
> That they been enemys of Cristes croys,
> Of whiche the ende is deeth, wombe is hir god!"
> O wombe! O bely! O stynkyng cod,
> Fulfilled of dong and of corrupcioun!
> At either ende of thee foul is the soun.
> How greet labour and cost is thee to fynde!
> Thise cookes, how they stampe, and streyne, and grynde,
> And turnen substaunce into accident,
> To fulfille al thy likerous talent!
> Out of the harde bones knokke they
> The mary, for they caste noght awey
> That may go thurgh the golet softe and swoote.
> Of spicerie of leef, and bark, and roote
> Shal been his sauce ymaked by delit,
> To make hym yet a newer appetit.
> But, certes, he that haunteth swiche delices
> Is deed, whil that he lyveth in tho vices.
>   A lecherous thyng is wyn, and dronkenesse
> Is ful of stryvyng and of wrecchednesse.
> O dronke man, disfigured is thy face,
> Sour is thy breeth, foul artow to embrace,
> And thurgh thy dronke nose semeth the soun
> As though thou seydest ay "Sampsoun, Sampsoun!"
> And yet, God woot, Sampsoun drank nevere no wyn.
> Thou fallest as it were a styked swyn;
> Thy tonge is lost, and al thyn honeste cure;
> For dronkenesse is verray sepulture
> Of mannes wit and his discrecioun.
> In whom that drynke hath dominacioun
> He kan no conseil kepe, it is no drede.
> Now kepe yow fro the white and fro the rede,
> And namely fro the white wyn of Lepe,
> That is to selle in Fysshstrete or in Chepe.
> This wyn of Spaigne crepeth subtilly
> In othere wynes, growynge faste by,
> Of which ther ryseth swich fumositee
> That whan a man hath dronken draughtes thre,
> And weneth that he be at hoom in Chepe,
> He is in Spaigne, right at the toune of Lepe,—
> Nat at the Rochele, ne at Burdeux toun;
> And thanne wol he seye "Sampsoun, Sampsoun!"

Or, (b) By what means does Chaucer reveal the Pardoner's personality in
The Pardoner's Tale?   **20**

NICCEA 1994

2 CONRAD: *Heart of Darkness*

Either, (a) 'Marlow had one fatal defect: he talks too much and sometimes in the wrong way'. How successful is Marlow as a narrator in *Heart of Darkness*? **20**

Or, (b) What does Conrad mean when he has Kurtz say 'The Horror! The Horror!'? **20**

3 PLATH: *Ariel*

Either, (a) 'Nihilistic and life-denying'. Is this a true appraisal of Sylvia Plath's poetry in *Ariel*? **20**

Or, (b) By what means does Sylvia Plath reveal her struggle to assert her independence in *Ariel*? **20**

4 E M FORSTER: *Howards End*

Either, (a) What is the importance to the novel of the house, Howards End? **20**

Or, (b) Comment on the importance to the novel as a whole of the concert at the Queen's Hall described in Chapter 5. (The episode is printed below to help you.) **20**

It will be generally admitted that Beethoven's Fifth Symphony is the most sublime noise that has ever penetrated into the ear of man. All sorts and conditions are satisfied by it. Whether you are like Mrs Munt, and tap surreptitiously when the tunes come — of course, not so as to disturb the others; or like Helen, who can see heroes and shipwrecks in the music's flood; or like Margaret, who can only see the music; or like Tibby, who is profoundly versed in counterpoint, and holds the full score open on his knee; or like their cousin, Fraulein Mosebach, who remembers all the time that Beethoven is 'echt Deutsch'; or like Fraulein Mosebach's young man, who can remember nothing but Fraulein Mosebach: in any case, the passion of your life becomes more vivid, and you are bound to admit that such a noise is cheap at two shillings. It is cheap, even if you hear it in the Queen's Hall, dreariest music-room in London, though not as dreary as the Free Trade Hall, Manchester; and even if you sit on the extreme left of that hall, so that the brass bumps at you before the rest of the orchestra arrives, it is still cheap.

'Who is Margaret talking to?' said Mrs Munt, at the conclusion of the first movement. She was again in London on a visit to Wickham Place.

Helen looked down the long line of their party, and said that she did not know.

'Would it be some young man or other whom she takes an interest in?'

'I expect so,' Helen replied. Music enwrapped her, and she could not enter into the distinction that divides young men whom one takes an interest in from young men that one knows.

'You girls are so wonderful in always having—oh dear! We mustn't talk.'

For the Andante had begun—very beautiful, but bearing a family likeness to all the other beautiful Andantes that Beethoven has written, and, to Helen's mind, rather disconnecting the heroes and shipwrecks of the first movement from the heroes and goblins of the third. She heard the tune through once, and then her attention wandered, and she gazed at the audience, or the organ, or the architecture. Much did she censure the attenuated Cupids who encircle the ceiling of the Queen's Hall, inclining each to each with vapid gesture, and clad in sallow pantaloons, on which the October sunlight struck. 'How awful to marry a man like those Cupids!' thought Helen. Here Beethoven started decorating his tune, so she heard him through once more, and then smiled at her cousin Frieda. But Frieda, listening to Classical Music, could not respond. Herr Liesecke, too, looked as if wild horses could not make him inattentive; there were lines across his forehead, his lips were parted, his pince-nez at right angles to his nose, and he had laid a thick, white hand on either knee. And next to her was Aunt Juley, so British, and wanting to tap. How interesting that row of people was! What diverse influences had gone to the making! Here Beethoven, after humming and hawing with great sweetness, said 'Heigho', and the Andante came to an end. Applause, and a round of wunderschoning and pracht volleying from the German contingent. Margaret started talking to her new young man; Helen said to her aunt: 'Now comes the wonderful movement: first of all the goblins, and then a trio of elephants dancing'; and Tibby implored the company generally to look out for the transitional passage on the drum.

'On the what, dear?'

'On the *drum*, Aunt Juley.'

'No; look out for the part where you think you have done with the goblins and they come back,' breathed Helen, as the music started with a goblin walking quietly over the universe, from end to end. Others followed him. They were not aggressive creatures; it was that that made them so terrible to Helen. They merely observed in passing that there was no such thing as splendour or heroism in the world. After the interlude of elephants dancing, they returned and made the observation for the second time. Helen could not contradict them, for, once at all events. she had felt the same, and had seen the reliable walls of youth collapse. Panic and emptiness! Panic and emptiness! The goblins were right.

Her brother raised his finger: it was the transitional passage on the drum.

For, as if things were going too far, Beethoven took hold of the goblins and made them do what he wanted. He appeared in person. He gave them a little push, and they began to walk in a major key instead of in a minor, and then—he blew with his mouth and they were scattered! Gusts of splendour, gods and demigods contending with vast swords, colour and fragrance broadcast on the field of battle, magnificent victory, magnificent death! Oh, it all burst before the girl, and she even stretched out her gloved hands as if it was tangible. Any fate was titanic: any contest desirable; conqueror and conquered would alike be applauded by the angels of the utmost stars.

And the goblins—they had not really been there at all? They were only the phantoms of cowardice and unbelief? One healthy human impulse would dispel them? Men like the Wilcoxes, or President Roosevelt, would say yes. Beethoven knew better. The goblins really had been there. They might return—and they did. It was as if the splendour of life might boil over and waste to steam and froth. In its dissolution one heard the terrible, ominous note, and a goblin, with increased malignity, walked quietly over the universe from end to end. Panic and emptiness! Panic and emptiness! Even the flaming ramparts of the world might fall.

Beethoven chose to make it all right in the end. He built the ramparts up. He blew with his mouth for the second time, and again the goblins were scattered. He brought back the gusts of splendour, the heroism, the youth, the magnificence of life and of death, and, amid vast roarings of a superhuman joy, he led his Fifth Symphony to its conclusion. But the goblins were there. They could return. He had said so bravely, and that is why one can trust Beethoven when he says other things.

PAPER 3   2 hours

Answer BOTH questions.

1 Printed below is an episode from *Candida*, a play written by George Bernard Shaw (1856–1950). James Morell is described by Shaw as 'a Christian Socialist clergyman of the Church of England' and a celebrated orator. Eugene Marchbanks, a young, self-styled poet, has been befriended by the Morells and has just declared to Morell his love for Candida, Morell's wife.

When you have read the passage, write a critical analysis of it. Consider such things as the personalities and attitudes of the characters, showing how these are revealed; aspects of the irony and humour of the passage; the tone, purposes and effects of the stage directions.   **20**

Morell That foolish boy can speak with the inspiration of a child and the cunning of a serpent. He has claimed that you belong to him and not to me; and, rightly or wrongly, I have come to fear that it may be true. I will not go about tortured with doubts and suspicions. I will not live with you and keep a secret from you. I will not suffer the intolerable degradation of jealousy. We have agreed—he and I—that you shall choose between us now. I await your decision.

Candida (slowly recoiling a step, her heart hardened by his rhetoric in spite of the sincere feeling behind it) Oh! I am to choose, am I? I suppose it is quite settled that I must belong to one or the other.

Morell (firmly) Quite. You must choose definitely.

Marchbanks (anxiously) Morell: you don't understand. She means that she belongs to herself.

Candida (turning on him) I mean that, and a good deal more, Master Eugene, as you will
both find out presently. And pray, my lords and masters, what have you to offer for my
choice? I am up for auction, it seems. What do you bid James?

Morell (reproachfully) Cand—(He breaks down: his eyes and throat fill with tears: the
orator becomes a wounded animal) I can't speak.

Candida (impulsively going to him) Ah, dearest—

Marchbanks (in wild alarm) Stop: it's not fair. You mustn't shew her that you suffer,
Morell. I am on the rack too; but I am not crying.

Morell (rallying all his forces) Yes: you are right. It is not for pity that I am bidding. (He
disengages himself from Candida).

Candida (retreating, chilled) I beg your pardon, James: I did not mean to touch you. I am
waiting to hear your bid.

Morell (with proud humility) I have nothing to offer you but my strength for your
defence, my honesty for your surety, my ability and industry for your livelihood, and
my authority and position for your dignity. That is all it becomes a man to offer to a
woman.

Candida (quite quietly) And you, Eugene? What do you offer?

Marchbanks My weakness. My desolation. My heart's need.

Candida (impressed) That's a good bid, Eugene. Now I know how to make my choice.
(She pauses and looks curiously from one to the other, as if weighing them. Morell,
whose lofty confidence has changed into heartbreaking dread at Eugene's bid, loses all
power of concealing his anxiety. Eugene, strung to the highest tension, does not move
a muscle.)

Morell (in a suffocated voice: the appeal bursting from the depths of his anguish) Candida!

Marchbanks (aside, in a flash of contempt) Coward!

Candida (significantly) I give myself to the weaker of the two.

(Eugene divines her meaning at once: his face whitens like steel in a furnace.)

Morell (bowing his head with the calm of collapse) I accept your sentence, Candida.

Candida Do you understand, Eugene?

Marchbanks Oh, I feel I'm lost. He cannot bear the burden.

Morell (incredulously, raising his head and voice with comic abruptness) Do you mean
me, Candida?

Candida (smiling a little) Let us sit and talk comfortably over it like three friends. (To
Morell) Sit down, dear. (Morell, quite lost, takes the chair from the fireside: the
children's chair) Bring me that chair, Eugene. (She indicates the easy chair. He fetches
it silently, even with something like cold strength, and places it next to Morell, a little
behind him. She sits down. He takes the visitor's chair himself, and sits, inscrutable.
When they are all settled she begins, throwing a spell of quietness on them by her
calm, sane, tender tone) You remember what you told me about yourself, Eugene: how
nobody has cared for you since your old nurse died: how those clever fashionable
sisters and successful brothers of yours were your mother's and father's pets: how
miserable you were at Eton: how your father is trying to starve you into returning to
Oxford: how you have had to live without comfort or welcome or refuge: always lonely,
and nearly always disliked and misunderstood, poor boy!

Marchbanks (faithful to the nobility of his lot) I had my books. I had Nature. And at last
I met you.

Candida Never mind that just at present. Now I want you to look at this other boy here:
my boy! spoiled from his cradle. We go once a fortnight to see his parents. You should
come with us, Eugene, to see the pictures of the hero of that household. James as a
baby! the most wonderful of all babies. James holding his first school prize, won at the
ripe age of eight! James as the captain of his eleven! James in his first frock coat! James
under all sorts of glorious circumstances! You know how strong he is (I hope he didn't
hurt you): how clever he is: how happy. (With deepening gravity) Ask James's mother
and his three sisters what it cost to save James the trouble of doing anything but be
strong and clever and happy. Ask me what it costs to be James's mother and three
sisters and wife and mother to his children all in one. Ask the tradesmen who want to
worry James and spoil his beautiful sermons who it is that puts them off. When there
is money to give, he gives it: when there is money to refuse, I refuse it. I build a castle
of comfort and indulgence and love for him, and stand sentinel always to keep little
vulgar cares out. I make him master here, though he does not know it, and could not
tell you a moment ago how it came to be so. (With sweet irony) And when he thought
I might go away with you, his only anxiety was—what should become of me! And to

tempt me to stay he offered me (leaning forward to stroke his hair caressingly at each phrase) his strength for my defence! his industry for my livelihood! his dignity for my position! his—(relenting) ah, I am mixing up your beautiful cadences and spoiling them, am I not, darling? (She lays her cheek fondly against his).

Morell (quite overcome, kneeling beside her chair and embracing her with boyish ingenuousness) It's all true. every word. What I am you have made me with the labour of your hands and the love of your heart. You are my wife, my mother, my sisters: you are the sum of all loving care to me.

Candida (in his arms, smiling, to Eugene) Am I your mother and sisters to you, Eugene?

Marchbanks (rising with a fierce gesture of disgust) Ah, never. Out, then, into the night with me!

Candida (rising quickly) You are not going like that, Eugene?

Marchbanks (with the ring of a man's voice—no longer a boy's—in the words) I know the hour when it strikes. I am impatient to do what must be done.

Morell (who has also risen) Candida: don't let him do anything rash.

Candida (confident, smiling at Eugene) Oh, there is no fear. He has learnt to live without happiness.

Marchbanks I no longer desire happiness: life is nobler than that. Parson James: I give you my happiness with both hands: I love you because you have filled the heart of the woman I loved. Goodbye. (He goes towards the door).

Candida One last word. (He stops, but without turning to her. She goes to him) How old are you, Eugene?

Marchbanks As old as the world now. This morning I was eighteen.

Candida Eighteen! Will you, for my sake, make a little poem out of the two sentences I am going to say to you? And will you promise to repeat it to yourself whenever you think of me?

Marchbanks (without moving) Say the sentences.

Candida When I am thirty, she will be forty-five. When I am sixty, she will be seventy-five.

NEAB 1994

2 Read the poem printed below, and then write a critical commentary on it, paying attention to such things as the subject matter, imagery, use of language, mood and tone. Offer comment on any further aspects of the poem which interest you. **20**

LAUNDRETTE

We sit nebulous in steam.
It calms the air and makes the windows stream
rippling the hinterland's big houses to a blur
of bedsits—not a patch on what they were before.

We stuff the tub, jam money in the slot,
sit back on rickle chairs not
reading. The paperbacks in our pockets curl.
Our eyes are riveted. Our own colours whirl.

We pour in smithereens of soap. The machine sobs
through its cycle. The rhythm throbs
and changes. Suds drool and slobber in the churn.
Our duds don't know which way to turn.

The dark shoves one man in,
lugging a bundle like a wandering Jew. Linen
washed in public here.
We let out of the bag who we are.

This youngwife has a fine stack of sheets, each pair
a present. She admires their clean cut air
of colourschemes and being chosen. Are the dyes fast?
This christening lather will be the first test.

This woman is deadpan before the rinse and sluice
of the family in a bagwash. Let them stew in their juice
to a final *fankle, twisted, wrung out into rope,
hard to unravel. She sees a kaleidoscope

For her to narrow her eyes and blow smoke at, his overalls
and pants ballooning, tangling with her smalls
and the teeshirts skinned from her wriggling son.
She has a weather eye for what might shrink or run.

This dour man does for himself. Before him,
half lost, his small possessions swim.
Cast off, random
they nose and nudge the porthole glass like flotsam.

Liz Lochhead

* Fankle: tangle

NEAB 1994

Please read the examiners' report below before reading the students' answers to Paper 3 on pp. 232–4.

EXAMINER'S REPORT ON PAPER 3: CRITICAL APPRECIATION

Question 1

As always, mark the answer as a whole. Do not sub-divide the maximum mark to provide notional sub-totals for the various aspects of the question. Candidates do not need to consider every aspect mentioned in the rubric or in the notes which follow in order to achieve a high mark. The quality of the comments made may be enough to justify a high mark even though the coverage is not comprehensive. (NB it may be particularly important with this passage for examiners to bear in mind the statement in the General Instructions: 'No scheme of marking can cover every case'.)

Personalities and attitudes (and dialogue)

NB all three characters are subtly complex and will not submit to crude stereotyping. None of them is presented by Shaw entirely unsympathetically, though he mocks the men, both through C and in his SD's.

Morell: at beginning of episode appears strong and (respectably?) proud, though not without pomp and a tendency to strike postures. Attempting to take charge. Very soon his anguish at the prospect of losing C undermines his confidence: his 'lofty confidence has changed into a heartbreaking dread'. He is not as perceptive as Marchbanks, who immediately 'divines...at once' the significance of C's decision. Has the honesty and integrity to acknowledge that C's assessment of his dependence on her is justified. His love for C seems genuine. In spite of his anxiety, cannot resist the temptation of rhetoric. A kind man.

Marchbanks: often seems both more perceptive and more mature than Morell, but at other times reverts to boyishness ('...it's not fair' and 'Coward!'). Posturing comparable with Morell's: postures as a struggling poet, but this struggling poet comes from a rich family and has had an expensive education. Speaks, for the most part, in romantically inflated language, calculated for its effect. It is suggested that his feeling for C is youthful infatuation. (C certainly suggests this in her final words to him, but then, she treats them both as boys!)

Candida: clearly the character with whom Shaw most closely sympathises. Controls the situation from first to last. She has a gentle strength: even though she mocks both men, she does so with a 'sweet irony' — and considerable wit. Clever. Shows affection for both men, but there is no doubt about her love for Morell. Her final words to Marchbanks are perhaps patronising, but inoffensively so, part of her desire to 'let him down lightly'. More mature than both men, whom she treats, and indeed addresses, as boys. Outdoes Morell in rhetoric, his own field — and then mischievously apologises for 'mixing up your beautiful cadences'. Remains calm and sensible.

The irony and humour

The situation is certainly unusual and in some ways preposterous, as Candida empha-sises. Essentially, C chooses the man she deems the weaker and more dependent of the two, though superficially, especially at first, he appears to be, and claims to be, the stronger. There is irony in the contrast between Morell's offer and Marchbanks's, but the sharpest irony is in C's responses to their offers, the more effective because it is, as Shaw tells us, a 'sweet irony', i.e. without malice. There is further irony (and we can't have too much of it in passages selected for this paper!) in the way that C takes control of the proceedings. Any comments on the humour of the situation should be rewarded. (For the wit and humour of the dialogue and of the stage directions see below.)

Stage Directions

Perceptive attention to the stage directions should be amply rewarded: the recognition that they are more than bald instructions to actors; their wit and humour; their often satiric purpose. The overall tone of the SD's is mocking of both men and admiring of C.

Question 2

Subject matter

A wry observation of people using a laundrette. Users sit clouded (anonymous?) in steam of washing. Laundrette surrounded by large houses, previously grand, but now turned into bed-sits. The customers have brought books to read, but leave them in their pockets and sit (on rickety chairs) staring at the clothes revolving. A solitary man enters, carrying a bag of clothes, like a refugee(?) carrying all his possessions. There are no secrets here: our washing gives us away. A newly married woman is washing for the first time some new sheets, wedding presents, knowing that this first wash will reveal whether the colours will run. Another older woman, a mother, watches without expression or interest ('Let them stew in their juice'); (fankle = tangle). It is perhaps suggested that as she stares at the clothes she sees her family who wear them. It may also be suggested that she is as indifferent to the family as to their clothes. The man is isolated; his few clothes are like lost articles floating in the sea. Suggestion of anonymity ('nebulous') in first line continued throughout poem: 'we', 'one man', 'this youngwife', 'this woman'. No communication among various users of laundrette. Each is self-involved. Mechanical nature of process is suggested: 'stuff the tub', 'jam money in the slot'; also inactivity and lack of interest: 'sit back' and 'Let them stew in their juice'.

Imagery and use of Language

In an attempt to be helpful and to avoid repetition, imagery and use of language are dealt with simultaneously here.

* 'nebulous': useful definition in Chambers: 'hazy, vague, formless (lit.. fig)'; suggestion that the identities and personalities of the laundrette-users have been clouded/ shrouded by the steam of the laundrette.
* 'hinterland': interesting use of geographical term.
* 'not a patch on what they were': ambivalent, I think, suggesting the fallen grandeur of the 'big houses' and the fact that they cannot now be seen clearly through the misted windows. This is the first of several colloquial sayings which the poet uses (cf. 'don't know which way to turn', 'Linen washed in public', 'let out of the bag', 'Let them stew in their juice', 'does for himself'). Perhaps this is a representation of the kind of language which the laundrette-users would use. Each of these expressions has a double meaning.
* 'stuff' and 'jam': vigorous verbs which paradoxically convey the indifference of the customers.
* 'rickle chairs': emphasises the seedy surroundings.
* 'paperbacks curl': foreshadows 'not reading' and 'Our eyes are riveted', all supporting the idea of mindless concentration on the washing process.
* 'colours': perhaps an oblique reference to the use of this term in washing powder advertisements.
* 'smithereens of soap': washing powder, tiny fragments of soap, emphasised by the alliteration, which continues with 'sobs' and 'cycle'.

- Candidates will no doubt be keen to point out the onomatopoeia in 'sobs', 'throbs', 'drool' and 'slobber'.
- 'Our duds don't know which way to turn': in keeping with the other colloquialisms; amusing suggestion of the clothes in the washer being turned this way and that (and being tangled?).
- 'The dark shoves one man in': indicating his reluctance and possibly his embarrassment.
- 'lugging a bundle like a wandering Jew': puzzling, but presumably compares him to a refugee with all his possessions in one bag.
- 'Linen washed in public here': play on the well-known phrase.
- 'let out of the bag': play on 'let the cat out of the bag' and taking one's clothing out of the bag.
- 'youngwife': written as one word — why? Perhaps to emphasise her sense of newly acquired status as a married woman, a view possibly supported by 'being chosen' in 1.19.(?). Or is 'being chosen' better taken as referring to the sheets, chosen as a wedding present?
- 'christening lather': their first wash.
- 'deadpan': this woman shows no interest, is older and more experienced than the 'youngwife' and 'has a weather eye for what might shrink or run'.
- 'the family in a bagwash': as suggested above, this probably suggests that the woman visualises her family as she stares at their clothes in the washer.
- 'Let them stew in their juice': may also apply to the family as well as their clothes, as indeed may 'fankle' (a Scots term), 'twisted' and 'hard to unravel'.
- 'kaleidoscope': the many colours of the washing.
- 'teeshirts skinned from her wriggling son': 'skinned' + 'wriggling' combine to form a vivid picture of undressing a young boy.
- 'does for himself': does his own washing/looks after himself/has nothing to do with the others (all women) who are there.
- 'small possessions': a pun on 'smalls'? — the marine imagery in the final stanza is worthy of comment.

Mood and tone

No fussy distinctions between them, please, since one must inevitably reflect the other.

- Reflects the tedium of the situation.
- Gloomy, but the poet's amusement relieves the gloom.
- Indifference, with possible exception of 'youngwife', to whom the experience is new.
- It is useful to bear in mind that the poet includes herself among the clientele of the laundrette and this is emphasised by the 'We' which begins the first three stanzas.
- The tone is of wry amusement, sympathetic because she is involved in the situation herself.

Other matters

Structure: moves from general observations in first three stanzas to individual portraits in rest of poem. Verse-form: give credit for anything sensible on this, but do not give any credit for material which is merely descriptive.

EXAMPLES OF MOCK EXAM ANSWERS
PAPER 1

A1 (a) It is amazing how quickly the characters are revealed in this opening to *Hamlet*. It is immediately obvious from the start that the soldiers are on edge, about what we do not know, but it is interesting to see how the men react under these conditions. At first, they seem not to trust each other, Francisco demanding that Barnardo reveal himself before he will trust him. However, once the two men are aware of the identity of each other, they show genuine tiredness. Barnardo finally impels Francisco to get to bed and Francisco in turn is grateful to Barnardo. Neither complains about the other being late or early, and they seem to genuinely care for each other.

However, as the play continues and Horatio and Marcellus join Barnardo on the platform, it is obvious that they are not there for a reunion party. They seem to be bothered about the appearance of something. Horatio saying 'What has this thing appear'd again tonight?' Yet all throughout they remain good friends and companions.

In the second half of the extract, Shakespeare reveals even more about the characters. Horatio is a scholar, whereas the others would seem to have more physical fighting abilities. We are also shown the soldiers' sound judgement. Marcellus comments on the ghost saying 'This bodes some strange eruption to our state.'

The themes of the play are also skilfully brought to our attention. Throughout the whole play there is a theme of war and instability, for example when Hamlet comes across the soldiers on their way to fight Norway. From the very beginning we are aware of this stress. The play begins upon the guard platform of a castle, with the guards there on edge. This would seem to indicate that they are worried about an attack on the castle.

This theme also comes across through the ghost. It is wearing a 'warlike form' and reminds the soldiers of wars they have fought in.

The theme of instability and its resulting from damage to the royal family also comes through. There is a dead king obviously upset because it has come back as a ghost. This immediately raises such questions as to why is the ghost upset? Why is he dead? Who is now on the throne? The upheaval of the royal family has created a very unstable atmosphere which comes across in the soldiers, and already this theme is beginning to show itself.

Shakespeare uses language and verse very skilfully in this passage. At the start, we have short sharp sentences, highlighting the uncomfortableness and fear of the soldiers and the sentences remain short mainly until the entrance of the ghost.

The ghost's silence is very effective. This silence maintains the ghost's mystical image, and this is just as skilful a use of language than having the ghost say something.

The speech of the soldiers is used to portray their feelings as mentioned earlier and also to show how the other feels. Barnardo tells Horatio 'You tremble and look pale'. This shows both the kindness of the men and the fear the ghost has instilled.

Because the soldiers do not speak in verse but simply like normal people, it means the audience can feel a greater affinity with them. They are just normal people doing their job, so we, the audience, can understand how shaken up they must be by the ghost.

Stage actions also play a big role in *Hamlet*. The fact that everything is taking place on a guard platform of a castle is effective, as mentioned earlier. Also the fact that there are people constantly coming and going during the first half of the passage shows the nervousness and activity of a country at war and shows the erratic nervous behaviour of the soldiers.

As an opening to a play, this passage is a wonderful example. There is conflict, human stress, a ghost, and many questions raised in just this one scene, encouraging the audience to stay and await the unfurling of this famous play.

Examiners' comments

13/20

Fairly thorough, but some odd expressions. You need a wider vocabulary and more detailed comments on staging and language.

A1 (b) (i) The extract shows that Leontes is a very jealous man and the onset of his jealousy is rapid in Act 1, scene 2. In Act 2, scene 2, Archidamus and Camillo, courtiers to the two kings, tell us through reported speech how close the two kings are and that they are like brothers.

But Leontes' jealousy and anger is so great that it consumes him and disease imagery is often used to show how his actions are poisoned by his jealous thoughts.

We also see him as a very proud man and he isn't upset about how his wife has been disloyal to him but concentrates on the shame of being cuckolded. This classical illusion shows the legend of how a cheated husband would grow horns as an outward sign of his wife's betrayal and he would be 'cuckolded'. This image is also linked to Leontes referring to his brows '... that is entertainment my bosom likes not, nor my brows'.

Much of Leontes' speech is spoken 'aside', so the characters are not aware of what Leontes is saying. Dramatic irony helps the audience to understand how tyrannical a figure Leontes is, as every move that Hermione and Polixenes make strengthens Leontes' belief that they are both betraying him and having a relationship. 'But to be paddling palms and pinching fingers'. Leontes even hates the way they look at each other and sigh deeply 'as 'twere the mort o' th' deer'. This simile shows that Leontes is imagining things, by thinking that they sigh because they're sad that they can't be together. A simile describes how they look at each other and Leontes sees it as two lovers gazing at each other, '...and making practis'd smiles, As in a looking-glass...'

Sexual imagery is also used to show that Leontes' jealousy has gone so far, that he thinks his best friend and wife are sleeping together. An important point is that Polixenes has been staying with them for nine months which makes it possible in Leontes' mind that the baby Hermione is carrying could be Polixenes' child. 'Too hot, too hot! To mingle friendship far is mingling bloods.'

The extent of Leontes' jealousy is shown through his suspicions of whether Mamillius is his son. He uses animal imagery to describe how animals are clean and associates it with Hermione, questioning her purity. He puts a pun on the word 'virginalling', suggesting that Hermione is sleeping with Polixenes. 'We must be neat...cleanly... And yet the steer, the heifer, and the calf, are all call'd neat'.

Leontes is upset that Polixenes agrees to stay when Hermione asks him to and Leontes says, in an 'aside', 'at my request he would not'.

Polixenes and Hermione are worried about Leontes. Polixenes calls him 'best brother', Hermione says, 'You look as if you held a brow of much distraction', which Leontes takes as a reference to being cuckolded.

Disease imagery, of sickness and affection, starting off in Leontes' thoughts and brain, end up affecting his actions, 'to the infection of my brains and hardening of my brows'.

Images of dream and reality, things he never thought could happen are happening. Life is becoming a nightmare. Lust is at the root of it all, Hermione and Polixenes' lust is causing him heartache now. 'Affection! thy intention stabs the centre: Thou dost make possible things not so held, communicat'st with dreams'.

Examiners' comments

8/10

Well done - thorough attempt.
You have commented well on the language element.

(ii) Many of the events are only made convincing within the context of the play itself and so require you to 'suspend your disbelief', as Paulina says in the final scene.

Emphasis is placed on coincidence in this play and this is what makes it work. But Shakespeare has written the play in such a way that unbelievable coincidences become believable events.

The ending seems to acquit Leontes' jealousy, the main event that started the chain reaction, as everyone is reunited and Leontes appears to have paid heavily and has deeply repented his actions.

The chain of coincidences starts with such events as Leontes' jealousy and it grows rapidly. Human nature makes it possible that two such good childhood friends end up hating each other. Leontes goes to the extent of trying to poison Polixenes and when he escapes back to Bohemia, Leontes sees this as proof that he was guilty.

It is also amazing that Leontes doesn't believe the Oracle, who is a representative of

God and says that Hermione is innocent. But his punishment comes in the form of Mamillius' death, who was heir to the throne and held great hope for the future.

When Archidamus is sent to kill the child Hermione has given birth to, he is killed himself and eaten by a bear. But the child, Perdita, survives and is brought up in Bohemia by a shepherd.

Polixenes' son, Prince Florizel, just happens to cross the shepherd's cottage when hunting and meets Perdita. They both fall in love and marry at the end of the play.

Paulina speaks her mind in front of Leontes, calling him a 'tyrant' and his courtiers 'sycophants'. But Leontes doesn't do anything and puts up with her harsh words.

When Hermione and Mamillius are dead, or Hermione is said to be dead, a Lord tells Paulina she has been too harsh towards Leontes and she backs down.

It is amazing the way in which Hermione is hidden for so many years and then brought back, to make Leontes realise how wrong he was and that he is truly sorry.

The ending is a happy one, with Camillo and Paulina paired off and the tragedy in the play seems very far away. The beginning, with Leontes' 'reign of terror' seems very distant at the ending, where Paulina tells him he must 'awake his faith'. Mistakes have been made but everyone has learned their lesson and it seems as if everyone's trying to play 'happy families'. The bond between the two families is strengthened by Florizel and Perdita who won't make the same mistakes as their elders and so represent hope for the future.

Examiners' comments

6/10

Good answer, but you must grasp dramatic significance.
Point your answer to the question, otherwise it's just narrative.

B2 (b) The judgement on women given by Hamlet applies to quite an extent in the presentation of Gertrude but only to some extent in the presentation of Ophelia. Both women have circumstances that differ in many ways, yet are the same in some ways.

Firstly, with Gertrude it can be said that this judgement is reflected in the presentation of her character. Gertrude is presented sometimes as being weak, dependent and unable to think and act on her own judgement alone. Gertrude is presented as a woman who cannot live without a man, a woman who is dependent on men and having a relationship with a man in her life and is therefore seen to be weak. This is all shown by the fact that she married so quickly after her first husband's death, seemingly going from having one man in her life to having another. The space of time between the funeral and the marriage is very short, only two months, and it is this as well as Hamlet's interpretation of the whole relationship that makes us believe that Gertrude is weak. 'The funeral bak'd meats did coldly furnish forth the marriage tables.'

Hamlet talks of how weak Gertrude is and how she used to be with her first husband, the short time between the marriage and the funeral, and how she is now. Hamlet says that Gertrude used to 'hang on' Old Hamlet's neck doting on him and looking at no one else, yet two months after his death she has married her husband's brother and is in a relationship which Hamlet perceives as being wrong and incestuous. It is because of this that we see Gertrude as being weak, as being unable to live without a man, and as being dependent on men.

Also in the closet scene in Act 3, Gertrude is portrayed as being weak in the face of confrontation and conflict. Gertrude is scared of her own son, believing he is going to harm her and reacts by being scared and calling for help and trying to get away from him or calm him down. Also the fact that Gertrude continues staying with Claudius after Hamlet has put these doubts in her head about his father's murder and allows Claudius to send Hamlet to England, can all be seen as signs of weakness, of not confronting problems and solving them, but instead pushing them out of sight and ignoring them.

However, there is another side to the way in which Gertrude is conveyed and that is of her not being presented as weak but rather as a victim of the circumstances in which she finds herself. Firstly, the quick marriage may have just been due to the fact that she was caught at a very weak time in her life. Gertrude's husband had died, she was left alone, in charge of the country, with a son to look after, whilst mourning for her husband, and it was Claudius who was comforting her. Gertrude turning to Claudius may have been a weak time for her or a genuine love for him and not just a sign of weakness and dependence.

Also the fact that Gertrude appeared weak when Hamlet confronted her is not surprising due to the nature of the confrontation. Gertrude was being confronted by her son whom she thought she knew, but who was acting in a way that was completely alien and frightening to her. Hamlet, to her, was acting in an angry, emotional, insane and dangerous way. His actions and his words were both alien and dangerous to her, and having never seen him like this before, it is unsurprising that she is a little weak, especially after he kills one of her close friends in an angry rage. It may not be due to weakness that she stays with Claudius and allows him to send Hamlet back. After all, can she believe without a doubt what Hamlet is saying, is he sane or mad? Gertrude would probably believe it to be for the best if Hamlet was not there, thereby not risking his own life or anyone else's. Also, Gertrude, it seems, only really wants a peaceful, happy ending. She didn't want all this, her hope that everything turns out nicely and idyllically is not really a sign of weakness. Even though Gertrude is presented as weak in the face of confrontation, the circumstances that she is in have to be taken into account.

Ophelia is fairly similar as she is presented as being 'weak' and the judgement is seen to apply to her, yet Ophelia is a victim of circumstance. Ophelia is seen to be weak because she does not stand up to her father or to Hamlet, she doesn't speak up for herself, and she seems to go mad rather quickly. However, she does not go mad quickly, instead the madness builds up gradually as a result of the immense pressure put on her by the circumstances she finds herself in and the people around her.

Opehlia at times does stand up for herself and appears to be bold, for example when talking to her brother and father about Hamlet and defending him. However, as a woman in those times, Ophelia has to obey her brother and father, she has to be obedient and dutiful and do things she may not want to do. Ophelia cannot be judged in these terms on a twentieth-century level as in her time she had to behave a certain way. That is why Ophelia can be seen as weak when she is not, by the very fact that she obeyed her father, who is very domineering, and stopped seeing Hamlet: "I shall obey, my Lord".

Also in the confrontation between Hamlet and herself, Ophelia can be seen as being weak as she starts to break down and says little even though at the beginning she showed strength in talking to Hamlet and returning his gifts. However, again it is the circumstances in which Ophelia finds herself that have to be looked at before saying that this judgement applies to her. Ophelia is already going slightly mad because of her father's treatment of her and because of her having to conform and to obey. The contrast in Hamlet's behaviour is also another big step towards her madness.

Ophelia's madness is not due to weakness, she is not really a victim of weakness but of circumstance. Ophelia's madness is helped every step of the way by her circumstances, and so much happens to Ophelia that it is not surprising that she goes mad. Firstly, she is unable to be her own person but has to be what others want her to be and has to obey them. Secondly, she sees her one true love in an altered state of mind, and then her father is killed by him and he is exiled. Both women are not completely weak, they are weak in some cases but are more victims of who they are and the circumstances they find themselves in.

Examiners' comments

14/20

A good exam answer — but at times your expression is repetitious and poor, which lowers your mark.

B3 (b) In many ways, *The Winter's Tale* is obvious because everything happens so quickly and unreasonably at the beginning, that the mistakes have to be realised later on. Leontes suddenly decided that Hermione and Polixenes were having an affair and then announced it to the court. His imagination kept enlarging the fantasy and he began to believe there was also a plot to kill him. This total over-exaggeration makes it obvious that he will eventually come to his senses and regret his rash actions.

The coincidences that happen are also obvious. Perdita is abandoned on a Bohemian rock and a bear appears, yet it eats Antigonus and not Perdita. On one hand this is feasible because she is necessary for the story to continue, yet on the other hand it seems unlikely that the bear would leave her. This point can be defended because Perdita is supposed to be protected by Hermione. Antigonus's dream said he would never see Paulina again if he abandoned Perdita, and as he didn't abandon her, so it should follow that the baby was protected from harm.

The coincidence that Perdita and Florizel happen to fall in love is also obvious, as is the fact that they will end up happily together. Out of anybody Florizel picked a shepherd's daughter to fall in love with. Again this can be accounted for by the fact that she is really royalty and so able to relate to him on the same level.

The main part of the play that appears careless is Leontes' sudden jealousy and accusations against Hermione. They had been married for a long time and they had always known Polixenes so it seems strange that he would suddenly overreact about their relationship.

The fact that Hermione talked Polixenes into staying in Sicilia after Leontes' refusal to let him do so, would spark off understandable jealousy, but Leontes' ideas about their affair and the way he deals with this is totally unreasonable and appears so to the audience. This action is counteracted by his remorse when Mamillius dies and he comes to his senses.

The fact that Mamillius died is also an unlikely and careless feature. It is necessary for the plot because it is what jolts Leontes back into reality, but it does seem strange that he would die of a broken heart.

When Hermione faints and Paulina announces she is dead it seems reasonable that Leontes would visit her because the audience also thinks that Hermione is dead. Yet later when it is discovered she is alive it is virtually impossible for Hermione to have seemed dead when Leontes visited her. This flaw in the play is covered because the scene where Leontes visits her is not shown.

'Time' appearing is also a flaw, not because it isn't possible to show, but because it is often unacceptable to the audience. This was partly overcome in the production with John Nettles by having a balloon come down with a note on it and Camillo reading out what time said. This made it fit in with the play more by having one of the characters take the time change.

The fact that Hermione lived is a positive part of the play because it means that Leontes can have his wife back after repenting for 16 years and that Perdita can see her mother. It is the way in which Hermione survived which is carelessly done and flawed.

If she had gone abroad then she may never have been discovered, but she lived close by in Sicilia and Paulina took food to her every day. With this happening it is almost impossible that she would not have been discovered. Yet it doesn't ruin the play because it isn't the main feature. The important part is that she is away for 16 years and then returns to Leontes who is unbelievably sorry for what he did.

Another part of the play that appears careless is jumping from tragedy straight into comedy with Autolycus. When seen or read for the first time it seems to be a flaw because of the lack of continuity. But when studied there are links between the two because Perdita is there and so are Camillo and Polixenes. As well as the characters there are references to the first part of the play. Camillo talks about wanting to return home after his time in Bohemia.

The play does appear to be 'obvious, careless and flawed' at first sight but when studied the actions and events can be explained and justified. If there is any doubt about whether the events are believable Paulina says that they have to be accepted – 'It is requir'd you do awake your faith'.

Examiners' comments

15/20

Well argued, but could have contained more close detail.
You must show in every paragraph that you've studied the text in detail.

C4 (b) 'The Sentry' is very effective in presenting an individual, namely the sentry on lookout during a shell attack. To begin with, Owen describes the context. The soldiers are in a dugout, knee deep in freezing water and slime, whilst outside there is a vicious shelling attack from the Germans. It is so vicious that it acts more like a person than a bombardment. Indeed Owen says that they were in a trench '...and he knew, and gave us shell on frantic shell...' as if the bombardment is a person.

Amidst all this, the sentry, looking out from the dugout, is hit in the eyes by shrapnel and falls screaming into the trench. The description of his suffering is grotesque, 'His eyes, huge – bulged like squids' is very effective in portraying the horror experienced by the men. The image of a man's eyes bulging like a squid's eyes is like a nightmare, and shows the horror of war.

What makes this poem even more effective is the fact that Owen, the narrator, is the officer in charge. He is responsible for this tortured man and has been with him for so long and through so much that he is more of a mother to him than his natural one. This responsibility highlights the suffering of the officer for he has to help this man and live amidst this man's screams and pain, and the screams and pain of many others like him.

What really upset Owen, however, is that he forgets the man lying there. The Germans start to invade, so he joins his men in shooting them rather than looking after the injured man. However, what he forgets then is ingrained in his memory for the rest of his life and haunts him. This also shows how people can be just as hurt by bombardment of the mind as by bombardment of the body and we are shown very effectively Owen's suffering.

'Dulce et Decorum est' is also effective in portraying the suffering of a man suffering from a gas attack. Again, Owen would seem to be the officer in charge. In the first section, we simply see events as if looking back. The language is very effective in portraying the horrors war has wrought on the soldiers: 'Knock kneed, coughing like hags, we cursed through sludge'. The soldiers look more like old women than the young men they are, and this is very effective in showing how much they have suffered.

From here on, Owen concentrates on the individual soldier unable to put his gas mask on in time. Through a haze of green, like a living nightmare, we are told of the man's 'froth-corrupted lungs', again through good use of language. In the latter part of the poem, Owen changes tense to the present saying '…In all my dreams, before my helpless sight he plunges at me, guttering, choking, drowning…'. This shows the suffering of the soldier, and also the suffering of the officer who must live with this nightmare forever.

In 'The Dead-Beat', a soldier is suffering for completely different reasons. Although he is not physically wounded he cannot get up even when threatened with a gun. He is considered to be malingering yet he eventually dies. This poem is written much more matter-of-factly, but is still just as effective, showing the naivety of the officer in charge, his fellow soldiers, the stretcher-bearers and the doctor. It is also horrific to have to accept that what a soldier sees and hears alone can lead to his death.

Again, Owen is the officer in charge and we can feel his guilt for threatening the soldier with a gun and for not understanding why he is ill.

Owen presents the individual soldier in two ways. Firstly, by describing the results of war on their minds and bodies. He also portrays them as poor men, little more than boys, forced into a war they have no interest in for all the wrong reasons. As he is the officer in charge in all three poems, he is able to make these observations legitimately as someone who actually experienced the war. Finally, he portrays the suffering of himself as an officer who lost so many 'sons' to the horrors of war.

Examiners' comments

16/20

Super general comments – you really are fluent but need the same kind of detail for all the poems that you've shown in 'The Sentry'

PAPER 2

1 (a) The Pardoner is a lay-person of the Roman Catholic Church which means he is unordained. However, he is a very skilled orator and I think he is a good storyteller because of the variety of content in his sermons. He preaches about vices and sins and illustrates these with many examples, which will appeal to everyone in his congregation.

It is also important to establish that the Pardoner has two audiences which he preaches to. The first audience is his church congregation which he preaches to and tries to make them buy his relics. His other audience, the other pilgrims who are travelling with him on a pilgrimage, are told the truth about how he preaches and cheats the poor out of their money. His motto is 'Radix malorum est cupiditas', which means 'money is the root of all evil'. This is rather hypocritical of him as he preaches only to gain money and cares 'nothing about correction of sin'.

He preaches against sins such as avarice, greed, drunkenness, lechery, gambling and blasphemy. Yet he describes the sins in such detail that he must have actually experienced and participated in such things himself. In the passage he describes the evil of eating rich foods that 'may go thurgh the golet softe and swoote'. Surely he must have tasted such foods himself to know the sensation of swallowing them and feeling them go softly and smoothly down your throat.

He also talks about the vices of drinking and how a man loses his senses and is unaware of what he's doing and how his face is 'disfigured'. Yet we know he drinks, because before starting his take in the Tabard Inn, he asks for a mug of 'Corny Ale'. He describes how a drunk man has sour breath and he is foul to embrace and also the sound he makes when he snores: 'thurgh thy dronke nose semeth the soun as though thou seydest ay "Sampsoun, Sampsoun!"'

He gives as an example the wine that is sold in the town, at Fish Street. He tells the audience how white Spanish wine, which is cheap, is mixed with expensive French wine and so people are cheated out of their money. He tells the people the truth, but adds an element of humour to the story, to get them over to his side and so ensure that they will trust him.

At the beginning of the tale the Pardoner describes to the pilgrims how he is able to cheat his congregation. First of all, he is a skilled orator and he speaks clearly and loudly describing his voice as a bell. He also describes himself as a bird, as he sticks his neck out and looks towards every person in the congregation as if he is looking directly at them.

He shows them documents which are supposed to be from the Pope, but he actually has no right to preach, as he hasn't been ordained. He also tries to impress the poor, uneducated people by speaking to them in Latin and this also flatters them as they think that he thinks they are capable of understanding him.

Some parts of his speech are clearly intended to shock and put fear into the people. He closely refers to stories from the Bible and also tells mythological stories and legends. This makes him appear very knowledgeable so they respect him and look up to him as a trustworthy educated preacher. He has a very good understanding of their lives and the fears and worries in their lives. He plays on these fears to profit from his knowledge. He tells a story of a bone that if put into water and left overnight will be able to cure your animals of diseases. Also if a man drinks the water he will not feel jealous about his wife sleeping with a few priests.

It is in such ways that he takes the people into his confidence (revealing the corruption of the Church) and hopes this will make them buy his relics.

Another story he tells is about a glove that will make your crops give a good yield if you wear it while sowing the seeds. People's livelihoods depended on their corn and animals, so people would want to buy such relics.

He preaches on a very wide range of sins from drinking and blasphemy to murder and lechery. Therefore, his sermons are applicable to everyone, as most people will have sworn in their lives. He makes them feel that their sins will be forgiven if they buy his relics. People would have very horrific ideas about hell as plays used to be put on to show what sinning would lead to and hell would be portrayed as a terrible place.

He tells stories such as how drunken Lot slept with his two daughters which would shock people, and also of how King Herod made an oath to kill John the Baptist when he was drunk. Such stories from the Bible would be believed by people because they were religious.

The Pardoner tells the pilgrims how he cheats the poor people of his congregation and thinks this will make the pilgrims trust him as he's telling them the truth. He uses crude language in the stories he tells them. He also tries to make his story humorous so that the pilgrims will laugh with him at the ignorant people of his congregation.

The pilgrims hear about how he will take money from a widow and her starving children just so that he can 'have a pretty wench in every town' and eat rich foods, not simple bread and water. We see how determined he is as he repeats the word 'will', but this is another example of how he doesn't practise what he preaches as he indulges in gluttony himself and warns others that it is sinful.

Examiners' comments

14/20

Good essay – you could have used other parts of the tale more. Don't over-use the passage you're given.
The examiner will be looking for an essay ranging throughout the whole of the tale.

3 (a) It could be perceived perhaps that Sylvia Plath's poetry is 'nihilistic and life-denying' because so much of her poetry centres on the negative theme of Death. However, although 'Death' could be seen as being negative, most of Sylvia Plath's poetry expresses positive connotations of Death.

Sylvia Plath's poems contain a variety of issues although most of them are often perceived as being autobiographical. Based upon her life, Plath's poetry reflects a troubled childhood, and the expression of intense pressures to achieve highly. These pressures and the failure of her marriage resulted in several suicide attempts, one of which was successful.

She bases her poems around these suicide attempts, and her will to die and rise above everything is apparent in her poems. Sylvia Plath writes 'Dying is like an art, I do it exceptionally well', and also 'the woman is perfected, her dead body shows the smile of accomplishment'. Both of the above quotes appear to be nihilistic and life-denying and to some extent they are. However, the latter of the two quotes also has an underlying element, an idea of women rising above men.

Often her poetry stresses the solidarity of women, the 'sisterhood' and 'hood of bone'. In 'The Applicant' Sylvia Plath shows how men cannot do without women, yet women are perceived as the subservient partner in a marriage, someone to 'bring teacups and roll away headaches'. In the poem 'Daddy', Sylvia says that women have 'lived like a foot' in his black shoe. This shows the restrictions put on women by male domination and authority. This is a reason why Sylvia Plath is so adored by feminists, who see her poetry as an inspiration for women.

Sylvia Plath's poetry is also not always 'life-denying' and seen as 'nihilistic' because she writes fondly of children; 'what is so real as the cry of a child?' and 'your nakedness shadows are safety' are illustrations of the positive ideas of childhood. In the poem 'Morning Song' Sylvia Plath's first line is 'Love set you going like a fat gold watch'. This simile expresses the love and value of a child with the use of 'gold'. Children also represent reality, their visions are not clouded or mirrored. They are 'pure' and 'innocent' creatures in contrast to adults and males in general.

Sylvia Plath's poetry also gives life; even when she talks of death she talks of life after death and the poem 'Lady Lazarus' exemplifies this point. In another poem there is a poignant line 'the blood jet in poetry'. This shows that the life source 'blood' inspires her to write about life. A part of life which follows life is death, the two are linked.

However, some of her poetry is 'nihilistic'. For example, the poem 'Daddy', in which the female voice relates herself to a Jew who is persecuted by her father and her husband, is nihilistic. Here her revenge is 'if I've killed one man, I've killed two'. Another example is the poem 'Tulips'. In this poem a gift of tulips, usually considered to be thoughtful and pleasant, has the opposite effect. The redness of the tulips are 'too excitable'. They remind the mother lying in bed of her 'loving associations', whom she thinks of in ironical terms. She feels she is a 'thirty-year-old cargo boat', whose role in life is to carry their 'baggage'. In this poem she refers to her children negatively as 'little smiling hooks'.

In yet another of her poems Sylvia Plath refers to a wedding ring as nothing but 'Lies. Lies and a grief'. Marriage here is associated with dishonesty and could reflect upon Plath's own marriage breakdown and the affair her husband Ted Hughes had.

One of her poems sees the closeness of her mother's relationship as an intrusion and is referred to as a 'barnacled umbilical cord'. In fact in the collection of poems in *Ariel*, Sylvia Plath managed to suggest that every member of her close family has a negative element to their personalities. This is shown in her parents, her husband, and her children.

Therefore, in conclusion, Sylvia Plath's poetry is to some extent 'nihilistic and life-denying', as some critics of her work would agree, but it is also positive, informative, historical, mythological and true to reality as well. The collection of poems in *Ariel* is truly a collection. There is not one main theme which bonds all of her poems together, they are different because each individual poem expresses a different point of view in a different way. Sylvia Plath's poetry does contain issues other than just death and its negative connotations. Sylvia Plath just adopts these different worldly issues such as religion, institutions, war and the solidarity of women, in a domestic fashion. By portraying these issues in a domestic way, Sylvia Plath can effectively achieve her aim by stressing her point through her poetry successfully.

18/20

A little weaker at the end, but on the whole excellent and very well researched. I am very impressed by this essay. Try to end on a strong, thought-provoking and perhaps controversial note.

4 (b) The concert plays an important part in the novel because it shows how the characters interpret the music in different ways just as they, later in the novel, tackle issues in different ways.

The Schlegels are all there and although they are seen to be basically one 'type' of person they are all interested in the music for different reasons. Mrs Munt likes the tune, which shows that she understands the obvious points but doesn't read too deeply into them. Helen is the opposite of this and sees 'heroes and shipwrecks' in the music. She is very passionate and loves the dramatic parts of the music, just as with her life she is interested in the impulsive and exciting parts. This is shown in the Oriton episode when she impulsively takes the Basts to Evie's wedding to force Henry to give Leonard a job.

Meg, despite being close to her sister, reacts differently to the music as she does in her life. She can 'only see the music' because she is a realistic person. The Oriton episode demonstrates this for when Helen gets very excited, Meg tells her it was idiotic to drag the Basts to Oriton and so makes Helen see sense.

This chapter is also significant and important because it introduces Leonard. Although he is not really mentioned much in this passage, he later talks to Meg then goes to Wickham Place to collect his umbrella and becomes a major part of the novel. He is at the concert to educate himself and to become culturally aware, whereas the Schlegels are there because they find the music entertaining and stimulating.

The meeting of Leonard also displays Meg's interest in people and her ability to interact with almost anyone. Mrs Munt recognises this and thinks that it is 'wonderful' that they meet so many people. Helen obviously sees this as normal because she is not surprised or very interested, due to her being enthralled by the music. It is only when the loud and dramatic part is over that she takes an interest in what is around her.

The Schlegels' interest in art and literature is highlighted obviously because they are at a concert, but also by the fact that when Helen is bored by one part, she starts to admire the architecture in the Hall.

Helen also has a vivid imagination because after the Andante is over she tells Aunt Juley that the next movement includes 'goblins' and 'elephants'. She can obviously see these images in the music because she 'stretched out her gloved hands as if it was tangible'.

Tibby, the youngest of the three, has a very different outlook on the music and on life. He has the score in front of him and is only interested in very specific parts of the symphony. He is very keen for everyone to listen for the 'transitional passage on the drum' which appears to be the only part he enjoys. His life reflects this because there are only specific parts of it that he takes an interest in. Food is his main love and he is often associated with it. Even when Helen visits him at Oxford and says she is leaving and wants Tibby to give 5000 pounds to Leonard, he asks if it's alright for him to eat his apple charlotte before it goes cold. Whereas Meg and Helen's main concerns are feelings and 'connecting', Tibby appears immune from this and may eat to compensate for his lack of emotions.

The Wilcoxes are also mentioned and their philosophies are displayed through the symphony's ending. The goblins disappear and Wilcox-types would say they never existed, but Beethoven and the Schlegels know that they are there somewhere and could easily return. The Wilcoxes are represented by 'panic and emptiness' and show no real emotions, whereas the Schlegels can enjoy the music. This is shown throughout the novel because the Wilcoxes have nothing if their fortress isn't built around them to protect them, whilst the Schlegels can always survive because they have inner strength.

16/20

You deal very well with this, but you've missed out important 'bits'.
Doesn't cover the themes adequately and you've missed out Forster's narrative 'voice'.

He is a vital presence in the novel – don't miss him out.
The tone, viewpoint and humour are entirely typical of the way he writes the whole novel.

PAPER 3

1 The way in which the characters are presented at the beginning of the passage alters as they are revealed more fully. Morell begins by sounding strong and makes Marchbanks appear ignorant and immature: 'That foolish boy'.

Yet Morell only sounds sure of himself because he feels he's in control and that Marchbanks is no threat to him. Once the truth is revealed, that Candida might not choose her husband, he breaks down and his weaker, vulnerable side is displayed.

Candida explains how her husband has had everything he ever wanted and has led a very sheltered life. This probably shows why he can't cope when he feels he will lose.

Unlike Marchbanks, Morell has no insight into how he is making people feel or about what people mean. He tells Candida that she must 'choose' one man and it is only Marchbanks who realises she doesn't want to feel like a possession. Later in the passage she says she'll choose the 'weaker of the two' and Morell doesn't even realise that she means him. He appears not to understand himself because he has always had his own way, and has never needed to recognise his failings.

Marchbanks is a contrasting character to Morell – he is more independent and realistic about himself. He immediately realises that Morell is the 'weaker' one and that he, with his hard life, is stronger. With this strong character also comes unhappiness, yet he is resigned to it. The stage direction says that he is 'faithful to the nobility of his lot'. Marchbanks is also a proud character, when Candida chooses Morell over him he just leaves and says he is pleased she is happy. Morell would have broken down and begged her to stay, as he virtually did earlier in the passage.

Candida is the link between the two very different men. She seems to be understood more by Marchbanks but chooses Morell because he needs her. This noble attitude makes her appear a strong and admirable character. Her strength is displayed when Marchbanks attempts to leave and Morell wants Candida to stop him and calm him down, showing that she is in control and has the power in this situation.

Her character also appears wise and sensitive. She chooses her husband because she knows he will be nothing without her, whereas Marchbanks has 'learnt to live without happiness'. Rather than callously throwing one of the men aside she (smiling) gets them to sit down so she can explain her decision to them both.

The stage directions help to reveal the characters because they explain what tone the lines are said in. Morell is for the majority of the time distraught and scared that she won't choose him. He is also made fun of throughout the passage, his offer to Candida is said '(with proud humility)' yet later his bid is mocked because it is self-centred. Candida explains this '(with sweet irony)'. These stage directions give an indication of how George Bernard Shaw makes fun of Morell's supposed dramatic lines by making them over-dramatic and too exaggerated for the situation. This is displayed when he feels she will go to Marchbanks when he speaks '(in suffocated voice: the appeal bursting from the depths of his anguish)'. Marchbanks' retort continues the over-dramatic exclamations as he speaks '(aside in a flash of contempt)'.

The tone of the play, shown mainly through stage directions, is ironic and displays exaggerated emotions.

The punctuation also helps to portray the ironic tone when describing James Morell's upbringing. After each of Candida's statements about how he was adored there is an exclamation mark, which indicates that his supposed amazing talents as a child were over-exaggerated because everything he did was considered great.

Candida refers to the two men as 'boys' which shows her position of authority and also gives the play a slightly humorous tone. She has one 'boy' who can't live without her and cries when she threatens to leave and another who is more admirable and a stronger character.

The three contrasting characters make the play interesting by showing how they interact with one another and it ends with Candida in control as always, and wisely showing Marchbanks that it is better that they are not together because of the age gap.

Examiners' comments

16/20

Very well answered!

2   The title 'Laundrette' sets the scene and then the poem fills in the details of who goes there and how they feel and what they do. The poem is written as if we are at the launderette, which gives the reader a personal insight into what is happening. It could also mean that 'we' is everybody who goes to the launderette because they all act in a similar way. 'We' all appear to watch the machines spinning the clothes around: 'We stuff the tub, jam money in the slot' because whoever 'We' are it is compulsory at a laundrette, so 'We' act as one.

The poem personifies the washing machines when they are in action – 'The machine sobs'. It is also described as a 'kaleidoscope' which effectively portrays how all the colours spin round and constantly change their pattern. This seems to interest everyone, at the laundrette they are 'riveted' by watching their clothes.

After explaining what happens in a laundrette and making everyone into clones of one another, the poet begins to pick out individual people who are washing their clothes. The first man is introduced by being shoved in by 'the dark'. This personification seems to show that people are drawn there just as they are mesmerised by watching their clothes spin round.

The poet has taken the common phrase 'washing your dirty linen in public' and effectively applied it to her poem - '...Linen washed in public here'. As well as being realistically true, because they bring their clothes to a public place, it is also true in the sense that a person's character and lifestyle can be analysed through their clothes. The poet again uses language associated with laundrettes to show that their characters are revealed – 'We let out of the bag who we are'.

The poem then begins analysing very different people who have the laundrette in common. The 'youngwife' appears very house proud and neat because she looks at her new sheets' 'clean cut air'. She wonders whether the colours will run and is now going to find out. It is almost as if a trip to the laundrette is an adventure of discovery for the wife.

The next woman is very different, she sounds older and the description of her and her washing contrasts to that of the 'youngwife', who is giving her fine sheets a 'christening lather'. This smart image is very different from that of the woman who is 'deadpan' with her 'bigwash'. Her clothes are 'fankle, twisted, wrung out into rope'. This description gives the impression of an older mother who is tired and worn down by her jobs and responsibilities. She also appears very experienced at washing and knows exactly what might shrink or run.

The final customer is a single man who 'does for himself'. His clothes are 'half lost' which seems to fit with his character because he is alone. His clothes are personified, they 'swim' in the machine and 'nudge the porthole glass' which gives the impression they are trying to get out and find someone.

The poem effectively shows the same task being viewed through different people in contrasting ways. The poem begins with 'we' but then shifts its focus to 'this woman' and 'him', which allows the poet to describe clothes to suit their characters rather than it being written in the first person.

The tone of the poem is fairly calm because it isn't telling an exciting story, but just describing different people at quite a slow pace. Enjambement helps to keep the pace slow because the rhyme at the end of the line is emphasised and creates a pause mid-sentence –

> We stuff the tub, jam the money in the **slot**
> sit back on rickle chairs **not**
> reading...

This regular rhyme scheme of rhyming couplets gives the poem rhythm and unity. The most noticeable line that doesn't rhyme is: 'We let out of the bag who we are'. This may be because it makes the line stand on its own and disconnects it from the general feeling of the poem. It is at the point where the emphasis changes from generally describing the laundrette to going into detail about individual people, so it could be breaking the poem subtly in half to show the distinction between the two points of view.

The mood of the poem isn't obvious to define, it isn't definitely happy or sad but just shows peoples' lives briefly. It is giving an insight into a laundrette and how all types of people go there so the mood is calm and quite relaxed in general. Later on it depends on the individual people but mainly it just describes average life in a variety of ways.

Examiners' comments

15/20

Good detail. Well done. A little more language detail needed, but you have tried well with this. Examine this carefully with the examiner's report on this paper.

GLOSSARY

Where a word is followed by q.v. (quod vide) it is listed elsewhere in the glossary.

Accent This is a word which can mean two different things:
- It may refer to the prominence given to a syllable by use of pitch.
- It also refers to the way words are pronounced e.g. with a Welsh accent or a Cornish accent etc.

Be careful not to confuse this term with dialect.

Aeneid An epic poem in Latin by Virgil (P Vergilius Maro, 70–19 BC), recounting the adventures of the legendary Trojan prince Aeneas after his escape from Troy, culminating in his settlement in Italy as the ancestor of the Romans.

Aesthetics The philosophy of taste, the study of the beautiful.
   Aesthetic (adj.), pertaining to the above.

Agnosticism The view that man cannot know anything but the material world; especially that he cannot prove, or disprove, the existence of God.
   An **Agnostic** (n.) professes **Agnostic** (adj.) views.

Alexandrine In English poetry, a line of verse having six (usually iambic) feet, e.g.

> That like a wounded snake drags its slow length along
>
> (Pope)

Alienation effect (Ger. Verfremdungseffekt) An effect in a play intended to remind the spectator that what he is watching is not reality, but an entertainment performed by actors. As used by Bertolt Brecht (1898–1956), it is achieved by satirical songs and comments addressed directly to the audience. As a Communist, Brecht professed a contempt for the bourgeois or romantic theatre's attempt to create an illusion of reality ('the willing suspension of disbelief', as Coleridge says) and was anxious that his audience should not miss the didactic point of his plays. It is of course quite untrue that Brecht 'invented' the **alienation effect**, which older dramatists regularly achieved by the use of choruses, asides, and soliloquies. The expression is perhaps more widely used than understood.

Allegory A greatly extended metaphor, in which events are related in terms of other events, real or fictitious, and frequently at tedious length. Thus, the medieval *Roman de la Rose*, or at least that part of it translated by Chaucer, describes in some 7,700 lines the attempt of a lover to win his lady in terms of getting into a garden and trying to pluck a particular rose.
   Allegorical (adj.)

Alliteration Repetition of the same initial consonant sound; the basis of Old English. and of much medieval English poetry, e.g.

> In a somer sesun, when softe was the sonne…
>
> (Langland, 14th century)

Alliterative (adj.)

Allusion The device of referring to characters and events in mythology, history and literature to evoke a certain atmosphere. The works of Chaucer, Shakespeare and Milton abound with allusions.

For example, this passage from Spenser's *The Faerie Queene* describes the garden of Adonis. It contains many mythological allusions derived from Plato and Aristotle.

> Great enimy to it, and to all the rest
> That in the Gardin of Adonis springs,
> Is wicked Tyme; who with his scythe addrest
> Does mow the flowring herbes and goodly things,
> And all their glory to the ground downe flings,
> Where they do wither, and are fowly mard:
> He flyes about, and with his flaggy winges
> Beates downe both leaves and buds without regard.
> Ne ever pitty may relent his malice hard.
>
> Yet pitty often did the gods relent,
> To see so faire thinges mard and spoiled quight;
> And their great mot her Venus did lament
> The losse of her deare brood, her deare delight;
> Her hart was pierst with pitty at the sight,
> When walking through the Gardin them she saw
> Yet no'te she find redresse for such despight:
> For all that lives is subject to that law:
> All things decay in time, and to their end doe draw.

Ambiguity Having a doubtful or double meaning. The word 'ambiguity' is also used to describe a device of style, especially of poetry, which permits two or more meanings to be kept in mind at the same time.

Ambiguous (adj.)

Ambivalence Having two contrasting values or qualities.

Anachronism A mistake in dating or timing, placing an event in its wrong historical setting, e.g. Shakespeare mentions doublets in Julius Caesar. The Elizabethan playwrights paid little attention to historical accuracy.

Analogy A likeness or comparison of a non-figurative kind, i.e. not based on simile or metaphor.

There is an analogy between our situation and that of the Roman Empire in its last days.

Analagous (adj.)

Analysis An examination of a literary form in detail, involving necessary division of a poem or prose into form, content, meaning, tone, diction, etc. Some people see this as destructive, but it is necessary for the establishment of values and is an important part in the constructive or creative process.

Anapaest In English poetry, a foot consisting of two unstressed syllables, followed by one stressed, e.g.

The Assyrian came down like a wolf on the fold

(Byron)

Anapaestic (adj.)

Anticlimax Arrangement of ideas in descending order of importance or power: a false climax or weak repetition, deliberately used for humorous effect, cf. **bathos**.

Antithesis An arrangement of words to produce an effect of balanced contrast, e.g.

He was neither elated by the prospect of success, nor depressed by the anticipation of failure.

Antithetical (adj.)

Aphorism A concise observation or statement. An aphorism is distinguished from an epigram by being more solemn and less witty.

Apostrophe Breaking a speech or composition to address or appeal to a person, often as part of personification, e.g.

> Thou, Nature, art my goddess! To thy law
> My services are bound.

> (Shakespeare, *King Lear*)

Apron stage Part of a stage projecting into the audience, beyond the line of the proscenium (q.v.).

Aristotelian Pertaining to the Greek philosopher Aristotle (384–322 BC), author of *The Poetics* (q.v.).

Art Originally, skill: hence **Artist**, a skilled artificer, e.g. 'the Tuscan artist', i.e. Galileo (Milton). Any particular skill which gives predominantly aesthetic pleasure (e.g. music, poetry, painting, sculpture. Popularly, painting (cf. **the Sciences**). Other combinations: the **Fine Arts**, the **Liberal** (q.v.) **Arts**.

Art for Art's sake A popular phrase thought to sum up the essence of aestheticism, namely, the view that art needs no justification but itself and is to be judged not, for example, by its moral tendency, but solely by whether it is successful art.

Assonance Correspondence of vowel sound, an essential feature of traditional English rhyming; more generally, correspondence of sound between words and syllables.

Atheism positively asserts that God does not exist.

Attitude A writer's attitude to his subject determines the tone of his writing: e.g. he may be solemn, flippant, indignant or detached.

Augustan (adj.) A word which began to be used in the early part of the 19th century to describe the early years of the 18th – the 'Age of Pope'; based on a fancied analogy between the England of Queen Anne and the Rome of Augustus, both being seen as distinguished by a high level of civilisation.

Ballad A narrative poem, sometimes of folk origin, anonymous, simple and direct with historical, romantic, tragic or supernatural settings.

  Ballad metre A four-line stanza with alternate four-stress and three-stress lines rhyming abcb or abab.

> It fell about the Martinmas,
> When the wind blew shrill and cauld,
> Said Edom o' Gordon to his men,
> 'We maun draw to a hauld'.

Banter (n. and vb.) To make fun of someone in a good-humoured way.

Baroque (adj.) Originally a florid or extravagant style of architecture developed in Catholic countries during the 17th–18th centuries; more generally, irregular, grotesque, odd.

Bathos Descent from the serious to the ludicrous; anticlimax. Sometimes deliberate:

> Not louder shrieks to pitying Heaven are cast
> When husbands, or when lapdogs, breathe their last

> (Pope)

Sometimes unconscious:

> Then Montrose asked the executioner how long his body would be suspended,
> Three hours was the answer, but Montrose was not the least offended.

> (McGonagall)

It is a matter of taste which type is the funnier.
Bathetic (adj.)

Blank verse Unrhymed verse: in English, usually in iambic pentameters.

Bombast Pompous, inflated language.
Bombastic (adj.)

Buffoonery Low jesting, clowning.
Buffoon (n.) a low jester.

Burlesque A composition which makes its target appear ridiculous by the methods of caricature; also vb. and adj. 'Pyramus and Thisbe' in *A Midsummer Night's Dream* is a burlesque of heroic drama.

Caesura In English prosody (q.v.), a pause about the middle of a line of verse.

Caricature A character, generally exaggerated, easily recognisable and never developing. Several of Dickens's and Thackeray's characters are caricatures.

Catastrophe The change producing the final event in a play: generally, the decisive misfortune in a tragedy.

Catharsis See Katharsis.

Chorus In ancient Greek drama, a body of performers who recited or chanted verses commenting on the action; in the modern theatre, any character, whether involved in the action or outside it, who serves as a commentator.

Ciceronian In the style of M. Tullius Cicero (106–43 BC) Roman orator; (adj.) eloquent in a stately fashion employing complex sentences (see **Periodic**).

Circumlocution A roundabout method of expression which may be a defect of style if the result does not justify the use of many words.

Classical This can have two meanings –

(1) The imitation in English of a Latin or Greek idiom. *Paradise Lost* abounds in this style.
(2) Meaning 'of the first class' – writers who lay emphasis on tradition, form and decorum, e.g. Ben Jonson, Milton, Samuel Johnson.

Cliché A trite or over-used phrase: 'at the end of the day', 'all things being equal' are two current examples of clichés.

Climax The 'building up' of a series of propositions, e.g.

> There is tears for his love; joy for his fortune; honour for his valour; and death for his ambition.

> (Shakespeare, *Julius Caesar*)

Generally, the culminating point of an action, especially in a play.

Comedy Originally, in the Greek theatre, referred to plays of an entertaining and satirical kind representing persons and situations in real life. In the 'Old Comedy' of Aristophanes (450–386 BC), the characters were often real personalities of the day like Socrates, represented on the stage in a ludicrous light; in the 'New Comedy' of Menander (340–292 BC), they were humorous stock types. Imitated in Latin by Plautus (254–184 BC) and Terence (190–159 BC), the New Comedy had a strong influence on Renaissance dramatists, e.g. the stock character of the 'miles gloriosus', or boastful but cowardly soldier, gave Shakespeare a hint for Pistol and Falstaff, and Jonson for Bobadill (in *Every Man in his Humour*). In the Middle Ages, just as 'tragedy' could be applied to non-dramatic works, so 'comedy' had a pretty wide application, e.g. the *Divine Comedy* of Dante (1265–1321). This non-specific use continues down to modern times. La Comedie Française, the French National Theatre, performs tragedy and comedy alike; Balzac (1799–1850) gave the resoundingly Dantesque title of *La Comédie Humaine* to his ambitious project of a series of interlocking novels giving a wide picture of contemporary life.

Comedian a writer of comedies, or an actor – usually in comedy, but not exclusively so in Shakespeare's day.

Comedienne an actress in comedies.

Comic (adj.) **Comical** (adj.) has acquired a rather trivial everyday quality, and should be used of life's little oddities. One would hardly speak of 'Jonson's comical invention'.

Conceit A fanciful notion or far-fetched comparison, much in favour in Metaphysical poetry. This example from Donne's *A Valediction Forbidding Mourning* is probably the most famous.

> If they be two, they are two so
> As stiff twin compasses are two;
> Thy soul, the fix'd foot, makes no show
> To move, but doth, if the other do.

Context Placing a passage in its context means saying what precedes and follows it. Normally, all words and phrases have to be studied in their contexts. Often the more general context has to be studied, too.

Couplet A couplet is a pair of lines rhyming together where the sense is self-contained. Pope wrote true or 'closed couplets' otherwise called 'heroic couplets'; as in:

> Hope springs eternal in the human breast;
> Man never is, but always to be blest.

Elizabethan dramatists frequently use the couplet to indicate the end of a scene. Shakespeare uses the rhyming couplet to finish his sonnets.

> So long as men can breathe or eyes can see
> So long lives this, and this gives life to thee.

(Sonnet XVIII)

Courtly love The medieval view of courtly love is seen in Chaucer's poetry especially *Troilus and Criseyde* and *The Knightes Tale*. Courtly love was aristocratic, secretive, and adulterous.

Crisis A decisive turning point, especially in the action of a play.

Criticism The appraisal, particularly of art, either favourably or unfavourably, hence **dramatic criticism, literary criticism**: popularly, hostile comment, fault-finding – perhaps because of the natural tendency of artists to consider all comment on their work as presumptuous, or proceeding from the malice and envy of the uncreative.

Critique (n.) An essay in criticism, a critical examination, usually of a work of literature or philosophy.

Culture Generally, the whole complex of factors producing a distinct way of life; in this sense one can speak of the culture of the Eskimos, or of teenage 'pop' culture; more specifically, the possession of knowledge and taste in artistic and intellectual matters.

Dactyl In English poetry, a foot containing one stressed syllable followed by two unstressed, e.g.

> Half a league, half a league, half a league onward

(Tennyson)

Dark Ages A vague term for the period in European history between the collapse of the Roman Empire in the West (5th century AD) and the emergence of the Frankish Empire of Charlemagne (9th century AD). In Northern Europe the 'darkness' lasted longer; but was not necessarily as total as popularly supposed.

239

Deism Belief in the existence of God, but rejection of the mystical and miraculous elements in, e.g., Christianity. A widespread attitude among 18th-century intellectuals.

Deist (n.); **Deistic** (adj.)

Dénouement (Fr. 'unknotting') The unravelling of the plot of a play or novel at the end.

Deus Ex Machina (Lat. 'a god from a machine') Originally refers to the practice, in some classical plays, of bringing on stage (or letting down upon it) a god in, e.g., a chariot, to bring about the dénoument; hence any unexpected person or event introduced to dispose of an apparently insoluble difficulty, especially at the end of a play. The end of Molière's *La Tartuffe* provides a striking example.

Dialect This refers to a system of grammar and vocabulary particular to a region or social class. Dialect has nothing to do with pronunciation (distinguishing it from accent).

Dialectic Argument intended to elucidate the truth; particularly the examination of contradictions, which leads to a synthesis in which all the elements of truth are brought together – a method notably employed by the German philosopher Hegel (1770–1831).

Dialectical (adj.) **Dialectical Materialism** The method of argument developed by Marxists, which employs Hegelian dialectic in the context of Marxist materialism (q.v.); highly esteemed by Communists as a way of arriving at conclusions known to be acceptable to the Party by methods which the Party has sanctified.

Diction Choice and arrangement of words.

Poetic diction a phrase often used of the artificial style, full of elaborate periphrasis (q.v.) favoured by 18th-century poets, and denounced by Wordsworth, e.g. 'the scaly tribe' for 'fish'.

Didactic (adj.) Teaching, giving instruction, usually of a morally improving kind. Bunyan's *Pilgrim's Progress* is a didactic work.

Discussion play A phrase coined to describe a type of play in which there is little action, but much discussion of issues considered by the dramatist to be important; wrongly supposed to be characteristic of the plays of Henrik Ibsen (1828–1906) and, with more justification, of those of George Bernard Shaw (1856–1950); in both cases presumed, without any truth, to be destructive of genuine dramatic interest.

Dramatic irony A device of style by which a character in a play is made to say something in ignorance of its full or deeper meaning. The audience, and usually the other characters, know more than the speaker and so are able to appreciate the comic or tragic irony of the speaker's situation.

A good example of dramatic irony is in *King Lear* when Lear, having divided his kingdom between his two elder daughters, assumes they will offer hospitality to him and his hundred knights. When Goneril refuses to do this, Lear curses her and says, 'Yet have I left a daughter'. The dramatic irony here is obvious to anyone who knows the play. Regan will be as harsh as Goneril and he has rejected Cordelia, the only daughter who really loves him.

Election (theological) Choice by God of certain individuals for salvation, not because of their merits or good works, but by His own sovereign will: the only evidence of an individual's election being his own conviction that divine **Grace** (q.v.) has been extended to him. Belief in election was widely accepted by Puritans, especially followers of the teaching of the French reformer Jean Calvin (1509–64).

The Elect the whole body of those so chosen.

Elegy A poem of lamentation or mourning, usually for the dead.

Elegiac (adj.) of a grave or melancholy nature, appropriate to an elegy.

Elements The four elements are earth, air, fire, and water, believed from the time of classical Greece down to the 17th century to be the basic constituents of matter.

Ellipsis Omission of words, as in note-taking, or in the conversation of Mr. Jingle in *Pickwick Papers*.

Emotive Can be used to describe language which excites the emotions. **Emotive** poetry tries to move the reader with its use of language.

Empathy This is the power of entering into the experience of or understanding objects or emotions outside ourselves; the power to project oneself into the object of contemplation. In Keats's odes he enters totally the world of his poem. In Coleridge's *The Rime of the Ancient Mariner*, his body beats as one with the sky and the sea:

> I looked upon the rotting sea,
> And drew my eyes away;
> I looked upon the rotting deck,
> And there the dead men lay.
>
> I looked to heaven, and tried to pray;
> But or ever a prayer had gusht,
> A wicked whisper came, and made
> My heart as dry as dust.
>
> I closed my lids, and kept them close,
> And the balls like pulses beat;
> For the sky and the sea, and the sea and the sky
> Lay like a load on my weary eye,
> And the dead were at my feet.

End-stopping Composing verses so that a pause dictated by the sense of the words comes at the end of a line; not necessarily shown by punctuation.

Enjambement (also spelt **Enjambment**) Continuation of the sense from one line of verse to the next without pause; running-on; the opposite of **End-stopping**.

Enlightenment, Age of A phrase used to describe particularly the early and middle years of the 18th century, a period marked by sceptical, rational, scientific and deistic attitudes among intellectuals who wished to be as different as possible from the 'fanatics' or 'enthusiasts' of the previous age; largely inspired in England by the philosophical writings of the third Earl of Shaftesbury, and well represented in e.g. the historian Gibbon; in France, in the work of Voltaire and the Encyclopaedists; in Germany by 'die Aufklärung'.

Epic A long poem recounting in an elevated style the exploits of legendary (usually semi-divine) heroes in remote times (See *Aeneid, Iliad, Odyssey*).

Epic (adj.) of the nature of epic poetry; pop., grand, heroic, on the largest scale.

Epic simile A long simile, worked out in elaborate detail, characteristic of epic poetry.

Epicurean A follower of the philosophical teaching of Epicurus (341–270 BC) who defined 'pleasure' as the supreme good in life; since the only kind of pleasure which most people can conceive of is that of the senses, the word has come to mean someone who lives only for sensual pleasures.

Epicurean (adj.)

> Epicurean cooks
> Sharpen with cloyless sauce his appetite

> (Shakespeare, *Antony and Cleopatra*)

Epigram A brief but pointed statement; in modern usage, implying also the quality of wit, e.g.

> All women become like their mothers; that is their tragedy. No man does; that's his.
>
> (Wilde, *Importance of Being Earnest*)

Epigrammatic (adj.)

Episode A coherent and substantially complete part of a longer narrative; not necessarily corresponding to Act, Scene, or Chapter.

Episodic (adj.) consisting of episodes: often used rather disparagingly to suggest a rambling, badly connected plot.

Epistle A letter (only humorously, in modern English); more particularly, a long discourse, didactic in purpose, addressed to a correspondent in letter form, e.g. the Epistles of St Paul, the *Epistle to Dr Arbuthnot* (Pope).

Epitaph An inscription on a tomb; hence, a composition in memory of the dead (usually short).

Erotic (adj.) Producing sexual excitement.

Eschatology (theol.) The study of the 'four last things: death, judgement, heaven and hell'.

Eschatological (adj.)

Essay A short composition, originally of a tentative or speculative kind (e.g. Bacon's *Essays*) on any topic: today assumed to be in prose, but not in the 18th century, e.g. Pope's *Essay on Man*, *Essay on Criticism*.

Eulogy A composition, written or spoken, in high praise of a person or thing, e.g. Enobarbus' description of Cleopatra's appearance on the River Cydnus in *Antony and Cleopatra*.

Eulogise (vb.)

Euphemism The expression of a distasteful idea in mild language; particularly common in connection with death, e.g. 'The deep damnation of his taking off' (*Macbeth*), 'liquidation' for killing'.

Euphemistic (adj.)

Euphony Melodiousness of sound, especially in words.

Euphuism Affected, over-elaborate style (from *Euphues*, a novel by John Lyly, 1553–1606).

Euphuistic (adj.)

Evocative 'Calling up certain feelings or memories'. Most imaginative poetry arouses evocative feelings.

Exegesis Exposition, explanation; originally of the Scriptures.

Existentialism In its modern, i.e. post-Second World War, sense, the view that one can only assert one's existence, and truly be said to live, by a positive act of will or choice, even if it be absurd in the eyes of others; popular among French writers and intellectuals of the War and post-War generation, e.g. Sartre (to whom the only possible choice presented itself as active engagement in Left-wing politics), Camus, Anouilh.

Existentialist (adj.) (n.)

Exposition With particular reference to novels and plays: the opening, considered as a setting forth of the situation and introduction of characters.

Expressionism A tendency, especially in German literature, which may be seen as beginning as a reaction against **Naturalism** (q.v.): marked by strong emotionalism ('Rausch'), aspirations towards moral and political regeneration, and a certain affinity with **Surrealism** (q.v.) in painting.

Expressionist (adj. and n.)

Fable A short story devised to convey a useful lesson, often employing animals as symbols, e.g. Aesop's and La Fontaine's *Fables*, Orwell's *Animal Farm*.

Fancy The lighter and more playful aspect of **Imagination** (q.v.); especially when expressed through the invention of decorative imagery. Much ink was spilt by Romantic (q.v.) critics in the attempt to define the difference between Fancy and Imagination.

> Let the winged Fancy roam
>
> (Keats)

Farce A work, especially a play, which seeks to provoke laughter by the unsubtle exhibition of ridiculous characters in absurd situations.

Figures of speech Expressions which deviate from the strictly literal or grammatical meaning of words. These figures of speech are not meant to be ornaments; they are the total meaning and inseparable from the poem itself.

Foot A group of syllables having a fixed stress pattern (in English verse), and constituting a unit comparable in some ways with a bar in music. The names traditionally given to feet in English verse are borrowed from the terminology of classical prosody, but it should be remembered that in Greek and Latin prosody the basis is not stress, but quantity, i.e. vowel length.

Free verse Poetical writings with no regular rhyme or rhythm.

Freudian Inspired by the work, in agreement with the ideas of Sigmund Freud (1856–1939), Austrian psychiatrist, whose exploration of the subconscious level of the mind, and particularly of the suppressed sexual motivation of much human behaviour, has had immense influence on 20th-century art and thought.

Genre (n.) In painting, a style depicting common daily life; may be applied to literature which possesses a similar quality. Also means a kind or style of writing.

Georgian Belonging to the 18th century, when all the kings of England were Georges, especially in references to architecture; but also applied to a period and style of English poetry immediately before the First World War (reign of George V).

Gothic In architecture it describes the buildings of the 12th to 15th centuries. In the 18th century the word was used to describe any work of art which appeared fantastic or eerie, as opposed to the classical ideal of orderliness. The 'Gothic novels' were those of Horace Walpole and Ann Radcliffe and were lampooned by Jane Austen in *Northanger Abbey*.

Graces Classical divinities, usually three in number, regarded as the bestowers of beauty and charm, and portrayed as women of exquisite beauty; often associated with the Muses (q.v.).

Grandiloquence Ridiculously elevated language, pomposity of style.

Graphology This is the study of the writing system of a language, e.g. when involved in a stylistic analysis of a newspaper article you might consider such features as stroke direction, size of lettering, spacing, colour and general layout.

Hedonism The belief that pleasure is the chief good (cf. **Epicureanism**).
    Hedonist (n.); **Hedonistic** (adj.)

Hero The chief personage in an epic poem; hence, the principal character in any play, novel, or poem.
    Heroic (adj.) Of the nature of epic.

Heroi-comic(al) (adj.) Having the quality of burlesque epic, ridiculing the epic subject and manner.
    Mock-heroic (q.v.)

Heroic couplet In English poetry, the closed or end-stopped couplet of iambic pentameters; employing a witty, epigrammatic and antithetical style, employed with great success in the later 17th and 18th centuries by, e.g. Dryden, Pope, Johnson; possibly so called because it was thought the most classical and 'correct' English metre. Pope used it for his translation of Homer.

Histrionic (from the Latin word for an actor in farce, *histrio*). Exaggerated, overdone, 'stagey', in the manner of a 'ham' actor.
　Histrionics (n. pl.) a display of overacting, not necessarily on the stage.

Homeric In the manner of Homer (9th century BC), supposed composer of the *Iliad* and *Odyssey* (q.v.).

Homophone A word having the same sound as another word, or words, but differing in meaning, e.g. 'soul', 'sole'; the basis of the kind of word-play known as a **Pun** (q.v.).

Horatian (adj.) In the manner of Horace (Q. Horatius Flaccus, 65–8 BC), marked by moderate epicureanism and good-humoured irony.

Horatian Ode An ode (q.v.) which possesses regularity of form and restraint of feeling, as opposed to the irregular or **Pindaric** (q.v.) ode. The most famous example in English poetry is Marvell's *Horatian Ode upon Cromwell's Return from Ireland*.

Hubris (n.) Pride, arrogance, excessive self-esteem: the quality of a tragic hero which, especially in Greek tragedy, invites divine displeasure.

Humane (adj.) Pertaining to those studies which civilise and refine; traditionally, the classics; hence 'literae humaniores' (Oxford).

Humanism The pursuit of humane studies; more particularly, the culture of the Renaissance scholar, based on 'human' as opposed to 'divine' learning, and giving pre-eminence to Greek and Latin over theology; (mod.) any system of thought which puts 'human' interests first; the 'religion of Humanity'; in schools today, **the humanities** means all vaguely cultural studies.
　Humanist (n.); **Humanistic** (adj.)

Humour Originally, one of the four fluids (**the humours**), phlegm, choler, blood and melancholy, supposed by ancient physicians to be secreted in the body, and to influence character, especially by an excess or deficiency of one in relation to the others; hence **Humorous** (adj.), behaving in the eccentric way attributed to an imbalance of the humours. On the Elizabethan stage, the 'humorous man' was a whimsical or absurd personage:

　The humorous man shall end his part in peace

(Shakespeare, Hamlet)

provoking laughter by his oddities; therefore 'humour' acquires the sense in which it is always used today: the ability to evoke, or to respond to, the comical aspects of human behaviour. Humour is generally distinguished from **Wit** (q.v.) which, in modern usage, has associations with cruel cleverness.

Humours, Comedy of Comedy of the kind particularly, though not exclusively associated with Ben Jonson (q.v.), which depends on the interaction of a group of humorous (in the Elizabethan sense) characters, usually of the most grotesque kind.

Hyperbole Rhetorical exaggeration, e.g.

　I lov'd Ophelia; forty thousand brothers
　Could not with all their quantity of love
　Make up my sum.

(Shakespeare, Hamlet)

　Hyperbolical (adj.)

Iambus In English poetry, a foot consisting of an unstressed followed by a stressed syllable:

> The curfew *tolls* the *knell* of *part*ing *day*
>
> (Grey, *Elegy*)

Iambic (adj.)

Idea (n.) Philosophically, as in **Platonism** (q.v.), an eternally existing pattern, of which the individual things we perceive in this world are imperfect copies; popularly, any concept in the mind.

Ideal (n.) (from idea) A thing conceived as perfect in its kind.

Idealism (n.) One of the many philosophical systems deriving ultimately from Plato, and generally opposed to **Materialism** (q.v.); popularly, aspiration to lofty objectives; in literature or art, the tendency to depict character, objects, and situations, as they should be rather than as they are, represented in, e.g., the character of the Poor Parson in the Prologue to the *Canterbury Tales*; the opposite to **Realism** (q.v.).

Idealist (n.); **Idealistic** (adj.)

Idiom A form of expression in current use. For example, 'He's easily taken in', 'I've run out of sugar'.

Idyll Originally a short poem describing a picturesque scene or incident, usually in rural life; later used to mean little more than 'episode', as in the title *Idylls of the King* (Tennyson), a series of episodes from the legend of King Arthur.

Idyllic (adj.). Generally used today to describe innocent, perfect happiness: perhaps because of the **Pastoral** (q.v.) associations of 'idyll'.

Iliad Epic poem by Homer describing an episode in the siege of Troy (Ilion): the 'wrath of Achilles' and the slaying of the Trojan hero, Hector.

Image In literary usage, a simile or metaphor; generally, any expression tending to create a 'picture in the mind'.

Imagery (n.) The images of a poem or other composition, considered collectively; the use of images.

Imagination (n.) That mental faculty by which we create and shape, particularly in literature; invention.

> ... imagination bodies forth
> the forms of things unknown
>
> (Shakespeare, *Midsummer Night's Dream*)

Generally held, especially by Romantic critics, to be a higher power than **Fancy** (q.v.).

Impressionism The name given to a style of painting which flourished, particularly in France, in the second half of the 19th century. Impressionism seeks to capture the 'feel' of a scene at a particular moment, conveying the effect of light, shape, and colour by bold brush-work, but not attempting to paint accurately observed detail; the term may be figuratively applied to literature, especially poetry, which avoids precise narration or description, and endeavours primarily to suggest atmosphere. There are affinities with **Symbolism** (q.v.).

Improvisation In speaking of drama, the making up of dialogue on the stage (apparently) on the spur of the moment; 'gagging'; particularly associated with the Italian Commedia dell' Arte of the 16th–17th centuries, in which conventional characters (Harlequin, Pantaloon) figured in predictable situations, but also a practice among Elizabethan stage clowns (and, indeed, clowns in all ages).

> Let those that play your clowns speak no more than is set down for them
>
> (Shakespeare, *Hamlet*)

Improvisation is popular also among many modern dramatists.

245

Interlude A late 15th- and 16th-century name for a short stage entertainment of the lighter kind, originally intended to fill a gap between the performance of the parts of a **Morality** or **Mystery** cycle (q.v.).

The International Phonetic Alphabet (IPA) A standard set of phonetic symbols created by the International Phonetic Association for use in practical phonetics.

Intrigue The **Plot** (q.v.) of a play or novel.

Intuition The immediate grasping of the truth, or what one believes to be the truth without the intervention of the reasoning process.
    Intuitional (adj.); **Intuitive** (adj.)

Invective (n.) A violent attack, denunciation; also adj.

Irony A restrained form of sarcasm or ridicule, usually taking the form of exaggerated praise, e.g.

> We were told that at Glenelg, on the seaside, we should come to a house of lime and slate and glass. This image of magnificence raised our expectation.

> (Dr Johnson, *Journey to the Western Islands*)

Jargon A form of technical language used by a small group of people. It often seems to be designed to confuse a lay audience! For example, 'one's view', 'interpersonal' and 'on-going' are used in business.

Johnsonian In the style of Dr Samuel Johnson (1709–84), poet, critic, lexicographer and conversationalist: expressed in a sententious, stately, periodic style; but also, on occasion, blunt and direct:

> Sir, we have done with civility; we are to be as rude as we please.

Jonsonian In the style of Ben(jamin) Jonson (1573–1637), poet and dramatist; particularly with reference to the Comedy of Humours (q.v.).

Juvenalian In the style of Juvenal (D Junius Juvenalis, 60–110 AD) Roman satirical poet: hitter, savage.

Kafkaesque (adj.) Relating to, or in the manner of, Franz Kafka (1883–1924), Czech–German–Jewish novelist. In his most famous novels, *The Trial* and *The Castle*, the protagonist grapples with incomprehensible accusations and obstacles, which he is never able to clear up, in a labyrinth of bureaucratic procedure; hence, generally, nightmarish.

Katharsis (Gk. n.) Purgation. Used by Aristotle in the *Poetics* (q.v.) to describe the purpose and effect of tragedy as 'through pity and fear effecting the proper purgation (katharsis) of these emotions.' It is not clear whether he thought that tragedy, by arousing pity and fear at the downfall of the tragic hero, purged the spectator of these ignoble emotions, or that it purged or purified those emotions of their baser elements. Often spelt **Catharsis** in English.
    K(C)athartic (adj.)

Laconic (adj.) Sparing of words, brief and pithy, as the ancient Spartans were reputed to be. (Laconia – name of the district of which Sparta was the principal city.)

Leitmotiv (Ger. n.) A musical theme associated with a character, especially in Wagnerian opera, which is introduced at appropriate moments, e.g., when the character appears on the stage; may be applied to an important idea which recurs frequently in a writer's work, e.g. the influence of heredity in Ibsen or in Zola.

Lexicographer (n.)

> A maker of dictionaries: a harmless drudge.

> (Dr Johnson)

Lexis The vocabulary of a language – a stock of words, usually listed in a dictionary.

Liberal (adj.) Originally, pertaining to those skills and studies considered worthy of a 'free' man, as opposed to those considered 'servile' or mechanical: a concept of immense influence, especially in education, from Renaissance times onward, the 'free' man being generally equated with the gentleman; hence such expressions as 'the liberal arts', a 'liberal education'; today generally taken to refer to the pursuit of general intellectual culture, not narrowly professional or technical.

Litotes (n.) Device of expressing something by the negative of its opposite: 'She is no shirker' (= 'She is a hard worker').

Lyric (n.) Originally, verses intended to be sung or chanted to the accompaniment of the lyre; song. Now generally applied to that kind of poetry which is felt to have the closest affinity to song; a short poem giving direct expression to personal feeling, creating an effect of spontaneity (though the poet has probably sweated blood over it), and employing great variety of metre and rhyme-pattern. It would be fair to say that most contemporary poetry is **Lyrical** (adj.), and that, when people think of 'poetry' (if they ever do) they have lyrical poetry in mind. The 'lyric' of a song means its words.

Machiavellianism The combination of craft and ruthlessness attributed to Niccolo Machiavelli (1469–1527), Italian statesman and writer on political subjects. His handbook for rulers, *The Prince*, was studied attentively throughout Renaissance Europe, though often publicly deplored.

> Though some speak openly against my books.
> Yet will they read me, and thereby attain
> To Peter's chair.
>
> (Marlowe, *The Jew of Malta*)

Popularly, 'Machiavel' was associated with 'Old Nick', The Devil.
Machiavellian (adj.)

Malapropism A verbal muddle, which takes its name from Mrs Malaprop, a character in *The Rivals*, a comedy by Richard Brinsley Sheridan (1751–1816). The lady may be allowed to explain herself:

> Sure, if I reprehend any thing in this world it is the use of my oracular tongue,
> and a nice derangement of epitaphs.

Mannerism (n.) Excessive addiction to a particular style in art or in literature.
Mannered (adj.), affected; **Mannerist** (n.)

Manners With reference to epic or dramatic poetry, distinctive varieties of disposition, as revealed in behaviour.

Manners, Comedy of Term used to describe a kind of comedy which represents in a ridiculous light the speech, customs, and affectations of fashionable people; best represented in English literature by so-called **Restoration** (q.v.) comedy, and by the later plays of Sheridan (q.v.).

Masochism (n.) Sexual pleasure derived through submission to physical maltreatment; the word derives from Sacher Masock, 19th-century Austrian novelist, who exploits this taste in his work.
Masochist (n.); **Masochistic** (adj.)

Materialism Philosophically, the doctrine that nothing exists except matter, and that man, in all his aspects, is merely a form or function of matter; more generally, devotion to material interests; the opposite to **Idealism** (q.v.).
Materialist (n.); **Materialistic** (adj.)

Medieval Belonging to the Middle Ages, a somewhat vague term for that period of time between the **Dark Ages** (q.v.) and the **Renaissance** (q.v.); approximately from the 10th–15th centuries.

Meiosis (Gk.n.) Understatement; a special kind of **irony** (q.v.) in which understatement, often negative, is employed for emphasis, e.g. Queen Victoria's celebrated 'We are not amused'; sometimes no irony is intended, and the intention is solely to add emphasis, e.g.

> Not seldom from the uproar I retired

> (Wordsworth)

Melancholy (n.) 'Black bile', one of the four Humours (q.v.): the lowness of depression of spirits (sometimes called melancholia) it was supposed to produce when secreted to excess. The most prestigeful of all the humours: in Elizabethan days supposed to be a distinctive mark of the superior or intellectual man:

> I'll be more proud, and melancholy and gentlemanlike than I have been.

> (Jonson, *Every Man in his Humour*)

The subject of a vast, rambling work of enormous erudition by Robert Burton (1577–1640), *The Anatomy of Melancholy*; supposed by other European nations in the 18th century and particularly in its most eccentric and suicidal forms, to be peculiarly the *English Malady*.

Melancholy (adj.); **Melancholiac** (n.) a person afflicted with melancholy (also adj.); **Melancholic** (adj.)

Melodrama Originally a play with songs and music, evidently devised to gratify popular taste; hence a play aiming to appeal to simple popular audiences, marked by exciting incident, strong but uncomplicated feeling. Melodrama has characters easily recognisable as 'good' and 'bad' characters and a happy ending; often spoken of rather condescendingly as the staple entertainment of the Victorian working class theatre, but dominates popular TV drama today.

Melodramatic (adj.)

Metaphor A kind of image in which the qualities of one object are suggested by direct association with another, e.g. 'a *tide* of woes'. It is often helpful to consider a metaphor as a compressed **simile** (q.v.), and to explain it by converting it into a simile, e.g. (to take the example given) 'woes as overwhelming and irresistible as an incoming tide, or a tidal wave'.

Metaphorical (adj.)

Metaphysics Originally, the world of Aristotle 'after the Physics'; hence, rather freely, the study of what is beyond the physical, material, or natural.

Metaphysical (adj.) pertaining to the immaterial or **transcendental** (q.v.); hence, popularly, far-fetched, strange. It was in this sense that Dr Johnson, in his *Life of Cowley*, bestowed on the early 17th-century English poets the name of the **Metaphysical Poets**, alluding to their fondness for strained or novel images, or **Conceits** (q.v.). The word is often used to suggest cloudy impractical speculation, e.g.

> the central opacity of Kantian metaphysics

> (Peacock)

> Ah, that is clearly a metaphysical speculation, and like most metaphysical speculations has little reference to the facts of real life as we know them
> (Wilde, *The Importance of Being Earnest*)

Metre Poetic rhythm divisible into regular feet.

Metrical (adj.)

Millenium (n.) The period of a thousand years during which, according to the *Book of Revelations*, Christ is to reign on earth; hence, a period of perfect happiness.

Miltonic (adj.) In the manner of John Milton (1608–74), author of *Paradise Lost*: grand, sublime, epic, in subject and style.

Mimetic (adj.) Of, or addicted to, imitation.

Miracle Play A type of religious drama which flourished in the later Middle Ages; originally written by clerks to present stories from the Scriptures in popular dramatic form, then collected into 'cycles' and presented on movable stages by the trade guilds during religious holidays.

Mock-heroic (adj.) Same as **Heroi-comical** (q.v.).

Morality Play A late development of the **Miracle** or **Mystery Play** (q.v.) in which the scriptural story is replaced by an allegory in which the characters are personified virtues and vices. The most famous of these plays is *Everyman*.

Morphology This is the branch of grammar which looks specifically at the structure of words.

Muses The nine goddesses attendant on Apollo, and thought of as the patronesses of the arts and sciences recognised by the Greeks. From Renaissance times down to the end of the 18th century it was customary for a poet to describe his inspiration as 'the/his Muse'; this is sometimes done today, facetiously.

> With Donne, whose Muse on dromedary trots
>
> (Coleridge)

Mystery Play As **Miracle Play** above. The derivation from 'mister', a skilled trade ('In youthe he lerned hadde a good myster' Chaucer), is not generally supported.

Mysticism The belief that man can attain direct communion with God in an ecstatic state usually induced by solitude, fasting, and prayer; hence, any attitude, experience, or belief which is claimed to be spiritually uplifting but is beyond rational explanation or comprehension.
   Mystic (n. and adj.); **Mystical** (adj.) (The words derive ultimately from the Greek for 'a person initiated into the Mysteries', secret rites performed in honour of a variety of gods.)

Myth (n.) A traditional story expressing the religious beliefs of a people, relating its supposed origins, or offering a supernatural explanation of natural phenomena. The figures of myth are presented as gods, demi-gods, and heroes, and are frequently referred to in the epic poetry of the people concerned; popularly, a story with no foundation in fact.
   Mythical (adj.)

Mythology A body or collection of myths; more rarely, the study of myth.
   Mythological (adj.)

Nature Originally, that which is in the normal course of things. The word, and its associated adjectives, **natural** and **unnatural**, has been used in a bewildering variety of meanings, according to period and context, e.g.

1 the nature or essential property of things;

2 the 'natural' order, with its hierarchical system of beings, thought by Medieval and later theologians to be divinely established – the Great Chain of Being;

3 normal human nature, life as it is –

> o'erstep not the modesty of nature
>
> (Shakespeare, *Hamlet*)

> First follow Nature
>
> (Pope)

4 the physical universe –

> Nature and Nature's laws lay hid in night
>
> (Pope)

5 especially to the Romantic poets, the natural world unmodified by man, its appearance and forms of life, thought of as inherently beautiful and ennobling –

> Nature then...to me was all in all

(Wordsworth)

6 the preceding meaning personified, again by Romantics –

> Let Nature be your teacher. She has a world of ready wealth.

(Wordsworth)

Naturalism In literature, a development in the later 19th century of the **Realism** of the mid-century. Purporting to represent nature as in **(3)** above, it carried to an extreme the idea of the novel as a kind of documentary study, particularly of the more squalid and miserable aspects of life, and was much influenced by the idea that individuals are merely the product of heredity and environment, and cannot choose their way of life; the most celebrated **naturalist** writer is Emile Zola (1840–1902).
Naturalistic (adj.)

Negative Capability Defined by Keats as a kind of receptive state of mind where

> a man is capable of being in uncertainties, mysteries, doubts, without any irritable reaching after fact and reason.

Nemesis Nemesis was the Greek goddess of vengeance or retribution. In literature the word means the principle of tragic poetic justice where evil brings its own punishment. Such happenings are seen in *Macbeth*.

Neo Prefix derived from the Greek for 'new': frequently used to describe a revival of something earlier, e.g. *neoclassicism*, to describe the culture and particularly the critical standards of the later 17th and early 18th centuries.

Neologism A newly coined word.

Nostalgia Home-sickness, longing for another place: sometimes extended in modern usage to a longing for another time.
Nostalgic (adj.)

Novel A prose fiction of substantial length, purporting to represent real contemporary life, which supplanted the fanciful **Romance** (q.v.) at the beginning of the 18th century. In English literature, Daniel Defoe (1659–1731) is often regarded as 'the father of the novel', though there are Elizabethan prototypes. Many critics associate the rapid growth of the novel with the increasing importance of the middle classes throughout the 18th and 19th centuries. In the last hundred years the novel has become the most widely employed literary form, has shown an increasing responsiveness to general intellectual and artistic movements, is widely used as a vehicle for all kinds of propaganda, and has accommodated every kind of experiment and eccentricity. One can hardly imagine what a novelist of an earlier age would make of, for example, a **Surrealist** (q .v.) novel like *Ulysses* (James Joyce, 1882–1941).

Number Old word for **metre** (q.v); in pl., verse, lines of verse:

> I lisp'd in numbers, for the numbers came

(Pope)

Objective (adj.) Treating a topic impartially, seeing it as it is, excluding one's own personal views and feelings – all of which is hardly possible in literature, and not always in the interpretation of what passes for scientific fact.
Objectivity (n.); Antonym, **Subjectivity** (q.v.)

Ode A lyrical poem of some length, in a dignified and serious style, often addressed to a person, or personification, or expressing a sustained meditation, e.g. *Ode on Intimations of Immortality* (Wordsworth). **Horatian** and **Pindaric odes** (q.v.). **Choric odes**: The verses assigned to the Chorus in a Greek play.

Odyssey Epic attributed to Homer, recounting the ten years' wanderings and adventures of the hero Odysseus, or Ulysses, on his return from the Trojan War.

Oedipus (literally, swollen-foot) Mythological king of Thebes, who read the riddle of the Sphinx, and, in ignorance, killed his father and married his mother; he blinded himself when his unwitting enormities came to light. The hero of probably the most celebrated Greek tragedy, the *Oedipus Rex* of Sophocles (497–105BC).

Omniscient narrator All-knowing narrator.

Onomatopoeia The invention or use of words whose sound suggests the meaning, e.g.

    The murmur of innumerable bees   (Tennyson)

    Onomatopoeic (adj.) Words like 'crash' and 'bang' are onomatopoeic.

Ottava Rima (Ital.) An eight-line stanza, consisting (in English poetry) of iambic pentameters rhyming abababcc; considered suitable for long narrative poems, and used with admirable dexterity by Byron (1788–1824) in *Don Juan*.

Ovidian In the manner of Ovid (P. Ovidius Naso, 43 BC–17 AD): ingenious, graceful, amatory – with reference to his *Art of Love*.

Oxymoron A figure of speech in which words of opposite meaning are joined together, e.g.

    A damned saint, an honourable villain   (Shakespeare, *Romeo and Juliet*)

Palladian (adj.) Relating to, or in the style of Andrea Palladio (1518–80), Italian architect, who may be said to have initiated the neoclassical tendency in architecture by his revival of the Roman style.

Panegyric (n.) A public speech, or composition, in high praise of some person or achievement; a eulogy or encomium.

Pantheism The belief that God is everything, and everything is God; that God and the universe are one: a view that accords well with the Romantic attitude to nature, and may be found in much of Wordsworth's early poetry, e.g., in the lines beginning

           And I have felt
      A presence that disturbs me with the joy
         Of elevated thoughts.   (*Tintern Abbey*)

    Pantheist (n.); **Pantheistic** (adj.)

Pantheon A temple dedicated to all the gods; the whole body of the gods, considered collectively.

Parable An allegory (q.v.) taking the form of a narrative which seeks to convey a moral or religious truth.

Paradox A statement contrary to popular opinion, apparently absurd or self-contradictory, but often containing a great deal of truth, e.g.

    It is always painful to part from people whom one has known for a very brief space of time. The absence of old friends one can endure with equanimity.
                (Wilde, *The Importance of Being Earnest*)

Paralinguistics The study of properties of communication (in support of meaning) such as tones of voice. Paralinguistics is not to be confused with Kinesics, which is the study of facial expression and physical gesture to communicate meaning.

Paraphrase To paraphrase a piece of poetry or part of a Shakespeare play means to render it into simple, modern English prose. Some people may feel that this destroys the whole appeal of poetry, but it may be of great practical value for two reasons:

1 It enables the meaning which exists in most poetry to be isolated and studied.

2 The difference between the paraphrase and the original will show the beauty of the poetry of the original lines.

Pararhyme Near-rhyme: the placing in the rhyming position, at the end of lines, words whose consonants are the same, or similar, but whose vowels are different: a device particularly associated with the poetry of Wilfred Owen (1893–1918):

> Wearied we keep awake because the night is silent:
> Low, drooping flares confuse our memory of the salient.

> (*Exposure*)

Parenthesis An explanatory or qualifying word, or group of words, inserted into a passage with which it has no grammatical connection, and enclosed between dashes or brackets.

Parentheses (pl.) The bracket signs; **Parenthetic(al)** (adj.)

Parody A composition which mimics the characteristic features of a writer's style and thought, in order to expose him to ridicule.

Pastoral (n.) A poem or other work which represents the life of shepherds, usually in an idealised light; extended to any work dealing with country life. Originally, i.e. in the period of the *Renaissance*, based on classical models, e.g. Spenser's *Shepheardes Calendar*, it became so much used as a ready-made form for trifling compositions, often allegorical, as to weary even those of strongly classical tastes; hence Dr Johnson's comment on Milton's pastoral elegy, *Lycidas*: 'its form is that of a pastoral; easy, vulgar, and therefore disgusting; whatever images it can supply are long ago exhausted', (*Life of Milton*).

Pastoral (adj.)

Pathetic Fallacy A phrase invented by John Ruskin (1819–1900) to describe the tendency to credit nature with human feelings.

> All violent feelings…produce in us a falseness in all our impressions of external things, which I would generally characterise as the Pathetic Fallacy

> (Ruskin, *Modern Painters*)

It is, of course, a leading feature of the Romantic poets, e.g. Wordsworth, with whom Ruskin was by no means out of sympathy.

Pathos (Gk. n.) Suffering feeling; hence that quality in a work of art which arouses pity and sadness; in earlier times was often used to describe one of the qualities of tragedy, but has been a good deal debased in modern usage, as may be seen particularly with **pathetic** (adj.) which now usually means, in popular speech, miserable, wretched, contemptible.

Pedant (n.) In Elizabethan English, a school master or tutor:

> like a pedant that keeps a school i'the church

> (Shakespeare, *Twelfth Night*)

but often, even in this period, with a pejorative suggestion of heavy learning unseasonably paraded, a quality never lacking in schoolteachers, least of all in Shakespeare's day.

Pedantic (adj.) **Pedantry** (n.) All these words are today wholly **pejorative** (q.v.).

Pejorative (adj.) (from Lat. 'peior', worse) Tending to the worse, conveying disapproval, disparaging.

Pentameter A line of verse having five feet.

Period (n.) The full stop at the end of a sentence. In **Rhetoric** (q.v.) a complete sentence, especially an elaborate one made up of many clauses. **Periodic** (adj.) used particularly to describe an ornate, stately style employing sentences of this kind, as in the historian Edmund Gibbon (1737–94), author of *The Decline and Fall of the Roman Empire*: a subject which evidently requires a majestic style.

Peripeteia (Gk. n.) A sudden change of fortune, as often in tragedy; a reversal of situation, e.g. the change in the relationship between Higgins and Eliza at the end of Bernard Shaw's *Pygmalion*.

Periphrasis (Gk. n.) Round-about expression, verbosity, circumlocution. Sometimes **periphrase** in English: (to be distinguished from **paraphrase**, (n.) expression of meaning in other words than those of the original).

Peroration (n.) The conclusion of a speech, in which the speaker usually 'gives it all he's got'.
    To **perorate** (vb.) To declaim, speak vehemently.

Persona (n.) From the Latin for a mask of the kind used by actors in the Greek and Roman theatre; hence, the outward presentation of one's character, one's 'image', as contemporary jargon has it, in life, or as a character in a play: which need not be the same as one's 'real' personality.

Personification (n.) A kind of metaphor in which an inanimate thing or an abstract idea is treated as something living, usually a human being; a favourite device of 18th- century poetry:

> Let not Ambition mock their useful toil
>
> (Gray, *Elegy in a Country Churchyard*)

Philistine (Ger.) 'Philister', a term used derisively by German students in the 19th century of persons not members of their, or any, university; possibly by allusion to the words, 'The Philistines be upon thee, Samson' (Judges, XVI), used in altercations between students and townspeople. Hence, anyone lacking **Liberal** (q.v.) culture, devoted to **material** (q.v.) interests; much used by, e.g., Matthew Arnold (1822–88), poet and critic, in deploring the **philistinism** (n.) of the British middle class.

Philosophy (n.) Literally, 'the love of wisdom'; the medieval university recognised three branches, constituting a field for advanced study leading to a Doctor's degree (hence PhD): (1) Natural, (2) Moral, and (3) Metaphysical Philosophy. (1) has become what we call 'science', (2) ethics, and (3) 'philosophy' in its accepted academic meaning, i.e. the study of 'the meaning of things', ultimate reality, first causes and principles. In Shakespeare's day, it sometimes meant knowledge acquired by the use of natural reason, as opposed to faith or revealed truth, which is why Hamlet tells Horatio:

> There are more things in heaven and earth, Horatio,
> Than are dreamt of in your philosophy

In the 18th century the word often implied **scepticism** (q.v.) in religious matters, especially in France. Today, popularly, the word is used to mean no more than a general attitude to life: 'my philosophy as a greengrocer…'. Since philosophers were supposed to rise above the petty concerns of other men, **philosophical** (adj.) and **philosophically** (adv.) have acquired a strong suggestion of resignation or **stoicism** (q.v.) in the face of misfortune.

Phonology The study of the sound systems of a language (see the section on phonetics in Chapter 4).

Picaresque (adj.) From Sp. 'picaro', a rogue; used to describe the type of novel which chronicles the adventures of a wandering rogue; popular in England, especially in the 18th century. Many of the best-known novels of this period fall into this category; the hero need not always be a rogue himself, but certain features are common to all: an episodic plot, full of complications, much diversity of scene and many characters, some of whom reappear at intervals, and plenty of lively pictures of low life. Example: any novel of Defoe's, Fielding's *Tom Jones*, Smollett's *Roderick Random*.

Pindaric (n.) An **ode** (q.v.) in the manner of Pindar (521–141 BC) Greek poet. The features of the English Pindaric, associated particularly with Abraham Cowley (1618–67), are a complex and irregular stanza, high-flown language, and a straining after intense and exalted feeling.

Plagiarise (vb.) To steal another writer's words and ideas and pass them off as one's own. **Plagiarism** (n.); **Plagiarised** (adj.); **Plagiarist** (n.); **Plagiary** (n.) hence the name of the character in Sheridan's *The Critic*, Sir Fretful Plagiary.

Platitude (n.) Flatness, commonplaceness in speech or writing; an expression having these qualities (cf. **cliché**).

Plato Greek philospher (429–347 BC), disciple of Socrates, whose views he purported to represent in his *Dialogues*.
   Platonism (n.) the philosophy of Plato, especially in its exposition of **idealism** (q.v.);   **Platonist** (n.i.)

Platonic Pertaining to the above; particularly with reference to purely spiritual love between the sexes, a meaning acquired in the 17th century: though originally 'amor platonicus' denoted male homosexuality.

Plot (n.) The plan of a play, novel or other work of fiction: its narrative framework, (cf. **intrigue**).

Poetaster (n.) A minor, or bad poet: a pretender to poetry. The name of a comedy by Ben Jonson ridiculing rival dramatists.

Poetic (adj.) In modern usage, extended to any prose which has the qualities of feeling, imagination, and language expected in poetry: also **Poetical** e.g. 'The most poetical account of a game of cricket I have ever read in a newspaper'.

Poetic licence The 'right' of poets to distort language, historical and geographical truths for the sake of their art. Shakespeare, for instance, invents coastlines for countries which are landlocked in *The Winter's Tale*.

Poetics, The Title of an incomplete treatise by Aristotle (q.v.), of immense influence on both criticism and the writing of plays: the part that survives deals principally with Tragedy and Epic. See also **Unities**.

Polymath (n.) One who knows many things: sometimes suggested to have been the ideal and highest type of **Renaissance** (q.v.) culture, e.g. Leonardo da Vinci.

Predestination The doctrine that God, being omniscient, has foreseen, and therefore ordained the fate of every human soul before birth; opposed by the view that God has given man Free Will to determine his salvation or damnation by his own acts.

Predestinarian (adj.) Theology is particularly associated with the teaching of Calvin, but has provided a meaty bone of contention in all ages.

> But I ne kan nat bulte it to the bren,
> As kan the hooly doctour Augustyn
> Boece, or the bisshope Bradwardyn.
> Whether that Goddes worthy forwityng
> Streyneth me nedely to doon a thyng...
>
> (Chaucer, *Nonne Preestes Tale*)

Pre-Raphaelite (n.) A member of the 'Pre-Raphaelite Brotherhood', a group of Mid-Victorian British poets and painters (Rossetti, Millais, Morris, Burne-Jones and others) who professed a great devotion to their concept of the Middle Ages, as opposed to the **Philistinism** of contemporary life. The name expressed the desire of the painters to go back to the supposedly pure, austere, and pious art of the period before Raphael of Urbino (1483–1520); they were therefore also rejecting **Renaissance** art.
Pre-Raphaelite (adj.); **Pre-Raphaelitism**.

Prolixity Unnecessarily long and tedious expression.

Proscenium (n.) In the modern theatre, the space between the main curtain and the orchestra, or front stalls; more generally, the line dividing the stage from the audience in a 'picture-frame' stage, marked, until the development of subtler forms of stage lighting, by footlights.

Prose (n.) Non-metrical (though not necessarily unrhythmical) language; is not verse.

Prosody The study or analysis of metre.

Protagonist (n.) The chief personage in a drama, or other work of fiction; the hero or heroine: should be used as far as possible in the singular only, though pl. is permissible where there is more than one character of the first importance.

Psychoanalysis (n.) The analysis of the mind; the approach to the psychiatric treatment of mentally disturbed patients by the analysis of dreams and suppressed memories, practised notably by **Freud** (q.v.).

Psychology The study of the mind; popularly the understanding of human nature.

Pun A joke or piece of word-play arising from a **Homophone** (q.v.):

> Not on thy sole, but on thy soul, harsh Jew,
> Thou makest thy knife Keen.

> (Shakespeare, *The Merchant of Venice*)

Puritan (n.) A reformed Protestant who wished to 'purge' or 'purify' the church of all unscriptural doctrine and Romish ritual; generally associated in the 16th and 17th centuries with Calvinist theology (see **Grace**, **Election**), sobriety of dress and speech, and disapproval of merry-making, whether in private or in public, as at the theatre; and equally generally suspected of hypocrisy. One of the most rumbustious satires on Puritanism is the character of Zeal-of-the-Land Busy in Jonson's *Bartholomew Fair*; anyone of ostentatiously austere life.
    Puritan (adj.); **Puritanical** (adj.); **Puritanism** (n.)

Quasi- (Lat. 'as if') A prefix signifying 'near', 'akin to', e.g. 'quasi-Romantic'.

Quatrain (n.) A stanza of four lines.

Quibble (n.) A jest involving some verbal hair-splitting, popular in Elizabethan drama, e.g.

> *First Clown*: There is no ancient gentleman but gardeners, ditchers, and grave-makers;
>   they hold up Adam's profession.
> *Sec. Clown*: Was he a gentleman?
> *First Clown*: A' was the first that ever bore arms.

> (Shakespeare, *Hamlet*)

Raillery (n.) Good-humoured mockery, **banter** (q.v.).

Rationalism The belief that reason is man's chief or only guide, especially in what concerns religion or the supernatural; the explanation of all questions by the application of reason; (philosophically) the view that reason, rather than sense, is the foundation of knowledge.
    Rational (adj.); **Rationalist** (n.); **Rationality** (n.) the state of being reasonable.
    To Rationalise (vb.) and **Rationalisation** (n.), connected with the idea of explaining by reason, or bringing into a 'reasonable' state by e.g. closing down redundant or profitless parts of a business, are often used today with a somewhat

pejorative flavour, suggesting the finding of plausible but specious explanations for unwelcome facts.

Realism Philosophically, any system of thought opposed to idealism; generally, the acceptance or representation of 'things as they are'; in literature, a tendency among mid-19th century novelists (especially in France) to give a scrupulous representation of life in all its aspects and to depict human nature as it really is, 'warts and all'; in some ways a reaction against **Romanticism** (q.v.) and a return to the attitude of 18th- century novelists. *Madame Bovary* (Gustave Flaubert, 1821–80) is often cited, not altogether fairly, as the great Realist novel, and the precursor of the kind of **Naturalism** (q.v.) associated with **Zola** (q.v.). Naturalism may be considered as a development of Realism.

Reason, Age of A descriptive phrase used of the early and middle years of the 18th century, when **Sceptical Rationalism** (q.v.) was much in favour with intellectuals, and 'rational' was a word of high commendation. Even Christianity was defended as a rational system of belief by its apologists.

Refrain Recurring phrase or line, especially at the end of a stanza. Many ballads have refrains at the end of each verse.

Regency (n. and adj.) Referring to the period at the beginning of the 19th century when, because of the madness of George III, his eldest son, later George IV, was head of state, with the title of Prince Regent; a period approximately that of the Napoleonic War and the years immediately after, and ending, technically, in 1820, with the death of George III; generally associated with frivolous and dissipated style of life among the upper classes, it was the age of Byron and 'Beau' Brummell – and also of Jane Austen; a 'Regency buck' – a man of fashion of the time, generally presented, especially by romantic lady novelists, as dashing, fascinating; also applied to styles of decoration, etc., of the time. In the history of French civilisation, 'Regency' usually refers to the period (1715–23) during which the Duke of Orleans was Regent for the young Louis XV; also associated with dissipation in high life. Regencies seem to go in for this.

Renaissance (Sometimes, though not often today, **Renascence**) Literally, 'rebirth'. The name given to what must still be reckoned the greatest movement in history of European art and culture. It began in Italy towards the end of the 14th century, with a turning away from medieval art and thought, and a rebirth of interest in the art and literature of the classical civilisations. New styles of painting, architecture, and sculpture, the revived study of Greek, and a new approach to Latin, all flourished under the patronage of wealthy Italian princes and Popes. A considerable impetus was given to the movement by the fall of Constantinople to the Turks in 1453, and the consequent flight to Italy of Byzantine scholars and Greek manuscripts. The wars of the French in Italy (1494–1525) did much to accelerate the spread of Renaissance culture into France (Leonardo spent his last years in Amboise), but it did not attain its full development in England until the reign of Elizabeth. The Renaissance man, at his most fully developed, is thought of as many-sided, with a highly cultivated mind and love of art, a delight in luxury and sensual pleasure, and often a ruthless ambition and cruelty.

Repartee (n.) A smart, clever retort; especially in plays, dialogue marked by this quality, e.g.

> *Algernon*: Come, old boy, you had much better have the thing out at once.
> *Jack*: My dear Algy, you talk exactly as if you were a dentist. It is very vulgar to talk   like a dentist when one isn't a dentist. It produces a false impression.
> *Algernon*: Well, that is exactly what dentists always do.

> (Wilde, *The Importance of Being Earnest*)

Restoration (n. and adj.) In English, referring to the period beginning with the Restoration of the Monarchy in 1660, and extended, especially in such expressions as **Restoration Drama** or **Restoration Comedy**, to the end of the 17th century, and even later: it being felt that the literature of this whole extended period is essentially of the same kind.

Rhapsody (n.) Earlier, a miscellany: today, a composition, in literature or in music, extravagant or enthusiastic in feeling, but deficient in form or control: the kind of composition in which the artist gives free rein to 'the spontaneous overflow of powerful feelings'.

Rhetoric In the medieval university, the formal study of the art of speech-making, as defined in rules and typical examples of figures of speech derived from ancient authorities like Quintilian (M. Fabius Quintilianus, 35–95 AD): a basic study, one of the lower division, or 'Trivium' (hence 'trivial') of the seven liberal arts – the other two being grammar and logic. In modern usage, the art of speech-making in general, or just eloquent public speaking; but often used pejoratively, to suggest empty noise, a flow of bombastic language – 'mere rhetoric'; similarly **Rhetorical** (adj.); **Rhetorician**.

Rococo (n. and adj.) The style of, particularly French, furniture, architecture, interior decoration, in the age of Louis XIV and XV, marked by much elaborate scroll-like decoration; generally, tastelessly florid and ornate.

Roman à clef Novel in which characters are real people, disguised.

Romance (Languages) Originally, 'romanz' (O. Fr.) was the name of the vernacular tongue of Roman Gaul, as opposed to the language of the Germanic invaders; hence, generally, the name of the whole group of European languages descended from Latin – French, Italian, Spanish, etc.

Romance (n.) In literature, a medieval verse tale of the kind written in a Romance language, recounting the adventures of a knightly hero, and expressing the ideals of the age of chivalry; or a later prose tale, often of great length, and containing something of the same spirit. 'Twelve vast French romances, neatly gilt', writes Pope, presumably referring to a work like *Le Grand Cyrus* by Mlle. de Scudery (1607–1701): destined to be supplanted as entertainment by the more realistic novel. Today, a 'romance' is usually a popular sentimental love story (*True Life Romances*), the love-affair, itself, or just a tall story – a sad comedown in the world.

Romanticism The name given to the attitudes which, building up throughout the second half of the 18th century, dominated the early years of the 19th century in every aspect of life and art. Essentially it involved a turning-away from the sceptical, rational, classically-moulded culture of the 18th century, in an effort to liberate the creative imagination. The Romantic artist was no longer a craftsman, mindful of form and precedent: he saw himself as a lonely dedicated figure, often wrung by self-torture and a sense of failure, who expressed his imagination in whatever way he pleased, and felt himself charged with a prophetic mission – 'one of the unacknowledged legislators of the world', as Shelley put it. Romanticism exploited all that was felt to be mysterious, remote, or terrifying – the medieval, the supernatural, the unexplored: it cherished dreams of social regeneration which coloured the political revolutions of the age, and, perhaps most important of all, at least in England, it established an attitude to nature discussed under **Nature** (5) and (6) which still influences us today.

Romantic (n.): **Romantic** (adj.) at the beginning of the 18th century, was virtually synonymous with 'absurd', but in the course of a century transformed its meaning first into 'picturesque' and finally into 'grand', e.g.

> But oh! that deep romantic chasm which slanted
> Down the green hill athwart a cedarn cover!

(Coleridge, *Kubla Khan*)

Sadism (n.) Sexual pleasure derived through the infliction of physical suffering on others, as described in the novels of the Marquis de Sade (1740–1814) celebrated French madman and (unless one shares his tastes) minor writer.

Sadist (n.): **Sadistic** (adj.)

Saga A medieval prose narrative or chronicle written in Norway or Iceland. The word is often used today as if it had some suggestion of 'epic' or heroic'; but, although the events related in thc original sagas are often the stuff of epic (like the discovery of North America from Greenland!), their style is remarkably plain and factual.

Satire (n.) The exposure in a ridiculous light of human vice and folly, professedly to 'chasten morals with ridicule': any work, in whatever form, which attempts this.

Scepticism Philosophically, the view that real knowledge, or truth, is unattainable. Generally, a doubting or disbelieving attitude, especially towards religion.

Scholasticism A general name for the theology and philosophy of the medieval university – based on the writings of the Fathers of the Church and the works of Aristotle in Latin translation.

Science Originally, knowledge in general, e.g. 'Fair Science frown'd not on his humble birth' (Gray, *Elegy*): the modern meaning was usually expressed by **Natural Science** (cf. **Natural Philosophy**, q.v.) but in the course of the 19th century the modern limitation gained the upper hand. The Sciences are those studies which investigate the phenomena of the physical world.

Sciolism Pretentiously superficial knowledge. **Sciolist** (n.); **Sciolistic** (adj.)

Semantics The study of meaning in a language, e.g. the relationship between words and the things they signify.

Senecan (adj.) Tragic in the manner of Seneca (L. Annacus Senecca), who wrote in imitation of the Greek tragedy, but in a violently rhetorical style, and with a much greater emphasis on blood and horror. It has been questioned if his plays were intended for stage performance, but he was much admired and imitated by Elizabethan dramatists.

Sensibility (n.) Power of perception through the senses, ability to feel; in the 18th and early 19th centuries, capacity for refined emotion, hence the title of Jane Austen's novel, *Sense and Sensibility*.

Sensible (adj.) almost invariably used to mean no more than 'perceptible to the senses' in Shakespeare and contemporary writers,

> Art thou not, fatal vision, sensible to feeling as to sight?
>
> (Shakespeare, *Macbeth*)

In the 18th century we find the modern meaning of 'possessing good, or common sense' appearing, as when Dr Johnson, having made his hearers giggle by saying 'the woman had a bottom of good sense', sternly corrected this to 'the woman was fundamentally sensible' (which is also capable of a ridiculous interpretation, though no one dared to laugh a second time). There is also the rather affected meaning of 'aware', as in 'I am very sensible of your kindness'.

Sensual Seeking, or producing, gratification of the senses through excessive indulgence. Always pejorative today, e.g. 'Free from sloth and sensual snare'.

Sensuous (adj.) Pertaining to, or affecting, the senses; readily responsive to stimulation of the senses; without the pejorative force of **Sensual** above, but used particularly of a temperament, or an effect, which is the opposite of austere. If it is desired to use a perfectly neutral word in reference to the operation of the senses, or the process of sensation, the best one is **Sensory** (adj.).

Sentimentalism In the 18th century, the provocation and indulgence of tearful emotion as a way of proving to oneself that one belonged to that superior category of mankind possessed of 'a feeling heart': as exploited by Samuel Richardson (1689–1761) in his novels, became very much of a vogue. Hundreds, perhaps thousands, of admirers of both sexes (including Dr Johnson!), both at home and abroad (particularly in Germany) wept agreeably over the distresses of his heroines, Pamela and Clarissa. For a time, **sentimental** (adj.) became an almost meaningless fashionable word, signifying little more than 'chic' or 'charming'. After Richardson, **sentiment** got on to the stage in the form of the **Sentimental Comedy**, of which the most successful English practitioner was Richard Cumberland (1732–1811).

> Retailing nightly to the yawning pit
> The purest morals, undefiled by wit

(Prologue to Sheridan's *The Critic*)

There was a contemporary craze for 'comedie larmoyante' in France. But the inevitable reaction set in, largely promoted by RB Sheridan (1751–1816), who brought Cumberland himself on stage in *The Critic* as Sir Fretful Plagiary, and satirised the **Man of Sentiment** splendidly in the character of Joseph Surface, in the *School for Scandal*. Joseph is never at a loss for an improving sentiment –

> To pity, without the power to relieve, is still more painful than to ask and be denied

– but is really a heartless and scheming hypocrite.

Sentimentality (n.) is today the best word to use to suggest the mawkish and excessive display of tender feeling.

To **sentimentalise** (vb.)

Shavian (adj.) In the manner of George Bernard Shaw (1856–1951), witty and paradoxical.

Simile A comparison intended to bring out the qualities of something by reference to those of something else, but, unlike metaphor, made explicitly, e.g. 'He tore through the house like a tornado'. All similes are introduced by 'like' or 'as'.

Soliloquy (n.) 'Speaking alone', speaking one's thoughts aloud, especially on the stage.

To **soliloquise** (vb.)

Solipsism The view that the only person of whose existence one can be sure is oneself.

Solipsist (n.)

Sonnet A poem of fourteen lines of iambic pentameters, of Italian origin, regularly used in English poetry from Tudor times. The Elizabethan or Shakespearean form (in which Shakespeare wrote all of his sequence of 154 sonnets) consists of three quatrains and a couplet, rhyming ababcdcdefefgg. The 'Italian' form used by most post-Elizabethan Sonneteers, e.g. Milton, Wordsworth, consists of a group of eight lines, or octave, followed by a group of six, or sestet, with different rhymes.

Spenserian stanza The stanza (q.v.) invented by Edmund Spenser (1552–99) for his long allegorical poem, *The Faerie Queene*: it consists of eight iambic pentameters and a final alexandrine, rhyming ababbcbcc.

Spleen (n.) The popular old name for the milt, or melt, a large ductless gland in the stomach which controls certain blood changes; in former days its function was not understood, and it was supposed to secrete the **melancholy humour** (q.v.); hence the name is transferred to the humour, and becomes another word for melancholy, peevishness, lowness of spirits, throughout the 18th century.

Standard English A prestigious dialect of the English language. There is no single accent associated with it.

Stanza (It. n.) A group of lines of verse arranged in a regular and recurring pattern, which fixes the number of lines (usually not less than four), the metre, and the rhyme scheme.

Stoicism from Gk. *stoa*, a porch or colonnade, and particularly the hall at Athens in which Zeno (c. 300 BC) lectured. The doctrine of Zeno that happiness was to be achieved by duty and self-denial, and that pleasure and pain were to be ignored by a virtuous man; hence, therefore, the patient uncomplaining endurance of misfortune; the opposite of **Epicureanism** (q.v.).
    Stoic (n.); **Stoical** (adj.)

Stress In English prosody, the emphatic pronunciation of certain syllables.

Style Those aspects of literature which concern form and expression rather than content: a writer's language, not his subject matter. Though the distinction between style and content is sometimes rather artificial, it is often necessary in criticism.
    Stylist (n.) particularly a writer whose style is felt to be distinctive and elegant.

Stylistic analysis This is the branch of linguistics which looks at styles of language. Stylistics attempts to establish principles which account for how texts create meaning, as a result of the choices made by individuals and groups in their use of language.

Stylistics (n.) The study of style.

Subjective (adj.) Treating a question exclusively from the writer's own point of view; coloured by his or her own feelings and prejudices; personal, not impartial: the opposite to **objective** (q.v.).
    Subjectivity (n.)

Surrealism A movement in art and literature which may be said to have effectively begun in the early 1920s; essentially a reaction of a kind that recurs periodically in the history of culture, against what is felt to be the stifling requirements of established convention, form, logic. The early surrealists set themselves the task of liberating from the subconscious level of the mind all its freakish, unconnected images, and letting them express themselves more or less spontaneously; later, perhaps, there is more of a tendency towards the deliberate assembly of haphazard images. In this aspect of surrealism one feels the influence of the psychoanalytical writings of **Freud** (q.v.). Another influence was surely the feeling that civilised Europe was disintegrated in the First World War:

> What is the city over the mountains
> Cracks and reforms and bursts in the violet air
> Falling towers
> Jerusalem Athens Alexandria
> Vienna London
>
> (TS Eliot, *The Waste Land*)

In the novel, the greatest surrealist achievement is James Joyce's *Ulysses*, also first published in 1922. Among surrealist painters may be mentioned Dali and Picasso. It should hardly be necessary to point out that Surrealism is the direct opposite of **Realism** (q.v.)
    Surrealist (n. and adj.)

Swiftian (adj.) In the manner of Jonathan Swift (1667–1745), Dean of St Patrick's, Dublin, author of *Gulliver's Travels*, etc.; bitterly satirical, misanthropic.

Symbolism The use of something to represent something else, especially the use of some material object to represent an abstract idea, e.g. the mace, or sceptre, to symbolise power, authority ('His (the king's) sceptre shows the force of temporal power', *Merchant of Venice*); the employment of **symbols** as a literary device. With particular reference to French poetry from about 1850, the term is used to describe a whole tendency or movement towards emotive suggestion rather than precise statement (see *Impressionism*), and the use of images as symbols of the poet's own inner state rather than as representations of the external world. The culmination of Symbolism is to be found in the poetry of Stéphane Mallarmé (1842–98).

Symbolist (n. and adj.); **Symbolic(al)** (adj.)

Sympathy Participation, or sharing, of another's feelings; particularly, in literary criticism, the association of the reader or spectator with a character in a work of fiction, or with the author himself; a **sympathetic** character is one we find congenial, and with whom we can to some degree identify ourselves.

To sympathise (vb.); Antonyms: Antipathy, Antipathetic.

Syntax The orderly arrangement of parts: particularly, in grammar, the orderly construction of sentences.

Tacitean (adj.) In the manner of Tacitus (Cornelius Tacitus, 55–120 AD). Roman historian; brief and sententious.

Tautology Useless and repetitious verbiage, the repetition of the same idea in different words, for example,

The Vase is unique and very rare.

He passed away and died.

Theme Leading idea in a novel, play or poem. Sometimes the theme is obvious: in Hardy, the struggle of the individual against fate; in Shakespeare's plays the themes are mixed – in *Hamlet*, two of the several themes are indecision and incestuous love.

Theology The study of God, divinity; a particular system of belief incorporating a God, or gods.

Theological (adj.); **Theologian** (n.)

Tirade (n.) A violent speech, long and denunciatory: a harangue.

Tone The prevailing feeling of any work of literature. This tone can be, e.g., humorous, satirical, cynical.

Tragedy A play which represents the downfall of a great man in a serious manner, using elevated and poetical language: this is essentially Aristotle's concept, as expressed in the **Poetics** (q.v.), as well as Shakespeare's; any story which ends in disaster: this was the medieval meaning – see Chaucer's *Monk's Tale*.

Tragic (adj.); **Tragedian** (n.) a writer of tragedy, or a performer in tragedies.

Transcendentalism A name given to any system of philosophy which is based, not on experience, but on the assumption that there exists 'something beyond', independent of man; recognising 'eternal verities' like 'the starry heavens above, and the moral law within', as the German philospher Immanuel Kant (1724–1804) puts it; a variety of **idealism** (q.v.); rather vaguely used to signify metaphysical (q.v.), abstract, treating of the supernatural.

Transcendental (adj.)

Trochee A foot of two syllables in which the stress falls on the first: the opposite to an **iambus** (q.v.) e.g.

Dante once prepared to paint an angel

(Browning)

Trochaic (adj.)

Unities, Dramatic Principles of dramatic construction elaborated from the *Poetics* (q.v.) of Aristotle. Aristotle says that the best plays observe 'unity of action', i.e., that they narrate only one coherent episode of one story; also, that tragedy 'endeavours to confine itself to a single revolution of the sun'. As interpreted by Neoclassical critics and dramatists, especially in the 17th century, this emerges as three inflexible rules of tragedy:

1 Unity of Action: no sub-plot or intermixture of 'comic staff with tragic sadness and gravity', as Milton says in his preface to *Samson Agonistes*;

2 Unity of Time: the action of the play must be confined within the supposed space of a natural day;

3 Unity of Place: the action was not to depart, except marginally, from the place where it was shown to begin. This last Unity was nowhere mentioned by Aristotle, but it is a logical complement to the others, since it cannot be supposed that the same group of characters (postulated by the Unity of Action) should in the course of a day remove from, say, Rome to Alexandria. The fact that the Unities were dogmatically asserted, and dramatists like Shakespeare roundly condemned for not understanding 'The Rules', by people who had never read a page of Aristotle, does not necessarily mean that their observance is not, in many plays, a source of dramatic strength. It is, however, true that the urgent advocates of the Unities seem to think that the dramatist's main task is to placate an imaginary spectator who goes to the theatre determined not to be taken in, and sits through the performance with stop-watch in hand.

Urbane (adj.) Smooth, polished, polite; having those qualities with which **Urban** or town-dwelling man credits himself, in contrast with those of the 'rustic, ruder than Gothic'.

Verse Metrical composition, poetry; a metrical line; a group of lines arranged in a recognisable pattern, approximately the same as **stanza** (q.v.).

Versification (n.) composition of verses.

Versifier (n.) a maker of verses; generally with some pejorative suggestion, e.g. 'a mere versifier' as opposed to a poet; a **poetaster** (q.v.).

Virgilian (adj.) Possessing the qualities associated with Virgil (see **Aeneid**), e.g. dignified eloquence, either of the epic kind or in dealing with country life, as Virgil does in the *Georgics*.

Wit (n.) Originally intelligence, intellect, reason; later, in the 17th century, high intelligence, great mental capacity, or the possessor of such qualities of mind: thus Dryden – 'Great wits are sure to madness near allied'; the 18th century develops the meaning which is now dominant: the ability to amuse, or the quality that amuses, by brilliant and unexpected play with words and ideas. Wit is essentially a matter of cleverness, of intellect, unlike **humour** (q.v.). Wit can be cruel and stinging; it often goes with satire: humour is rarely to be found in such company.

Wordsworthian (adj.) In the manner of William Wordsworth (1770–1850), especially to suggest a reverent or mystical attitude towards Nature.

Zolaesque (adj.) In the manner of Emile Zola, French novelist. See **Naturalism**.

INDEX